PREPARING [
TWENTY-FIRST

PAUL KENNEDY was brought up in Newcastle and taught for many years at the University of East Anglia before taking up his present post of Dilworth Professor of History at Yale University. His previous books include *Strategy and Diplomacy*, *The Realities Behind Diplomacy 1870–1914*, *The Rise and Fall of British Naval Mastery* and *The Rise and Fall of the Great Powers*, which has been translated into twenty-three languages. He lives in Hamden, Connecticut.

from the reviews:

'Every generation or so, the British humanities seem to throw up an intellectual figure with a big idea who catches the imagination of the global chattering classes . . . from Edmund Burke through Macaulay and the Fabians and H. G. Wells and Keynes and Arnold Toynbee to Paul Kennedy.'
MARTIN WALKER, *Guardian*

'Kennedy's brave and extremely readable survey is immensely valuable for two reasons. It identifies, inter-relates and illustrates the components of the world crisis with dazzling clarity, and Kennedy has the humility of a good historian.'
ANGUS CALDER, *Scotland on Sunday*

'Thought-provoking: an ambitious attempt to analyse the deeper trends – demographic, environmental and technological – that underpin the fortunes of all nations . . . Kennedy deserves the credit for tackling big and important issues. His book is an antidote to the excessive optimism of analysts who argue that the end of communism and revived faith in market forces must result in a brighter future.'
MICHAEL PROWSE, *Financial Times*

'Kennedy's book is based on an astonishing mass of material. He humanises statistics culled from rebarbative official reports. He enlivens us with snippets from *Harper's* and TV commentators. This makes for lively reading . . . We must hope that this present book will strengthen President Clinton's professed concern about the fate of the world tomorrow.'
RAYMOND CARR, *Spectator*

'A headying, dizzying experience . . . Kennedy is one of the few intellectuals writing today who's willing to grapple with *all* the complexities of *all* global or national problems.'
San Francisco Chronicle

'Kennedy brings together information and argument in a clear and arresting fashion . . . Throughout *Preparing for the Twenty-First Century* he takes care to avoid the traps inherent in a survey of this kind. He does not exaggerate. He brings no ideological baggage. He sets out the case, and balances the arguments.'
CRISPIN TICKELL, *TLS*

'A bold attempt at future-gazing . . . if you're attracted to *fin de siècle* pessimism it's compulsive stuff'
DAVID STAFFORD, *Scotsman*

'It is impossible not to admire the sweep, scope and interdisciplinary daring of Kennedy's work'
VERNON BOGDANOR, *Times Higher*

'Kennedy's vision has a far-reaching sweep . . . the book's impact is crushing . . . A tour de force, required reading for anyone who wants to take the measure of 21st-century realities.'
New York Times

'A powerful and persuasively argued account of the dilemmas facing humankind as the second millennium approaches'
FERGUS PYLE, *Irish Times*

'Instead of trying to find patterns in history and project them into the present, Kennedy tries to find dynamic processes in the present and project them into the future. He asks whether the world – its nation-states, its transnational institutions and its economy – is organised to withstand the impact of these processes, and concludes that it is not.'
NEAL ASCHERSON, *Independent*

Paul Kennedy

PREPARING FOR THE TWENTY-FIRST CENTURY

FontanaPress
An Imprint of HarperCollins*Publishers*

Fontana Press
An Imprint of HarperCollins*Publishers*
77–85 Fulham Palace Road,
Hammersmith, London W6 8JB

Published by Fontana Press 1994

1 3 5 7 9 8 6 4 2

First published in Great Britain by
HarperCollins*Publishers* 1993

ISBN 0 00 686298 5

Set in Electra and Fenice

Printed in Great Britain by
HarperCollinsManufacturing Glasgow

*To the Hamden under-fifteen
Boys' Soccer Team from their Coach*

FOREWORD
AND
ACKNOWLEDGMENTS

This book had its origins in a debate which took place between me and a large group of economists at the Brookings Institution in Washington in the spring of 1988, and which centered upon my newly published work *The Rise and Fall of the Great Powers.* In the course of a lively evening, one critic—not known to me—declared that he couldn't understand why such a fuss was being made about *Rise and Fall* by everyone. It was, after all, a very traditional sort of book, focusing upon the nation-state as the central actor in world affairs. Why hadn't I used my time better, to write about much more important and interesting issues, those forces for global change like population growth, the impact of technology, environmental damage, and migration, which were *trans*national in nature and threatened to affect the lives of us all, peasants as well as premiers?

I left it to others that evening to weigh in with opinions about why *Rise and Fall* might be of some pertinence, especially in the American presidential campaign of 1988, but I found my critic's comment sufficiently arousing to begin initial readings in subjects (global warming, demography, robotics, biotech) that were then totally foreign to me. Before long, I was making clippings of newspaper and journal articles upon those subjects and filing them away. After a further while, I realized that I had the makings of a new book, very different from *Rise and Fall* in its subject matter and structure and yet—as I explain in Chapter 1—closely related in its concerns and purpose. Both are an attempt to write what David Landes calls "large History." Whether the present work provokes the same interest as the previous study will be for the reader to say.

In the course of researching and preparing this book, I have become obliged to an embarrassingly large group of individuals, only a few of whom can be mentioned here. I am deeply indebted to Sheila Klein and Sue McClain, who once again typed repeated drafts of the manuscript with wonderful efficiency and dispatch. Old friends Gordon Lee and J. R. Jones read and commented on every aspect of the initial draft, then upon the revisions. Jonathan Spence, Richard Crockatt, David Stowe, W. H. McNeill, Paul Golob, André Malabré, James O'Sullivan, Bill Foltz, and Bill Cronon read and made notes on parts or all of this work. Kenneth Keller, Bill Nordhaus, and Maria Angulo tried to keep me from going too far wrong in my coverage of environmental issues.

I was also blessed by the assistance of a large number of Yale graduate students. For the past few years, Maarten Pereboom, Karen Donfried, Richard Drayton, Geoff Wawro, Kevin Smith, Fred Logevall, and Reynolds Salerno have successively grappled with the mountains of files, documents, correspondence, and other materials, reducing them to some order. David Rans did statistical analysis for me. My son John Kennedy took a summer off to reorganize and list the entire archive. Fred Logevall and Reynolds Salerno prepared the bibliography and checked the endnote references.

When, in the summer of 1990, it became clear that I was being overwhelmed by the sheer mass of literature upon the subjects I proposed to cover, I was rescued by a group of five research assistants, all Yale students. Zhikai Gao, with wonderful computing skills, organized a computer search of the literature held in the Sterling Library's extensive collections, providing the results to the rest of us. Tony Cahill investigated and prepared an extensive report on environmental issues. Gary Miller did the same on comparative education. Sameetah Agha reported on robotics, automation, high technology, and related issues, as well as advising on the developing world, Islam, India, and China. David Stowe was amazingly efficient in providing reports on demography, globalization, and biotech agriculture and also gave more general assistance. Without these five, the work would never have been completed. I remain, of course, solely responsible for all lingering errors, as well as for the general and specific arguments made in the text.

I am especially indebted to my literary agents, Bruce Hunter and Claire Smith, who have supported me throughout the project. Stuart Proffitt, my London editor at HarperCollins, has also been wonderfully supportive throughout this project, exchanging ideas and information, reading and gently criticizing the various drafts, and helping to give an overall shape to the work. I know the completed manuscript arrived later than he would have wished, but I hope he will find that the extensive revisions have been worthwhile.

My two greatest critics, Jason Epstein of Random House and my wife, Cath, deserve special mention. Being edited by the former is the literary equivalent of Marine Corps boot camp, but although the process of revision is a painful one, there is no doubt in my mind that the manuscript benefited immensely from Jason's line-by-line editing and from his insistence that the chapter themes be much more closely interrelated than they were in the first draft.

The manuscript was also vastly improved by the many amendments suggested by my wife; the Part Two chapters especially benefited from her advice.

This is dedicated to the Hamden under-fifteen Boys' Soccer Team, which I have had the pleasure of coaching for the past four years and hope to be with until they go to college. Coaching can be frustrating at times—usually when the team loses—but it is also a wonderful escape from one's books, files, and statistics. Some authors can be single-minded scholars. This one cannot; but I feel much the better, and much refreshed, for having been coach as well as professor during the writing of this work.

Paul Kennedy
Hamden/Branford, Connecticut
May 1992

CONTENTS

PART THREE:
CONCLUSION

TABLES AND CHARTS

PART 1

GENERAL TRENDS

1

PROLOGUE: OLD CHALLENGES
AND NEW CHALLENGES

TWO HUNDRED YEARS AGO, AS THE EIGH-
teenth century was drawing to a close, observers of social and political
trends in Europe were deeply troubled. A revolutionary tide, which had
first surged in France in 1789, was spreading to neighboring states,
bringing down regimes from Italy to the Netherlands. Instead of peaceful constitutional change to a more representative political system, here
a revolution was feeding upon itself, producing demagogues, angry
street mobs, violence, and a new pan-European war. As a consequence,
authorities in nations as different as Georgian Britain and czarist Russia
reacted by suppressing revolutionary tendencies. Moderate voices, as
happens so often, found themselves scorned by the left and threatened
by the right.

Although the French Revolution had specific causes—for example,
worsening state finances during the 1780s—many felt that there were
deeper reasons for these social upheavals. One such was obvious to
anyone who visited Europe's crowded cities or noted the growing
incidence of rural underemployment: it was the sheer press of human
beings, all needing food, clothing, shelter, and work in societies not well
equipped to meet those demands, at least on such a scale. Countryside
hovels teemed with young children. Town authorities grappled with a
rising tide of homeless vagrants. In the larger cities, a floating popula-

tion of tens of thousands of unemployed slept on the ground overnight and poured into the streets the next day. Jails, pauper houses, foundling hospitals, and lunatic asylums were packed with human casualties who had not yet arrived at their common grave.

Concerned observers did not need statistics to know that their societies were experiencing a population boom. Had the data been available—the taking of a national census was only just being introduced around this time—the figures would have confirmed their judgment. The population of Europe (including Russia) had been about 100 million in 1650, was almost 170 million a century later, and by 1800 was well past 200 million.[1] The population of England and Wales grew by a mere 1 percent in the 1720s, by 4 percent in the 1750s, and by over 10 percent per decade as 1800 approached—and was still accelerating.[2] The major cities, swelled by the drift of population from the countryside, grew even faster. On the eve of the French Revolution, Paris had a total of between 600,000 and 700,000 people, including up to 100,000 vagrants—combustible materials for a social explosion. London's total was even larger, its 575,000 inhabitants of 1750 having become 900,000 by 1801, including a mass of the bustling street hawkers, pickpockets, urchins, and felons so well captured in contemporary prints. With more and more "have-nots" being born in a world of relatively few "haves," was it any wonder that the authorities were fearful and tightened up restrictions upon public assemblies, pamphleteering, "combinations" of workers, and other potentially subversive activities?

This late-eighteenth-century surge in population, which was also taking place in countries as far removed as China and America, had various causes. An inexplicable decline in the virulence of diseases like smallpox was one. So also was the increasing use of vaccination techniques. Improvements in food supply and diet, at least in parts of Western Europe, were another cause. In certain societies, women were marrying younger.[3] Whatever the exact combination of reasons, there were many more children in most parts of the world than there had been a century earlier. As the population expanded, it pressed upon existing resources.

The prospect of a growing mismatch between people and resources deeply troubled a learned and inquisitive English country curate named

Thomas Robert Malthus, who in 1798 committed his thoughts to paper in a work which has made him world-famous. In his *Essay on Population,* * Malthus focused upon what appeared to him the greatest problem facing the human species: "that the power of population is indefinitely greater than the power in the earth to produce subsistence for man."[4] This was so, he argued, because the populations of Britain, France, and America were doubling every twenty-five years whereas— although fresh land was also being opened up—there was no certainty that food supplies could increase at the same rate repeatedly. Indeed, while the output of farm produce might conceivably be doubled over the following twenty-five years, to suppose such a doubling could occur again, and again, and again was "contrary to all our knowledge of the qualities of land."[5] As Britain's population geometrically increased from 7 million† to 14 million over the next quarter century, and to 28 million over the following quarter century, and then to 56 million and 112 million, Malthus forecast there would be an ever greater gap between the people's food demands and the land's capacity to meet them. The result, he feared, would be increasing starvation and deprivation, mass deaths through famine and disease, and a rending of the social fabric.

It is not necessary here to follow all the debates between Malthus and his contemporaries, except to note that he had deliberately penned his *Essay* to contest the arguments of certain writers (Godwin, Condorcet) about the perfectibility of man. Those optimists had concluded that while things were troubled at the moment, the growth of human understanding, the capacity for self-improvement, and breakthroughs in knowledge would one day lead to a society that was much more equitable, free of crime and disease, free even of war.[6] The pessimistic Malthus, by contrast, felt that population growth meant that the human condition would worsen, with the existing gap between the "haves" and the "have-nots" exacerbated by the pressures upon the earth's resources.

This debate between optimists and pessimists has, in one form or

---

*More accurately, *An Essay on the Principle of Population as It Affects the Future Improvement of Society* (London, 1798). This is also known as Malthus's "first" essay on population, since it was rewritten in 1803 and there were later editions.

†It was actually larger, about 10 million, at this time.

another, been with us since then, and, this study will argue, it is even more pertinent today than when Malthus composed his *Essay.* As for that debate of two hundred years ago, the optimists were proved correct, although not necessarily for all the reasons they had advanced. While advocates of the perfectibility of man suffered frequent disappointments as the nineteenth and (especially) the twentieth centuries unfolded, Malthus's pessimistic, mathematical reasonings ignored a number of factors, so his forecast of "gigantic inevitable famine" was off the mark, at least as far as his native Britain was concerned. To be sure, the British Isles in the early nineteenth century felt some negative consequences of the population explosion: poverty in rural regions was widespread, and while millions decided to remain there, many more drifted into the towns and cities for work; sprawling slums of jerry-built houses, lacking water, light, heat, and sanitation, sprang up in the new manufacturing towns; hordes of children lacked adequate health care, nutrition, clothing, and education; gangs of unemployed agrarian workers attacked the new farming machines that had thrown them out of work; social protest was common, especially in years when poor harvests drove up the price of bread, and large-scale demonstrations (like the one held at Peterloo in 1819) were fiercely suppressed by authorities fearful of a Jacobin revolution.

Nevertheless, *three* developments permitted the British people to escape the fate Malthus predicted for them. The first was emigration: people left the British Isles in vast numbers, in search of better conditions elsewhere. While only slightly more than 200,000 emigrated in the 1820s, that figure trebled in the following decade and reached almost 2.5 million in the 1850s. Between 1815 and 1914, around 20 million Britons left the country,[7] a massive exodus relative to the overall population. (By 1900, the British population was about 41 million; without emigration, it would have been over 70 million.) More important than absolute numbers, however, was the fact that the British were not prevented by domestic or foreign authorities from migration. Apart from those who headed to the labor-hungry United States, millions also streamed to colonies rich in land and resources (in Canada, Australasia, southern Africa) and inhabited by peoples who could not long resist Western military technology. Existing communications— the long-range sailing ship, followed by the steamship and the railway—

permitted hundreds of thousands of families to cross the globe, in discomfort surely, but also in relative security. There was thus no need to linger in the hovels and slums of England or Scotland, borne down by the press of numbers.*

The second development was that just as Malthus was writing his *Essay*, there occurred significant improvements in British farming output—so significant, indeed, that the whole process was later called the Agricultural Revolution.[8] Far from being a sudden event (as the word "revolution" suggests), the process consisted of piecemeal improvements—rotation of crops, new breeding techniques, better estate management, new agricultural implements, introduction of the potato, enclosure of common lands and draining of wetlands, better publicity about these new farming methods, enhanced communications and access to markets—cumulatively raising the quantity and the quality of the food supply to the British nation, enhancing its well-being, reducing mortality rates, and also contributing to the population increase. In due course, the steadily expanding numbers of people could not fully be supplied from these augmented domestic sources; in that sense, Malthus was correct. However, by the third quarter of the nineteenth century, British demand for grains, meat, and other foodstuffs could be supplied from the farms established by earlier emigrants to North America, Australia, and elsewhere—such produce being transported in refrigerated steamships. Contrary to Malthus's forebodings, "the power in the earth" was able to match "the power of population," thanks to the ingenuity of his own countrymen.

The third and most important development was that just a decade or two before Malthus composed his *Essay*, Britain entered the first stages of the Industrial Revolution, that vast leap forward in productivity which followed from the substitution of mechanical devices for human skills, and of inanimate power (steam, then electricity) for animal and human strength.[9] Even in their early forms, power-driven looms could produce twenty times the output of a hand worker, while a power-driven "mule" (a spinning machine) had two hundred times the capacity of a spinning wheel. Moreover, the coal needed to fuel

---

*In the case of the Highland clearances, of course, the emigration was more involuntary than voluntary.

those machines and the manufactures flowing from the newly established factories in which the machines were grouped could be hauled
by locomotives possessing the capacity of hundreds of packhorses. No
earlier technological breakthroughs produced anything like the rise in
output that flowed from the Industrial Revolution.

While the coming of steam power had many consequences, short-
term and long-term, its greatest was to save at least parts of the human
race from the dire results of the population explosion that so worried
Malthus. The Industrial Revolution boosted productivity to such a
degree that both national wealth and general purchasing power outran
the rise in the numbers of people. During the nineteenth century as
a whole, the British population grew *fourfold*, whereas the national
product grew *fourteenfold*. [10]

This is not to say that the material benefits were immediate or, for
that matter, evenly distributed. Industrialization brought early gains to
the entrepreneurs, inventors, mill owners, and their financial backers
who realized that the new methods of manufacture would lead to
enhanced profits. But apart from the critical issue of providing jobs for
the expanding populace, it did not greatly benefit the first or second
generation of workers, who, suffering under awful conditions in factories and mines, were organized alongside their machines in a strict,
time-driven system of labor unlike anything known previously. The
difference clearly was between the short term and the long term. Only
the later generations of workers gained from the general increase in
prosperity that flowed from industrialization, for which their parents
and grandparents paid so heavily. It was little wonder that Karl Marx—
and Marx's followers elsewhere more recently—forecast that the
proletarianization of a people would lead to a revolution against the
classes in power, and did not foresee that things might improve over
time. Marx—an angry critic of Malthus—was even worse at the art of
prediction.

Because the new technology and system of production turned Britain into the workshop of the world, its people steadily became richer.
With earnings from rising British exports—5 million pounds' worth of
textile exports of the 1780s had been transformed into almost 40
million pounds' worth by the 1820s[11]—Britain was able to purchase
the foodstuffs, raw materials, and other goods its population needed,

and to transport those products more swiftly on more sophisticated ships. Possessing greater manufacturing efficiency than any other society at that time and enjoying ever-higher standards of living, many Britons became proponents of laissez-faire economics and of an "open" trading order in which national boundaries and ownership counted for less and less. Perhaps the great English economist Jevons best captured this mood when he exulted in 1865:

> The plains of North America and Russia are our cornfields; Chicago and Odessa our granaries; Canada and the Baltic are our timber forests; Australasia contains our sheep farms, and in Argentina and on the western prairies of North America are our herds of oxen; Peru sends her silver, and the gold of South Africa and Australia flows to London; the Hindus and the Chinese grow tea for us, and our coffee, sugar and spice plantations are all in the Indies. Spain and France are our vineyards and the Mediterranean our fruit garden, and our cotton grounds, which for long have occupied the Southern United States, are now being extended everywhere in the warm regions of the earth.[12]

In many ways, this was one of the great success stories of the human race, very different from, but as important as, the coming of representative government or the rise of religious tolerance. The Industrial Revolution, together with the earlier Scientific Revolution of detached research and inquiry, created a built-in upward spiral of economic growth and technological advance. New inventions, new manufacturing techniques, new forms of transport, and new capital tended to stimulate each other. For example, the creation of the large, iron-hulled steamship in the middle of the nineteenth century was both a product of the twin revolutions in science and industry and a means to improve global communications, food supply, migration, and so on. Since then, the interaction of technological change and industrial development has been unstoppable.[13]

Thus, "the power of population" was answered, not so much by "the power in the earth" itself, but by the power of technology—the capacity of the human mind to find new ways of doing things, to invent new devices, to organize production in improved forms, to quicken the pace of moving goods and ideas from one place to another, to stimulate fresh approaches to old problems. Malthus was absolutely correct to see that a doubling of a country's population every twenty-five years would involve a race between consumption and resources; but he missed the power of science and technology to create improvements in the transportation of people, goods, and services, to enhance agricultural output, and to stimulate breakthroughs in the manufacture of wares, so that fresh resources were harnessed and invented to meet the growing demands of a vigorous population. Moreover, the rising standards of living led to social changes—more years at school, improvements in the status of women, enhanced consumption, growing urbanization of the population—all of which tend to decrease the average number of children born per family. In other words, Britain went through a "demographic transition" that eventually led to a stabilization of the population, a century or more later. The geometric increase in numbers, it turned out, lasted only a few generations.

In sum, the British people escaped their Malthusian trap via three doors: migration, agricultural revolution, and industrialization. It is equally important to notice, however, that this escape was not very common. Certain countries—Belgium, Germany, the United States—imitated British practices and followed the upward spiral of increased productivity, wealth, and standards of living. However, many other countries were not so fortunate and, constrained either by internal or external forces, steadily lost ground. Ireland, disadvantaged in many ways (alien political control, lack of infrastructure, lack of coal, low per capita levels of consumption, depressed agriculture), was unable to solve "the central problem of the age . . . how to feed and clothe and employ generations of children outnumbering by far those of any earlier time."[14] By the 1840s, starvation and emigration had reduced population by about one-fifth.

India is another case in point, and much closer to Malthus's model. Its population also doubled and redoubled in the nineteenth century, but on a much less productive base. Furthermore, because the Indian states had been unable to resist Britain's East India Company militarily, their subjects could do little when British machine-made textiles—not only cheaper but of better quality than native cloth—poured into the country, driving out traditional domestic producers in the process.* The awful result, according to one calculation, was that whereas the British and Indian peoples had roughly similar per capita levels of industrialization at the onset of the Industrial Revolution (1750), India's level was only one-hundredth of the United Kingdom's by 1900.[15] Industrialization and modernization certainly caused problems in Western societies, but they paled in comparison with "the lot of those who increase their numbers without passing through an industrial revolution."[16]

There was, it is worth noting, another solution in Malthus's time to the problem of excess population, namely, internal unrest followed by external aggression. In France, popular discontents smashed an *ancien régime* that was less well structured than Britain in agriculture, industry, and commerce, and in its social framework and attitudes, to sustain rapid demographic growth. By the time the French Revolution's early hopes had been destroyed by terror, reaction, and then Bonapartism, an enormous number of young, energetic, and frustrated Frenchmen were being deployed in armies of occupation *outside* France, where many if not most of them died from combat or disease. Territorial conquest thus played its traditional role as a vent for overpopulation, social tensions, and political frustrations—although over the long run it could not compete with Britain's combination of technological innovation, economic growth, and colonial acquisitions.[17] Still, the record indicates that among the possible consequences of rapid population growth, social turbulence and territorial expansion are as plausible as any.

Those same interrelated issues—overpopulation, pressure upon the land, migration, and social instability on the one hand, and technology's power both to increase productivity and to displace traditional occupations on the other—still confront us today, with greater force than ever. In other words, we should see the demographic and economic conditions of the late eighteenth century as a metaphor for the challenges facing our present global society, two centuries after Malthus's ponderings. It is imperative, moreover, that we come to under-

---

*India imported a mere 1 million yards of cotton fabrics in 1814, but that figure had risen to 51 million yards by 1830 and to a staggering 995 million yards by 1870.

stand the *interconnectedness* of these issues in today's comparable dilemma. The real differences are not in the nature of our global problems, but in their greater intensity now compared with the late eighteenth century. The earth again confronts a population explosion, not in the developed societies of northwestern Europe but in the poverty-stricken regions of Africa, Central America, the Middle East, India, and China, involving *billions* rather than millions of people. At the same time, we are witnessing a knowledge explosion in an extraordinary number of fields of technology and production. In both respects, the impact is larger, and much more swiftly and widely felt. In the eighteenth century, the global population was adding another quarter of a billion people every seventy-five years; today, such an increase occurs every three years. Meanwhile, our integrated world of science and communications has immensely quickened the pace of technological change.

Although few, if any, of our political leaders appear willing to face the fact, the greatest test for human society as it confronts the twenty-first century is how to use "the power of technology" to meet the demands thrown up by "the power of population"; that is, how to find effective global solutions in order to free the poorer three-quarters of humankind from the growing Malthusian trap of malnutrition, starvation, resource depletion, unrest, enforced migration, and armed conflict—developments that will also endanger the richer nations, if less directly.

This problem is more sobering, because of the geographic disjunction between where the population pressures are and where the technological resources are. In late-eighteenth-century England, population explosion and technology explosion were occurring in the same society, and interacted with each other in ultimately beneficial ways: the increased population stimulated demand for food, and encouraged investment in agriculture; industrialization boosted national wealth, and that in turn led to increased purchases of textiles, kitchen goods, foodstuffs. The challenge posed by one of these great forces for change was thus answered by the other force. Increased demand was met by enhanced supply, demonstrating that a swift-growing population will not necessarily lead to lower per capita standards of living if its productivity is increasing at an equal or faster pace.

In today's world, however, there is no longer such a geographic overlap. The technology explosion is taking place overwhelmingly in economically advanced societies, many of which possess slow-growing or even declining populations. However, the demographic boom is occurring in countries with limited technological resources, very few scientists and skilled workers, inadequate investment in research and development, and few or no successful corporations; in many cases, their governing elites have no interest in technology, and cultural and ideological prejudices are much more tilted against change than they were in the England of the Industrial Revolution.

Even those differences of circumstance do not capture the full dimensions of the present global dilemma, since two further difficulties also need to be noted. The first is that population pressure in many developing countries is causing a depletion of local agricultural resources (overgrazing of the African savannahs, erosion of the Amazonian rain forests, salinization of the land from India to Kazakhstan) just when more farm output is needed. Even Malthus assumed that the food supply would continue to grow, albeit not at the same rate as the populace itself; presumably his writings would have been even gloomier had he conceived of possible decrease in "the power of the land" as occurs in Africa today. Secondly, there are indications that some of the "First" World's new technologies, far from rescuing the booming populations of the developing world, may harm poorer countries, by making redundant certain economic activities—just as the spinning jenny put Indian handloom weavers out of work on the other side of the globe. New scientific breakthroughs often create structural problems of transferring their benefits from the "haves" to the "have-nots" within that society; today's global community is presented with a far larger challenge, as advanced technologies threaten to undermine the economies of developing societies.

This book has many similarities to, and yet is very different from, *The Rise and Fall of the Great Powers*. To begin with, while the present study is not itself a historical work, it does rely upon the perspective of history, in that the developments analyzed here are not completely new. In both books, the reader is offered an analysis of broad-based forces for change that influence international events. Eschewing the historical detail of *Rise and Fall*, this study has shifted its focus somewhat, to consider the human race's encounter with technology, economic change, and population growth. Yet each in its way is an attempt to place world affairs in the largest possible context.

Secondly, while this work is not greatly concerned with military conflict, armed forces, the balance of power, and traditional ways of thinking about national security, it will argue that some of the newer forces for change bearing down upon our planet could cause instability and conflict in the future, and that governments and peoples need to reconsider their older definitions of what constitutes a threat to national and international security. Regardless of whether the Cold War is over or whether an end can be brought to Middle East rivalries, there now exist vast *non*military threats to the safety and well-being of the peoples of this planet which deserve attention.

Thirdly, because the focus here is upon transnational developments, less attention is paid to the nation-states themselves and to the diplomatic/alliance systems within which they traditionally operate. This does not mean that what decision-makers in Washington and Moscow do is unimportant, or that the future of specific territorial units like Japan and the European Community is insignificant, or that the global trends are such that it is irrelevant whether one lives in Switzerland or Chad. Different regions and countries of the globe are differently structured—in terms of geographic location, skill levels of the population, national resources, capital assets—and are either better or worse prepared to respond to the transnational challenges which all confront. Furthermore, structures within a certain country may mean that the impact of a new technology is more severe—or more beneficial—than in a nation with different structures; biotech farming, to give an obvious example, may be beneficial to a high-tech, food-importing country like Japan but potentially disastrous to developing nations like Ghana or Costa Rica that rely upon crop exports. Just where a people is located on this planet and how well endowed are its human and technological resources will greatly affect its prospects in the face of impending global transformations.

It is for that reason, therefore, that whereas the chapters in Part One analyze the dimensions of the transnational forces for change, those in Part Two examine the specific consequences for some of the most important parts of the globe—China and India, the developing nations, Europe, the erstwhile USSR, Japan, and the United States. Just as in Malthus's time, the various peoples of the globe are not poised along the same level starting line as they prepare to move out of one century into the next; and many of them are very badly handicapped indeed.

This suggests at first sight that History is, once again, producing its lists of winners and losers. Economic change and technological development, like wars or sporting tournaments, are usually not beneficial to all. Progress, welcomed by optimistic voices from the Enlightenment to our present age, benefits those groups or nations that are able to take advantage of the newer methods and science, just as it damages others that are less prepared technologically, culturally, and politically to respond to change. As with the Industrial Revolution in England, technological progress can have a trickle-down effect, so that the standards of living of all members of society improve over time; yet that was never a satisfactory explanation to the unemployed handloom weavers of 1795, nor is it likely to satisfy their equivalents in the world today.

In addition to attempting the tricky task of assessing potential winners and losers, this work also asks whether today's global forces for change are not moving us beyond our traditional guidelines into a remarkable new set of circumstances—one in which human social organizations may be unequal to the challenges posed by overpopulation, environmental damage, and technology-driven revolutions and where the issue of winners and losers may to some degree become irrelevant. If, for example, the continued abuse of the developing world's environment leads to global warming, or if there is a massive flood of economic refugees from the poorer to the richer parts of the world, everyone will suffer, in various ways. In sum, just as nation-state rivalries are being overtaken by bigger issues, we may have to think about the future on a far broader scale than has characterized thinking about international politics in the past. Even if Great Powers still seek to rise, or at least not to fall, their endeavors could well occur in a world so damaged as to render much of that effort pointless.

• • • •

Because this work deals primarily with broad global trends, environmental issues, demographic patterns, and technological breakthroughs, it might appear that I pay insufficient attention to the intangible and nonmaterial dimensions of our human and social existence—to our spiritual and cultural values. This may be true of the general themes in Part One, but a careful reading of the regional case studies in Part Two will indicate how significant those dimensions are to understanding why different societies react differently to new challenges. In fact, the most important influence on a nation's responsiveness to change probably is its social attitudes, religious beliefs, and culture. Students of past civilizations that failed to adjust to the challenge of modernization point, in example after example, to the obstacles which hindered new developments: a distaste for industry and manufacture, a Mandarin suspicion of trade and enterprise, an ideological or religious opposition to Western, capitalist mores, power structures which favored courtiers, the bureaucracy, the military, and the church, and legal and taxation systems (or even outright plunder) that discriminated against entrepreneurs and in favor of officeholders.[18]

It has often been assumed by Western writers that these obstacles are characteristic of Oriental and African societies—in contrast to European societies, whose adoption of rationalism, scientific method, and experimentation led over time to their domination of the world.[19] With the extraordinary successes of Japan in recent decades in the fields of invention, design, manufacturing, and finance, that assumption looks more dubious than ever. Granted that certain regions of the world (New Guinea, the Kalahari Desert) pose natural obstacles to development, it nonetheless seems fair to assume that most peoples of the world, *if they so choose,* can respond positively to the challenge of change. But the very phrase "if they so choose" implies an adoption of those features that explain Holland's success in the seventeenth century and Japan's success in the late twentieth: the existence of a market economy, at least to the extent that merchants and entrepreneurs are not discriminated against, deterred, and preyed upon; the absence of rigid, doctrinal orthodoxy; the freedom to inquire, to dispute, to experiment; a belief in the possibilities of improvement; a concern for the practical rather than the abstract; a rationalism that defies mandarin codes, religious dogma, and traditional folklore. A society dominated by fundamentalist mullahs or by conservative land-owning barons is as unlikely to embrace change in the twentieth century as it was in the fifteenth.

Cultural obstacles to change are common in all societies, for the obvious reason that an impending transformation threatens existing habits, ways of life, beliefs, and social prejudices. They are as likely to occur in advanced societies as in underdeveloped ones. Indeed, countries (or elites within countries) which have passed their peak in world or regional affairs and are being overtaken economically by faster-growing nations often exhibit the greatest reluctance to change. The reasons are partly practical, but psychological and cultural as well. Having risen to the top under specific historical conditions, declining nations find it difficult to accept altered circumstances: that there are now different ways of organizing industry, educating the young, distributing resources, and making policy decisions—and that those new ways are more successful. To respond to change might mean altering one's own social priorities, educational system, patterns of consumption and saving, even basic beliefs about the relationship between the individual and society. Concerned Americans, struggling today with the issue of how to meet "the Japanese challenge," know how complicated and deep-rooted such cultural and social obstacles are.[20]

The structure of this book is relatively simple. The first part analyzes certain major forces for change bearing down upon our world and discusses the general implications of those transformations. Though this book is arranged in discrete chapters, I hope that the reader will see the interconnectedness of the population explosion and increased illegal migration, the robotics revolution and global labor demand, technology and shrinking national sovereignty. Since the global population explosion is so powerful in its implications, I examine it first; but I immediately follow it with an analysis of how new technologies (computers, satellites, information/communications) are globalizing world business and changing the way companies operate—this juxtaposition to show the gulf between developments in the overpopulated poor parts of the world and those in technologically advanced rich parts. I pursue the same theme in Chapter 4 (on biotech agriculture) and Chapter 5 (on robotics), which respectively explore why our contemporary agricultural revolution and industrial/technology revolution might aggravate the population explosion rather than—as in Malthus's England—mitigate it. Since all this points to the prospect of an ever-widening rift between rich and poor countries, Chapter 6 discusses the way in which widespread environmental damage, and in particular global warming, may compel developed societies, at last understanding the connectedness of demographic, environmental, and technological trends, to aid their poorer cousins. Part One concludes with a chapter exploring the extent to which transnational changes are affecting the position of the nation-state itself.

The second part of this book examines the different regions of the globe and their respective capacities to deal with newer challenges. I selected the countries/regions not only because of their importance but also because of their very different situations: Japan is increasingly seen as the leading technology-driven society; India and China, with over one-third of the world's population, grapple with the task of checking population growth and harnessing technology; smaller countries in the developing world (East Asia, Latin America, Muslim nations, and sub-Saharan Africa are examined here) show marked differences in their response to demographic and technological challenges; the erstwhile USSR confronts these global forces as its former unity disintegrates, whereas the European Community has to deal with transnational developments *and* strive after further integration; and finally, the United States, well equipped militarily, faces radically new challenges of a nonmilitary sort. Each chapter discusses, prospectively, a range of outcomes for the country or region in question.

The third and final part again switches focus, to reflect upon the most important question of all: if we are being challenged by major forces for change, how can a society best "prepare" itself for the coming twenty-first century? What characteristics, what strengths, are desirable for a people to possess in such fast-changing and unpredictable times? This seems a more sensible line of inquiry than to engage in the politically exciting but misleading question "Who will be number one in 2025 (or 2050)?" because it allows for the possibility that societies will adapt to change and focus upon the process of acquiring, or building upon, desirable characteristics. Whether the countries and regions concerned adapt and acquire those strengths remains, as ever, an open question. Human beings make their own history even if, as Marx reminded us, they do so under circumstances influenced by the past.

It is important to emphasize the time horizon that informs the present work. Some critics of my discussion of America's "relative decline" in *The Rise and Fall of the Great Powers* misread the text to conclude it referred to today rather than a generation hence. Similarly, those unconvinced by the potential of robots (Chapter 5) might fail to understand that the relatively few examples of today's automated factories may not be dissimilar from the few factory prototypes existing when Malthus penned his first *Essay*; the broader adoption was at least a generation away. In this book, because most demographic projections go to 2025, a range of about thirty years is assumed in discussing either transnational trends or a particular region's prospects. Estimates beyond that time are much more dubious. Moreover, the exercise is complicated by the fact that some of these forces for change are moving at a faster pace than others: for example, whereas the population of Norway will change only slowly, who can foresee how far the biotech revolution will take us in the next quarter century? Similarly, if great social convulsions (including wars) do break out early in the next century, how will they affect the fate of nations, or the speed of the transnational trends discussed here?

Preparing for the Twenty-first Century does not assume, therefore, that there is an ideal blueprint or marching plan which, if followed, will enable societies to grapple with the next few decades of enormous change. It *does* assume that the impending transformations—particularly the race between demography and technology—will affect some societies and classes more than others, in both positive and negative ways, simply because of the uneven pattern of change and of the human race's differentiated responses to it. Finally, it does not contend that change is, of itself, a good thing, but rather that it is likely to produce both beneficial *and* adverse consequences. Still, if we can at least understand the transformations bearing down upon our planet, we might be able to consider how best to prepare for them.

2

THE DEMOGRAPHIC EXPLOSION

THE EARTH, UNLIKE ITS NEIGHBORING planets, is covered with a film of matter called life. The film itself "is exceedingly thin, so thin that its weight can scarcely be more than one-billionth that of the planet which supports it. . . . [It is] so insignificant in size that it would be detectable only with the greatest difficulty by beings on other planets, and would certainly be unnoticeable to observers elsewhere in our galaxy. . . ."[1] Within that film, coexisting alongside plants, animals, insects, crops, and other organisms, is the human race. It assumed the form of *Homo sapiens* some half a million years ago, well after the emergence of many of the other members of the earth's film of life. But because of the human race's growth and its economic activities, it now risks endangering the delicate envelope of matter that makes this planet unique.

The *physical* impact of the human race's expansion upon the natural environment and in particular upon the earth's atmosphere is so critical an issue that a later chapter will be devoted to it.* This chapter will focus upon demographic change, its implications for human societies, and the range of outcomes that could result from the great regional disparities in population growth.

*See Chapter 6, "The Dangers to Our Natural Environment."

21

As will be seen, these regional disparities are the most critical aspect of all. Were the earth's population expanding and devouring resources at an equal pace across the planet, that would be serious enough. But that different peoples are experiencing very different demographic patterns—some expanding fast, some stagnant, some in absolute decline—is altogether more problematic. Such imbalances influence how the various races of the globe view one another; they affect international and domestic politics, the social fabric, and the politics of food, energy, and migration. Moreover, unlike certain other global developments treated in this book—global warming, for example, or production of biogenetically altered foodstuffs—the contours of the demographic explosion are already reasonably clear.

While there remains a *range* of estimates of what the earth's total population will be in the years 2025 and 2050, the raw figures are daunting, especially when placed in historical perspective. In 1825, as Malthus was making the final amendments to his original *Essay on Population,* about 1 billion human beings occupied the planet, the race having taken thousands of years to reach that total. By then, however, industrialization and modern medicine were permitting population to rise at an increasingly faster rate. In the following hundred years the world's population doubled to 2 billion, and in the following half century (from 1925 to 1976) it doubled again, to 4 billion. By 1990, the figure had advanced to 5.3 billion.[2] It is true that the increase has slowed in recent decades, because overall fertility rates are decreasing in many countries. Even among today's fast-expanding populations of the developing world, demographers expect average family sizes to decline in the future, as urbanization and other factors cause a demographic transition and numbers begin to stabilize. But that is decades away—*even if* those forecasts are correct—and since the globe's enlarging population continues to beget more people than those who die, the effect is like a giant supertanker at sea beginning to slow down. As it decelerates, it still has a considerable way to go before it stops. Before we reach what is termed "global replacement fertility" levels, which United Nations authorities believe may occur around 2045, the population supertanker will have moved a long way.

Just how far will that be? Because regional birth and death rates change over time, demographers use complex formulae to calculate

Chart 1. World Population Increase, 1750–2100
(in billions)

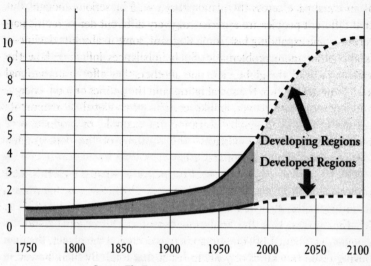

Source: *The Economist*, January 20, 1990, p. 19

these trends, and then offer three possible variants (high, middle, low). According to the middle one, by 2025—a year in which perhaps about half of the readers of this book may still be alive—the earth will contain a population of 8.5 billion people.[3] Even with the low variant of 7.6 billion, our population will have increased by almost one half. If the high variant is correct, the population will be nearly double what it is today, reaching 9.4 billion. One calculation, by the World Bank, suggests the total population of the earth may "stabilize" at between 10 and 11 billion people in the second half of the twenty-first century, but others have put the total as high as 14.5 billion.[4]

Another way of understanding these figures is to consider the increase in world population each year. In the 1950–55 period, the annual addition to world population was about 47 million—slightly more than the population of England and Wales today. In the 1985–90 period, the earth's enlarged population was adding about 88 million people annually—equal to the population of Mexico today. If future global fertility follows the high estimate, the years 1995–2000 could see annual increases of around 112 million—equal to the present Nigerian population.[5]

Mention of Mexico and Nigeria brings us to the crux of the problem: that these increases are taking place overwhelmingly in developing countries. In fact, between now and 2025, around 95 percent of all global population growth will take place in them. Concealed within the estimate that the world's "average" annual population growth rate in the years 1990–95 will be 1.7 percent lie some startling differences, ranging from Europe's small increase (0.22 percent per year) to Africa's far swifter rate of expansion (3.0 percent per year).[6] Perhaps the most dramatic way of expressing this difference is to note that in 1950 Africa's population was half of Europe's, by 1985 it had drawn level (at about 480 million each), and by 2025 it is expected to be three times Europe's (1.58 billion to 512 million).[7]

Why are the populations of certain countries growing so fast? The simple answer is that they are now in the same position as England and France were in Malthus's time—that is, they are basically agrarian societies in their first generation of enjoying a significant decrease in mortality rates. Historically, fertility rates in agrarian societies are usually very high, but so too are mortality rates, especially among the young. "Of 1,000 newborn children, 200 to 400 normally die within a year," and many of the others die before reaching the age of seven.[8] There was thus a reason for couples in preindustrial, agrarian societies to marry young and to have lots of children—on the twin assumption that each child would enhance the family labor force but that many of them would perish in their early years.

It is therefore easy to imagine what happens to the population of an agrarian society when mortality rates shrink, as they did in nineteenth-century Europe and are doing today, at a far faster rate, in large parts of the developing world: the total number of surviving human beings explodes within a few decades. In Tunisia, to take one example, the infant death rate (i.e., deaths before first birthday, per thousand live births) dropped from 138 to 59 between the years 1965–70 and the years 1985–90, and the child death rate (i.e., deaths of children under five, per thousand live births) dropped from 210 to 99 in the same period. Not surprisingly, Tunisia's overall population *doubled* in size in the three decades 1960–1990.[9] What also changes is the balance between old and young. In Kenya today, 52 percent of the population are less than fifteen, and only 2.8 percent are over sixty-five.

The irony is that this population explosion is chiefly the result of Western health practices, especially immunization and antibiotics, as well as the use of DDT to reduce mosquito-borne malaria. As mortality rates plunged after 1960, the number of children surviving infancy and early childhood quickly increased; in addition, populations began to enjoy increased average life expectancy because of improvements in food output. In retrospect, and especially with Europe's own nineteenth-century experience in mind, this demographic explosion was entirely predictable. Yesterday's perfectly natural wish to cut infant mortality in the developing world has resulted in today's unintended consequences, this time involving numbers far beyond those imagined by Malthus. For example, in the poorest and also the fastest-growing continent of all, Africa, which now contains about 650 million people, the total (as noted above) is forecast to increase almost threefold, to 1.58 billion, by 2025. Nigeria could expand from 113 to 301 million, Kenya from 25 to 77 million, Tanzania from 27 to 84 million, Zaire from 36 to 99 million, *without* corresponding increases in resources—indeed, with resources shrinking.[10]

Elsewhere in the developing world, the likely increases are almost as large. China's total may rise only (!) from today's 1.13 billion to about 1.5 billion in 2025, whereas the faster-growing population of India may reach the same total from today's 853 million. Given the approximate nature of these statistics and possible changes in both the birth and death rates of the two countries, it is conceivable that India might possess the world's largest population in 2025—for the first time in recorded history—and then eventually total 2 billion people. In addition to these demographic giants, other nations will contain unprecedentedly high populations by the third decade of the next century: Pakistan with 267 million, Indonesia with 263 million, Brazil with 245 million, Mexico with 150 million, Iran with 122 million.[11]

Behind these raw statistics lies the reality: human beings, each requiring daily two to three thousand calories and four and a half pounds of water, though getting much less except in reasonably well-off countries. The citizens of well-to-do societies get a glimpse of the poverty in which millions are forced to live in television broadcasts of famine

in (say) Ethiopia, or in *National Geographic* magazine's photographs
of slum cities in Latin America: the stricken landscape, the squalor, the
attenuated limbs, the signs of disease, above all, the thousands and
thousands of young children. If the sights are pitiful now, how will they
seem when those regions possess three times as many human beings as
today?

Of the twin manifestations of mass poverty, on the land and in the
cities, the latter is of rising concern because of the tendency for the
young and the mobile to abandon agricultural society. In 1985 about
32 percent of the population of the developing world lived in urban
areas, but that figure is expected to rise to 40 percent by 2000 and to
around 57 percent in 2025. Now 1.4 billion people are living in the
urban areas of developing countries; there will be a crushing 4.1 billion
in 2025. By that time Latin America will be the most urbanized region
of the world, with nearly 85 percent of its population living in cities;
in Africa the figure will be around 58 percent and in Asia about 53
percent. Even by the end of this present century, there will exist twenty
megacities with populations of 11 million or more, of which seventeen
will be in the developing world. Leading that list will be Mexico City,
with an estimated 24.4 million in 2000, followed by São Paulo with
23.6 million, Calcutta with 16 million, Bombay with 15.4 million, and
Shanghai with 14.7 million.

This trend involves not simply a question of numbers but also a
potential change in our social and cultural assumptions about urban
living. For thousands of years, cities (Nineveh, Tyre, Rome, Constanti-
nople, Venice, Amsterdam, London, New York, Tokyo) were centers
of wealth, creativity, and cultural activities, where the upper and middle classes resided, building fine houses, impressive boulevards, monuments, parks, concert halls. Many European cities such as Stockholm
or Copenhagen, which remain attractive to their prosperous residents,
will no doubt continue to function in that way; by contrast, Asian,
Latin American, and Central American megacities of 20 million inhabitants have become increasingly centers of poverty and social collapse.
Already, the sheer concentrations of people—143,000 per square mile
in Lagos, Nigeria, and 130,000 per square mile in Djakarta, Indonesia,
compared with New York's mere 11,400 per square mile—make it

inconceivable that their inhabitants will enjoy the benefits offered by traditional European cities.[12]

Consider, for example, the burdens that will be placed on such cities' already inadequate (or nonexistent) housing, sanitation, transportation, food distribution, and communications systems if their populations double and treble in size. In many of these countries a disproportionate amount of the nation's limited wealth is owned by the governing elites, who will find it difficult to buy off the discontents of the fast-growing urban masses. How the crowded populations will be fed, especially in times of famine, and what will happen to the always sensitive relationship between city and country are not at all clear; but even if food is available, will it be possible to give these billions of young people decent health and education and, afterward, to provide new jobs at the rate needed to prevent mass unemployment and social unrest? The phenomenon is roughly similar to that crowd of 100,000 vagrants who roamed the streets of Paris in the 1780s, but today's numbers are fantastically larger. At present, the labor force in developing countries totals around 1.76 billion, but it will rise to more than 3.1 billion in 2025—implying a need for 38–40 million new jobs *every year.*[13] Over time, urbanization leads to a decline in the rate of population increase. But the real challenge comes in the next twenty to forty years, when urbanization in the developing world will exacerbate all of the problems associated with high population density, producing miserable living conditions for the vast majority of human beings at present in their infancy or soon to be born.

There remains one random—and tragic—factor which may significantly affect these statistical projections: the AIDS epidemic, which is especially prevalent in the continent of its origin, Africa. AIDS is caused by a human immunodeficiency virus (HIV) that weakens the body's immune systems and makes it unable to fight sicknesses. The problem in estimating the demographic impact of AIDS is that perhaps eight or nine years may pass before an HIV-infected person produces symptoms, after which point the fatality rate approaches 100 percent. The graph of an AIDS epidemic therefore looks something like an iceberg. "Those who have the disease are the part of the iceberg above the water. But the much larger and deadlier part of the iceberg is composed of those who are HIV-positive but who have not yet developed the disease."[14] There also exist many individuals who, aware or unaware of being infected, pass on the infection.

While the estimated number of AIDS cases in Africa in 1988 was only about 100,000, it was believed that that figure probably represented only 5 percent or less of those already HIV-infected. Death by AIDS could therefore total some 2 million Africans in the 1990s, yet even that sounds far too low an estimate, given the flood of recent reports on this problem. One, by the World Health Organization, calculates that as many as 25–30 percent of pregnant women in certain African countries tested HIV-positive, and offers evidence that entire families suffer from the disease.[15] Only recently, the World Health Organization abandoned its earlier estimate that 25–30 million people globally would be HIV-positive by 2000, raising the total to 40 million (including many more in Asia); fully 90 percent of AIDS victims would then be in developing countries, principally among the most impoverished.[16] A 1992 report, by Harvard epidemiologists, raised the total to 100 million, with more in Asia than Africa.

If there is no cure found for AIDS in the next few years, then Africa's high fertility rates could be checked by worsening mortality rates. One recent article on this subject reports that in contrast to the World Bank's assessment that the annual population growth in Central and East Africa may slow to 2.75 percent early in the next century, "some AIDS researchers predict growth as low as 1 percent, or even, on the bleakest of guesses, an absolute decline by the year 2010"; another talks of "more people dying than being born" in Uganda and neighboring states after 2000, and wonders whether it is wise to be pressing for increased population control![17] While that would represent a classic Malthusian check upon population expansion, it is worth noting that those estimates seem unduly bleak compared with earlier forecasts, in which demographic modelers had assumed that HIV prevalence rates in Africa would peak at somewhere between 20 and 30 percent of the adult population, implying that an AIDS epidemic might cut an initial population growth rate of (say) 3 percent down to nearly 2 percent per year.[18] Africa's overall population would still be growing rapidly, therefore, but in the midst of an appalling scene in which millions of people were dying of disease. Moreover, unlike most of the other afflictions that devastate Africa, AIDS strikes disproportionately among adults, that is, among the productive and (to some degree) educated parts of the population; it thus deals a severe economic blow to the societies in question, in addition to causing great human suffering.

Apart from the special horror of the AIDS epidemic, the chief problem remains: how can poor agrarian societies deal with excessively-rapid population growth? The Malthusian answer would be that, eventually, nature intervenes: increasing famine, a struggle to gain foodstuffs and resources, open conflict, war, and disease would reduce—perhaps drastically reduce—the size of the population. Yet, as we have seen, just as Malthus was composing his *Essay on Population* the Industrial Revolution was creating a medium-to-long-term escape for the fast-growing British population of his time: increased industrial productivity and urbanization led to increased per capita income, which gradually altered the life-styles and reproductive patterns of most families and slowed population growth.

Among the countries once crudely described as part of the "Third World," a few have recently imitated the pattern that occurred in Britain two centuries ago. These are the Newly Industrialized Economies (NIEs) of East Asia, like Singapore, Taiwan, and South Korea, and perhaps also some of their larger neighbors such as Malaysia. Partly stimulated by and partly in imitation of Japan's own fabulous economic growth, these East Asian states have achieved a fast, export-led expansion, with GNPs that in recent decades have grown by more than 10 percent each year (which implies a doubling every seven years). Although their annual growth rates are now 6 or 7 percent, that is considerably more than the global average, and the decline probably indicates that their economies are moving beyond their adolescent stage. With their own steel mills, shipyards, electronics firms, national airlines, and (in the case of Taiwan and South Korea) very considerable trade surpluses, they are becoming richer year by year, with per capita GNP fast approaching those of European countries such as Portugal, Spain, and Greece.

Moreover, as East Asian standards of living have increased, total fertility rates have tumbled,* in South Korea's case from 4.5 in 1965–70 to 2.0 in 1985–90, and in Singapore's case from 3.5 to 1.7 over the same period, so that several governments now have pro-natalist population policies as in some mature economies. Mortality rates have also dropped; infant death rates and average life expectancy levels are close to those of Europe and the United States. Unsurprisingly, the percentage of couples using contraceptives is much higher than in Africa or South Asia. In such other measures of an "advanced" society as male *and* female literacy levels, sanitation services, and so on, the East Asian economies are far removed from the desperate conditions of most other developing nations.[19] If trends continue, South Korea and Taiwan may be among the healthiest and richest nations in the world early next century.

Is not this, then, the solution to the problem—to encourage the rise of "trading states" throughout the developing world, on the assumption that they would enjoy the benefits that came to the Dutch and the British in centuries past, and now have come to Japan and Korea?[20] Yet as soon as that question is posed, one begins to see the difficulties. Previous and present trading states—Venice, the Dutch Republic, Britain, Japan, Singapore, Taiwan—were relatively small countries with a favorable geographical position, a skilled population, and an openness to foreign techniques and fashions. That can hardly be said of Zaire, Iran, Mali, Afghanistan, or Ethiopia, where a combination of structural and cultural hindrances at present blocks development.†

Furthermore, just as Britain's original industrial expansion was not achieved without cost, so also have there been considerable costs following the growth of Japan, Taiwan, and Korea. As we shall see later, atmospheric pollution, erosion of the forests and wetlands, surging demand for foodstuffs and raw materials, vast increases in CO_2 emissions, and the conversion of small coastal towns into giant shipyards and steel mills all cause environmental damage, not just in the industrial regions themselves but also abroad, as East Asian companies imi-

---

*A society's total fertility rate is an estimate of the number of children on average that a woman will have in that society.

†For an elaboration of this argument, see Chapter 10, "Winners and Losers in the Developing World."

tate their European and American equivalents in a relentless demand for ores, oil, gas, timber, and other materials from the developing world. As a nation like Korea reaches a European standard of living, it also consumes energy and foodstuffs at a European level. Given their relatively small size, the East Asian NIEs are not a major cause of global degradation, especially as compared with the resources consumed by the West. But if, for example, the per capita consumption of 1.2 billion Chinese reached that of Japan or the United States, the environmental damage would be colossal.

This issue of "population and economic growth" has led to considerable disagreement between demographers and economists. During the 1960s, it was common to suggest a negative correlation between demographic growth and economic development: more meant worse, because of the cost of raising children, the reduced amount of capital per head of population, and the diversion of investment from growth-related activities to meeting the increased social demands of a larger population.[21] In the early 1980s, a revisionist and pro-natalist school typified by Julian Simon's book *The Ultimate Resource* argued that "[i]n the longer run . . . per capita income is likely to be higher with a growing population than with a stationary one, both in more-developed and less-developed countries."[22] According to this viewpoint, while there may be short-term costs associated with looking after and educating lots of young children, over the longer term there will be a larger population of productive workers between fifteen and sixty-four years old. Given the ingenuity and inventiveness of human beings, the more of them there are, the better; if on average there are two or three really creative people in every hundred, better to have a population of 100 million than 1 million.

That population growth encourages economic expansion is true in some cases, but not in others. The chief weakness lies not in the argument per se, but in the context in which population growth occurs. Rates of population growth in many less developed countries today far exceed the moderate levels that the revisionist, pro-natalist school believes are conducive to economic expansion. Total fertility rates of 2.5 are one thing; Nigeria's 7.0, Syria's 7.8, and Rwanda's 8.3 are quite another.

In addition, it is increasingly clear that population growth affects the natural world and can affect the social order and international system. Not only does a demographic explosion hurt the masses of overcrowded and undernourished youngsters who compose that boom, but it does great damage in other spheres. Human activity and ecological damage will be discussed in more detail later, but the main outlines can be stated here. The overall consensus—with the exception of a few revisionists—is that the projected growth in the world's population cannot be sustained *with our current patterns and levels of consumption.* Unlike animals and birds, human beings destroy forests, burn fossil fuels, drain wetlands, pollute rivers and oceans, and ransack the earth for ores, oil, and other raw materials. It is therefore important whether the planet contains 4 billion people engaged in these activities, as it did in 1975, or 8 to 9 billion, as is likely in 2025.

With 95 percent of the anticipated population increase between now and 2025 expected to occur in developing countries, it might appear that the main problem is *there.* If the inhabitants of Africa, Central America, and other developing areas would temper their fast-breeding habits, the argument goes, they would not only require less of the earth's food, but would also cause less damage to its rain forests, water supply, and ecosystem in general. Moreover, because those activities contribute to global warming, the population explosion in the southern hemisphere threatens to affect more developed countries of the North.

Yet even if that is true, developed Northern regions place much greater stress per capita upon the earth's resources than do developing countries, simply because the former consume so much more. Thus, the consumption of oil in the United States—with only 4 percent of the world's population—equals one-quarter of total world annual production; in 1989, the United States consumed 6.3 billion barrels of oil, ten times the consumption of Britain or Canada, and hundreds of times that of most Third World countries, which make do on very little. The same imbalance in consumption is true of a range of other items, from paper to beef. According to one calculation, the average American baby represents twice the environmental damage of a Swedish child, three times that of an Italian, thirteen times that of a Brazilian, thirty-five times that of an Indian, and 280 (!) times that of a Chadian or Haitian because its level of consumption throughout its life will be so much greater.[23] That is not a comfortable statistic for anyone with a conscience.

From the viewpoint of environmentalists, therefore, the earth is under a twofold attack from human beings—the excessive demands and wasteful habits of affluent populations of developed countries, and the billions of new mouths born in the developing world who (very naturally) aspire to increase their own consumption levels. This in turn has led a number of environmentalist voices—the Worldwatch Institute, Greenpeace, the United Nations Population Fund—to portray the entire issue as a race against time. In their view, if we do nothing to stabilize the world's total population, curb the profligate use of energy, foodstuffs, and other raw materials, and control damage to the environment, as soon as possible, then before very long we will have so overpopulated and ransacked the earth that we will pay a heavy price for our collective neglect.[24]

This viewpoint, which challenges the assumption that growth is desirable and economic output is the most useful measure of a country's material success, has provoked counterattacks from many economists. In the optimists' opinion, natural resources are not an absolute amount that is steadily being depleted; rather, many resources are created through human inventiveness and labor, and technology has an infinite capacity for producing new resources. The scarcity of a commodity, such as petroleum, leads to the search for (and discovery of) fresh stocks and the creation of alternative forms of energy, alarm at the levels of world food production leads to significant increases in agricultural productivity from breakthroughs in biotechnology, and so on. Just as Malthus was incorrect in his predictions, so will today's doomsayers be proved wrong.[25]

Only time will tell which of these positions is more accurate, but the world's population was less than a billion when Malthus first wrote his *Essay;* now it is heading, at the least, toward 7 or 8 billion, perhaps to well over 10 billion. If the optimists are right, the world will simply contain many more prosperous people, even if that prosperity is unevenly distributed. If they are wrong, the human race as a whole could

suffer more from a careless pursuit of economic growth than it may lose
by modifying its present habits.

Even before the world is in a position to judge the outcome of this
debate—in, say, 2025—it may be grappling with another potential
consequence of the global population explosion: its impact upon national security. Traditionally, that concern focused upon the availability
of military manpower; a declining population means fewer recruits for
the armed forces, which, if rival nations enjoy a greater fertility rate,
places the country in a state of relative strategical weakness.[26] Thus,
a few years ago, NATO planners were warning that the West's declining age cohorts of fit young men would reduce the size of its armed
forces. Not only have *perestroika* reforms and East-West arms accords
made such fears seem irrelevant, but the NATO planners ignored the
Soviet Union's own demographic problems. Even by the 1970s, differences emerged in total fertility rates between the nearly stagnant Russian population and the fast-growing populations of the southern
republics, where a heady combination of local nationalism, the Muslim
religion and way of life, ignorance of the Russian language, and a
profound dislike of Moscow's control was alarming Soviet military
manpower planners.[27] Now that those republics are independent, the
immediate problem may have disappeared; but the larger issue, that
some ethnic groups are growing much faster than their neighbors,
remains.

Still, the problem of military manpower is probably less urgent than
the other important implication of population change upon international security: the prospect of demographically driven social unrest,
political instability, and regional wars. As noted earlier, behind many
well-known historical upheavals—the outward thrust of the Vikings,
the expansion of Elizabethan England, the French Revolution, Wilhel-
mine *Weltpolitik*, the turbulences that rack Central America and the
Middle East today—the societies involved were experiencing population explosions, and often having difficulty in absorbing increasing
numbers of energetic young men.[28] Sometimes the unfulfilled expectations of a new generation exploded into violence and revolution. In

other instances, those energies were diverted by nimble and ambitious political leaders into *foreign* adventures and conquests.*

Those in developed countries who complain about the shrinking of their fertility rates—their "birth dearth"[29]—may wish to consider the places in the world nowadays experiencing the most serious unrest: Central America, South Africa, Southeast Asia, Afghanistan/Kashmir, the Middle East, Northern Ireland, the rimlands of the former USSR, the Horn of Africa. In all those regions, there exist fast-growing, youthful populations with pent-up social and economic expectations. It is surely no coincidence that the Palestinian *intifada*—"the war of stones" waged by teenage youth against the Israeli occupying forces—began in the Gaza Strip, with its population density of 4,206 persons per square mile (compared with 530 in Israel).[30] Obviously, ideological rivalries, racial and religious hatreds, and lots of other factors also contribute to these civil and regional wars. Nevertheless, the social effects of a population explosion appear to form the context within which such bitter struggles swiftly escalate. While this was as true in ancient Macedonia as in the Near East today, what has changed is the *momentum* of population growth, nowadays involving tens of millions of people rather than the thousands of Alexander the Great's day. What sort of future do we face if social turbulence increases at the same pace as the world's population?

While the demographic explosion (combined with reduced resources) is the greatest problem facing developing regions, many developed nations confront the opposite problem of stagnant or even negative population growth. These countries, with high standards of living and superior health care, now enjoy low mortality rates. To maintain a nation's overall size, a "replacement fertility" rate of approximately 2.1 children per woman is needed.† Current statistics from the United

---

*I use the words "often" and "sometimes" here because I'm not arguing that a population explosion *will* or *must* lead to instability or expansion. Other factors (nature of regime, geographic opportunity, state of economy) also play a role.

†This allows for the fact that a small number of girls die early, and that roughly half of births are male and thus excludable from reproduction calculations.

Nations Population Division indicate, however, that most developed nations have experienced lower fertility rates since the late 1960s; for example, Italy's rate has dropped from 2.5 to 1.5, and Spain's from 2.9 to 1.7.[31]

The most obvious cause of this decline is the changed position and expectations of women in Western societies, with larger numbers entering higher education, and then careers. Childbirth is delayed and the number of offspring reduced—something made possible by the availability of sophisticated methods of contraception. These trends interact with the effects of urbanization upon reproduction, especially in large cities. Whether because more sophisticated and career-ambitious couples tend to live in cities, or—more likely—because human beings find it hard to bring up children in cramped tenement housing where there is little place for their energies, urbanization leads over time to a reduction in fertility rates. But the key modifier is, indeed, "over time." Long before cities become the places in which those rates decline, they attract millions seeking employment, social improvement, and escape from the trials of an overpopulated, underresourced agricultural society.

The obvious implication arising from these different age structures is that whereas developing nations have the burden of supporting millions younger than fifteen, developed nations have to look after fast-increasing millions older than sixty-five. The reason for this is simple enough. The age structure of a swiftly growing society is a pyramid, as shown for Mexico in Chart 2, with the broad base representing the large numbers under twenty years old, and the narrow peak representing the small numbers of elderly. If a sharp reduction in the fertility rate takes place, the pyramid's base will become narrower, leaving a relatively smaller number of young people to sustain a relatively larger group of older ones.

Whereas in the poorest African countries only 2 or 3 percent of the population are over sixty-five, in the rich and healthy nations the proportion is far higher—Norway has 16.4 percent, for example, and Sweden 18.3 percent.[32] The average for richer countries* as a whole

---

*"Richer" here refers to the twenty-odd members of the Organization for Economic Cooperation and Development (OECD).

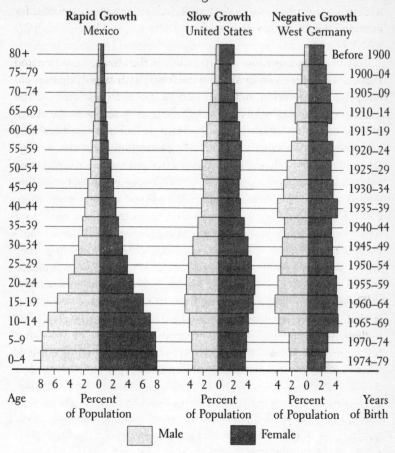

Chart 2. Age Structures

is steadily rising, partly because their total fertility rates are declining and partly because of improved health-care techniques for the elderly: by 2010 around 15.3 percent of their populations will be over sixty-five, and that figure will come close to 22 percent by 2040. This may one day pose an additional obstacle to international—or, rather, North-South—understanding, for as prosperous societies grapple with the problem of allocating more and more resources to the elderly, the rest of the globe begs for help dealing with the demands flowing from the boom in young children and infants.

Not all advanced economies are equally affected by the problem of excessively aging populations. In the United States, for example, the continued inflow of immigrants and the relatively high fertility rates of ethnic-minority families mean not only that overall population is expected to grow, but also that the bottom segments of the age-structure pyramid will not drastically narrow. And in Scandinavia, excellent maternity support systems appear to be stemming earlier declines in fertility rates. But other developed countries, such as Germany, Italy, and Japan, already grapple with the consequences of a large rise in the number of their elderly at the same time as their juvenile population is shrinking.

In macroeconomic terms, this is not a welcome development. On the whole, members of a population aged between fifteen and sixty-four tend to create wealth and place fewer demands upon health and social services. Old people, like the very young, tend to consume resources and place higher demands upon health and social services. Some of this financial burden can be anticipated (in richer societies, at least) by national savings and pensions schemes. Nevertheless, in countries where more and more expensive techniques are being used to prolong the lives of those *over seventy-five,* the question is whether these resources might better be invested elsewhere, such as in preventive medicine for the very young or improved educational facilities. Finally, there is the concern that the age structure and spending priorities of a country with a high "elderly dependency ratio" may be a drag upon overall production increases, weakening it relative to societies with a larger proportion of people at work and greater investment of resources in manufacturing and industry.

Still, the subject is too complex to say that all the consequences of this aging trend must be detrimental. A shrinking work force may stimulate a large investment in automation and other labor-saving devices, as in Japan at present.* An aging population may also save more, and thus increase aggregate national savings—although the evi-

*See Chapters 5 and 8.

dence here is not conclusive, since old people might also draw down their personal savings over time. A society with fewer youths is likely to have less crime and may be less prone to go to war, although it will also have fewer potential recruits for the armed services if it is threatened by external foes. How does one weigh the advantages against the disadvantages?

Ironically, all those consequences, negative and positive, will one day affect the peoples of the developing world, if they survive their present demographic explosion. Over the long run, the problem of aging populations in more developed and less developed countries is the same. The differences are in timing, and in scale. The median age of Europeans at present is 33.9 years; yet the median age of Mexico's population is projected to be 33.4 years by 2020. More dramatic still is the case of China, which for years has been trying to control its population growth by such vigorous means as the one-child policy. As a consequence of its relative success, "China in 2025 will have as big a share of over-sixties as Europe in 2010."[33] Whether both areas will have the same per capita resources to allocate to their over-sixties is a different question, especially when one considers the massive quantitative differences. About one-fifth of Italy's population in 2010 will be over sixty-five, or 11 million out of 55 million people. If China's population reaches 1.5 billion in 2025, then, by the same ratio, there will be 300 million elderly dependents, but there is no evidence that provision is being made to support such numbers.

So far, this issue of aging societies has been discussed almost exclusively as a cluster of practical and physical problems; but there is the further issue of deep-rooted cultural and racial anxieties, nicely described in one work as "the fear of population decline."[34] This phenomenon has a long history, including many examples from late-nineteenth-century Europe and the United States of writings and political movements agitating about the "decay" of the species, the fear that a certain race or culture will be overwhelmed in a sea of "lesser" peoples. Central to this anxiety is the belief that one's own racial and linguistic group has a special place in History, unique features within, and contributions to, world civilization, which must be preserved by the continued health and growth in population of the people in question. Should the fertility rate shrink, therefore, it is all too easy for

cultural pessimists to proclaim that the nation is heading for decline
and to agitate for methods to reverse the perceived "biological degener-
acy."[35]

The usual consequence of these anxieties has been efforts to advance
pro-natalist policies, encouraging women to have many more children.
Such efforts range from punitive legislation (forbidding abortion and
contraception), to more practical measures (child allowances, prenatal
and natal care, ensuring release time for working women who are
pregnant), to exhortations and propaganda (awarding medals and titles—
"Heroine of the Soviet Union," for example—to mothers who bore five
or, better still, ten children). These campaigns have been advocated by
right and left, arch-patriotic conservatives urging the same pro-natalist
policies as officials in certain socialist states, with only the liberal "middle" opposing attempts to interfere in a family's desire to choose its
own size.[36]

The obverse side of this anxiety is, of course, a resentment against
other peoples who reproduce at a much faster pace—the assumption
being that, as in a Darwinian struggle, the faster-growing species will
encroach upon, and eventually overwhelm, a population with static or
declining numbers. Such fears are especially prevalent when there
occurs differential growth of ethnic groups within the same country,
since that (it is presumed) may eventually alter the economic and
political balances. Israeli anxieties that the Arab population within
Israel's own (enlarged) boundaries is growing faster than the Jewish
population, the alteration in the Christian-Muslim population balance
in Lebanon (to the Muslims' advantage), and tensions and apprehensions in places as far apart as Quebec and Fiji all remind us of the
political dimensions of population decline. Occasionally, an understanding of these trends may also lead to positive results; to what
extent, one wonders, was the South African government's decision to
abandon apartheid influenced by its recognition of the whites' shrinking share of the total population, from one-fifth in 1951 to one-seventh
in the early 1980s and to a projected one-ninth or one-eleventh by
2020?[37] Overall, however, there appear to have been many more examples of intransigence and conflict, rather than compromise, when a
people has perceived it is in relative demographic decline.

. . .

There is one other response when a population explosion combines with a relative diminution of material resources: people can move out, to places where opportunities beckon. One form of migration is the drift of population from the countryside to the cities, as is happening in the developing world today. While that causes social problems in the cities themselves, most governments and their publics appear much more concerned about a very different form of migration, that from one country to another.

One reason for this concern is material. Because human beings (unlike migrating birds) require so much food, clothing, and shelter and demand many other items, migration always raises the issue of the allocation of resources. If food and land are plentiful, as in the Great Plains in nineteenth-century America, there may be less of a problem (except from the viewpoint of a Plains Indian); if the resources are believed to be more limited, as is felt in many European countries today, more migration will obviously raise the problem of providing for the immigrants. Moreover, large-scale immigration raises the fear of losing control of national boundaries and traditional sovereignty, the fear that an ethnically homogeneous or "pure" race will be altered through intermarriage, the fear not merely of foreign peoples but also of strange ways of life, religious norms, and cultural habits, of the newcomers encroaching upon the property, educational system, and social benefits owned and largely paid for by the natives. More recently, concern has been expressed that illegal immigration into (for example) the United States is responsible for outbreaks of old and new diseases—cholera, measles, AIDS—which place a further strain upon the health-care system as well as provoking new resentments against migrants. Finally, there is always the resident population's fear that if the immigration continues, they themselves may one day become a minority.

Much of the recent concern about uncontrolled migration has been expressed by European nations or by such European offshoots as Australia and the United States, which is very ironic historically. After all, several hundred years ago Europe itself was the source of the most important migratory movement in world history. Its first manifestations occurred centuries earlier, in such forms as the eastward expansion of Germanic settlers and the westward and southward conquests of the Iberian states.[38] But it was the Industrial Revolution in Europe, simultaneously sustaining massive growth in population *and* producing enhanced forms of transportation and weaponry, that really stimulated the continent's outward thrust. Between 1846 and 1890, people emigrated from Europe at an average rate of 377,000 per year, but between 1891 and 1910 emigration soared to an average rate of 911,000 per year. Indeed, between 1846 and 1930, over 50 million Europeans sought a new life overseas. Since the European populations *at home* were also expanding rapidly in this period, their share of total world population steadily increased; according to one calculation, "the Caucasian population was about 22 percent of the human species in 1800, and about 35 percent in 1930."[39] This was the demographic foundation of what would later be termed "the world revolution of Westernization."[40] Whether they liked it or not, other societies across the planet were compelled to respond to the expansion of Western man, his politics, ideas, and economics. Many of them, of course, fell under the direct political control of the European immigrants.

The basic difference today is that whereas that earlier migration went from the technologically advanced societies into less advanced societies,* contemporary migrations chiefly move from less developed societies toward Europe, North America, and Australasia. Given the global imbalances in population trends, this movement ought in principle to help all concerned. Migration from the less developed countries should lower population pressure and unemployment at home, while offsetting the economic problems of negative population growth and an aging work force in the developed countries. Why, then, should North America not allow the influx of millions of families from south of the Rio Grande; or labor-short Japan admit vast numbers of willing workers from Southeast Asia; or the European Community, with its graying populations, welcome the millions of unemployed of North Africa? Since most of Europe has a negative replacement fertility rate

---

*The great exception here was the United States, which, by the mid-nineteenth century at least, was clearly technologically more advanced than Ireland, Italy, Poland, Russia, and other societies from which its immigrants came.

and the populations of Algeria, Morocco, and Tunisia are expected to double over the next few decades, this seems—as *The Economist* put it, no doubt tongue-in-cheek—"the perfect match."[41]

The reason for *The Economist*'s ironic comment on such migration flows is that its editors are well aware of how unpopular immigrants are in countries which lack America's "melting pot" traditions. During the boom years of the 1950s and 1960s, many European nations encouraged guest workers from southern Italy and Portugal, then Turkey, Yugoslavia, North Africa, and other less developed economies. Such guest workers not only provided the nonskilled labor in the factories and at the building sites but also the lower-paid jobs in health care, public transport, sanitation, and related fields. But the problem was that the host countries sought *labor* and got *people*: workers who, joined by their families, required housing and education and medical attention; people who conglomerated in a certain part of the city— usually the area with the cheapest housing—and brought to such districts their restaurants, shops, temples and mosques, foreign habits, foreign cooking, foreign skin. When the host economies slowed down in the late 1970s, it was impossible to return all these guest workers to their countries of origin; and many of them were still useful to their employers. By 1985, therefore, of the 30 million who had traveled to Europe to find work during the preceding decades, a full 5 million remained, whose families brought the total number of permanent immigrants to 13 million.

Although the laws of host countries officially ban discrimination, a nativist prejudice against immigrant communities clearly exists—in Britain against Indians and Pakistanis, in France against Algerians and Moroccans, in Germany against Turks, and in parts of the United States against Latin Americans and Asians. The root of these tensions lies in foreignness, or, to use another word, race. White Americans have no problem in welcoming to their shores many thousands of well-educated professionals from Scandinavia, Britain, and Germany, just as Australians welcomed British (as opposed to Chinese) immigrants, the European colonial states did not oppose the return of ex-settlers from Angola, Rhodesia, and Algeria (though British governments had a different response to Ugandans, Indians, and Hong Kong Chinese), the Germans had little difficulty in the immigration of former *Auslands-*

deutsche, and Israel actively embraces Jewish (but not Arab) immigrants.[42]

Given the political and social tensions that the *relatively limited* transnational migration has recently provoked, there is reason to be concerned should a massive surge in population occur from one country to another. In view of the imbalances in demographic trends between "have" and "have-not" societies, it seems unlikely that there will not be great waves of migration in the twenty-first century. The raw statistics alone suggest that conclusion. Australia, whose 1990 population of 16.7 million is expected to rise gently to 22.7 million by 2025, lies next to an Indonesia whose population is forecast to grow from 180 million to 263 million in the same period. The southern European states of Spain, Portugal, France, Italy, and Greece, whose combined populations are estimated to increase by a mere 5 million between 1990 and 2025, lie close to North African countries (Morocco, Algeria, Tunisia, Libya, Egypt) whose populations are forecast to grow by 108 million in those years. The United States' population is forecast to rise 25 percent by 2025, while its southern neighbors Mexico and Guatemala may grow 88 percent and 225 percent respectively in the same period.[43]

A recent study of "population and security" has suggested that because the territories of the globe are now divided among standing governments controlling their own boundaries, the amount of migration is (and will be) much less than it was a century ago.[44] While it is clear that nations nowadays make greater efforts to restrict immigration (and, in some cases, to prevent emigration), desperate migrants are unlikely to be deterred. Neither the U.S. Immigration and Naturalization Act of 1986 nor patrols along the Mexican border have stemmed the northward flow of migrants, which have again risen to well over a million each year. In July 1991, under pressure from a resentful home population, an embarrassed French government announced a series of stricter measures to reduce illegal migration, including chartering aircraft to deport the migrants; but with right-wing opposition leaders denouncing "the noise and the smell" of the 4 million mainly Arab immigrants, and government ministers themselves admitting the difficulty of accepting more newcomers when the country has a 9.5 percent unemployment rate, the controversy gave the impression that

France had *lost control* of its borders.[45] Furthermore, throughout Western Europe there is concern that the European Community, which permits internal migration and residency, will weaken a member nation's control over the inflow of population from other EC states and reduce its ability to check illegal immigrants. At present, as many as 15 million men, women, and children are living in camps as far apart as Central Europe and Southeast Asia, hoping for somewhere to go. While they, and those already on the move via Mexico and Turkey, may encounter obstacles, many of them are getting through. Often they are aided and sheltered by relations who have already made the trek. And they are increasingly stimulated, as we shall see, by the information revolution, which means that "[p]eople now, even if they are very poor, know how people live in other parts of the world," and will attempt to get there, by land, sea, or air.[46]

These push factors in the overpopulated developing world are compounded by the pull factor of population decline in the more developed societies. Today, as in the past, "billions of peasants and ex-peasants . . . are ready and eager to move into places vacated by wealthier, urbanized populations."[47] As the better-off families of the northern hemisphere individually decide that having only one or at the most two children is sufficient, they may not recognize that they are in a small way vacating future space (that is, jobs, parts of inner cities, shares of population, shares of market preferences) to faster-growing ethnic groups both inside and outside their national boundaries. But that, in fact, is what they are doing.

Enhanced efforts to control migration, therefore, are unlikely to succeed in the face of the momentous tilt in the global demographic balances. Perhaps the most compelling statistic of all is that while the industrial democracies accounted for more than one-fifth of the earth's population in 1950, that share had dropped to one-sixth by 1985 and is forecast to shrivel to less than one-tenth by 2025. By that time, only two of them (the United States and Japan) will be among the top twenty most populous countries, and the rest of the industrial democracies will almost all be regarded as "little countries."[48] This relative diminution of their share of world population presents the industrial democracies with their greatest dilemma over the next thirty years. If the developing world manages to raise its output and standards of living, the West's proportion of economic output, global power, and political influence will decline steadily, simply because of the force of numbers; which in turn has raised the interesting question of whether "Western values"—a liberal social culture, human rights, religious tolerance, democracy, market forces—will maintain their prevailing position in a world overwhelmingly peopled by societies which did not experience the rational scientific and liberal assumptions of the Enlightenment.[49] Yet if the developing world remains caught in its poverty trap, the more developed countries will come under siege from tens of millions of migrants and refugees eager to reside among the prosperous but aging populations of the democracies. Either way, the results are likely to be painful for the richest one-sixth of the earth's population that now enjoys a disproportionate five-sixths of its wealth.

This issue of global demographic imbalances between richer and poorer societies forms the backdrop to all of the other important forces for change that are taking place. There is little doubt that we are witnessing today, in major regions of the world, a population explosion analogous to—but hundreds of times bigger than—that which occurred in Malthus's England. Moreover, it is also occurring at a time of stupendous technological changes in the way we manufacture, grow things, trade, and communicate—changes which will now be examined, not only to consider them on their own terms, but also to see how they might mitigate or aggravate an impending demographic disaster.

3

THE COMMUNICATIONS AND FINANCIAL REVOLUTION AND THE RISE OF THE MULTINATIONAL CORPORATION

ANY ATTEMPT TO ESTIMATE WHETHER today's new technologies can solve an impending demographic crisis needs to be placed in context. The critical issues are which groups and individuals create, control, and have access to the new discoveries, and what are the general economic circumstances in which these scientific breakthroughs occur. This chapter will argue that the world economy is becoming much more integrated and much richer overall, although the creation and enjoyment of that wealth are very uneven. However, it will also argue that the main creators and controllers of technology have increasingly become large, multinational corporations with more global reach than global responsibility. Far from producing a solution to the gap between the world's "haves" and "have-nots," the changing structures of international business and investment may exacerbate them.

The tremendous expansion of the world economy in recent decades is the result of a number of interrelated causes. The most obvious, especially as compared with the troubled interwar years, is that after 1945 a system was set up by the major trading nations to ensure a reasonable degree of financial and economic stability and to restrict protectionist tendencies. With the U.S. dollar as the world currency, America became the "lender of last resort," as the City of London had been in the late nineteenth century, whereas there had been no such lender in the 1920s and 1930s. In addition, the postwar decades saw a remarkably long period of stability in Great Power relationships, at least to the extent that the world's most powerful nations have not gone to war with each other.

This stability, together with the need to rebuild economies after the ravages of World War II, led to an unprecedented rate of growth in world industrial output. Between 1953 and 1975, output grew on average at a remarkable 6 percent a year overall (4 percent per capita), and even in the 1973–80 period the average increase was 2.4 percent a year, which was very respectable by historical standards. Table 1 gives a sense of this dizzy rise, especially compared with the lackluster growth of world manufacturing industries in the inter-war years.

Table 1. Production of World Manufacturing Industries, 1900–80[1]

	Total Production	Annual Growth Rate (%)
1900	100.0	2.6
1913	172.4	4.3
1928	250.8	2.5
1938	311.4	2.2
1953	567.7	4.1
1963	950.1	5.3
1973	1730.6	6.2
1980	3041.6	2.4

These increases refer only to manufacturing. The growth in services such as advertising, banking, catering, and insurance was even greater, as such activities came to occupy an ever-increasing share of the GNP of most advanced economies (well over 70 percent in the United States). Agricultural trade, too, has grown steadily since 1945, as has the international demand for raw materials (especially oil). Given the decades of Great Power stability and the general growth in prosperity, tourism and travel boomed as well, becoming one of the world's greatest industries and employers. In consequence, the global economy grew more since 1945 than in all world history prior to World War II; in fact, world real GNP quadrupled—from 2 trillion to about 8 trillion U.S. dollars—from 1950 to 1980 alone.

Global economic growth has, however, been much more beneficial for the average inhabitant of an advanced industrial economy than for someone living in the developing world. By 1991 the per capita Gross Domestic Product of Switzerland had soared to $36,300, with Sweden ($32,600), Japan ($29,000), and Germany ($27,900) not far behind.* By contrast, India's per capita GDP languishes at a mere $360, and Nigeria's is only $278.[2] And there are, in Saharan and sub-Saharan Africa, as well as in South and Southeast Asia, dozens of countries with even lower average per capita GDPs.[3] The grotesqueness of this disparity in wealth—a citizen of Switzerland enjoys on average several hundred times the income of a native of Ethiopia—is mirrored in the differential rates of child mortality, life expectancy, and access to education. After nearly five decades of unprecedented global economic growth, the world heads toward the twenty-first century with *more than a billion people living in poverty*—an awful enough figure until one realizes that those billion are people "struggling to survive on less than $370 a year,"[4] not the billions of human beings who live in countries like Botswana or Guatemala where the per capita GDP is a relatively satisfactory $750 or a comfortable $1,000 each year—levels that would horrify inhabitants of the "First" World.

This uneven surge in global prosperity has occurred at the same time as—and has interacted with—the emergence of large multinational companies which are increasingly less attached to the particular interests and values of their country of origin. As they compete against rival firms for world market shares, they have developed a strategy of directing investment and production from one part of the earth to another, with the help of revolutionary communications and financial technologies that have created a global marketplace for goods and services. Already important in today's world, these corporations will be even more significant in the future, as Cold War trading barriers break down and the global economy becomes increasingly integrated.[5]

Companies with international rather than national interests are not new. They existed, in embryonic form, in the cosmopolitan private banks of the late nineteenth and early twentieth centuries, whose growth was assisted by the earlier "communications revolution" of the

---

*Followed by Austria ($24,800), the United States ($23,100), and Canada ($23,100). All figures are rounded to the nearest $100 and are at current exchange rates. Germany refers to West Germany only.

telegraph and by the absence of major Great Power coalition wars. The House of Rothschild in 1900, for example, had branches in Frankfurt, Vienna, Paris, and London in daily contact with one another. Lloyds of London before 1914 insured most of the German shipping industry and was prepared to pay out compensation for losses even in the event of an Anglo-German war. Again, earlier examples abound of multinational companies such as Lever Bros. (the forerunners of Unilever), with production facilities ranging from West Africa to India; or of major oil companies, scouring the globe for fresh sources of petroleum and switching the refined products from one market to another. Ford also went "global" when it decided to manufacture cars and trucks on both sides of the Atlantic.

But today's globalization is distinguished from those earlier examples by the sheer quantity and extent of the multinational firms in our expanded and integrated global economy. As noted above, they emerged in a postwar international economic order that reduced protectionism and encouraged a recovery of world trade, and were further stimulated in the 1970s by the United States' decision to abandon the gold standard, followed by a general liberalization of exchange controls, at first only in a few countries, later in many others. This not only provided more liquidity for world trade, but increased the flow of transnational capital investments, as companies invested abroad without constraints imposed by central banks.

Although this financial liberalization helped to expand world commerce, it also produced another effect: the increasing separation of financial flows from trade in manufactures and services. More and more, foreign-currency transactions took place not because a company was paying for foreign goods or investing in foreign assembly, but because investors were speculating in a particular currency or other financial instruments. This surge in global capital flows beyond those required to finance the boom in world industry and commerce is intimately connected with two further occurrences: the deregulation of world money markets, and the revolution in global communications as a result of new technologies. Without the vast increase in the power of computers, computer software, satellites, fiber-optic cables, and high-speed electronic transfers, global markets could not act as one, and economic and other information—politics, ideas, culture, revolutions, consumer trends—could not be delivered instantaneously to the more than 200,000 monitors connected into this global communications system. And all this, according to some pundits, may be only the initial phase.[6]

Except among black marketers and drug dealers, the physical handling of large amounts of currency notes is rapidly becoming redundant. Flows of paper have been replaced by electronic transactions that take place around the clock, picked up in one capital market when another shuts down for the night. From one major exchange to another—Tokyo, Hong Kong and Singapore, London, Frankfurt and Zurich, New York, Chicago, and Toronto—trading in yen futures or in General Motors stock goes on twenty-four hours a day and creates a single market. Daily foreign exchange flows amount to around *one trillion* dollars, and far outweigh the sums employed for the international purchase of goods and services or investments in overseas plants. Indeed, by the late 1980s, more than 90 percent of this trading in the world's foreign exchanges was unrelated to trade or capital investment.[7]

Within this system, and largely because of it, many successful companies are internationalizing themselves. Given a global market, competition among firms—whether automobile producers, aircraft manufacturers, pharmaceutical companies, makers of computer hardware, or publishing houses—is driving them to sell and produce in all of the major economic regions of the world. Not only does the company benefit from economies of scale, but it hopes to protect itself from the vagaries of currency fluctuations, differentiated economic growth, and political interference. A recession in Europe will be of less concern to a firm which also operates in booming East Asian markets than to one exclusively dependent upon European sales. A company interested in developing goods banned by certain bureaucracies (in the biotech industry especially) can switch its manufacture to parts of the world lacking such regulations. A multinational corporation, fretting at the "voluntary controls" imposed by governments to protect indigenous firms from open competition, can often get around those barriers by setting up plants *inside* the protected territory. Once a multinational breaches protectionist obstacles, it is likely to enjoy handsome profit opportunities, at least in the early years, in the newly accessible market.

Even research and product development is being shifted—from the United States to Switzerland, from Germany to California—when it suits a company's needs. For the same motives, large companies rush in to acquire small, innovative firms on the other side of the globe, to forestall preemption by their competitors.

A popular and somewhat shallow interpretation of these trends—put forward not coincidentally by people involved in international consulting and banking—is that the economic consequences of globalization can only be beneficial. In this interpretation, whereas government restrictions previously prevented the consumer from purchasing the best goods, free trade now permits individuals and companies to buy and sell on a world market. Moreover, not only firms but cities, regions, and countries will play a role in this process of global openness and competitiveness, at least if they understand the rules—that is, to invite investment and manufacturing, keep restrictions (including taxes) to a minimum, and provide a well-trained work force and modern infrastructure. If these rules are followed, the multinationals will flock to your door.[8] The result will be an upward surge in wealth creation, a development in which no one loses.

This optimistic interpretation also applauds the way in which the revolution in communications is influencing politics and society. In a world with more than 600 million television sets, viewers are as much consumers of news and ideas as they are of commercial goods. Thus governments of authoritarian states find it increasingly difficult to keep their people in ignorance. Chernobyl was swiftly photographed by a French *commercial* satellite, and then transmitted all over the world— including within the Soviet Union itself. The Chinese government's suppression of the students in Tiananmen Square and the outside world's shock at that event were immediately reported back *into* China by radio, television, and fax messages. As Communist regimes in Eastern Europe fell late in 1989, reports and pictures of each government's demise led to similar events in neighboring states.[9] In other words, just as television in the 1960s helped to shape American public perception and policy concerning civil rights and the Vietnam War, so the spread of the same technology around the world is leading to similar transformations of values.[10] Knowledge and openness, it is assumed, brings with it truth, honesty, fairness, and democracy.

Such a vision of a prosperous and harmonious world economic order, founded upon laissez-faire, twenty-four-hour-a-day trading, and all-pervasive television, seems breathtakingly naive in the light of this planet's demographic, environmental, and regional problems. Cheering references to the way in which the "discriminating consumer" can nowadays buy a Mont Blanc pen or a Vuitton suitcase without regard to that product's country of origin[11] recall Jevons's enthusiasm a century ago about the easy purchase of Argentine beef and Chinese tea.* In both cases, there is a failure to recognize that newer technologies may not benefit all, that the vast majority of the world's population may not be able to purchase the goods in question, and that profound changes both in economic production and in communications can bring disadvantages as well as advantages in their wake.

Since globalization has recently attracted immense publicity, it has become easier to identify which groups and interests are already being hurt by the process or are likely to be affected in the future: economic nationalists, interest groups and companies that wish to protect their domestic markets, workers whose jobs are made redundant when a multinational company moves its assembly and manufacturing elsewhere, and localities in which employment (especially of skilled labor) shrinks. There is, in addition, reason for concern about the volatility of the vast, computer-driven system of financial trading. Finally, since enthusiasts of globalization seem to focus overwhelmingly upon what it means for the "triad" of prosperous societies in North America, Europe, and Japan,[12] they devote less attention to the prospect of a further marginalization of four-fifths of the earth's population not well prepared for these new commercial and financial trends.

To today's economic nationalists, globalization threatens to undermine the assumed integrity of the nation-state as the central organizing unit of domestic and external affairs. The implications of this challenge will be further discussed in Chapter 7, but the general reason for this unease is clear: like illegal migration or global warming, the internationalization of manufacturing and finance erodes a people's capacity to control its own affairs. The idea that we are entering an era in which there will be no national products or technologies, no national corpora-

*See above, p. 9.

tions, and no national industries is bewildering to all who think in traditional terms. In the United States in particular, which for so long has possessed much more of a self-contained economy than, for example, the Netherlands or Britain, it must be unsettling to hear that "as almost every factor of production—money, technology, factories, and equipment—moves effortlessly across borders, the very idea of an American economy is becoming meaningless, as are the notions of an American corporation, American capital, American products, and American technology."[13] If products are no longer "American," what is the point of trying to measure the balance of merchandise trade, or the gap in U.S.-Japan commerce in high-technology goods? While the enthusiasts of globalization want national governments and their agencies to become invisible in the marketplace, many others are made uneasy by such a disappearance. The older ways are more familiar, more comforting—and besides, the people you know and can appeal to (Congress, Parliament, the Treasury) still seem to be in control of economic affairs.

These are not just theoretical concerns but practical, everyday ones, at least for businessmen and politicians struggling to protect certain interests from the effects of globalization. Examples here would be the attempts by Chrysler and Hyster (which makes forklift trucks) to reduce the competition from Japanese rivals by pressing for voluntary restraint agreements or special import duties because American manufacturing was being hurt by unfair foreign practices—a strategy which backfired when it was revealed that Hyster's own "American" forklift trucks contained more foreign parts than those they had identified as "Japanese," and that Chrysler cars contained the highest percentage of foreign-made parts of any made by the big three auto manufacturers.[14]

Consider also the problems that attend efforts by France and Italy to restrict the Japanese share of their home automobile market to a mere 2 percent or 5 percent. Such protectionism was possible when those two countries were still economically sovereign entities. The creation of a tariff-free Economic Community means, however, that Japanese automobiles assembled in Britain—with more than 80 percent local parts—cannot be excluded without a quarrel with the European Commission in Brussels. Nor is this the end of the dilemma, for if Japanese car makers export automobiles to the French and Italian markets from their *American* plants, protectionist politicians in Paris and Italy could find themselves in a dispute with the United States; and the U.S. Department of Commerce, better known for its "Japan-bashing," could be interceding in third markets on behalf of a Japanese company. While the Japanese firms might be operating according to what is now airily termed "the new logic of the global marketplace," these developments suggest that local polities and authorities are increasingly ceding control of their economic destiny. Indeed, the real "logic" of the borderless world is that nobody is in control—except, perhaps, the managers of multinational corporations, whose responsibility is to their shareholders, who, one might argue, have become the new sovereigns, investing in whatever company gives the highest returns.

If major corporations have largely broken free from their national roots, this is even more true of the fast-moving, twenty-four-hour-a-day, border-crossing, profit-hunting system of international finance, in which vast sums of capital—described by one investment authority as "the most purely rational thing there is"[15]—move in and out of a country or a stock according to perceptions of that entity's prospects.

Yet even if money is the most purely rational thing there is, it does not follow that it is immune to instability, panics, and financial flight. Forty years ago, foreign exchange ratios reflected the fundamentals of individual countries' trade balances, and most of the current exchanges that were made related to the flow of goods. Today, the daily volume of foreign exchange trading is *several hundred times* larger than the value of traded goods, and the relationship has altered. Across the world, millions of individual investors, companies, and banks speculate in currencies, many of them automatically following computer-generated indicators that reveal whether (say) the dollar is increasing or decreasing in value relative to other currencies. These players swiftly react to economic data such as the latest trade figures or a rise in interest rates, incidentally making it more difficult for governments and central banks to implement what may be necessary fiscal measures out of fear that international investors may find them unwelcome; a marked reduction in interest rates, judged by a government to be helpful to its country's industries and employment, may be ruled out or at least trimmed because of concern over its effect on the nation's currency. Still more do these investors react to political turbulence such as the threat of a war, or a political assassination. Were the event to be particularly serious—a major earthquake in Tokyo, or the death of the president of the United States—currency markets could be swiftly and seriously destabilized.

The ideological implications of this global system are debated more in Europe than in the laissez-faire United States. The reality nowadays is that any government which offends international finance's demand for unrestricted gain—by increasing personal taxes, for example, or by raising fees on financial transactions—will find its capital has fled and its currency weakened. From the difficulties of the Wilson government in the late 1960s, to the Mitterrand administration's failed attempt to "go it alone" in its economic policies of the early 1980s, to the experiences of innumerable regimes in the developing world, the message is clear: if you do not follow the rules of the market, your economy will suffer. But the market's message ignores important considerations. If, say, a French Socialist government is conscientiously attempting to provide better schools, health care, housing, and public utilities for its citizenry, by what means can it raise the necessary funds without alarming international investors who may be not at all interested in the well-being of those citizens but merely in their own profits? The rational market, by its very nature, is not concerned with social justice and fairness.

Political issues aside, there are practical problems in endowing a single currency—the U.S. dollar—with such an overwhelming responsibility within the international financial system. In the 1940s and 1950s, there was no alternative to that arrangement, which in any case rested upon firm foundations: the U.S. economy was strong, it enjoyed a national current-account surplus, and America was by far the world's largest creditor nation; its budgetary deficits were small, currencies were in fixed relation to one another (and to gold), and foreign-exchange dealings were controlled. There was thus much less room for volatility in the financial markets, at the same time as capital flows were relatively small. Today, none of those conditions applies. The American share of world assets is significantly smaller; the United States has run large current-account deficits for many years, covered by borrowing from abroad, which has made it an international debtor in a spectacularly brief period of time; the amount of speculative capital in the system is much larger and is under far less institutional control; and American political leadership has become used to huge budgetary and current-accounts deficits without having to face the discipline of the markets, which would be the fate of politicians in countries not benefiting from the special position of the U.S. dollar.

Orthodox economists offer many reasons why the present financial system will continue. As American deficits grow, foreigners simply hold more dollars. For various structural reasons, it is argued, no other currency can replace the dollar—at least not in the foreseeable future. Therefore, the position of the U.S. dollar remains "unassailable," according to the optimists.[16] History shows, however, that previous international monetary regimes—such as the one that revolved around the gold standard, the pound sterling, and the City of London prior to 1914—became ever more difficult to sustain when the hub economy itself began to lose its relative strength and competitiveness.[17] Current economic trends—the diminution of the American share of global assets, the rise of such other currencies as the yen and the ECU, the emergence of new financial centers, the increasing share of American national wealth needed for debt repayment—suggest that the post-1945 international monetary regime may also be drawing to a close, *without* an adequate successor system in view.

Ultimately, all these concerns are about credit. The system itself has to be believed in. If its credibility fails because more and more people become doubtful about American indebtedness or the value of the dollar or the volatility of the Tokyo stock market, those worries could explode in panic—especially when the system itself can rush hundreds of billions of dollars in and out of a currency in half a day's trading. Central banks and finance ministries have put emergency controls in place to avoid a financial "meltdown," but such controls have not yet been fully tested, and their very existence reflects fear on the part of those monitoring this vast, free-flowing flood of capital that people might one day cease to believe in the system.

What have these financial matters to do with preparing for the year 2025, and with the larger problems facing our global society? At first glance, the investment calculations of a multinational company's strategic planners and the daily maneuvers of Tokyo speculators may appear to overlap little with the challenges facing a West African groundnut producer or a Malaysian tin miner. If this is true, it means that the great gap between the rich and poor in today's world is increasing; how, indeed, will a technologically sophisticated, transnational, corporate culture, loyal to no government and beyond the reach of local regulation, coexist with the polyglot, hungry, and dissatisfied masses foreshadowed by a world population of 8 or 10 billion?[18] Moreover, if profound financial instability does occur as a consequence of the fast-flowing but irresponsible system of monetary exchanges, severe shocks to the international trading order are likely to depress developing world commodity prices—coffee, cocoa, ores—most of all. That was a lesson of the 1930s, and of the post-oil-shock 1970s. The continued dependence of developing countries upon such exports suggests that the same would be true today. Events in Central America may have little impact upon Wall Street, but Wall Street's actions could have serious consequences for the developing world.

Even within the industrial democracies themselves, the globalization of production, investment, and services has serious consequences. Until recently, many large companies still retained the characteristics of the typical post-1945 corporation: located in a particular region, the provider of jobs to its skilled blue-collar work force and to layers of managers, the provider also of philanthropic and social goods to the "company town." Although examples still exist of such localist and paternalist firms, many have been compelled by international competition to discard all such loyalties to the town, the region, or the country. "The United States," one prominent American executive observed, "does not have an automatic call on our resources. There is no mind-set that puts the country first."[19] In consequence, states, regions, cities, and townships have become "bidders" for the presence of a new factory, or, more often, the retention of an existing plant which a multinational company may be thinking of moving. If the community in question can offer enough inducements—tax concessions, operating subsidies, training grants—as did Danville, Illinois, in 1983 in a bid to win a new forklift assembly plant, it may succeed, at least for a while; if it does not make enough concessions, like Portland, Oregon, in the same bidding war, it will lose. If a union at one plant is willing to agree to the demands of the corporation—as did the General Motors workers in Arlington, Texas, thereby contributing to the closure of the firm's factory in Ypsilanti, Michigan, where the union was less cooperative—it may survive, until the next time.[20] Since communities and unions are bidding for the same jobs, it follows that one region's enhanced (or retained) employment means another region's rising unemployment. Winner or loser, it is clear that there is "uneven bargaining power" between communities and the globalized company.[21]

Within the developed world, globalization also affects the career expectations of individuals and the structure of employment generally. In the United States, which has opened itself to laissez-faire forces more readily than other industrial democracies, lawyers, biotechnology engineers, economics editors, software designers, and strategic planners are in demand because they contribute a high "added value" to whatever they are working upon. The demand for their services is international—the request for the software design, or legal brief, or "op-ed" commentary upon a diplomatic crisis may come from anywhere in the developed world—just as the means of communicating this knowledge (via Express Mail, or fax) are also international. Unlike the fast-food server, or the local policeman or schoolteacher, or the blue-collar worker, these creators and conveyors of high-added-value information are no longer linked to a regional or even a national economy. They have become functioning and prosperous parts of a borderless world—and, like the growing number of their equivalents in Europe, Japan, and Australasia, will remain so just as long as their education, skills, expertise, and inventiveness are in demand from distant consumers.

Much more important, in social and political terms, is the fate of the four-fifths of Americans who are not in such international demand. Skilled blue-collar employees—the core of the traditional high-per-capita-income U.S. work force, and the backbone of the Democratic Party—have lost jobs in the millions as American firms wilted under international competition or relocated industrial production to other countries with lower labor costs. During the 1980s, the United Auto Workers lost 500,000 members even as companies like General Motors were adding to employment abroad.[22] At the same time as high-paying blue-collar jobs were disappearing, millions of new jobs were being created across the United States. Unfortunately, the vast majority of those positions were low-paid casual or unprotected jobs requiring few skills and offering little opportunity, such as work in fast-food stores, gas stations, discount supermarkets, hotels, and cleaning and gardening services. An increasing majority of Americans have found their real standards of living—like the real level of national productivity—stagnating since the mid-1970s. Just as the gap between the upper one-fifth and lower four-fifths of global society has increased, so also, though less drastically, has the upper one-fifth in American society detached itself from the rest.

Although it is too early yet to be certain, these changes in American society—and in societies that go the "American way"—may also affect the debate on North-South relations. A family whose chief wage-earner has lost his job because the factory was moved to Mexico or Thailand is unlikely to be sympathetic to pleas for enhanced development aid to poorer countries. Employees who lack a college education and scramble to retain their low-paying positions as hospital janitors or office cleaners will resent the infiltration of immigrants (whether legal or illegal) willing to work longer hours and for less money. Politicians in constituencies suffering from factory closings by multinationals will be tempted—are already tempted—to push for greater protection of the home market, regardless of what that means for the developing world. Well-heeled professionals, who are college-educated, drive Volvos, contribute to Oxfam, and are sympathetic to environmental concerns, may increasingly recognize the need for unpopular reforms to counter worrying global trends; but that is unlikely to be true for most of their fellow citizens, who are finding it hard to preserve their standards of living.

The implications for the developing world of the financial and communications revolutions and the rise of the multinational corporations are even more sobering. So much of the breathlessly enthusiastic literature about the benefits of globalization focuses upon what is happening in

Europe, North America, and Japan, plus certain extensions of that triad (South Korea, Brazil, Australia). But little is said about the rest of the world. From the perspective of laissez-faire theory—from Adam Smith and Cobden to Kenichi Ohmae today[23]—such countries presumably become relevant only when they learn the lessons of the marketplace and possess those features which allow them to compete in the border-less world: a well-educated population, lots of engineers, designers and other professionals, a sophisticated financial structure, good communications, enormous deposits of knowledge (libraries, computers, laboratories), adequate capital and entrepreneurs, and perhaps a fledgling multinational corporation or two. If this has happened in South Korea, why can't it happen in every country of the world?

Chapter 10 argues that this beguiling theory is too abstract. Not merely would it require the ending of corrupt regimes, excess spending on the military, bureaucratic ineptitude, protection of special interests, lack of legal protection, religious fundamentalism, and all the other obstacles to commerce which exist in many countries in Central America, the Middle East, and sub-Saharan Africa. It would also involve a transformation of the dominant value systems in many developing world societies that are antithetical to the norms of Western rationalism, scientific inquiry, legal theory, and capitalism. Until such a profound change occurs, it is hard to foresee when Ethiopian-based or Philippine-based multinational companies, flush with funds and talented personnel, will begin to move into Japan or New England, making strategic acquisitions as they take *their* historic turn at the center of the global economic stage.

Accepting the logic of the global marketplace will also be difficult because of the structural obstacles that cramp many of today's developing nations. The idealized picture, in which hyperefficient multinational corporations compete to bring their latest products to discriminating consumers across the globe while governments become all but invisible, makes seductive reading; but it ignores the fact that what most poorer nations need is not simply the liberating effects of free-market economics, but also enormous investments in social improvement. In a predominantly agrarian, land-locked African country whose population is doubling every twenty-five years, the most urgent needs would appear to be family planning, environmental protection, health care, education, and basic infrastructure—which free-market, multinational corporations are not likely to be interested in financing. In other words, huge public funds are required—whether in Central Africa or Eastern Europe—before conditions become attractive to investment managers of Japanese and American companies. But how such public funds are to be provided is rarely if ever touched upon by the fans of globalization.

Moreover, if a developing country does manage to reconstitute itself on the East Asian model and enjoys a rise in foreign investment, production, exports, and standards of living, then it could in turn become steadily more susceptible to the relocation of branch plants and jobs as multinationals search for still cheaper regions for manufacture and assembly. According to borderless-world theories, this is not a problem; if the principles of supply and demand really work efficiently, deindustrialization and unemployment ought not to last for long: "In this interlinked economy, there is no such thing as absolute winners and losers. A loser becomes relatively attractive as its currency gets weaker and an unemployed work force emerges that is available at reasonable cost."[24] Just as an American automobile company would be willing to move assembly plants *back* to the United States if its currency and labor costs fell far enough, so would an obliging multinational return to (say) Malaysia or Brazil when it became cheap enough again. Such unimaginative reasoning does not consider whether the working populations and governments of newly industrializing countries are likely to remain complacent when multinational corporations move elsewhere, as happened to a large extent in northern England and the Ohio Valley. An angry native reaction and a backlash against being treated as the economic pawns of First World companies are equally plausible.

Poorer societies may come to resent cosmopolitan capitalism for two further reasons, both of them consequences of the financial/communications/multinational revolution. The first is the possibility that the transmission of information from one part of the globe to another via 1.5 billion radios and 600 million television sets may not necessarily lead to universal enthusiasm for the Western way of life, as some optimistic commentators have suggested. It is a remarkable technical and manufacturing achievement that as the 1980s ended, billions of people from the Inner Mongolian plain to the Andean mountains were able for the first time to see the world outside via television.[25] It is also true that the information revolution played a critical role in the demise of Communist societies that had visibly failed to keep up with the West.

Still, it is less certain that the poorest four-fifths of the world will necessarily emulate the Western prosperity that it sees on television. If domestic obstacles to reform remain entrenched, as appears likely in many developing societies, one response could be a vast migration to the richer parts of the globe, while others retreat into fundamentalism and reject Western values (especially its conspicuous consumerism). There could also be growing bafflement and resentment in developing countries at the structural obstacles to achieving the standards of living enjoyed by industrial democracies. Instead of creating masses of discriminating consumers of Vuitton suitcases, the coming of a telecommunications revolution to developing countries could well cause billions of "have-nots" to feel ever more angry at the "haves"—including the engineers and managers of multinational companies in their midst.

Globalized communications, moreover, work in many ways. The Islamic fundamentalist revolution against the shah of Iran was orchestrated from Paris by the Ayatollah Khomeini through audiotaped sermons that were widely distributed in his native country. Television also has complex consequences. While viewers in the developing world gape at the riches displayed in programs like *Dallas* and *Brideshead Revisited,* the peoples of the industrial democracies are exposed to frequent coverage of the dreadful poverty, malnutrition, and other effects of wars and natural disasters that continue to afflict Africa, the Middle East, and elsewhere. In the case of a terrible disaster, like the Ethiopian famine of 1985, this sometimes produces a broad public response from horrified viewers in the North. Again, the graphic footage of Kurdish families fleeing the wrath of Saddam Hussein in early 1991—and the reactions of European governments and American public opinion—forced the White House to help create enclaves for the Kurdish refugees.

But television is constantly in search of newer and more dramatic topics, and coverage of such events swiftly fades. Moreover, as mentioned above, individuals who have suffered economically because of competition from developing countries or who believe that the domestic ills of their own society require attention first may be less eager to support moves to assist poorer nations—especially if a significant redistribution of resources is involved. Disaster relief is one thing, structural adjustments are another. Nevertheless, given that 95 percent of future population growth will occur in developing countries, the basic issue remains: how will the peoples of this planet relate to each other at the dawn of the twenty-first century as increasing billions of poverty-stricken peasants view (but do not share) the North's wealth, while millions of prosperous families in the industrial democracies are exposed to the demographic and environmental disasters that their fellow human beings are suffering? Will it produce reforms—or apathy and resentment?

A further consequence of globalization, which will be discussed in detail in the following chapters on biotechnology and robotics, is that companies in the developed world are investing in new technologies which could greatly harm poorer societies, by providing substitutes for millions of jobs in agriculture and industry. Such investment is driven by the same profit-seeking motives that have propelled technological innovation since the Industrial Revolution at least; but just as the intentional creation of the power-driven textile factory, the steel mill, and the railway had profound, *unintended* results for domestic and foreign populations, so also are some of today's emerging technologies likely to have profound consequences for contemporary societies, especially in the developing world. As the twenty-first century approaches, therefore, the peoples of the earth seem to be discovering that their lives are ever more affected by forces which are, in the full meaning of the word, irresponsible.

4

WORLD AGRICULTURE AND THE
BIOTECHNOLOGY REVOLUTION

AS "GLOBALIZED" BUSINESS EMERGES IN
richer countries while population pressures increase in poorer ones, is
there any way that human ingenuity can reverse this ominous mismatch? At the least, could not the problem of widespread malnutrition
be tackled by new inventions? The second reason that Malthus's dire
predictions about England's future were proved wrong, it will be re-
membered, was a so-called Agricultural Revolution which enhanced
"the power in the earth." What are the prospects of another such
escape, this time for the vastly larger populations of the developing
world? During the 1980s alone, an additional 842 million people were
added to the earth's population,[1] while croplands were eliminated to
make way for roads and buildings, soil erosion and degradation caused
millions of acres of farmland to be abandoned, and careless irrigation
led to widespread salinization of the soil. This makes a significant
increase in productivity of the remaining farmland all the more urgent,
for otherwise malnutrition and starvation will increase.

Until recently, it appeared that global agricultural output was expanding nicely. From 1950 to 1984, food production rose faster than
ever before in human history. World grain harvests rose 2.6 times in
those years, which was more than the increase in global population.

Production of root crops, meat, milk, fish, fruits, and vegetables also expanded, in response to worldwide demand for food caused by population growth and enhanced standards of living. Millions of additional acres were cultivated, and newer machines, more fertilizer, better irrigation, and crop rotation were introduced to farming across the world.

The best example of this change was what came to be known as the "green revolution" in Asia, where, in addition to improved mechanization and fertilization, great advances occurred because of biotechnological breeding of newer strains of plants. New hybrid rice strains turned out to be more durable—more resistant to diseases and pests—and produced higher yields. Some new rices yielded two to three times more than traditional varieties. Moreover, because the new strains were readily made available to developing countries by International Agricultural Research Centers, there took place a superb example of international research and applied agricultural science. In consequence, world rice production rose from 257 million tonnes in 1965 to 468 million tonnes twenty years later. "Miracle rice" was said to have averted famines, weaned poor countries off dependence on imported food, and provided political stability.[2] Being swifter and more widespread, the green revolution had a far greater impact than Britain's eighteenth-century agricultural revolution.

Since 1984, however, the pace of increase in global agricultural production has slowed considerably, partly because of intense droughts in the United States and elsewhere that occurred in 1988. Instead of the roughly 3 percent annual increases in grain output of the 1950–84 years, overall production rose by only 1 percent annually between 1984 and 1989. Global production of root crops peaked in 1984 and has declined since then, because of overuse of fertilizers (which seem to expand crop growth for a while, before it levels off), attacks by new diseases, the deterioration of soil quality, and the fact that there was less suitable land available for further planting.[3] Moreover, recent figures indicate that the yields of some crops, especially rice, have now also leveled, suggesting that the miracle increases have run their course.[4] Scientific breakthroughs could reverse this trend; on the other hand, if the reduction of forests and other habitats causes further loss of plant species and reduced biological diversity, that could cut hopes of producing improved strains.*

Overall, global food production continues to increase, but more slowly than before. Production of cereal, the most important food crop, has not kept up with population growth. The period 1984–89 may be too short to show a long-term trend—there was also a similar worry in the early 1970s—but if cereal production continues to rise at about 1 percent a year on average and global population at 1.7 percent a year, the predictable results will soon be felt. This is particularly true in Africa, where the seemingly impressive 23 percent rise in total food production from 1976–78 to 1986–88 has been outpaced by higher population growth, so that per capita food production actually declined 8 percent over that decade.[5] In the Middle East and Latin America, rises in food production have been matched by population increases, a situation which could worsen. Political convulsions in Eastern and Central Europe and the backwardness of agriculture there and in the former USSR make matters worse.

Because global food consumption has exceeded production for a number of years, reserves of carryover stocks have been falling, as Chart 3 indicates for cereals.

1988 may have been a freakishly hot and dry summer, but if the United States experiences further droughts, the reserve stocks upon which more than a hundred food-importing countries rely will fall still further. Thus, we may be at the beginning of an ominous long-term trend in which population grows faster than food production. According to the Worldwatch Institute, increases of 28 million tons of grain are needed each year merely to keep pace with population growth, yet recently the annual net gain has been closer to 15 million tons. This means that the number of seriously undernourished people in the world has been rising, decade upon decade, so that it is now well over 500 million.[6]

In industrialized nations, where massive protectionist subsidies have led to "butter mountains," "wine lakes," silos and even aircraft hangars

---

*In general, a strain of crop such as wheat and rice will lose its resistance to disease and pests about 5 to 15 years after introduction and need to be replaced by new strains.

Chart 3. World Cereal Carryover Stocks

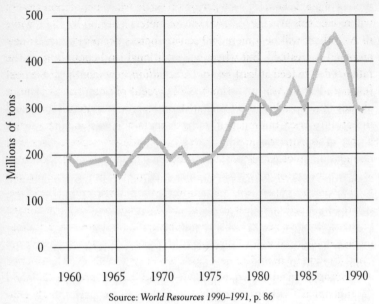

Source: *World Resources 1990–1991*, p. 86

bursting with surplus grain, it may be hard to imagine that there is an impending shortage as farmers idle millions of hectares of cropland. Yet while such additional capacity exists, the use of that land might still not solve the key problem, which is how poorer nations will *pay* for the food they have to import. Because of reduced stocks, world wheat and rice prices have risen considerably since 1986–87, while developing world currencies have fallen in value. Since northern-hemisphere farmers won't grow crops without compensation, an international mechanism would be required to transfer the crops to those nations in a sustained way. While a lot of food aid is donated at present, much more is needed to meet the doubling and trebling of African and Asian populations. But this does not solve the larger problem: an increase in food aid merely increases the dependency of poorer peoples upon their richer cousins, whereas a failure to supply such aid could intensify migration out of food-deficit countries.

Another way to help poorer nations feed their people would be to augment the amount of cropland. While there are now 2,800 square meters of arable land for each person on earth, world population growth will reduce this average to 1,700 square meters a person by 2025, while in Asia there will be a mere 900 square meters per person unless new cropland is created.[7] But where will additional land come from at the rate needed to feed at least two or three *billion* new mouths in the next few decades? In Asia, an estimated 82 percent of potential cropland is already under production. There are large reserves of potential cropland in Latin America, but much of this is marginal soil, unsuitable for major crops, or is Amazonian rain forest, which deserves protection, not denudation; in other regions, too, additional cropland could only come at the expense of forests, accelerating global warming and putting further pressure upon world agriculture in the longer term. In Africa, where food needs are greatest, widespread overgrazing and soil damage have resulted in a net loss of land suitable for agriculture, and few areas receive enough rainfall to support grain crops. Thus spare agricultural capacity lies chiefly in the developed world, especially North America and Europe, not in the countries where the food is most needed; and "cornucopian" writings about this general reserve capacity rarely consider the problem of *global* supply and demand. Moreover, if the forecasts about land degradation and the drawing-down of the water tables are correct,* the Great Plains of the American Midwest may not long provide grain surpluses to feed a world of eight or ten billion people.

Another possibility is to increase the efficiency of farmers in poorer countries. In some East Asian rice fields, up to 40 percent of fertilizers are wasted because of inefficient application, while poor crop management, storage, and handling wastes up to 20 percent of rice grown.[8] The average African farmer produces only 600 kilograms of cereals a year, compared to 80,000 kilograms, or 130 times as much, per agricultural worker in North America. Clearly, there *are* many ways to increase agricultural efficiency in the poorer areas of the world, including better training and instruction, improved access to markets, more skillful handling of seeds, better crops, fertilizers, and farm machinery, and ecologically sound agroforestry. Even so, such piecemeal and local

*See below, pp. 99, 319–20.

improvements must overcome stubborn geographical, economic, and social obstacles; after all, the American farmer is 130-fold more productive than his African counterpart because he owns far larger tracts of land, enjoys a more favorable growing climate and better infrastructure, is much more highly capitalized, uses modern machinery and quality fertilizers and seeds, has access to much more information, and so on. If the conditions of the African farmer were similar, Africa would not be a "developing" continent. The final cruel point is that if African farmers *were* as productive as their American counterparts, there would be a massive displacement of labor, with little prospect of employment by industry or services. In sum, rural poverty in Africa, Asia, and elsewhere will not be solved by technical fixes, if structural and cultural aspects of the problem remain unattended.

Because none of these more traditional solutions seems adequate, attention in recent years has focused upon biotechnology as a possible answer. Biotechnology means "any technique that uses living organisms or processes to make or modify products, to improve plants or animals, or to develop microorganisms for specific uses."[9] It has developed from the remarkable breakthroughs made by scientists since the 1950s in understanding the genetic code. Genes exist in all life processes and contribute to the inheritance of specific characteristics, whether a human being's tendency to overweight or a plant's susceptibility to a certain pest. Scientists can isolate, clone, and study the structure of the gene and seek to understand its relationship to the processes of living things. Genetic engineers are now able to insert into the DNA of a living cell a new gene to improve the organism's strength, or size, or resistance.[10]

Although medical biotechnology has attracted twenty times more capital investment than agricultural biotechnology, it is the latter's potential to improve and possibly even transform agriculture that is important here. This use of biotechnology can be seen as an entirely new stage in humankind's attempts to produce more crops and plants. For thousands of years, farmers have sought to improve their plants and livestock by selective breeding, guessing that some sort of internal element improves desirable characteristics or suppresses unwanted ones. According to one estimate, 70 percent of the increased corn yields in the United States from 1930 to 1980 derived from selective breeding. Today genetic engineers believe that in months or years they can achieve by genetic manipulation improvements in yields that would take decades using conventional plant-breeding techniques.[11]

Given all the publicity about the biotech revolution in agriculture, those achievements need not be described in detail here. They range from inserting a bovine growth hormone into cattle to increase their milk output to genetic alterations of the reproductive cells of fish, poultry, sheep, and pigs; from creating plants that are resistant to viruses or insects to engineering crops that are impervious to certain weedkillers, allowing farmers to spray indiscriminately; from creating faster-growing tropical crops like bamboo to experiments to produce plants that would fix their own nitrogen, thereby reducing the need for chemical-based nitrogen.[12]* Such breakthroughs, when presented by the popular media, all too often suggest that we have reached another watershed in technology and productivity, with beneficial results to all.

As will be argued in the rest of this chapter, such a conclusion is naive. Biotechnology is by no means a menace, but it will produce winners and losers, as all earlier technology-driven revolutions have done.

Some of the concerns about this new technology have less to do with its economic impacts than with health and environmental issues. Hogs into which growth hormones have been inserted are subject to gastric ulcers, arthritis, dermatitis, and other diseases, which makes them not only unappealing but possibly dangerous for human consumption.[13] Herbicide-resistant crops could increase the indiscriminate spraying of "designer" herbicides, which will then be carried away in the atmosphere or water drainage system. Moreover, if weeds and pests develop a resistance to these new biological enemies—as they have done to many chemical agents—the biotech companies will have to invent improved variants, thereby producing a "treadmill" in their effort to subdue nature.

---

*As will be evident from the rest of this chapter, the time horizon for the commercial applications of these inventions varies enormously. Some are in use now. Others are merely prototypes, and it will be years before they are fully ready *and* receive governmental approval.

There is also danger, scientists warn, in the increasing genetic uniformity of key plants. Traditional farmers cultivated hundreds, even thousands, of types of grass seeds, potatoes, and the like. Modern farmers purchase plants redesigned by genetic engineers who blend the best attributes from various seeds into a new one to increase productivity and meet consumer taste. If, however, billions of rows of essentially identical corn are planted each year, the entire crop becomes vulnerable to a single pest or disease. In 1970, an unexpected epidemic of corn leaf blight destroyed half the crop from Florida to Texas; and as recently as 1984 a new bacterial disease forced the destruction of millions of Florida citrus trees and seedlings. The biotech revolution will enhance yields, therefore, but may also increase the risk of costly crop failures.

Another environmental concern is that biotech agriculture will encourage the *evasion* of fundamental ecological reforms. To put it bluntly, if crop species can be developed that thrive in salty soil or in hot, dry climates, will farmers ignore the sources of environmental damage and simply wait for scientists to engineer new seeds for new conditions? Would genetically modified fish, able to flourish in acidified lakes, undercut the determination to clean up air and water? Instead of dealing with global warming, or the salinization of the soil through excessive irrigation, or the too-swift reduction of the bamboo forests, scientists are inventing plants that attempt to "collaborate" with the environmental changes that human activities are causing. Rather than encouraging farmers to work *with* nature, environmentalists protest, high-yield agriculture has now incorporated biotechnology into its arsenal of weapons, without confronting the larger question of ecological damage.[14] Ironically, a counterargument has been put that because natural habitats for wild plants are disappearing so fast, it is becoming more necessary to develop alternative sources in the laboratory[15]—suggesting that as population pressures erode rain forests and other plant habitats, the greater will be humankind's reliance upon laboratory-based rather than natural produce.

·   ·   ·

The potential economic impacts of biotechnology are critically important, both for farming in general and for North-South relations. The
new technology is occurring at a time when global agriculture is facing
two very different—indeed, contradictory—structural crises. The rich
countries suffer from overproduction; the poorest suffer from too little
production. This imbalance is nothing new, and the differences between food-surplus and food-deficit peoples were historically one of the
earliest and greatest stimuli to international trade. What *is* new is the
sheer size of the imbalances, and of the populations affected by them.

Also new—and very different from the gentleman farmers who were
responsible for the Agricultural Revolution in Malthus's time—is the
existence of large agrichemical and biotech corporations, racing to offer
new products. Like multinational companies in other fields, they see
their task as bringing new goods to a world market, without worrying
about the regional impacts—and social consequences—of this further
stage in the product cycle.[16] Because they compete with one another,
these companies prefer to shroud their research in secrecy and restrict
its use by patents, which is a major difference from the green revolution
of the 1960s, in which the technological breakthroughs were created
in the public sector—like the UN-funded International Potato Center
in Perú—and access to them was relatively unproblematic.[17] In deny-
ing their knowledge to rivals in the developed world—or requiring
them to pay a fee for its use—the biotech industry is making it more
difficult for the developing world to acquire those research techniques.

For large companies engaged in biotech research, the future looks
extraordinarily attractive; a totally new industry is emerging as the lines
begin to blur between farmers, seed growers, fertilizer companies, food-
processing plants, and the other distinct parts of the process of getting
cereals and livestock from the farm to the kitchen table. This vertical
integration among biotech corporations is qualitatively different from
previous types of integration. Chemical companies are now able not
only to grow their own feedstocks from patented microbes or seeds, but
also to use biotech for food processing. DNA has been described as a
new corporate resource that can be patented and owned, designed in
the laboratory, and used to replace raw materials; it also can reduce
labor costs, circumvent erratic variables like weather, and produce large

numbers of scarce materials cheaply. It possesses a language common
to chemistry, pharmacology, energy, food, and agriculture, and can be
used broadly and efficiently by corporations involved in many fields of
high-value-added biological and chemical research.[18]

Precisely because the range of biotech applications is so vast, it is
difficult to think through its larger consequences. What needs to be
kept in mind, however, is the distinction between biotechnology which
enhances food output *in the field,* and the newer science which is
creating synthetic products *in vitro,* in the laboratory. Both have profound implications, but it is the latter—obviously, still very experimental and regarded by many scientists as being a long way off—which
could bring the more serious consequences.

Like the steam engine and electricity, biotechnology seems likely to
introduce a new historical era and greatly change the way people live.
It offers new products and improved ways of creating existing ones. It
opens new markets, reduces the costs of many manufactures and services, and might alter the pattern of international trade. It could
change the way national economies are structured, how investment
capital is allocated, and the spectrum of scientific knowledge. It will
create many new jobs and eliminate many traditional ones.

And the latter effect is, of course, a major problem for global society
and employment. Land, natural resources, and labor have been regarded for millennia as the chief "factors" of economic production, but
this is becoming less true as mankind depends increasingly upon service
industries, laboratories, and automated factories. Given the need to
increase food production *and* the existence of powerful forces embracing the new technology, the biotech movement is unlikely to be halted.
But we need to think through the consequent "trivialization" of agriculture, and the possibility that crops will no longer be grown naturally
outdoors, anxiously cared for by millions of independent peasants and
farmers: that instead they will be the biomass feedstocks for downstream processing by the same companies that designed the seeds and
embryos to begin with.[19] To the consumer, biogenetically manufactured food may taste the same; indeed, it will be genetically instructed
to taste that way. To the farmers of the world, however, such a revolution in food production will be viewed differently. Like the handloom

weavers or coach builders of the nineteenth century, they are threatened with redundancy.

In the developed world, biotech farming is likely to exacerbate commercial relations among the big three trading blocs. While Japan is a food importer, the United States and the European Community have large agricultural surpluses. All three blocs provide subsidies to their farming sectors and quarrel among themselves over protectionism. Although farming is an inherently economic issue, that is not the whole story. Self-sufficiency in agriculture is frequently justified by reasons of national security (e.g., in France), or by a cultural attachment to a particular home-grown crop (e.g., rice in Japan). In all cases, there is a belief—by no means confined to residents of the countryside—that family and village farming represent continuity, stability, and closeness to nature that ought to be protected in a world of bewildering change.

But economic interests also influence the politics of farming in the developed world. Although the percentage of the population engaged in agriculture is not large in developed countries—3 percent in the United States, 4.8 percent in (West) Germany, 2.1 percent in Britain, 6.7 percent in France, 8 percent in Japan, 9.1 percent in Italy—farming lobbies remain enormously influential. From Wisconsin to Normandy, from Upper Bavaria to Kyushu, politicians fear they have little prospect of reelection if they are not seen to be protecting local farmers. Income and price supports given to growers in the industrial countries amount to about $250 billion each year.

Because farmers form such a differentiated industry, their attitudes to the biotech revolution are mixed. Some, chiefly larger operations, have embraced the package of products offered by biotech companies, whereas small farmers have fought against the trend or have only selectively adopted the new technology. National differences also count. Because of the United States' more relaxed policy toward biotech inventions, isoglucose took over one third of the American sugar market within ten years. By contrast, the European Community, traditionally more protectionist in agriculture, erected strict quotas for isoglucose in 1979; had it been allowed to penetrate the market in Europe to the extent it did in America, it is calculated that a substitution of

2.8 million tons of sugar would have resulted, equal to the entire sugar-beet acreage of West Germany.[20]

A second example concerns the introduction of the bovine growth hormone, which pits four of the largest companies in this field—Monsanto, Upjohn, Eli Lilly, and American Cyanamid—against American dairy farmers, or rather against *some* dairy farmers. Should the drug be widely adopted, the number of cows needed to meet America's milk requirements would likely drop from 10.8 million to 7.5 million by the year 2000 and the number of commercial dairy farms would be halved.[21] But while Wisconsin and Minnesota have banned the use of bovine growth hormone, Vermont has approved its use, which raises the issue of a differentiated response to new technology, something not, of course, confined to agriculture.[22] What if certain states or countries encourage new methods while others oppose them? One consequence, in the age of multinational corporations, will be that companies transfer their R&D efforts—and the attendant flow of young scientific talent—to hospitable countries; already, for example, major German pharmaceutical firms have chosen to locate their DNA research in the United States because of restrictions in Germany itself.[23]

Among farming communities in the developed world there exists—understandably—a deep anxiety about the possibility of *in vitro* laboratory production of basic items of food. It is one thing to have a genetically engineered tomato that is pest-resistant or doesn't go soft quickly; it is another to learn that some biotech firms may be creating *in vitro* tomato pulp, orange juice, apple sauce, and tobacco that don't have to be farmed at all. Even if this research is merely experimental at present and faces the obstacle of large production costs, the implications of replacing the traditional citrus or tobacco industry with synthetic products are so enormous—affecting growers, truckers, perhaps even the large foodstore companies themselves*—that this development, when it eventually occurs, might be heavily resisted.[24]

Nevertheless, it could be that richer nations with food deficits will embrace the biotech revolution to save foreign exchange on imported agricultural goods, whereas food-surplus countries will restrict the

---

*The argument here being that some of the *in vitro* produce could come from a relatively small biotech company, thus threatening the existing operations of large food-processing and foodstore firms.

technology out of deference to their farming constituencies. Here, of course, the contrast between Japan's position and that of the United States and Europe could not be more marked; Japan's difficult geography is exactly the sort of terrain that crop biotechnology is designed to enhance, while animal growth hormones would benefit Japan's consumers—now moving more toward a meat diet—and contribute to national self-sufficiency in food. This could be why Japanese ministries are seeking to eliminate the millions of inefficient, part-time farmers on the one hand yet encouraging massive investments in biotechnology (including buy-outs of or joint ventures with American companies) on the other.[25]

Such a differentiated response could lead to further tensions over agricultural trade, as food exporting countries like Australia and the United States find that their produce, while needed by developing countries unable to pay for it, is not required by rich nations increasingly able to create their own biotech substitutes at home. Japanese-American relations, already soured by other commercial quarrels, would only worsen if Japan were no longer a major market for American farm exports.

It could also lead to the emergence of two biotechnological "regimes" in the world, in one of which genetic engineering was encouraged and in the other restricted. As suggested above, industry and investment would move to those areas where the opportunity for making new products was not prevented. Thus, while inhabitants of the first regime struggled to deal with the dislocating effects of technological change, those in the second would anxiously debate whether they were going to be left behind as the rest of the world embraced a new technological paradigm.[26]

In addition, the widespread acceptance of biotech farming even of the nonlaboratory-based sort may exacerbate North-South relations. Were innovative techniques to enhance production of agricultural goods made by developing countries, which then attempted to increase food exports to consumers in the industrial democracies, farmers in the developed world would feel even more threatened than they do now. The labor costs of raising beef or growing fruit in Brazil are surely lower than in Kansas or Bavaria; but if depressed world food prices made many farmers redundant in richer countries, they would regard developing world competitors with as much hostility as industrial workers who discover that the local factory is being relocated to a cheap-labor country. Here again, the familiar pattern of winners and losers is in sight.

To the developing world itself, biotech agriculture offers the greatest mix of advantages and disadvantages. The gap between population increases and overall food output which has recently developed would be narrowed again if the biotech revolution works. Such a revolution could improve the caloric intake and the living standards of the poorer three-quarters of the world's population and would permit growing in areas of the developing world where the soil is too dry, too shallow, or too high in chemical residues like salt to allow traditional farming. For example, the invention of a hybrid banana that resists black sigatoka disease could have a swift local effect in parts of Africa, where bananas are a staple crop. Biotechnology could also offset environmental damage, if plentiful food supplies reduced today's pressures upon marginal land. Above all, it could remove the "Malthusian trap" confronting poorer societies.

Furthermore, developing countries and their scientists can make substantial contributions in biotechnology, something that is much less likely in robotics or global finance. Many biotech projects are much more research-intensive than capital-intensive, as in the case of Vietnamese farmers who profitably adapted French tissue-culture technology by propagating potato plants from tissue ordered from the International Potato Center.[27]

Even in expensive biotech fields, developing countries have committed funds and personnel. China and India have undertaken the most advanced use of biogas energy sources. There are also joint ventures with companies in the developed world, such as a project between China and International Embryos to boost dairy cattle using embryo transfers, or a French–Costa Rican initiative to turn some 140,000 tons of waste bananas each year into animal feed. Joint ventures and collaborations are also taking place among developing countries, independently of Western assistance.[28] All this is piecemeal and incremental, but the results can add up.

Yet biotechnology also challenges the developing world's chances of improving its relative economic position. DNA-related research—genetic engineering—offers the best prospect of raising overall food output, but it is very costly and is undertaken almost exclusively by agrichemical and biotech companies in the developed world. The promises of enhanced milk yields from the bovine growth hormone are not practical for most livestock owners in poor countries, because the treatment requires skilled technicians and costs as much per year as many people spend on food. In addition, treated animals require large, high-quality, consistent rations of feed and must be given frequent injections, which is unlikely in societies where vaccination of human beings against disease is still far from routine.[29] Herbicides make economic sense in high-capital agriculture and when labor costs are steep, but would be too expensive in lands where labor is abundant and cheap.

Yet even if farmers in developing countries *were* able to afford the newer methods of biotech farming, they would become dependent—like many of their equivalents in the developed world—upon Western corporations for the necessary hormones, seeds, fertilizers, and herbicides. In the words of one critic, the "gene revolution" in the developing world, should it occur, will probably involve extracting genetic resources from less developed countries, incorporating those resources into commercial plant and animal varieties in company laboratories, and later reselling the improved varieties to the less developed countries for a considerable profit.[30] Already there are heated charges that the developing world's genetic resources are being ransacked by the "biological imperialism" of large corporations.[31]

Finally, the possibility of an *in vitro* revolution increasingly permits such companies to produce in their laboratories crops traditionally grown in developing countries. Efforts are now under way not merely to improve the genetic quality of tropical foodstuffs for Western consumers—cocoa, palm oil, vanillin, and sugar—but also to find laboratory substitutes. Such substitutes would drastically reduce major sources of export income for the developing world, and threaten employment just as more and more fifteen-to-twenty-year-olds are looking for work. For example, sugarcane has been replaced by isoglucose or other super-sweeteners, yet the natural product provides a livelihood for millions of inhabitants of the developing world. Vanilla, a major export of Madagascar (per capita GNP $280), can be made by chemists. Barbasco, a plant which produces steroids, was once grown extensively in Mexico but is now manufactured by a chemical process. The export of coconut oil, upon which one-quarter of the Philippine population is at least partially dependent, is threatened with replacement by genetically engineered soybean or rapeseed. It is bad enough for a developing country to be dependent upon a monocultural export like cocoa or sugar, the prices of which fluctuate sharply, but it will be far worse if such produce is no longer needed by foreign consumers who can obtain it from domestic laboratories. The *in vitro* production of rubber, were it to become a reality, could throw an estimated 16 million people out of work in Malaysia, Indonesia, and other rubber-growing countries— with obvious implications for their political stability.[32]

Over the longer term, then, the biotech revolution potentially implies a significant relocation of agricultural production (or its substitutes) out of the developing world, worsening its trading position, indebtedness, and general dependence upon richer countries. Moreover, even if developing countries overcame all the obstacles (lack of laboratories, scientists, supply systems, patented information) and were able to develop their own *in vitro* production, millions of agricultural jobs would be at risk, with mass redundancies provoking a peasant backlash.[33]

With the experts divided in their forecasts, there is clearly great uncertainty about the outcome of the leapfrog race between population growth and agricultural production. The global imbalances in diet and health, bad as they are now, may, as many expect, get much worse. It is also possible that because of new technologies, agriculture stands on the verge of another great advance in productivity which will contradict the prophecies of the doomsters.[34] But even if that is true, the cornucopia will not necessarily reach all who need feeding, while millions of traditional farmers—in developed as well as developing countries—will be hurt as new techniques replace old ways. Whatever the consequences of an expanding world population, farming as we know it seems on its way out.

Paradoxically, then, biotech offers the prospect of both easing *and* complicating the global dilemma. There is no doubt that the world needs continued increases in agricultural productivity. Just as the world could not feed itself today with the farming methods of the 1940s, so farmers can hardly expect to meet the increased global demand in thirty or forty years' time with their present techniques of producing food. Without another agricultural revolution, the fate of the peoples of the developing world especially looks grim. This is why biotechnology, despite all the reservations discussed above, seems such an attractive solution and is clearly poised for further advances; the genie is now out of the bottle and affecting human life in all sorts of ways. What seems much less clear is whether global society can handle the economic and social consequences of a large-scale switch to biotech farming and food processing. On present evidence, that doesn't look likely.

5

ROBOTICS, AUTOMATION, AND A
NEW INDUSTRIAL REVOLUTION

STEAM-DRIVEN MANUFACTURE, WHICH
began to spread across northern and central England in the late eighteenth and early nineteenth centuries, naturally attracted the attention of many foreigners. Displaying fascination, enthusiasm, and sometimes apprehension, European and American visitors observed the brave new world of industrial production in which steam engines converted heat into work through machines. What impressed people about these machines was that they were "rapid, regular, precise, tireless."[1] Provided the supply of coal was maintained and the machines kept in order, they never flagged in the way that human beings, oxen, and horses did when their "animate" energy was exhausted. Machines could work all day, and through the night; they could work nonstop for weeks, if necessary.

But the real significance of the Industrial Revolution—and the reason observers were so awed by it—was that it placed these steam-driven machines and their human attendants within a *factory system*. Hitherto, most forms of manufacture were decentralized, house-based activities, involving everything from urban candlestick makers to rural handloom weavers, usually paid by piecework. Specialist crafts, from potters to haberdashers, were similarly arranged. Even the largest projects—building a warship, or a palace—were in a way idiosyncratic, irregular enterprises, subject to various interruptions. In a factory system, however, workers were assembled together and required to labor in a standardized fashion to a rhythm *set by the machines*; they worked in fixed "shifts" of ten or twelve or more hours, and were paid an hourly rate. Because the machines' requirements were supreme, the laborers had to live nearby, in employer-provided row houses. The factory system thus begat an urban proletariat, the succeeding generations of which knew less and less of their forebears' preindustrial way of life.

It is easy to understand why foreign observers viewed the new manufacturing with apprehension as well as fascination. The Industrial Revolution clearly enhanced the power of Great Britain, especially during the Revolutionary and Napoleonic wars, when booming exports sustained the coalition forces in their epic struggle against France.[2] A country capable of imitating the British system would also enjoy a relative rise in productivity and national power, whereas states unable to industrialize would be hurt. Industrialization thus gave a fresh twist to the age-old competition among the Great Powers.

A second and larger reason for apprehension was concern about the effects of industrialization upon one's own society. The clanking, steaming new machines might be marvels to watch, but it was clear that working in a factory was hell—not just because of unhealthy conditions, but because of the strict regimen of work. Could the preindustrial inhabitants of the Rhineland or Silesia be turned into a city-dwelling proletariat without inviting social convulsions? Worse still, how would one deal with the mass of craftsmen, handloom weavers, and the like who lost their jobs to the factory system, or influential guilds fighting hard against their redundancy?[3] To fail to match English practices was problem enough; to imitate them would mean profound changes in the way one lived, worked, and earned one's keep.

This dilemma is worth recalling because, two centuries later, we may be on the brink of another revolutionary change in how industrial goods are made—a change led this time not by England but by Japan, involving the replacement of human beings in the factory by robots and other automated equipment. For two hundred years, manufacture and assembly have been amended in all sorts of ways; but whatever the innovations of Taylor and Ford, or "just-in-time" production, the key element was human beings coming together in a place of work. Now we are witnessing a technology-driven revolution which breaks from that process; by replacing factory workers with robots to increase productivity, automation takes more and more human beings *out* of the factory until perhaps only a few supervising engineers remain. If that aim is achieved, the wheel will have come full circle. The industrial "serfs" of the factory system, whose working conditions appalled foreign observers in the England of the 1820s, will finally have been replaced by robots, whose linguistic root is the Czech word for serf, *robotnik.*[4]

Like steam power itself, robotics has many applications, of varying complexity. Apart from simple devices not controlled by a computer and considering only *programmable* machines, there are immense differences of sophistication among industrial robots, field robots, and intelligent robots. The first are fixed machines with manipulators primed to do various tasks automatically, such as spot welding or spray painting. Field robots, by contrast, are designed to operate in an unstructured environment and possess sensors to allow them to move around, respond to an obstacle, and so on; they are often used in operations too difficult or hazardous for human beings, such as mining, fire fighting, treating a contaminated plant, and undersea work; some are steered by teleoperated remote control. Finally, there is the new, exciting field of third-generation intelligent robots, experimental computerized machines designed to use artificial intelligence (the so-called knowledge-based systems) to solve problems as human beings do.[5]

Obviously, the more complex and expensive the task, the further robots are from actual replacement of human beings. The majority of industrial robots are employed in automobile p¹.nts—cutting pieces of metal, spot welding, painting—since that industry is the classic example of a factory-line production and assembly system requiring its workers to perform uniform, repetitive movements, like automata.[6] The same is true for the assembly of the components of a radio or CD player. Jobs needing independent actions, like schoolteaching or police work, are not going to be accomplished by machines. Lawyers, doctors, and professors will ensure that automatic emulation will not happen in their fields.

Although most of this chapter discusses the potential impact of industrial robots, it is worth noting that the use of field robots and intelligent robots is also influenced by economic consideration. In the United States, where the costs of long-term medical care are spiraling upward, hospitals are examining the purchase of robots able to move specimens in a laboratory, decontaminate surgical instruments, deliver medications from the pharmacy, and so on.[7] Again, because it will take hundreds of billions of dollars to clean hazardous waste across America, robots are now being recruited; field robots were developed to inspect, take samples from, and clean up the contaminated Three Mile Island plant after its 1979 accident. Other machines have been created for space exploration, for deep-sea mining, and even to act as "sentry robots" equipped with remote-imaging and intruder-detection sensors as well as alarm/communications systems.[8]

In the United States and Europe, most attention has focused upon exotic robotics: machines that can traverse the moon's surface, or play chess. While that research is very important, the fascination for robots in the Jules Verne tradition distracts from the automation of the *manufacturing* industry, to achieve improvements in efficiency and productivity. Industrial robots for assembly or metal-cutting may seem less interesting than robots that play chess, but their long-term effects—economic, demographic, and upon shares of world output—promise to be more significant.

Before considering those effects, however, we should understand why some industrial societies have embraced the new machines while others have not. Why, especially, has Japan become the world leader in robotics whereas the United States—which created much of the original technology and whose scientists still provide new ideas for the future of robotics—has allowed its share of this industry to be eroded? At first sight, Japan's superiority over America in robotics is a further example of what has occurred in related industries such as microprocessors, computers, and electrical goods. Japan possesses many strengths: a highly educated work force, a long-term commitment to develop key industries, easily available capital at low interest rates, high levels of R&D investment, masses of engineers, and a dedication to top-quality design and efficient production. Cutthroat competition among firms in Japan's automobile and electrical-goods industries drove them to invest in new machines to increase productivity; a government-encouraged leasing company (JAROL) offered advice and machines at low cost; and the robots were carefully integrated into a factory culture already practicing "just-in-time" production techniques.[9]

In the United States, conditions were far less favorable, despite the early breakthroughs achieved by companies such as Unimation and Cincinnati Milacron. The government's hands-off policy toward business meant that no help came from that source. No equivalent body existed to do JAROL's work of leasing, publicizing, and advising upon the use of robots. The costs of raising capital in America were greater than in Japan or Germany, and American companies were under pressure from Wall Street to keep profits high (even if this meant investing less). After initial enthusiasm in automated assembly by the major automobile companies, new investment in manufacturing as a whole fell sharply in the mid to late 1980s.[10] The result was a drastic shakeout of the robotics industry; more than half the fifty or so companies making robots in 1985 disappeared by 1990.[11] Those left were acquired by or forced to merge with foreign companies. By 1991 no independent American robotics manufacturers were left.

While a similar tale can be told of other American industries, the different response of Japan and America to robotics was heavily influenced by a special factor: demography. The chief reason for Japan's commitment to automation has been a serious labor shortage, which existed as long ago as the mid-1960s and threatened to reduce Japan's export-led boom. Demographic changes since then—not to mention those to come—are significantly altering the number of Japanese available for manufacturing work. The economic advantages of employing industrial robots are now overwhelming, as the cost of a robot has decreased sharply and the time needed for a return on investment has shrunk accordingly. "If a robot replaces one worker for one shift per day, the payout is roughly four years. If a robot is used for two shifts, it will pay for itself in two years, and if used round the clock, in just over one year."[12]

Yet automated production could not have occurred so easily without the special structure of Japanese industry and the state of management-labor relations. Most large companies in Japan have a policy of lifetime employment, so that a worker whose job has been taken over by a robot will not be fired, but retrained and relocated inside the firm or in related companies within these industrial conglomerates. Moreover, robots were initially deployed in repetitive and/or dangerous jobs, such as cutting metal, spot welding, painting, and transporting spare parts, which relieved workers of unpleasant tasks *and* promised enhanced productivity to be reflected in annual bonuses. Finally, Japanese trade unions traditionally work with management to enhance quality control and ensure that their company does better than its rivals. If robots helped Toyota or Kawasaki Heavy Industries to crush the competition, they would be warmly welcomed.

Not only did Japanese industry ease its labor shortages without destroying the social peace, it also avoided the path followed by German firms—or, for that matter, companies in New York and California—of importing large numbers of guest workers. Japan's commitment to its racial homogeneity was thus preserved, since mechanical "serfs" could do the work instead, while Japanese workers were retrained for other tasks. Whatever migration occurs from South to North in the future, therefore, Japan plans to be much less affected than the United States and Europe while still ensuring its industrial competitiveness.

The contrast with the American experience could not be more marked. Although rising labor costs led U.S. automobile companies to invest in robots during the early 1980s, America has no overall labor shortage; in addition, average wages now are considerably less than those in Japan. Moreover, robots often proved disappointing. To make them work effectively requires significant changes in factory layout and in redesigning products so that robots can handle them more easily. The more sophisticated the robot, the more redesign is required, so that many American firms eventually chose to retain the older methods— and the workers—and to sell off their new machines. In other words, there was no compelling demographic reason for companies to embrace robotics, even if the result was smaller productivity increases in the United States than in Japan.

Finally, American unions see robots as a threat to employment, suspicions well justified, for American industry does not usually retrain workers whose jobs have been made redundant. Following the 1981–82 recession, for example, as many as 2 million Americans with outdated skills lost their jobs. In cities like Pittsburgh, where one might imagine that robots would be welcomed to improve productivity, hundreds of thousands of skilled workers were fired as the 1980s unfolded.[13] While machines that replaced such arduous work as welding were tolerated, in general American labor has opposed robots—and the companies know it.

Therefore, the dominant place in robotics is now firmly occupied by Japan, as shown in Table 2.

Table 2. World Industrial Robot Population, End of
1988[14]

Japan	176,000
Western Europe	48,000
USA	33,000
Eastern Europe, Southeast Asia, rest of world	23,000
Total	280,000

Because Japan has spent much more than any other country on automation since 1988, its lead has grown further. With only 0.3 percent of the world's land and 2.5 percent of its population, it possessed around 65 or 70 percent of the world's industrial robots,[15] recalling that other island country, mid-Victorian Britain, which produced five-sevenths of the world's steel and half its iron.

How significant are the productivity increases coming from automation? A few years ago Nissan upgraded its automobile plants in the Tokyo area with a highly sophisticated method of assembly, using robots. Formerly it took eleven months and cost Nissan 4 billion yen to retool its body assembly for a new car model; now it takes a quarter the time and costs about a third as much[16]—which is the chief reason that Japanese auto productivity continues to rise. Perhaps the famous FANUC manufacturing plant near Mount Fuji comes closest to representing the "factory of the future." Before 1982, a work force of 108 people and thirty-two robots produced about six thousand spindle motors and servo motors each month. After a radical redesign and further automation of the factory, it now employs only sixty people and has 101 robots to produce ten thousand servo motors a month—a *threefold* improvement in productivity which handsomely repays the initial investment. Yet even that is regarded merely as an interim step toward full automation by FANUC's management.[17]

Although the increases in productivity are incremental, they become significant over time, producing not only a steady flow of orders for the Japanese robotics industry, but also a cumulative increase in the quality and efficiency of Japanese manufacturing. Robots do not require heating or air-conditioning; they can work in the dark, and save electricity; they do not become sloppy or tired. They contribute to a greater flexibility in manufacturing, since they can be reprogrammed for different tasks or to assemble different models. Because their movements are perfectly controlled, they do not waste materials—robot spray painters, for example, use up to 30 percent less paint than human workers.

All this suggests that we may be witnessing the beginnings of a new industrial revolution, involving the automation of the manufacturing process. In many ways, the similarities between the steam engine and the robot are striking. Both are a new way of making things that simultaneously reduces the physical efforts of workers *and* enhances overall productivity; a process that creates new jobs and eliminates many others; and a stimulus to social change as well as to new definitions of work.[18] Like the steam engine, robotics affect international competitiveness, raising the per capita output of nations that invest heavily in the newer technology and weakening the long-term relative position of those unable to do the same.

Another similarity seems to be the strong impression made upon visitors who witness the new technology for the first time. Like aghast observers at Britain's early steam-driven factories, foreign visitors* to the FANUC automated factory appear awed by the sight of robots moving around inside the building, clicking and whirring as they solder circuit boards, examining their work with camera eyes, passing items from one robot to another, work which continues after dark, when the lights are dimmed.[19] Both steam engine and robot, people could sense, brought promise and peril to manufacturing.

Since robotics is still in its early stages and heavily concentrated in one country, less attention has been paid to its implications for developed and developing nations in (say) thirty years' time than has been devoted

*About two thousand people a month visit the FANUC factories, which must make it one of the most popular industrial sights in the world.

to biotech or demographic change. Despite the publicity given to FANUC's wonder robots, the use of robotics in Japanese manufacturing is undramatic and incremental as factory after factory installs additional machines. It is also much less headline-catching than breakthroughs in aerospace or supercomputing. Interestingly, although American industry is increasingly dependent upon Japanese robots, few politicians denounce this imbalance as they bemoan America's dependence on foreign-made chips or laptop computers. Even the term "robotics revolution" may be questioned by American businessmen who have had problems using them or see little advantage in the new machines when labor is relatively cheap.

Within developed nations, robotics is likely to progress most where there exists a strong "engineering culture," high per capita average living standards (and therefore high labor costs), and a shrinking pool of skilled workers because of demographic slowdown; after Japan, the leading contenders are Germany and Sweden, each with traditional strengths in machine tools, electrical engineering, and high-quality automobiles. Robotics is less likely to progress in countries where investment in manufacturing remains low, or where trade unions fear robots as job-replacers. Robotics is also unlikely to flourish in the states of the former Soviet Union, for, although the USSR claimed to possess tens of thousands of industrial robots, a top-notch robotics industry cannot function efficiently in an economy backward in computers and microprocessors. In any case, with millions of citizens of the erstwhile Soviet Union looking for work, robots are the last thing that is needed. The economics of investing in automation and a country's demographic and social structures always seem to provide the key.

Since automation increases manufacturing productivity, it adds to the relative power of companies and nations which can automate *and* handle the social consequences. In the global scramble for market shares in the three great economic zones of North America, Europe, and East Asia, robotics threatens to widen the already significant productivity gap between the Nissans and Toyotas on the one hand and the Peugeots, Fiats, and Chryslers on the other. As European bureaucrats and American car manufacturers scramble to meet East Asia's challenge in manufacturing and high technology by imposing import restrictions to give themselves a breathing space of five or ten years in which to catch up, robotics makes their task harder, perhaps impossible, so long as Japan's companies invest more than everyone else in the future. A further consequence of robotics, then, could be to shift the global economic balances away from Britain, France, Italy, and the United States and toward Japan and Germany.

If Europe's and America's responses to robotics are sporadic and hesitant, they are much better prepared to compete—at least in terms of physical and intellectual assets—than societies in the developing world. As with global finance, biotechnology, and multinationals, we are once again looking at a technology-driven revolution that could keep poorer countries at the bottom of the heap, or weaken them further.

Since a few developing countries appear to be detaching themselves from the Third World and catching up with the First,* the following discussion focuses on the fate of the really poor, overpopulated societies of South Asia, Africa, and Central America, not the NIEs of East Asia, which are in a different category. Except for Taiwan,† figures are not available on robotics in the NIEs, but they will probably reflect a more general technology indicator, such as semiconductor production. In that field, South Korea, Taiwan, Singapore, and Hong Kong are making very swift progress, since their governments have targeted electronics and computers as key industries for export-led growth. Because Japanese competitors have invested heavily in robotics—to beat the low-labor-cost products of the NIEs—that may encourage the latter to go heavily into automation. Obviously, it is not yet worthwhile in countries where wages remain low; but the explosion of workers' earnings in recent years in (say) South Korea and the steady decline in fertility rates bring automation closer.

To create its own robotics revolution, a developing country needs surplus capital, a large supply of engineers and scientists, and a labor shortage. Alas, countries in the developing world have few capital resources, and interest payments on international debts result in a net

*See Chapter 10, "Winners and Losers in the Developing World."
†In 1988, Taiwan possessed 682 industrial robots, which was more than European states such as Switzerland, Austria, and Norway.

outflow of capital each year. They also have relatively few engineers and scientists.[20] Finally, since their major problem is a massive surplus of labor, there is no economic or social rationale—from the viewpoint of their troubled governments, at least—in encouraging *labor-saving* systems of manufacture.

If there is little prospect that an indigenous robotics industry will arise in the developing world, might multinational companies establish automated manufacturing in those countries to obtain low-cost production? After all, some of the less developed and most populous countries of Asia—Indonesia, Thailand, Malaysia, China itself—have experienced rapid industrialization, faster than everywhere else in the world, and now export many manufactured goods. This economic growth is due to the relocation of manufacturing to those countries by firms like Fujitsu and Motorola, to take advantage of lower labor costs. Components of, say, a radio or record player are sent to a company's plant in Southeast Asia, where it is assembled and packaged for re-export. Such work improves the developing country's balance of payments, although it also creates unusual employment patterns, since these electronics companies employ almost entirely unskilled and semiskilled female workers.[21] The problem of young, frustrated men without work remains, and may be compounded. Moreover, such an employment structure creates little incentive for the training of native scientists and engineers.

Nevertheless, industrialization does bring *overall* benefits to Southeast Asia—export-led growth, a higher standard of living, a rising number of consumers of manufactures—especially when compared with Africa or the Middle East, where investment by multinational companies is negligible. Even if these developing countries have been "relegated to assembling pieces of high-tech equipment largely for consumption in industrial countries,"[22] that is better than no industrial employment at all.

But what prospect is there of a move by multinationals to *automated* assembly, instead of low-labor-cost assembly, in their developing world plants? Given the structure of the robotics industry, that seems unlikely at present, since it would require a skilled work force (systems engineers, trained maintenance crew), which most developing countries do not have; it would also require adequate infrastructure, power supplies, telecommunications, water, roads, and ports, which many poorer countries desperately lack. In any case, why invest in automated assembly in (say) Indonesia if it retains its cheap labor advantage? Moreover, even if automation did occur—despite all the problems noted above— it would then pose the same threat to local factory employment as it does in other parts of the world.

The final irony—and an awful future possibility—is that low-labor assembly plants established by foreign companies in Southeast Asia may one day be undermined by an intensification of the robotics revolution in Japan. This might seem farfetched at the moment, although at least one writer on "high technology and international labor markets" has argued that labor-saving technology, intensively used, could make the manufacturing of steel, heavy equipment, machines, and even textiles competitive again in industrial countries.[23]

As one indicator of how robotics might permit manufacturing to return to a developed country—or, in this case, not abandon it— consider the remarkable turnaround achieved by a single radio-cassette-recorder factory in Sendai, Japan, in 1985. Suffering from the rise in the value of the yen, acute labor shortages at home, and fierce competition from low-labor competitors in Southeast Asia, the company was in deep trouble. Rejecting the idea of relocating production to cheaper countries, the management embarked upon massive automation—the installation of no fewer than 850 industrial robots. Within a short while, the assembly line required only sixteen workers to reach full production compared with 340 (!) before automation, restoring the company's competitiveness even against Southeast Asian rivals whose wages were a fraction of those in Japan.[24] The "serfs" in the low-labor assembly plants abroad were outbid by automated "serfs" at home. If that was already possible in the mid-1980s, what degree of manufacturing efficiency might the robotics revolution achieve by 2020?

Whether or not the members of the Association of Southeast Asian Nations that are the home of foreign-owned assembly plants will escape from this challenge is impossible to judge at present; probably the more adept of them will. The main point is that multinational corporations in certain industries, already switching production from one country to another according to differentiated labor costs, will gain the further advantage of assessing whether developing-world wages are greater or less than the robot's "costs" in the automated factory back home. After all, the theory of the borderless world encourages managers to be constantly weighing the relative advantage of production in one part of the globe as opposed to others.[25] With the robotics revolution, Fujitsu assembly plants abroad might one day return to Japan and Motorola factories to America. In any event, such decisions will not be made by developing countries or their governments.

The mass replacement of factory workers will not happen overnight. Just as it took decades for the early steam engines to advance from mere curiosities and "wonder machines" to the center of the manufacturing process, so it may take a generation or more before the robotics revolution makes its full impact; and there is always the increase in cheap labor supplies to slow the pace of automation in many societies. Nevertheless, the longer-term implications are disturbing and threaten to exacerbate the global dilemma. If the biotech revolution can make redundant certain forms of farming, the robotics revolution could eliminate many types of factory-assembly and manufacturing jobs. In both cases, multinational companies become the beneficiaries of the reduced value of land and labor. Marvelous though the technologies behind the new agricultural and industrial revolutions may be, they neither offer solutions to the global demographic crisis nor bridge the gap between North and South. For all the difficulties it faced, Malthus's England perhaps had an easier time of it.

6

THE DANGERS TO OUR NATURAL ENVIRONMENT

WHY SHOULD AFFLUENT SOCIETIES IN the northern hemisphere care about the population explosion in the developing world and the spread of mass poverty there? Of what practical concern is it to the farmers of Kansas or the housewives of Tokyo—who have their own problems—that Ethiopians starve and Bangladeshis are overwhelmed by floods? After all, enormous gaps have existed between rich and poor since at least the time of the pharaohs, and famines and natural disasters are common to all centuries. If the sight of human distress on television causes individuals to donate to relief agencies, that is a nice thing; but why should more be done, if that implies changes in one's own prosperity and life-style?

Since poverty has always existed yet never persuaded the rich to curb their life-styles in favor of the poor, it would (alas) be unrealistic to reply that the North's affluent societies should do more because global malnutrition is an affront to human dignity; it was ever so. More practical reasons are needed to show why existing aid and relief are insufficient. One was already given in Chapter 2, that the demographic imbalance between poor and rich societies is producing a migratory flood from the former to the latter, and today's disturbing social and racial reactions to that may be small compared with what happens in a world of 8 to 10 billion people.

During the past decade or so, a second practical answer has emerged to the question "Why should rich societies care about the fate of far-off poor peoples?" It is that economic activities in the developing world, whether the work of billions of peasant farmers or of emerging factory enterprises, are adding to the damage to the world's ecosystem. Because the earth's thin film of life is entire and interconnected, damage inflicted upon the atmosphere by activity in the tropics could have serious effects not just locally but everywhere. The environmental issue, like the threat of mass migration, means that—perhaps for the first time—what the South does can hurt the North.

There is, of course, nothing new in the damage human beings inflict upon their environment and the suffering that follows. In the crowded cities of early-modern Europe—and in the even more crowded cities of Asia—garbage was thrown into the streets, rivers were polluted, and deaths by disease multiplied. Entire forests were cut down to provide fuel, housing, ships, so that the ecology of a whole region, and people's livelihoods in it, steadily altered. The burning of coal and brown coal (lignite), especially by early industry, dirtied the atmosphere and worsened people's health; in one week of December 1873, a great London "smog" killed an estimated seven hundred people with respiratory problems. Human beings have built dams, drained wetlands, diverted rivers, cleared bush and scrublands, and permitted overgrazing of grasslands since ancient times.

But the environmental crisis we now confront is quantitatively and qualitatively different from anything before, simply because so many people have been inflicting damage on the world's ecosystem during the present century that the system as a whole—not simply its various parts—may be in danger. Around 1900, the world was home to about 1.6 billion people. In some regions in the northern hemisphere, where coal was burned as the chief source of energy, pollution and environmental damage were common. Sprawling industrial conurbations in northern England and the Midlands, the Ruhr region, New York, Pittsburgh, and elsewhere emitted a pall of smoke, soot, and ash; salmon and trout had long abandoned the local rivers; buildings bore a coat of grimy soot while their inhabitants spluttered and choked in the foul air around them. Nevertheless, these problems appeared to be local. The well-to-do could escape to their country houses or seaside resorts, where the air was fresh and the waters clean. The more energetic could take strenuous walking holidays in the Swiss Alps or the upper Hudson Valley. If they were really adventurous, they could "explore" Africa, inner Asia, the Brazilian jungle, or the East Indies and observe huge regions virtually untouched by human activity.

By the middle of this century, the world's population had risen to 2.5 billion. What was more, industrialization had increased faster, almost threefold, reaching out to many more areas: Eastern Europe, the Soviet Union, Australia, Japan, India, and other parts of Asia. Alongside the vastly increased use of coal, there occurred an even more spectacular expansion in the use of fuel oils. Thousands of aircraft and ships and millions of motor vehicles poured their emissions into the atmosphere as they drew the different parts of the world together and transported more and more people into hitherto undamaged regions. As soot and ash began to pollute the air around Indian or Brazilian ironworks, the forests in their hinterlands wilted under the human onslaught of building roads, constructing airstrips, and felling woodlands for timber and grazing. In many developing countries, mixed (and reasonably balanced) ecologies were replaced by vast swaths of monocultural production.

As we enter the 1990s, the trends have intensified; world population has more than doubled since the 1950s, yet world economic activity has more than quadrupled. The population surge in developing countries has encroached upon jungles, wetlands, and broad grazing regions, as more and more people exploit surrounding natural resources. That pressure is intensified by further industrialization in Asia and elsewhere: new factories, assembly plants, road systems, airports, and housing complexes not only reduce the amount of natural land but contribute to the demand for more energy (especially electricity) and more automobiles and trucks, infrastructure, foodstuffs, paper and packaging, cement, steel, ores, and so on. All of this increases the ecological damage: more polluted rivers and dead lakes, smog-covered cities, industrial waste, soil erosion, and devastated forests litter the earth. Since midcentury alone, it is estimated that the world has lost nearly one-fifth of the topsoil from its cropland, one-fifth of its tropical rain forests, and some tens of thousands of its plant and animal species. And each new investigation of "The Earth as Transformed by Human Action" reveals the mounting pressures.[1]

Yet while the consequences of this onslaught produce growing concern, it is difficult to see how it can be halted at the local level. Consider, for example, the efforts of a pastoralist farmer in East Africa to maintain himself and his family. Everything depends upon his livestock— *the* measure of wealth in that society—and thus upon his ability to feed his animals. Few grains or other cattle fodder are grown in the region, and in any case it would be too expensive to purchase them. Instead, these herdsmen rely upon grazing and browsing on the grasslands, which at first sight seems natural enough; however, *numbers* now make all the difference. According to the Worldwatch Institute, 238 million Africans relied on 272 million livestock in 1950, but by 1987 the human population had increased to 604 million and the livestock to 543 million. "In a continent where grain is scarce, 183 million cattle, 197 million sheep, and 163 million goats are supported almost entirely by grazing and browsing. . . . As grasslands deteriorate, soil erosion accelerates, further reducing the carrying capacity and setting in motion a self-reinforcing cycle of ecological degradation and deepening human poverty."[2] But how is this cycle to be broken? By taking away the livestock? By inviting the herdsman and his family to move to more temperate climates such as Bavaria or Maryland? Either option is, for political reasons, impossible.

Again, how does one prevent the world's tropical forests from coming under assault, not just by peasant loggers, but also by large-scale indigenous enterprises wanting to clear these woodlands for grazing and crop-growing? Some of this is done illegally, but the greater part is open. In Brazil, much recent deforestation followed government decisions to subsidize forest clearing in the Amazon region.[3] The Indonesian government, in public advertisements, explains that "because its 170 million people have the same aspirations as anyone in the United States, 20 percent of its forests must be converted to plantations to produce teak, rubber, rice, coffee, and other agricultural crops."[4] Whether the deforestation is centrally organized or the result of the individual endeavors of millions of peasants, the results are ominous. In the Himalayas, the doubling of the population in recent decades led to greatly increased demands for fuel wood, fodder, and agricultural land—which in turn caused a massive deforestation (half of the forest reserves were lost between 1950 and 1980), and then to a tremendous increase in soil erosion. It is further alleged, by indignant Indians, that this contributes to siltation and flooding among the densely populated regions down the Ganges and Brahmaputra rivers, hundreds of miles from the cause.[5]

It is also worth noting that the lands now coming under pressure are almost invariably of marginal or temporary utility—unlike the rich Midwest prairies opened in the nineteenth century. The gains are therefore problematic and short-term because of soil erosion and the limited rainfall, whereas the damage threatens to be permanent.

What does this mean globally? About one-third of the land area of the earth (deserts, paved cities) supports little biological activity, one-third is forests and savannahs, and one-third is cropland and pasture.[6] The pasture areas of the world have been shrinking since the mid-1970s as overgrazing converts them to desert; even the share of cropland is falling because of degradation and conversion to nonfarm uses (roads, towns, airstrips, etc.). Most important of all, the rain forests are being cut back at a faster pace than ever. In 1980, it was estimated that the annual rate of deforestation in the tropics was approximately 11.4 million hectares; and one much more alarming (and perhaps unreasonably large) estimate raised that total to 20.4 million hectares of tropical forest annually—equal to the size of Panama.[7]

The disappearance of tropical forests (especially in Latin America, which contains almost 60 percent of them) is of concern to environmentalists for several reasons. The first is the destruction of the way of life of many innocent tribes. It is also the case that these forests have the world's greatest store of plant and animal species by far—Panama itself has as many plant species as the whole of Europe—and the destruction of this fantastic array of biodiversity would deal a heavy blow to humankind's constant need to keep renewing (and improving) pest-resistant and productive crops.[8] Population pressure leading to deforestation would thus curb global agriculture's ability to renew itself—and to provide for the additional billions of consumers. It would also be a blow to the fecundity and fascination of life itself. And all this is happening *so quickly*. According to an alarmed appeal sent to Latin American presidents in July 1991 by Gabriel García Márquez and other distinguished signatories, "by the year 2000 three-quarters of America's tropical forests may have been felled, and 50 percent of their species lost forever. What Nature created in the course of millions of years will be destroyed by us in little more than forty years."[9]

The increasing pollution of the earth's atmosphere is a further result of population growth and a desire to increase living standards. In the planned economies of the Soviet Union and Eastern Europe, for example, the post-1945 political leadership was determined to catch up industrially with the West; hence, utmost priority was given to heavy industry—iron, steel, cement, machinery—regardless of the ecological consequences. After systematic concealment by Communist regimes, the full extent of the damage has only recently become clear. Whole areas of Poland, Czechoslovakia, and the East German provinces were enveloped for decades in a heavy blue haze from industrial emissions, streams and lakes were fishless, the Danube became a deadly sump, and the buildings of many historic towns and cities were blackened by pollution. The forests in particular suffered, as millions of trees were killed or damaged. Even if the collapse of the Communist regimes and the closing of many of the antiquated factories and steel mills will slow environmental deterioration, the resources of the new regimes are at present inadequate to clean up the mess.[10]

Similar damage occurs in parts of the developing world that are also striving to catch up. Again, there are few controls over pollution and the emphasis is upon growth rather than public health and safety. China increased its coal output more than twenty times between 1949 and 1982, while in India emissions of sulfur dioxide from coal and oil have nearly tripled since the early 1960s.[11] According to the World Health Organization, leading cities with excessive amounts of sulfur dioxide and other pollutants include New Delhi, Beijing, Teheran, and Shenyang. In Mexico City, seven out of ten newborns have excessively high lead levels in their blood. Famous monuments, like the Taj Mahal and the temples, murals, and megaliths of the Mayans, are suffering from atmospheric pollution.[12]

Agricultural and industrial development have also affected the quantity and quality of the earth's water supplies. The larger cause, once again, is the increase in global population this century from 1.6 billion to more than 5 billion, with the consequent rise in demand for water. In virtually every city in the developing world, a combination of overpopulation, the reckless pace of industrialization, and an almost complete lack of sewerage and purification plants has destroyed what were once pure waters. The rise in world population has also encouraged massive investments in irrigation. Land under irrigation doubled between 1900 and 1950 and has increased more than two-and-a-half-fold since then, to reach a global total of some 250 million hectares, much of this in developing countries where the population increase is greatest and where often great seasonal or regional variations occur in the supply of water. Nations such as China, Egypt, India, Indonesia, and Peru now rely upon irrigated land for more than half their domestic food production.[13]

Irrigation has proved a boon to millions of the world's peasants and their families, but, like the use of pesticides, the new technology also brings disadvantages. Each year, a vast amount of water—estimated at six times the annual flow of the Mississippi—is removed from the earth's rivers, streams, and underground aquifers to water crops. Over time, this has led to waterlogged and salted lands, declining and contaminated aquifers, shrinking lakes and inland seas, and the destruction of wildlife and fish habitats.[14]

Because all water contains concentrations of salt, a field heavily irrigated throughout the year will receive considerable salt additions per hectare. In India, some 20 million hectares (36 percent of all irrigated land) are estimated to have had their yields reduced due to salinization, and an additional 7 million hectares have been abandoned as salty wasteland. What was originally conceived as a method of increasing crop yields has produced a very different result.[15]

Gigantic schemes to divert the natural flow of water have also created problems. One of the most spectacular was the Soviet effort to boost agricultural output in the Central Asian republics by diverting water from the two great rivers (the Amu Darya and Syr Darya) flowing into the Aral Sea. The rewards from this action seemed clear enough; most of the Soviet cotton crop, as well as rice, fruit, and vegetables, is grown here—but the dry climate requires irrigation. After thirty years of reduced inflow, however, the Aral Sea has dropped fourteen meters and has shrunk from 67,000 to 40,000 square kilometers, losing 40 percent of its area and 60 percent (!) of its volume. Mineral concentrations, especially of salt, have tripled, killing all marine life. The exposed land is now a salty desert, in the midst of which lie the sad former coastal towns of Aralsk and Muinak.[16]

Another example is the ambitious scheme of the Saudi Arabian government to make the desert glisten with water, in order to diversify its economy and invest its oil revenues. Following hefty farm subsidies and the massive extraction of underground water, *twenty times* as much land was under cultivation in 1988 as in 1975, and wheat output had increased about *a thousandfold.* Amazingly, Saudi Arabia is now a surplus producer of wheat, eggs, and dairy products. But the water is nonrenewable from aquifers that accumulated over thousands of years. In less than a decade, this water reserve has dropped by a fifth, and according to one estimate it may be totally exhausted by the year 2007.[17]

Despite very different ideologies, then, Soviet and Saudi leaders favored modernization policies which devastated a natural resource, and called upon technology to implement their grandiose projects. This has also been true across the developing world, from India to Nigeria, where the evidence accumulates of damage inflicted upon land, air, and water by human actions. In some cases, the governments in question have begun to amend affairs: proposals have been made to try to increase water levels in the Aral Sea, despite the engineering costs and the fact that valuable farmland may lose its irrigation; and the Saudi government is rushing ahead with ever more expensive desalination programs. But few other countries in the developing world have the political power or money to alter their earlier modernization plans— unless, perhaps, as will be discussed below, as part of a larger, global bargain.

•   •   •

All this environmental damage in the developing world was long preceded, of course, by equally unwise measures in developed countries. The smoke hanging over today's Chinese cities and the poor health of the work force are similar to conditions in mid-nineteenth-century Manchester. As recently as 1952 a notorious London smog claimed four thousand lives and left tens of thousands ill—finally provoking the British "Clean Air Act" two years later; efforts by developed countries to control auto emissions are more recent than that. Even today, as many as 150 million people in the United States breathe air considered unhealthful by the Environmental Protection Agency. Public buildings, from U.S. Civil War memorials to the Acropolis, are being steadily eaten away. Pollutants like "acid rain" are carried by the winds from Britain and Germany into Scandinavia, or from the Midwest of the United States into Canada, where tens of thousands of lakes have become strongly acidified. And the depletion of the Arabian aquifers bears comparison with what is happening to the massive Ogallala Aquifer that stretches from Texas to South Dakota and supports one-fifth of the irrigated cropland of the United States. Its depletion has caused many farmers to take land out of irrigation, and parts of the countryside are reverting to the condition they were in before pumping began—raising serious questions about the future of this substantial regional farming economy.[18]

Despite such problems, the rise of environmentally conscious "green" movements in the developed world—whether as a distinct political party in Germany, or at least in the emergence of public pressures upon authorities by Friends of the Earth and Greenpeace—has challenged the old policies of neglect. Respected bodies like the World Resources Institute, popular annuals such as *State of the World*, countless scientific investigations into environmental change, congressional and parliamentary hearings, and reports by governmental environmental agencies have had a significant impact upon politics and legislation in this field. Rivers and buildings are being cleaned up, factory emissions are being controlled, reforestation programs are under way, overfishing is increasingly banned, chemical and nuclear wastes are being treated, and recycling of used material is much more commonplace. As a result, many towns and regions in Europe and North America are, environmentally, a lot more pleasant to inhabit than they were a quarter century ago.

May it not be possible, then, for developing countries to imitate the developed world's recent efforts to repair environmental damage? And if not, why should that bother the inhabitants of Wisconsin or Jutland? Surely, one might think, the damage inflicted on African savannahs or Chinese rivers will be felt only by the local inhabitants, not by peoples five thousand miles away who have at last decided to tidy up their own backyards. If the peoples of the developing world opt to hurt their local environments, shouldn't they be left to do so?

Clearly, the chief reasons that developing societies cannot suddenly institute "green" policies are economic and demographic. It is relatively easy for concerned Scandinavians to divert some of their high per capita income into nonnuclear electricity or cleaning up the rivers. But it is much more difficult for societies whose average incomes are a mere one-hundredth that of Sweden to find the capital and skilled personnel to implement environmentally sound policies. Since the damage is caused either by the population explosion or by industrial emissions, the only way the former could be stopped would be by halting population growth, which simply isn't going to happen in South Asia, Africa, and Central America in the near future; and the only way to check industrial emissions would be to *reverse* industrialization, which many developing societies see as their only chance to escape from their demographically driven poverty trap. If Malthus's England had to endure the early unpleasant side effects of an industrial revolution in order to become prosperous, who can ask Mexico and India to refrain from attempting the same? And who can stop them from doing it? The answer is no one, least of all an inhabitant of the developed world.

While the local and national damage inflicted by acid rain, overgrazing, and water depletion is serious enough, concerned environmentalists nowadays point to what may be the most profound threat of all over the long term: the prospect that human economic activities are creating a dangerous "greenhouse effect" of global warming, with consequences for the earth's entire ecosystem and for the way of life of rich and poor societies alike.[19] If true, then precisely because *that* sort of damage is no longer local, it would inevitably concern Wisconsin and Jutland as well as Bombay and Amazonia.

The scientific theory behind global warming is relatively straightforward and relates to that thin "film of matter" which clothes our planet. In thermodynamic terms, the earth is a closed system, meaning that no material enters or leaves it except for the sun's radiant energy; and the only processes that can occur are those in which material is changed from one form to another. For example, burning autumn's fall of leaves or using up a tank full of gasoline on a lengthy car journey does not *eliminate* that material, it merely transfers it elsewhere in a different form. If this closed system is to run indefinitely, therefore, the transformation process must ultimately constitute a closed cycle, in which material returns to its original form: new resource becomes useful matter which becomes waste which is then absorbed back into the ecosystem to become future raw material. When functioning properly, it is a beautiful and wonderful self-sustaining cycle of life.[20]

It doesn't function properly when one or more of the sequential steps in the cycle is out of balance, thus producing a bottleneck. In earlier centuries, bottlenecks usually occurred in the conversion of raw material to useful matter: population and demand for fresh resources were growing, but the inhabitants of the system were unable to meet that demand (which then led to Malthusian "checks" upon population). Later, technological breakthroughs in consequence of the scientific and industrial revolutions produced new forms of conversion—the steam engine, internal combustion, electricity—and solved that bottleneck to a large degree. It also contributed to the gathering pace of global population growth after 1750, which in turn produced our present dilemma. For the more people you need to support on earth and the better you want them to live, the faster you have to drive the transforming system: hence the enormous growth of world economic activity in recent decades, and the corresponding increase in changing raw resources into useful matter. The problem is that as we have run the ecosystem faster and faster, driven by need and helped by technology, the bottleneck appears to have shifted to the waste-disposal step. Run the system harder and the waste—CO_2 emissions, CFCs (chlorofluorocarbons), acidified forests, polluted rivers—gets worse. Moreover, for various reasons, using technology to remove that bottleneck is likely to be altogether harder than applying human knowledge to capture useful energy and "make" things. Feeding coal to steam engines is easier than absorbing CO_2 emissions into the ecosystem.

How does global warming relate to this basic understanding of the earth as a closed system? Essentially, it concerns the interactions between the sun's heat and certain "greenhouse gases" in our atmosphere. The sun's energy comes to us through radiation, but almost all of that radiant energy is either reflected or reradiated back to space; if it were not, the earth would just keep heating up forever. When it is functioning properly, therefore, a uniquely balanced system exists. But if—as scientists now believe is happening—the composition of the trace gases in our atmosphere is altered by human activity, then more reradiated heat is being "trapped" (as within the glass of a greenhouse), which not only warms up the atmospheric gases but everything else as well. At the same time, scientists are also concerned that the ozone layer, which protects the earth and its inhabitants from harmful solar radiation, is being significantly depleted by chemical emissions like CFCs. The wider the "ozone hole," whether it be over Antarctica or New England, the more vulnerable human beings are, say, to skin cancer.

It is important to understand that global warming per se has always been with us, and is vital to life. Without our atmosphere, the earth's temperature would be about $-18°$ C, not the comfortable average temperature of $15°$ C that it is. Those 33 degrees of Celsius temperature are why the earth isn't cold and dead like Mars, which, if it ever had an atmosphere, lost it long ago and is lifeless and frozen. On the other hand, Venus, whose atmosphere is overwhelmingly made up of carbon dioxide, is hotter than a baker's oven ($450°$ C), making life impossible. While Mars is a deep freeze and Venus is a furnace, the earth is wrapped in that thin film of matter—including its vital atmospheric gases—that permits life. Should the content of those gases alter dramatically, we would either return to an ice age *or* find our temperatures rising to uncomfortable, or perhaps disastrous, levels.[21]

This latter possibility is the focus of today's earnest debate upon the greenhouse effect. In the last ice age, the earth's temperature averaged about 9° C colder than today, and the CO_2 level was only 190 to 200 parts per million. By the early nineteenth century, the CO_2 level had gradually increased to about 280 parts per million. It was then, however, that humankind began to use great amounts of coal, oil, and natural gas for heat and energy, pouring far larger amounts of carbons into the atmosphere. The clearing and burning of forests—for habitation, grazing, cultivation, and fuel—also added greatly to the process: burning a forest not only increases CO_2 levels, it also reduces the amount of plant life available for photosynthesis.

Atmospheric CO_2 concentrations have risen by about 70 parts per million during the past century and now total around 350 ppm. More than half of that increase has occurred during the past thirty years, which suggests that sheer population numbers are affecting the size of the increases. If the present growth rate of 0.3 or 0.4 percent per year continues, some scientists predict, carbon dioxide levels will be as high as 550 or even 600 ppm by the middle of the twenty-first century, leading to significant rises in the earth's average temperature.[22]

Given the complexity of our biosphere and of the countless interactions between the earth's air, sea, and land, considerable scientific uncertainty still exists about what may be happening to the environment. The computerized models and simulations of the atmosphere, which are extraordinarily complex, are usually simulations for the globe as a whole and much less helpful in allowing scholars to draw conclusions about a particular region. Measurement itself is also a problem: many recording stations may have been affected by "urban heat" as cities and suburbs expanded. Furthermore, individual features of the process of global warming are not very well understood. Would an increase in clouds, for example, warm the globe or cool it? Couldn't an increase in sunspot activity have caused the increase in temperatures? Might not some pollutants (sulfate aerosols) actually reflect the sun's radiation and *counter* global warming? How will ocean currents be affected by global warming? Won't the eruptions of volcanoes like Mount Pinatubo, which in 1991 spewed tons of dirt into the atmosphere, slow the forecast rise in the earth's temperatures? Would twice the level of carbon dioxide in the atmosphere actually increase the size and fertility of plant life—as has already occurred in controlled experiments in laboratories, and may also be taking place in northern Europe's forests—or will there be dangerous side effects? In any case, would that growth in vegetation be merely short-term, falling away as the enhanced CO_2 levels brought rises in the earth's temperature that would ultimately curtail agricultural production?

These uncertainties have encouraged a wide range of opinions on the subject of global warming. Concerned environmentalists believe that we are significantly changing the atmospheric gases, that a rise in global temperatures is inevitable, and that—to reduce the damage to our ecosystem—drastic changes should occur in our way of life in order to cut atmospheric emissions. That stance is vigorously contested by more skeptical scientists and laissez-faire economists, who are opposed to limiting growth and to governmental interference in how businesses operate and individuals live. Like the debate between neo-Malthusians and "cornucopians" over global agricultural prospects, much of the literature upon the greenhouse effect has therefore become very ideological, as each side denounces the other's "special agenda."[23]

Despite these varied responses, the scientific consensus is that average global temperatures are between 0.3° C and 0.7° C warmer than they were a century ago. This is a modest rise, but the real concern is the rising pace of temperature increase in the *next* century, especially as world population and industrial activity grow. It is estimated that double the CO_2 levels will produce average temperature increases of between 1.5° C and 4.5° C by the middle of the twenty-first century. The difference between the "low" and the "high" figures is considerable, but even at a compromise figure of 2.5° C or 3.0° C, most scientists in this field hold that there would be serious consequences. Even at the lower figure of 1.5° C, the Intergovernmental Panel on Climate Change warns, "the rate of change is likely to be greater than that which has occurred on earth any time since the end of the last ice age. . . ."[24]

For example, if substantial global warming occurs, the earth's sea levels could rise, simply because a warmer liquid has more volume than an equivalent mass of cold liquid. If the ocean warms up, then, it cannot help but "overflow" its basin and advance upon the shore. A warmer earth would also mean a net loss in the ice mass of the glaciers of the world, as more ice melts than is replaced by snow each year. In the warming after the last ice age, sea levels rose at the stupendous rate of about fourteen feet per century and covered vast areas of hitherto exposed land.[25]

Although scholars still debate what is happening to the all-important Antarctic ice fields (which contain 90 percent of the world's ice), most scientific studies believe that the sea level will rise as temperatures do—although estimates of the *extent* of that rise differ enormously.[26] Because of the configuration of the earth's landmass, however, even a relatively small rise (say, of up to a meter) would be significant; the geometry of beaches and offshore areas and the dynamics of waves mean that a one-meter rise in sea level can be expected to produce a shoreline retreat of about one hundred meters. Storms would push large amounts of water inland, flooding hitherto safe areas, and seawater would penetrate farther inland and upriver, contaminating freshwater aquifers.

Global warming could affect agriculture and land use, too, although the scientific evidence here also is complicated, incomplete, and at times bewilderingly contradictory. If, for example, global warming means that plants fade in the hotter temperatures but flourish in latitudes which formerly had been too chilly, does that imply a geographical relocation rather than a net reduction? And if this transformation is gradual, will farmers survive by planting crops that are more heat-resistant than those planted a decade earlier? Will agricultural pests become more rampant if global warming allows certain species to expand from the tropics, or would they be inhibited by the higher CO_2 environment?[27] Will the greenhouse effect mean that certain crops, stimulated by the increased levels of CO_2, experience greater agricultural output—and would those gains be sufficient to cancel out the losses in vegetation and foodstuffs elsewhere because of a temperature increase? Little of this is clear at present, although once again most scientists guess that the effects of global warming will be deleterious rather than beneficial.

· · ·

This conclusion is particularly worrying for countries in the developing world. If significant sea-level rises occur in the next century, many developing nations are going to be badly hurt. For example, the 177,000 inhabitants of the Maldive Islands would find themselves entirely inundated should there be a two-meter rise in sea level; the same would be true of many atolls in the Pacific Ocean. Even more important for our purposes—for thinking through the political implica- tions of these broad forces for global change—is the plight of countries such as Egypt, Bangladesh, and parts of China, where large populations reside on low-lying deltas. Egypt is already damaged environmentally from saltwater penetration because of the reduced flow of Nile water from the Aswan High Dam, and only 3.5 percent of its land is arable. A one-meter rise in sea level would take between 12 and 15 percent of that territory and turn almost 8 million people into refugees, while the loss of farmland would add to food shortages. With a one-meter rise in sea level, Bangladesh would lose 11.5 percent of its land, where 8.5 million people now live.[28] This does not include areas exposed to devastating storm floods, the likelihood of which would be increased because of both higher sea level and the possible greater intensity of the monsoons.*

As is usually the case, poverty compounds the problem. Egypt's per capita GNP is about $700 and Bangladesh's is a mere $170, one- hundredth that of wealthy European and North American countries.[29] Both Egypt and Bangladesh are on the United Nations list of the ten countries most threatened by sea-level rise, the other eight being Gambia, Indonesia, the Maldives, Mozambique, Pakistan, Senegal, Suriname, and Thailand. That does not mean that the developed countries are safely high and dry, for the water creeps up on both the rich and poor, and is as much a threat to the expensive housing and industry around Tokyo Bay and the Lower Rhine as it is to the Ban- gladesh deltas. The UN list includes those countries that will suffer

*The hypothesis here is that if global warming further heated up the hot air over the Tibetan plateau, the subsequent movements of the air masses could strengthen the intensity of the monsoon, causing more flooding. More generally, scientists suspect that while the increase in global temperatures will be a relatively gradual process, changes in the atmosphere could well produce increased storm activity, more "freak" weather, and so on, in line with "chaos theory." When critical thresholds—not known in advance—are crossed, instability is likely.

because of *their inability to pay* for either protective measures or a planned relocation to higher ground. Richer countries will pour funds into the defense of their own coastlines—one estimate is that to protect only developed land and the barrier islands of the United States from a one-meter rise in sea level could cost more than $100 billion[30]— though much of this expense may ultimately be in vain and the funds might be better allocated for different environmental purposes.

As we saw earlier, the populations of Egypt and Bangladesh are projected to increase greatly over the next few decades, in Egypt from 54 million (1990) to 94 million (2025), in Bangladesh from 115 million to 235 million during the same period.[31] Thus, the population growth and economic activity that trigger the greenhouse effect may also eventually cause a shrinkage of land area in places struggling with a demographic explosion of their own. The impending tragedies are unlikely to remain local in their impacts. If Egypt collapses under a growing population and a shrinking land base, the repercussions— political and military, as well as social—could greatly affect its neighbors in Israel and Europe. If Bangladesh is devastated by storm surges and inundations, millions upon millions of refugees may pour across the border into the already most heavily populated provinces of India, adding immensely to the latter's problems. The world is already used to the flood of refugees from civil war. There may soon be an even larger flood of environmental refugees as societies break down or experience civil war in the face of natural catastrophes. Already, numerous scholars are pointing to the significance of "environmental changes as causes of acute conflict."[32]

The possible effect of global warming upon agriculture in the developing world is a further cause of worry. Higher temperatures will exacerbate water use, and may interact with atmospheric pollution, overgrazing, and forest depletion; it is also likely to reduce the biodiversity of plant species. Moreover, increases in CO_2 will affect different crops in different ways, favoring temperate-region plants such as wheat and potatoes, but bringing much less benefit to corn and millet, which are critically important staples in Africa. The largest concern is about rice, whose fertility swiftly declines if daytime temperatures go over 35° C (95° F). In many rice-growing Asian countries, the average temperatures in the growing seasons are already close to the limit. A significant rise in global temperatures, say a 4.5° C increase at the "top end" of most estimates, would make current strains of rice unviable and might result in widespread starvation. This is potentially a dilemma for China, which has to consider the effect of increased CO_2 from its industrialization on its agricultural output over the longer term. Higher temperatures, reduced soil moisture, and a decline in rice fertility levels are disturbing to leaders seeking to industrialize, but also feed, a country of well over a billion people.

On the other hand, our earlier analysis of the impacts of biotechnology upon agriculture noted that recombinant DNA technology has opened up many more possibilities in adapting species to new environmental conditions; and there are also ingenious ways, developed by Israeli scientists, to produce good yields with low water inputs. These are not trivial developments, and some of the potentially most useful agricultural research is being done in this area. But the fact remains that they are expensive approaches, more easily available to biotech companies and agribusinesses in developed countries than to peasants in the developing world. For the latter, global warming, if it is coming, seems to threaten yet more trouble.

While the potential damage that global warming might inflict upon richer countries may be less severe, it is certainly worth taking seriously. Switzerland and Montana would not suffer from a rise in the sea level, but the low-lying regions of Louisiana, New Jersey, the Netherlands, and other parts of the developed world would be affected. A rise of one meter in the sea level would cause the United States alone to lose up to eight thousand square miles of wetlands and ten thousand square miles of dry land—a larger area than Vermont or Massachusetts—if no protective measures were instituted.[33] The fight to preserve Venice would be made more complicated, and other valuable cities and towns near the water's edge would be threatened. In many cases, higher seawalls could be built, costing enormous sums and, of course, doing nothing to address the causes of global warming.

The effect on agriculture could also be serious. The estimated increase of 1.5–4.5° C in temperature is an average for the earth as a whole, but the temperature rises are expected to be higher in the middle latitudes where most prosperous countries are located. A number of studies expect that increased temperature will reduce soil moisture in such regions as the North American Great Plains, Siberia, Western Europe, and Canada, where earlier snowmelt will be followed by a more intense evaporation as temperatures rise in the summer; there might also be less spring rain, at least in the Great Plains area.[34] This has global implications, because the United States, Canada, and France produce almost 75 percent of the world's grain exports, filling the needs of food-deficient countries across the world and providing an emergency reserve in times of famine. Should there be a reduction in overall agricultural output, the surplus nations would not be hurt— except in their balance of payments—as much as countries that require imports. While a rich country like Japan could easily pay the higher cost of scarce grain and soybeans, poverty-stricken developing countries could not.[35]

Can regions in which higher temperatures increase agricultural yields make up the deficits elsewhere? Probably, yes; Ontario and Alberta, for example, are expected to experience increased yields of corn, barley, soybeans, and hay if temperatures rise, although food output in their southern parts would suffer as moisture declines;[36] there may also be enhanced crop yields in Northern and Western Europe. None of this will provide satisfaction to the farmers of Oklahoma or southern Italy, who face the prospect of increasingly arid lands. Yet even if there is some compensation in a *global* sense as a poleward shift in the growing zones brings new lands under cultivation, this is unlikely to be enough. Unfortunately, in Siberia and northern Canada much of the soil is thin and highly acidified by centuries of decomposing evergreen needles—so that even if temperatures did rise, it is unlikely that crops would grow as well in those regions as they do in the rich soils of Iowa and the Ukraine. Global warming may also thaw vast tracts of frozen soil and permafrost, causing immense subsidence and swamping and releasing huge amounts of ancient, ice-locked methane and CO_2 into the atmosphere—accelerating the greenhouse effect and creating an ever-worsening cycle of ecological damage.[37]

. . . .

All of this suggests the need for reform and, even before that, for better understanding of the *interconnectedness* of the global changes now affecting our planet. Just as we have to realize that the earth is a closed system thermodynamically, so also ought we to comprehend the linkages which our varied human actions—demographic, economic, social—have created. Because of the population explosion and humankind's striving for higher living standards, we may now be subjecting our ecosystem to more pressure than it can take; but as it shows increasing signs of stress it in turn *threatens* us, rich and poor alike, with the consequences of having tampered too much with the earth's thin film of matter.

Those consequences—rises in sea level, depleted agriculture, reduced water flows, increased health hazards (skin cancer, city smogs), more turbulent weather, social strains—all suggest that both developed and developing nations have good reason to worry about global warming. Governments, farmers, and scientists currently have tended to prefer a policy of *adaptation,* turning to new heat and drought-resistant crops and installing ambitious new irrigation systems. But little of that appears to be adequate, given the sheer dislocation involved, even for those who potentially gain. Schemes such as the diversion of Rocky Mountain rivers to make up for the decline in the level of the Ogallala Aquifer would be horrendously expensive, with unpredictable environmental consequences elsewhere; and poorer countries simply can't pay for large irrigation schemes. Newer, genetically altered crops are simply too expensive for most farmers of the world, and in any case the basic problem—of environmental stress—would continue to be evaded by their use.

The alternative way of dealing with global warming is by *prevention,* that is, by changing how we live. Some changes are already under way, or are at least agreed upon. Energy intensity—the ratio of energy demand to real GDP—has been falling in advanced economies because of greater efficiency. Many nations, meeting in Montreal in 1987, agreed to end the production of CFCs by the year 2000, and rich countries have agreed in principle to finance the cost to poorer countries of this transition to newer technologies.[38] Local efforts are being made to reduce methane emissions, from capturing the gas from landfills by piping, to developing new rice breeds that produce less methane, to building enclosed feed lots for cattle. In the same way, many countries—and even townships—have imposed measures to reduce industrial emissions, cut automobile exhaust, and so on. Much of this is being done to address local atmospheric problems, but some reforms also help improve the global warming situation.

Yet such efforts are probably not enough. The CFC replacements (HCFCs) bring technical problems of their own. Moreover, the rate of carbon emissions has been growing at about 3 percent annually, which, if it continues, will double its atmospheric concentration by 2025. An atmospheric concentration of CO_2 double or more the preindustrial level is well beyond the gloomiest "ranges" and scenarios developed by climate modelers. In consequence, one concerned researcher has pointed out, "[a] frighteningly large gap looms between projected growth rates in carbon emissions and the level that atmospheric scientists believe is necessary to maintain a climate that can meet human needs."[39]

If this is to be reversed, or even slowed, full-scale cooperation between rich and poor countries is required, simply because virtually every nation contributes to the collective worsening of our atmosphere. In developed countries, the emissions from millions of automobiles and trucks, power stations, aircraft, and industry pour carbons into the air. In developing countries such as China and India, a heavy reliance upon coal does the same. Throughout the tropics, deforestation and burnings add to the toll. Moreover, it is not only carbon dioxide that is being released in such historically high proportions into the atmosphere. Methane (CH_4), which has twenty to thirty times the capacity to absorb heat as CO_2, comes from such varied sources as landfills, flooded rice fields, and cows' stomachs. Man-made CFCs, used since the 1930s in refrigeration, air-conditioning, and insulation, are up to sixteen thousand times more effective than CO_2 in absorbing heat and (until they are eliminated) contribute some 20 percent of man-made additions to the atmosphere.*

As will be seen in Table 3, each country's contribution to global

*As compared with 50 percent from carbon dioxide, and around 16 percent from methane. Another two sources are tropospheric ozone (8 percent) and nitrous oxide (6 percent).

warming is different. India and China burn lots of coal (generating carbon dioxide) and possess large numbers of cattle or pigs (generating methane), but use relatively few CFCs, especially in relation to the size of their population. Brazil, where so much forestland is cleared by burning each year, has recently been putting huge amounts of carbon dioxide into the atmosphere, but its contributions of methane and CFCs are much more modest—although one purpose of clearing tropical forests is to ranch more cattle (methane). Japan has lots of automobiles, but few cattle. And the United States is profligate in every category.

Many studies have shown what can be done.[40] A worldwide program to create and restore forests would lead to the absorption of large amounts of carbon—a forest of new trees sequesters about 5.5 tons of carbon per hectare as it grows—which would help offset the amounts emitted by deforestation.* Alternative energy sources (wind, photovoltaic, geothermal, biomass-sourced) could be much more extensively developed; photovoltaic power in particular looks enormously attractive as an inexhaustible and nonpolluting fuel if the conversion costs can be further reduced. Above all, however, it is of critical importance to reduce the 6 billion tons of carbon being poured into the atmosphere each year; this implies far greater energy-efficient technologies, from light bulbs to automobile engines to manufacturing plants. Developing countries have to be assisted, through the transfer of modern techniques, in adopting a "noncarbon" path toward industrialization. And the industrial nations have to make substantial reductions in the amount of greenhouse gases produced by their factories, houses, power stations, and automobiles.

But is such an effort possible? Since rich and poor nations alike contribute to atmospheric pollution, it is politically inconceivable—as well as environmentally ineffective—that only some reduce greenhouse-gas emissions while others ignore their responsibilities. Local measures are fine, but, globally, there is little point in Canada's adopting "clean" policies if the United States remains "dirty," or if the rain forests of Colombia are protected while those in Brazil are destroyed,

---

*At the moment, however, about ten tropical trees are being cut down for every one planted; in Africa, the ratio is twenty-nine to one.

Table 3. Top Twenty-five Countries with the Highest Greenhouse Gas
Net Emissions, 1987

(Carbon Dioxide Heating Equivalents, 000 metric tonnes of carbon)

Greenhouse Gases

Country	Greenhouse Index Rank	Carbon Dioxide	Methane	CFCs(a)	Total	Percent of Total
United States	1	540,000	130,000	350,000	1,000,000	17.6
USSR	2	450,000	60,000	180,000	690,000	12.0
Brazil	3	560,000	28,000	16,000	610,000	10.5
China	4	260,000	90,000	32,000	380,000	6.6
India	5	130,000	98,000	700	230,000	3.9
Japan	6	110,000	12,000	100,000	220,000	3.9
Germany, Fed. Rep.	7	79,000	8,000	75,000	160,000	2.8
United Kingdom	8	69,000	14,000	71,000	150,000	2.7
Indonesia	9	110,000	19,000	9,500	140,000	2.4
France	10	41,000	13,000	69,000	120,000	2.1
Italy	11	45,000	5,800	71,000	120,000	2.1
Canada	12	48,000	33,000	36,000	120,000	2.0
Mexico	13	49,000	20,000	9,100	78,000	1.4
Myanmar	14	68,000	9,000	0	77,000	1.3
Poland	15	56,000	7,400	13,000	76,000	1.3
Spain	16	21,000	4,200	48,000	73,000	1.3
Colombia	17	60,000	4,100	5,200	69,000	1.2
Thailand	18	48,000	16,000	3,500	67,000	1.2
Australia	19	28,000	14,000	21,000	63,000	1.1
German Dem. Rep.	20	39,000	2,100	20,000	62,000	1.1
Nigeria	21	32,000	3,100	18,000	53,000	0.9
South Africa	22	34,000	7,800	5,800	47,000	0.8
Côte d'Ivoire	23	44,000	550	2,000	47,000	0.8
Netherlands	24	16,000	8,800	18,000	43,000	0.7
Saudi Arabia	25	20,000	15,000	6,600	42,000	0.7

Source: *World Resources 1990–91,* p. 15

or if India agrees to control carbon dioxide emissions while China's
continue to rise. The sacrifices have to be global; more than that, they
must be as *equitable* as possible, allowing for differing standards of
income. Poor woodcroppers in India or African peasants whose animals
are overgrazing the savannahs are unlikely to be tempted to change
their ways unless societies one hundred times richer make a proportion-

ate sacrifice and offer adequate subsidies to replace lost income. Why, indeed, should developing countries worry about the greenhouse effect when they face—in their view—more immediate local issues like land erosion, desertification, limited access to clean water, colossal international debts, rising protectionism against their exports, inadequate technology transfer, etc.? How many desperate Ethiopians and Kashmiris have time to *care* about the opening of an "ozone hole" over North America?

All this returns us once again to politics, culture, and North-South relations. Global warming involves issues of wealth creation and distribution, of immediate gratification versus long-term gain, of traditional assumptions and modes of living versus newer realities, of international cooperation in place of independent isolationist policies. Like all the related matters discussed in this book, global warming forces us to confront the problem of a world divided into rich and poor.

Three instances illustrate just how sensitive the politics of global warming will be. The first, already mentioned, is the determination of China and India to have their own industrial revolution. Given their huge populations and the economic growth that they have to sustain, they may become the two largest contributors of greenhouse-gas emissions early next century. It is, therefore, desperately important to slow—better, to reverse—the level of emissions. Yet since the per capita GNP of both countries is so low, since their governments are wrestling with a population explosion and a rise in social and economic expectations, and since industrialization is regarded as the chief way to improve national product, how can either society be expected to adopt a "noncarbon" path to growth without enormous assistance from other countries? Even if that assistance should be forthcoming—and many developed countries are delinquent in their contributions to the Montreal Protocol Fund—would New Delhi and Beijing accept such restraint upon their economic sovereignty? Would they agree that they had to be more environmentally responsible than Europe and America were when they first industrialized?

This brings us to a second touchy issue, the destruction of the Latin

American rain forests. Today most people are aware of the implications of that process: the decline in biological diversity, the rise in carbon dioxide emissions from the burning of the trees, the reduction in the amount of plant and animal life. Yet the destruction is such that by the year 2000 three-quarters of America's tropical forests may have been felled. When, in 1988, satellite photos showed the extent of the burning, followed closely thereafter by news of the murder of union organizer Francisco Mendez (who had tried to prevent ranchers from destroying the forest), U.S. congressmen supported the idea of putting pressure upon Brazil—for example, by opposing international funds for a highway through the forests. This transformed the issue into one of North-South politics; Brazilian officials angrily pointed out that North Americans had not halted the destruction of their own forests over the past three centuries, that Brazil intended to develop its economy as any temperate economy would, and that, in any case, U.S. citizens use fifteen times more energy than Brazilians. Before preaching to others, America ought to set a better example.[41] In fact, Brazil now no longer subsidizes forest clearing, but it and its neighbors are still asking for a comprehensive North-South "deal" on this issue.

The third issue is the North's disproportionate contribution to greenhouse-gas emissions, especially carbon dioxide. According to the U.S. Environmental Protection Agency, to stabilize atmospheric concentrations of CO_2 at the present level, carbon emissions must be reduced by 50 to 80 percent, back to the level of the 1950s.[42] Otherwise there is little prospect of avoiding global warming, no matter what happens in Brazil and China. The obstacle here is not so much industrial emissions. Eliminating CFC and CO_2 emissions from factories and supermarkets is costly, and often opposed on that ground by American companies and Republican administrations, yet a great deal can and is being done. The real issue is the need to cut the emissions by vehicle engine combustion. Here the United States is particularly profligate, with 4 percent of world population devouring one-quarter or more of the world's fuel and being number one in greenhouse-gas emissions. Because they waste so much of the world's energy supplies, Americans would have to cut back far more than (say) Norwegians, by measures including stiff rises in gasoline prices, heavy investment in fuel-economy combustion, severe penalties on "gas-guzzling" automobiles, and the development of comprehensive public transportation systems. Yet however logical such a policy is on environmental grounds, it will be much easier to enact in the Netherlands or even Japan than in the United States. Never having had to conserve energy before—apart from during the few temporary "oil shocks" of the 1970s—many Americans would react angrily to strict restrictions on their right to drive, and emit engine exhaust, as they pleased.

Given the nature of American politics, it is difficult at present to imagine much leadership in Washington on global-warming issues.[43] Instead, there is a tendency to point to the differing scientific opinions in this matter, to suggest that fears about the greenhouse effect have been exaggerated, and to indicate that it would be unwise to devote funds and alter life-styles to meet circumstances that might not actually occur;[44] and, as noted above, those arguments are supported by skeptical scientists and economists.[45] All this has the *international* effect of making the United States appear indifferent to cooperation with other industrial democracies concerned with global warming, as occurred during the June 1992 Rio "summit" on environmental issues.

In theory, then, a number of measures could be instituted in both rich and poor countries to slow the rise in greenhouse-gas emissions. The UN Conference on Trade and Development is working on proposals for a forestry convention, a biodiversity convention, and a climate-change convention. Ingenious articles in Worldwatch Institute publications point to the merits of switching from automobiles to bicycles and invite readers to "cycle into the future."[46] Much of this writing might appear eccentric or quixotic on first reading, and the international agreements will be only as strong as the signatories permit, but behind it there lies a concern that there really is a long-term threat to our atmosphere, driven by overpopulation and industrialization. If global warming is as serious as some of the forecasts suggest, it will present our children and, more likely, our grandchildren with severe environmental problems.

And that, ironically, is the main obstacle to reform. Environmentalists are asking today's societies, in rich and poor countries, to make drastic changes—in their economic expectations, way of life, social behavior—in order to avoid deleterious effects a generation or two *in the future*; they are asking them to alter their own assumptions and life-styles now for the sake of their descendants' in thirty or fifty years' time. Since political leaders in many countries find it hard to call on their constituents for sacrifices even for immediate purposes (e.g., reducing the national debt, abolishing farm supports), few outside Northern Europe are likely to implement dramatic measures in response to global warming. One recent estimate, by UN environment authorities, that developing countries would need $125 billion a year to pay for new environmental programs—$70 billion more than *all* the financial assistance they now receive—was swiftly trimmed to a request for an additional $5 to $10 billion a year, in recognition of today's political and economic realities.[47] What is much more likely, therefore, is a number of piecemeal international agreements on environmental matters, especially if further droughts and other evidence of a rise in temperatures occur. That such measures will halt the destruction of the rain forests, the draining of aquifers, the profligate use of petroleum, and all our other dangerous habits seems unlikely—which cannot be good news for the future of the earth's thin film of life.

7

THE FUTURE OF THE
NATION-STATE

THE PRECEDING CHAPTERS DISCUSSED
demographic, environmental, and technological changes, all transnational in nature, which are bearing down upon human society. Chapters following this will discuss the likely impacts of those forces upon
specific regions and nations in light of their ability to respond to such
challenges. Not only are countries variably endowed geographically
with respect to size, location, and natural resources, their respective
inhabitants also differ greatly in their histories, cultural attitudes, social
structures, and economic prowess. Some of them are therefore better
prepared than others to deal with rising sea levels, or the biotech
revolution, or even demographic change. Inequality among nations
remains.

But before considering the prospects of different continents as the
twenty-first century approaches, we must address one further general
issue: what do these transnational developments mean for the future
of the nation-state itself, which is the organizing unit that people
normally turn to when challenged by something new? After all, to
plunge immediately into chapters upon the relative capacities of (say)
the German and Ethiopian states to grapple with global changes would
miss the point that most of those trends are so far-reaching that perhaps
no government agency is well equipped to handle them. Are not the

important "actors" in world affairs nowadays the global corporations? Isn't technology creating winners and losers—in employment, and career paths—regardless of where one lives? In an age of twenty-four-hour-a-day currency trading or, for that matter, global warming, have national bodies such as cabinets or commerce departments much relevance? And if they don't, how is it possible to think that countries as a whole can organize to face the century ahead?

For most citizens, the idea that not simply specific industries or activities but nation-states themselves are becoming anachronistic would be profoundly disturbing. It is true that nation-states as we know them are relatively recent creations, first appearing in the "new monarchies" of early-modern Europe such as Spain, France, and England.[1] In view of today's argument that people may be increasingly turning from national governments either to transnational or subnational agencies to achieve their goals,* it is ironic to note that the early-modern monarchies emerged from, and then subdued, a patchwork quilt of dukedoms, principalities, free cities, and other localized authorities such as Burgundy, Aragon, and Navarre; and that as they consolidated power internally, the nation-states also asserted themselves against transnational institutions like the papacy, monastic and knightly orders, and the Hanseatic League—the last being, in many ways, a sort of early multinational corporation.[2] Neither authority from above nor independence below could be tolerated in such egoistical states as Henry VIII's England or Louis XIV's France. Even where authority was shared internally—as between the English crown and parliament—the fact remained that both were national institutions.

As the modern nation evolved, it steadily acquired its basic characteristics, familiar to us now but often novel at the time and opposed by groups marginalized or overtaken by this process of state formation. The "ideal" type of state—for there were exceptions such as the multiethnic, multiterritorial Habsburg Empire—occupied a coherent geographical area, like France or Sweden. It therefore possessed recog-

*See below, pp. 131–33.

nizable national boundaries which, over time, were increasingly supervised by state employees such as customs officers, border police, and
immigration authorities. It, along with its fellow nation-states, was
recognized in international law and diplomacy as "sovereign"—there
was nothing above it—which was hardly surprising, since that law
consisted of norms which, at least in principle, countries had agreed to
observe. Each state evolved symbols (flag, anthem, historical figures
and events, special holidays) to reinforce consciousness of national
identity. While its schoolchildren studied universal subjects such as
mathematics, science, geography, other elements in the curriculum
(especially history) had a national focus, just as teaching itself followed
a national pattern. The national language steadily encroached upon
such regional tongues as Breton, Welsh, and Catalan, though the
resistance was often deep and determined.[3]

Institutionally and economically, too, the nation-state was at the
center of things. Adult males were conscripted or induced into the
armed services, which steadily changed from private feudal levies into
standing national institutions. As state spending rose to meet internal
and external needs, financial bodies like a national bank and a treasury
department evolved, national assemblies arose to vote on annual budgets, a national taxation system emerged, and national currency units
replaced older measures. The mercantilist economic system, intended
to boost a country's stock of capital, was also deliberately aimed at
making the nation strong and self-sufficient.[4] Reliance upon foreign
supplies of textiles, iron, grain, and other goods was reduced by making
them domestically, creating jobs, and lessening the outflow of specie.
Navigation acts strove to ensure that all seaborne trade was carried in
domestically owned vessels, crewed by one's own nationals. Knowledge
about how to manufacture, say, porcelain, or new types of textile
machinery, was kept from foreigners. All these actions, in the view of
people like Pitt, Colbert, and Frederick the Great, would enhance
national power and consciousness.

Apart from internal revolution, then, the only real threat to the
nation-state could come from another state seeking to enhance *its*
relative power, or from a coalition of hostile states. To ensure national
security, governments relied upon a mixture of military and diplomatic
measures—keeping a standing army, building a fleet, forming alliances

or ententes against a common rival. Wars, when they occurred, could be expensive, but they also served to boost patriotic fervor; denouncing the "overwhelming ambition" of France or the guile of "perfidious" Albion was always a good way to increase national solidarity.[5] By the beginning of the present century, nationalistic feelings were being reinforced by renewed naval and arms races, colonial rivalries, the agitations of the yellow press and chauvinistic pressure groups, and the social-Darwinistic notions of an international "struggle for survival." It was little wonder, therefore, that many of the citizens of the European powers marched willingly to war when those antagonisms exploded in 1914.[6]

This steady enhancement of the power and authority of the nation-state was not without certain counterforces. Despite governmental claims of national unity, in Ulster, Alsace, Catalonia, the Alto Adige, Silesia, Bosnia, and myriad other places, ancient ethnic rivalries and local patriotisms simmered beneath the surface. From Adam Smith's *The Wealth of Nations* (1776) onward, increasing numbers of economists, bankers, and businessmen argued that people everywhere would be better off if the hand of the mercantilist, protectionist state were removed from economic affairs and commerce and investment operated according to market criteria rather than governmental desires. The cosmopolitan ideology of liberalism was joined (and challenged), later in the nineteenth century, by a transnational workers' movement called Marxism. Each of these viewpoints opposed the claimed autonomy of the nation-state; yet whenever a grave international crisis occurred—as in 1914, and again in 1939—they were thrust aside. Diplomatic treaties (Versailles, Locarno, the Washington and London naval accords) and institutions (the League of Nations, the Permanent Court of Arbitration at the Hague) were similarly powerless to prevent egoistic sovereign states from going to war.

With the two great "total wars"[7] of this century fought by developed economies and organized by modern bureaucracies, the triumph of the nation-state seemed complete. Even liberal, democratic systems insisted on conscription. Citizens' loyalties were claimed totally; dealing with the enemy was treason, and all prewar trade was frozen. Controls were imposed upon industry and investment, currency dealing, even labor strikes, as the state-at-war sought to extract the maximum production possible from its people. World War I produced the passport—a proof of an individual's nationality but, interestingly, owned by the government, which could recall it when deemed necessary. World War II produced the "gross national product," an economist's device to allow the state full scrutiny of productive activity. In both conflicts, governments steadily augmented controls over information. Even great works of art reflected national need and resolve, as in Olivier's patriotic interpretation of *Henry V* or Shostakovitch's Eighth Symphony.

After 1945 these trends ebbed somewhat in the economic sphere but continued strong in political life. International financial and trading arrangements such as the International Monetary Fund, the World Bank, and the General Agreement on Tariffs and Trade sought to check a recurrence of the damage caused by interwar protectionism and autarky; foreign trade and investment flows boomed. But the rising tensions produced by the Cold War badly affected the climate of international relations and pointed to the continued importance of "national" security. The United Nations, devised as an improved version of the League, suffered accordingly as the superpowers squabbled over, and vetoed, one another's motions. External threats were studied by national security councils or similarly named bodies; wherever an American president went—even on vacation—his "national security adviser" was at his side. National security was used to justify almost everything, from building a highway system to providing science and technology scholarships. It was also used negatively, to withhold certain information, ban specified immigrants, forbid trade and travel with particular countries, suspend technology transfers. At the height of the Cold War, as both the USSR and the United States poured hundreds of billions of dollars each year into defense spending, observers wondered whether each had not become a "national security state"; others, concerned by the massive diversion of capital, R&D, scientists, engineers, and technicians into the arms race, feared for the effect upon long-term national competitiveness.[8]

Such ways of thinking still have a powerful hold today. During Cold War tensions, it was of course easy to argue that threats to one's people were primarily military in nature, and that the nation-state remained the central actor in world affairs. Even with that conflict removed, national security experts and Pentagon officials can still find many potential threats to international stability—and grounds for maintaining large defense forces. The existence of tens of thousands of nuclear warheads in the successor states of the Soviet Union, and the fact that their ownership is uncertain; the possibility of another breakdown in Arab-Israeli relations; ethnic conflict in the Balkans and elsewhere; volatile regimes in Libya, Iraq, and North Korea; the emergence of regional great powers like India and China; the proliferation of sophisticated weaponry to "trouble spots" around the globe—all these imply the continued need for military power, controlled by the nation-state and its instruments (Pentagon, National Security Council, Joint Chiefs of Staff), working in conjunction with international security structures (NATO, U.S.-Japan Defense Treaty, etc.).

These traditional assumptions are coming under increasing pressure, however, simply because of the way our world is changing. With the Cold War over, many writers now argue that military rivalries and arms races are being replaced by economic rivalries, technology races, and various forms of commercial warfare. In consequence, the language used to describe international trade and investment today has become increasingly military in nature; industries are described as coming "under siege," markets are "captured" or "surrendered," and comparative rates of R&D expenditures or of shares of high-technology goods are scrutinized as anxiously as the relative sizes of battlefleets before 1914.[9] Even national security experts now admit the importance of the economic dimensions of power and concede that traditional instruments such as armies and navies cannot be deployed against economic challenges. Yet although that shift seems novel, in fact the older way of thinking remains: the nation-state is still at the center of things, engaged in a ceaseless jostling for advantage against other nation-states. A neomercantilist world order remains, even if recourse to war is no longer regarded as an option.*

. . .

*Except in the extremist literature: see G. Friedman and M. Lebard, *The Coming War with Japan* (New York, 1991).

Yet, as we have seen in the preceding chapters, other experts on international trends are pointing to different causes for concern and to fresh threats to security. Overpopulation in the poorer countries of the world could produce resource wars, exacerbate ethnic tensions, contribute to social instabilities, and fuel external expansionism. A migratory flood from the poorer and more troubled parts of the globe to the richer and more peaceful will bring not only social costs, but also rising racial antagonisms. Differentiated population growth rates of ethnic groups within the same national borders are likely to heighten already existing tensions. The effects of the population explosion on the ecosystem might threaten national interests. In addition to increasing the risk of resource wars over diminishing stocks of water, grazing land, timber, and the like, environmental damage threatens economic prosperity and public health. Moreover, such damage cuts into global food production as world population increases by almost a billion per decade, which could cause massive global hunger and lead to further social and political instabilities, resource wars, and deteriorating relations between the richer and poorer peoples of the earth.[10]

The nation-state and its security are also potentially threatened by the new international division of production and labor. The logic of the global marketplace pays no attention to *where* a product is made, but defense planners—in keeping with traditional national security thinking—are more concerned. Is it not vital, they argue, for a country to maintain its own electronics and computer industry, to preserve shipping and aerospace, to be able to produce its own software for both military and nonmilitary purposes?[11] Unwelcome economic trends may affect national power indirectly as well. A country could be badly damaged if its dairy or beef industry—perhaps a source of large export earnings—were devastated by the advent of biotech methods of food production elsewhere; or if its automobile industry—another major source of national earnings and wealth—were wiped out by the invasion of the home market by more efficient foreign rivals; or if high-tech designs and production moved to other countries, and the national industrial base eroded.

The international financial revolution brings its own challenges to the assumed sovereignty of the nation-state. The borderless world implies a certain surrender of a nation's control over both its own currency and its fiscal policies. That surrender might bring prosperity, but if the international financial system is unstable, there is little or no authority to control potential massive currency flows. With the volume of daily currency exchanges well in excess of the GNPs of many countries, individual governments and finance ministries have much less command over the system than they had a quarter century ago. Simply the awareness of the market's disapproval of certain measures (like raising taxes) can deter so-called sovereign governments from implementing them.

Although very different in form, these various trends from global warming to twenty-four-hour-a-day trading are *transnational* by nature, crossing borders all over the globe, affecting distant societies, and reminding us that the earth, for all its divisions, is a single unit. They are largely out of the control of the authorities of the traditional nation-state, both in the direct sense that countries cannot prevent incoming atmospheric drift and in the indirect sense that if they banned such activities as biotech farming, robotics, and foreign-exchange dealing, that would not stop them operating elsewhere. Finally, these challenges cannot be met by military force, which is the normal way states have handled threats to their security. Carrier task forces and armored divisions have their uses, but they are unable to prevent the global demographic explosion, stop the greenhouse effect, halt foreign-exchange dealings, ban automated factories and biotech farming in foreign countries, and so on.

These developments, together with such secondary challenges as international terrorism and drugs, have suggested to some writers that "new" threats to national and international security are taking the place of the "old" threats of nuclear warfare and large-scale conventional war, and that governments should therefore cease their obsession with military dangers and concentrate instead upon measures to deal with very different challenges to the national well-being.[12]

Such a suggestion probably exaggerates the extent of the recent changes in world affairs. It makes much more sense to think of these newer threats to our way of life as *coming alongside* the older and more traditional threats to security, rather than replacing them. Even if the Soviet-American arms race loses its significance, there will still be many nuclear weapons on this planet; the nuclear powers themselves will also remain, and if attempts to halt proliferation are not successful, they will be joined in the future by other nations, perhaps less scrupulous and almost certainly located in more turbulent regions of the globe than Western Europe and North America. Regional conflicts, driven by their own socioeconomic, cultural, or ethnic dynamic, are unlikely to fade away and in many parts of the world may well increase in number and scope as the struggle for resources intensifies. After all, the continued relevance of nation-states and military power was amply demonstrated in the 1990–91 Gulf War.

Armed forces will remain, therefore, and on occasions will be used. But this traditional military dimension to "security" will increasingly coexist with the nonmilitary dimensions described above, compelling politicians and their publics to redefine their terminology and rethink their policies. On some occasions, indeed, we might also expect the "new" and the "old" security issues to combine; social instabilities caused by population pressure and resource depletion could take place in regions (Southwest Asia, for example) where arms proliferation, ethnic tensions, and territorial disputes have long been a threat to peace.[13] Meanwhile the winding-down of the nuclear arms race may, ironically, produce two distinct types of threat: the more traditional problem of how to prevent hundreds or thousands of former Soviet warheads and missiles from falling into the "wrong" hands, and the newer, perhaps equally difficult task of dealing with masses of nuclear waste, which are a profound ecological hazard. In both cases, one suspects, statesmen and their advisers are hastily scrambling to think through the implications of these new threats, and only the most sanguine observer can assume that they will get it right on every occasion. But what would "getting it wrong" mean?

In this larger and more integrated sense, "national" security becomes increasingly inseparable from "international" security, and both assume a much broader definition; in place of the narrower military concept there is emerging a larger definition which can encompass a whole spectrum of challenges, old and new. Indeed, we may eventually come to agree that a threat to national security means anything on the globe which challenges a people's health, economic well-being, social stability, and political peace.[14]

The problem with such an all-encompassing definition is, however, that it lacks the drama, the clarity, and the immediacy of a military threat to national security. When an enemy army is ravaging an ally or one's homeland is targeted by thousands of missiles, public opinion is relatively easily mobilized. But many people still distinguish between "high politics" (that is, clear threats to the nation) and "low politics" (economic quarrels, environmental reform proposals, trade negotiations); and while the issues of low politics are now attracting lots of attention, it still may be more difficult to convince publics and politicians to make the necessary sacrifices to meet new threats than it was in the period of bipolar antagonism.[15]

These global changes also call into question the usefulness of the nation-state itself. The key autonomous actor in political and international affairs for the past few centuries appears not just to be losing its control and integrity, but to be the *wrong sort* of unit to handle the newer circumstances. For some problems, it is too large to operate effectively; for others, it is too small. In consequence, there are pressures for a "relocation of authority" both upward and downward, creating structures that might respond better to today's and tomorrow's forces for change.[16]

The relocation of authority upward and outward from the nation-state has attracted the greater attention. This refers not only to the *re*emergence of transnational players such as the large corporations and banks, or to the rise of a global communications system largely outside the control of individual governments. It also refers to the increased role of international institutions and agreements, the reasoning being that if the new challenges are global, they can be met successfully only on a global scale, through transnational agencies and commonly agreed policies, ranging from greater cooperation and consultation among the leading industrial democracies (the G-7 summits), to treaties banning the use of CFCs, to the enhancement of the roles and resources of such international agencies as the United Nations, UNESCO, the World Bank, and the IMF. Insofar as the latter can contribute to peace and stability—for example, in the increasing use of United Nations peace-keeping forces in so many regional trouble spots—this is a welcome development; and if they do turn out to be generally successful (a big if in the case of places like Bosnia), that could further enhance the status of international bodies *vis-à-vis* purely national instruments and policies.

Also emerging are supranational organizations of a regional sort, especially for commercial purposes. While forecasts of the impending division of the developed world into three trading blocs and their satellites may be premature, the creation of something such as a North American Free Trade zone (Mexico, United States, Canada) does involve agreements to reduce national economic integrity; within the borders of the zone itself, national differences will begin to blur. This process is even more advanced in the European Community, whose home governments and parliaments have agreed to cede large areas of traditional national sovereignty in order to gain greater economic and political unity; and it is precisely because they have already gone so far that there exists deep political controversy between integrationists and those opposed to the further erosion of national powers.*

The relocation of authority from the nation-state to smaller units is also chiefly driven by economic and technological developments. The breakdown of borders across Europe, for example, permits the emergence (in many cases, the *re*emergence) of regional economic zones, which had been barred by national customs and tariff systems. As new trading relationships develop, the former ones fade; Slovenia trades increasingly with Austria and less with Serbia, Alsace-Lorraine becomes more integrated with Baden-Württemberg than with Paris, northern Italy develops closer links with Alpine states than with Calabria or Sicily. Individual American states, often frustrated by the lack of interest shown by the federal government, open their own "missions" in Tokyo and Brussels in order to conduct investment and trade diplomacy. Russian cities like St. Petersburg declare themselves free-trade zones in order to attract foreign investment.

Many of these developments are innocent enough, and welcomed by free-market economists on the grounds that unrestricted trade follows its own natural (and more beneficial) course. But this relocation of

*See Chapter 12, "Europe and the Future."

authority downward also carries with it the risk of national disintegration—at least in societies where ethnic rivalries and disputed boundaries fuel regional differences. While the most spectacular examples of this decay of national cohesion have recently been witnessed in the Soviet Union and Yugoslavia, there are many examples elsewhere in the world. In much of Africa, the European-style state system is breaking down, borders are permeated, regional and ethnic rivalries are on the rise. This issue of center versus provinces, or unity versus diversity, also drives observer nations into different political positions; a culturally homogeneous Germany might incline to sympathize with the autonomist claims of Slovenes and Croats in Yugoslavia, whereas governments with their own regional/ethnic problems (e.g., Spain) are understandably nervous about encouraging separatist movements anywhere. In all of the tense debates over international intervention—for example, to assist the Kurds—there runs this larger issue of the legality and integrity of the nation-state.

In the light of the broad global trends discussed in the preceding chapters, we should not be surprised if further internal and regional conflicts break out. With population pressures building up in various parts of the globe, the struggle for resources intensifying, and the communications revolution often fueling ethnic animosities rather than producing world citizens, the challenges to national authority—especially in the poorer parts of the world—may well intensify. Two centuries ago, Immanuel Kant observed that nature employed two means to separate peoples: "differences of language and of religion," both tending to produce "mutual hatred and pretexts for war." Within time, Kant hoped, the "progress of civilization" would finally lead to peaceful agreement among all.[17] Perhaps it will one day; but the evidence at present suggests that we have a long way to go, and that the progress of "civilization" is not keeping pace with those trends which are transforming our planet and challenging our traditional political arrangements. On the contrary, fundamentalist forces, partly in reaction to globalization, gather strength to lash back, while even in democracies, nationalist and antiforeign political movements gain ground—all of which hurts their long-term chances of "preparing" for the future.

. . .

This leaves humankind with a conundrum. For all the discussion about the relocation of authority and group loyalties, the older structures exist—and, indeed, in some places are increasingly clung to. There may have been a certain erosion of the powers of the nation-state in recent decades, but the nation-state remains the primary locus of identity of most people; regardless of who their employer is and what they do for a living, individuals pay taxes to the state, are subject to its laws, serve (if need be) in its armed forces, and can travel only by having its passport.* Moreover, as new challenges emerge—be it illegal migration or biotech farming—peoples turn instinctively (at least in the democracies) to their own governments to find "solutions." The global demographic explosion, atmospheric pollution, and technology-driven change each have their own transnational momentum; but it is national governments and assemblies which decide whether to abolish currency controls, permit biotechnology, cut factory emissions, or support a population policy. This does not mean that they will always be successful; in fact, a major argument of this book is that the nature of the new challenges makes it much more difficult than previously for governments to control events. But they still provide the chief institution through which societies will try to respond to change. Finally, if there is to be coordinated action by the peoples of this world, for example, to halt the destruction of the tropical rain forests or reduce methane emissions, then inter*national* agreements, negotiated by the participating governments, are clearly required.

In sum, even if the autonomy and functions of the state have been eroded by transnational trends, no adequate substitute has emerged to replace it as the key unit in responding to global change. How the political leadership of the nation prepares its people for the twenty-first century remains of vital importance even when the traditional instruments of state are weakening—which is why it is now necessary to consider the prospects of individual countries and regions as they respond, or fail to respond, to the challenges of the coming century.

*Or, in the case of Europeans, by having an EC passport.

PART 2

REGIONAL IMPACTS

8

THE JAPANESE "PLAN" FOR
A POST-2000 WORLD

ASSUMING THE DIMENSIONS OF OUR GLO-
bal predicament outlined above to be roughly correct—that there will
be a continuing population explosion in the poorer parts of the world
leading to increased environmental damage and social stress, while
globalization and newer technologies arising in rich countries may
undermine traditional methods (and locations) of agriculture, manufacturing, and business in general—how can any people hope to remain
unscathed? Even if the global economy is creating three immensely
powerful and privileged trading blocs, in Europe, North America, and
Japan, can they—regardless of how well they "prepare" internally for
the future—isolate themselves from the turbulences caused by worldwide change? Can they exist as islands of prosperity in a sea of discontents?

As we consider the prospects of the various countries and regions of
the earth—in this chapter, specifically Japan—we shall see that complete isolation from the "fallout" from global trends is impossible,
although the Japanese will undoubtedly strive to be more successful
than other advanced economies in meeting new challenges. Already,
Japan is viewed by many commentators as the country best prepared
for tomorrow's technologically driven global changes,[1] although the
very notion of "Japan as number one" has also drawn criticism from

authors more impressed by Japanese weaknesses than strengths.[2] Both strong and weak points are discussed here—as they will be in later chapters, which consider the prospects of other countries. While each region and nation is examined separately in order to provide a reasonably detailed assessment, their position relative to other societies—and, of course, to the general, transnational forces described in Part One— needs to be kept constantly in mind.

The overall conclusion of this chapter is that because of the way their society and economy are organized, the Japanese are probably the people least likely to be hurt by gross and direct damage from global overpopulation, mass migration, and environmental disasters on the one hand or from the globalization of production on the other; but even such a successful nation as Japan will find it hard to escape the larger repercussions of demographic and technological change.

Japan's achievement in creating wealth, decade after decade since 1945 and at a pace unequaled by any other large power (and very few smaller ones), rests upon strong foundations. These include the social and racial coherence of the Japanese people themselves, who have seldom intermarried with other ethnic groups and have enjoyed a lengthy period of relative isolation from international affairs. This cohesion manifests itself not only in a powerful sense of national identity and cultural uniqueness, but also—and, to Western eyes, more impressively—in an emphasis upon social harmony, the need for consensus, generational deference, and the subordination of individual desires to the good of the collectivity. As a result of such social norms, so the argument goes, the Japanese suffer far fewer murders, crimes of violence, and strikes, a greater degree of family and intergenerational bonding, and a higher average life expectancy than people in most Occidental societies. Having suppressed individualist impulses to a large degree, the Japanese function more effectively as a team or, rather, as members of many teams—the family, the school, the company, and the nation.[3]

Education is a critical element in Japan, as it is in other Confucian-influenced societies of East Asia. But while the Japanese emphasize the acquisition of knowledge, they lay even greater stress upon learning as a group activity; rather than encouraging individual excellence, the Japanese seek to ensure that all members of the class attain the required standard levels of literacy and numeracy. Teachers are a highly valued asset in Japan, deference to them is strong, and every year there are many more highly qualified applicants for schoolteaching jobs than places available. Learning in schools is reinforced by further study, at home or in "crammer" *(juku)* institutes, with the emphasis upon factual acquisition rather than the free flow of debate and ideas. Competition to get into prestigious universities is intense, harrowing for the student and eagerly supported by the family. Measured by standards of comparative economic advantage and wealth creation, the results are impressive.[4] Fresh cadres of school leavers, possessing high competency and encouraged to "fit in" to the company which recruits them, become members of a disciplined and skilled work force dedicated to improving the firm's productivity. The more talented will be steered toward careers which underpin a flourishing manufacturing and high-technology base: engineers of all types, scientists, computer specialists, R&D personnel; in other words, people who help to *make* things. By contrast, there are far fewer lawyers and management consultants, who provide services rather than produce goods.

Official statistics confirm this impression of a purposeful, utilitarian education system. The entire Japanese school structure, which consists of around 1.3 million teachers educating 27 million pupils in some 66,000 schools,[5] is tightly controlled and regulated by a powerful Ministry of Education; course offerings, textbooks, teachers' salaries, and even a school's physical plant are under its supervision. While this creates a rigidity and conformity that many other societies would find oppressive, the important fact is that high general standards are set, which everyone strives to reach. Almost all Japanese children (92 percent) attend kindergarten, where the early socializing process begins. Everyone in Japan then receives at least nine years of compulsory education, with the vast majority continuing into high school; and a full 90 percent or more of the population graduate from high school, a rate well above those in the United States, Britain, and most other countries. One result of this is that Japan currently has an illiteracy rate of a minuscule 0.7 percent. Moreover, because Japanese children go to school for many more days each year—about 220 (including Saturday half-days) compared with about 180 in the United States—and because they study longer during each school day, a fourteen-year-old Japanese child has been exposed to as much teaching as an American student of seventeen or eighteen. Japanese children score very highly in international standardized tests measuring mathematical or scientific ability (especially since so much of what they learn is in those fields); yet even on standard intelligence tests, the *average* Japanese student scores 117, compared to 100 for Americans and Europeans.[6]

In higher education the pressures are much less intense, even in the better universities, and the Japanese record is mixed. Receiving a lesser share of total education funding than in other industrialized nations, and with small graduate programs, Japanese universities and colleges have hitherto not done well in creative research; as of 1987, Japanese had won only four Nobel Prizes in science compared with 142 for the United States. This may change as the Japanese allocate much larger sums to pure research than in the past, but it is likely that the greatest amount of scientific investigation in Japan will continue to be carried out in laboratories and institutes of giant corporations, with "pure" knowledge purchased or copied from elsewhere. It is an indication of its preference for the practical that Japan leads the world in the proportion of qualified scientists and engineers (about 60,000 per million people); almost 800,000 Japanese are engaged in research and development, more than in Britain, France, and Germany combined.[7]

Japan's financial and fiscal structures also contribute to the national purpose of wealth creation. Not only does the tax system encourage private savings, but the high cost of housing and the need to save for old age ensure a high level of personal savings. This traditionally has provided banks and insurance companies with masses of capital, then lent at low rates to Japanese manufacturers, giving them a cost advantage over foreign rivals. In addition, banks and companies possess an intricate web of crossholdings of each other's stock, allowing the managers of a firm to plan a long-term strategy—often involving heavy capital investment, and without much regard for quarterly profit returns—to bring new products to the consumer and enhance market shares. These advantages were reinforced, at least until recently, by the government's policy of discouraging imports and of keeping the yen's value low, and by manufacturing companies' intimate links with domestic suppliers for components and ancillary services.[8]

This combination made it difficult for many foreign companies to compete with their Japanese rivals; American firms, for example, had to contend with a less highly skilled and less docile work force, the higher cost of capital, dependency upon the immediate profit-seeking tendencies of Wall Street investors, *and* the built-in difficulties of penetrating the Japanese home market. In addition to these extraneous advantages, Japanese companies also benefited from the quality of so many of their products and of the production system itself. The fanatical attention given to consumer tastes, to efficient and pleasing designs, to "lean production" on the factory floor, to quality control, and to after-sales service is noted in study after study.[9] Much of this passion, it seems, is driven by the strong competitiveness between rival Japanese firms; as Honda challenges Toyota and Nissan, as Olympus Optical battles with Pentax and Ricoh, the planners and personnel in each company devote great efforts to ensuring that their products will be the best. That is, of course, the ideal of competitive capitalist enterprise everywhere, but in Japan it is taken close to its limits.[10]

The result of this economic expansion—and in many ways the driving force behind it—has been the emergence of a number of giant Japanese corporations that possess vast amounts of capital and a world strategy for making and selling their goods. Most of them have used their large bank balances to install ever more sophisticated equipment in order to export competitively as the yen strengthens further; capital spending in Japan recently has exceeded that of the United States in absolute terms, an eye-opening fact when one considers that the American population is twice as large.[11] Ambitious corporations with "industrial intelligence" staffs to scour the world for new products and ideas have bought out foreign companies, established laboratories and research centers in Europe and North America, and funded the research of academics and scientists in different parts of the globe. When foreign experts declare Japan to be deficient in a certain field (luxury cars, computer software, supercomputers), intense efforts are made to eliminate that deficiency.[12] In much the same way, forecasts of increasing European protectionism swiftly stimulated Japanese companies to make heavy European investments, in order to manufacture *within* the EC's boundaries before the further integration of 1992.[13]

The results of Japan's manufacturing miracle have benefited not simply bosses and bankers, but the country itself. Its GNP, one-third of Britain's and a mere one-twentieth that of the United States in 1951, is now about three times Britain's GNP and close to two-thirds of the American total at current exchange rates; moreover, forecasters expect the Japanese economy to grow faster than America's, and probably faster than Europe's, for the rest of the century.[14] Individual Japanese possess a much higher standard of living than they did thirty years ago, a rise reflected not only in their heightened consumer spending, but even more spectacularly in Japanese purchases and travel abroad. As its economy has strengthened, so also has the purchasing power of its currency; whereas visitors to Japan wilt at the cost of everyday goods and services, the Japanese have found foreign countries and their assets (from farmland to Impressionist paintings) relatively cheap. Like Switzerland and several other Northern European countries, therefore, Japan has become a high-per-capita-income society, which is the ultimate economic fruit of enhancing overall productivity.

While enterprising firms have driven the Japanese economy forward, this expansion was clearly assisted by the macroeconomic and structural features mentioned earlier, such as the education system and low interest rates. In addition, many companies enjoyed the support of the Ministry for International Trade and Industry (MITI) in identifying new product areas, collecting information, and funding and sharing scientific research.[15] A further advantage was Japan's virtually demilitarized status after 1945; sheltered under the American strategic umbrella, Japan has spent only 1 percent of its GNP upon defense annually (as compared with American totals that have ranged from 5 to 10 percent and beyond).[16] "Savings" in that sphere have released funds for the continued modernization of its industry. While Japan does not have much in the way of *hard* power (tanks, aircraft), it possesses a growing amount of *soft* power, or nonmilitary influence,[17] as can be seen in its enhanced position within the IMF and World Bank, its acquisition of Hollywood studios and European computer firms, the size of the Tokyo stock market, and the fact that Japan is now the world's largest donor of foreign aid, so that many developing countries now look to Tokyo for assistance, loans, and investments. As politicians from developing countries hasten to Japan, a rising flood of Japanese businessmen, tourists, manufacturers, and capital penetrates most parts of the globe, in a manner reminiscent of Britain's mid-to-late-Victorian expansionism.[18] In the fastest-growing region of all, the western Pacific and East Asia, more and more economies are drawn into a Japan-dominated trading and investment bloc, raising fears that Japan is achieving a "Greater East Asia Co-Prosperity Sphere" by peaceful commercial means with greater success than it ever managed by its warlike expansion of the 1930s.[19] If it has come so far in the space of two generations, how much further will it have grown in wealth, influence, and power in forty years' time?

All this will be familiar to students of international economic affairs. Yet while the achievements are undoubted, they appear to have been gained at high cost to Japanese society itself. Japan's vaunted social harmony, some observers feel, has been secured by insisting upon conformism and deference to the point of repression. Instead of encouraging creativity, the entire educational experience is based upon memorization of facts and "group think"—features which reappear in factory and business organizations, where an unquestioned harmony is supposed to prevail. The system is rigid and hierarchical (the more important the boss, the deeper one's bow to him), and it accords enormous privileges to a select group of *males* who own the large corporations, run the bureaucracies, and manage the ruling Liberal Party. By contrast, the great majority of the Japanese population has to content itself with cramped accommodations, excessive work hours, group calisthenics, and the consolations of national pride. Women are meant to take care of the home, manage the savings, and ensure the children's after-school education.[20]

Furthermore, the emphasis upon uniqueness and "Japanness" reflects not simply a sense of cultural identity but, more disturbingly, a deep streak of racism, which is particularly manifested in Japanese views of Koreans, Chinese, American blacks, and many other ethnic groups abroad, as well as the *burakumin* ("outcasts") at home. Cultural exclusivity makes it difficult for Japan to offer transcendental values to other peoples in the way (it is avowed) that Athens, Renaissance Italy, and the modern United States have contributed to world civilization.[21]

"Japan Inc." has also systematically avoided the rules of international free trade. For decades, foreign goods that rivaled Japanese products were kept out of the home market, either by discriminatory tariffs or (when that led to protests by other nations) by a variety of less obvious obstacles—the distribution system, for example, or the fixing of bids and contracts in private. Unlike that other enormously successful exporting nation Germany, Japan until recently did not import very much, apart from raw materials or goods which it did not manufacture itself (Boeing aircraft, luxury automobiles), which led to its enormous trade surpluses. In industry after industry, American and European critics complain, Japan has targeted a product made elsewhere, bought the foreign expertise required to understand the technology (whether in the form of MIT professors or software engineers), given its manufacturers all manner of support to permit them to catch up, and only then favored free trade in that sector; in other cases, it is claimed, it has hurt foreign rivals by "dumping" goods at below-market prices abroad while keeping them highly priced in the protected home market.[22]

The greatest foreign "victim" of these Japanese business practices, at least measured by the decibels of complaints, is the United States, which in recent years has experienced annual merchandise trade deficits with Japan of as much as $40 to $50 billion, has seen some of its key industries eclipsed by Japanese competition, and has reacted with growing concern as Japan has bought up ever more American assets. This is not only a massive historic irony, in that the American post-1945 occupation encouraged Japan to abandon "militarism" in favor of peaceful commercial pursuits, but a contemporary political irony, since the United States provides strategic security to an ally that contributes much less to the common defense while eroding America's own industrial base. In consequence, U.S. congressmen regularly complain about Japan's status as a "free rider" and press for a greater contribution to international security, a field in which Japan has appeared indecisive and unimpressive as compared with middle-sized European powers like Britain or France—confirming, to those critical of Tokyo policies, that the Japanese are interested only in making money.*

Furthermore, the popular image of all-conquering Japanese corporations ignores many less impressive aspects of its society and economy. The thousands of small family firms and mom-and-pop stores are inefficient, the distribution network is clogged by special interests, and Japanese farming is uncompetitive, having survived only because of special protection which keeps food prices much higher than in North America. The average per capita income of the Japanese people therefore conceals the fact that their real purchasing power is reduced by the high costs of food, consumer goods, land, and housing. Japan also lags behind many other nations in public facilities, sewage disposal, and places of recreation. The global triumph of Japanese capitalism is not yet reflected in *overall* productivity—which is still less than America's—or in the people's quality of life compared with that in certain other advanced industrial societies like Denmark and Canada.[23] In any case, much of the *measure* of Japanese wealth in recent years has rested upon extraordinarily high property prices and almost equally inflated stock prices—that is, on paper assets which can fall deeply in value yet have been used by banks to "leverage" Japan's aggressive spending on acquisitions across the globe, some of which have yet to prove profitable. By the early 1990s, much of the nominal rise in values of the preceding decade had been lost, particularly affecting bank shares, raising the issue of whether Japan's large overseas investments might have to be sold off to increase bank liquidity at home. Should this all end in a crash, not only would Japan's wealth decline, but that collapse might also damage international money and credit networks.

Finally, many of the factors accounting for Japan's post-1950 economic success are themselves beginning to change, which could reduce Japanese growth rates. By far the most important of these is the demo-

*On the other hand, there has always been confusion about whether a large-scale enhancement of Japanese *military power*, together with a reduction in the American strategic presence in the Pacific, really would be wise. Critics who point to Japan's "one-dimensional" strength (i.e., economic power), and to the way it has exploited that position, are among the first to caution against building up the Japanese armed forces—which leaves Tokyo both accused of not spending enough on national security and simultaneously warned not to contemplate large defense increases. Even when Japan paid large amounts of money to finance the 1991 war against Iraq, many foreign critics were unimpressed.

graphic transformation, the consequences of which are discussed in more detail below. Japan will have far more elderly people in the early twenty-first century than now, and the country's traditionally high savings ratios may decline significantly as a result; and, with available capital reduced, Japanese firms may no longer be able to count upon low-interest loans as an advantage over foreign rivals. In addition, any further rise in the value of the yen could force Japanese corporations to move manufacturing offshore, to lower-cost countries. As that happens, the Japanese—like the British and the Americans before them—may increasingly lose their "manufacturing culture," a development already evident in the numbers of talented youths nowadays heading into merchant banking rather than engineering. Caught in the traditional "scissor" of higher costs at home and increasing competition from newly industrializing countries overseas, Japan Inc. could sooner or later find that its special advantages have disappeared.[24]

Throughout the commentaries upon Japan's prospects, there runs an underlying question: is it "special" or "not normal" compared with other advanced industrial societies?[25] Of course, the question itself raises the issue of whether there really is a "normal" Western or American capitalist system from which the Japanese are deviating. This literature suggests that the Japanese way of life has posed a challenge especially to Americans, who worry at being eclipsed economically but are even more worried that they might have to alter their own habits—concerning education, individualism, the role of women—in order to match the Japanese challenge.[26] (Far better, perhaps, to press the Japanese themselves to change *their* habits). The issue of Japan's uniqueness is complicated not merely by untestable claims of superiority by Japanese nationalists, but also by the differing approaches of foreign "experts." Whereas foreigners resident in Japan for many years have generally concluded that the Japanese do have special cultural assumptions which affect economic performance, classical Western economists believe that sooner or later, all countries function according to universal principles. Rational economic man has always found culture difficult to quantify.[27]

Behind this debate lies a larger historical issue: is Japan a normal country which will lose its present advantages one day, or has it found a way of defying laws concerning comparative national advantage and can it thus avoid what might be termed a late-Victorian fate? The phrase refers to the dilemma that faced the British a century ago when they began to lose their early industrial lead as other countries imitated them. In theory, at least, Britain could have avoided being overtaken if its economy had repeatedly switched into ever-higher-added-value production, abandoning the older sectors to foreign competitors. But that in turn would have needed some form of national planning and a long-term economic strategy, and also a constant upgrading of Britain's educational system, its output of scientists, technologists, and engineers, and its levels of investment in research and development, all of which were necessary to keep ahead of the field. Because British society did *not* choose to reorganize itself in that way, its late-Victorian economy was steadily overtaken by others and Britain lost its place as workshop of the world.[28]

According to some economists, the evidence of Japan's own long-term relative decline already exists in the aging of the population; the consumer spending, tourist outflows, and reduction in overall savings rates; the rise in imported manufactures, the shift of production to other parts of the world, and the reduction in its current-accounts surpluses; the steady structural move out of industrial production and into services; the emergence of Tokyo as a global financial center, a latter-day version of the City of London in Victorian times, but one resting upon less secure (because more speculative) foundations; the volatility of its stock market, no longer immune from steep declines; and the changes in cultural attitudes, career choices, and the role of women and other indications of a deep national metamorphosis. The Japanese sun may still be shining brightly, but it is now past the noon hour and beginning to set.[29]

On the other hand, there is also evidence that, while making certain ostensible changes to please internal and external critics (increasing domestic consumption, reducing trade surpluses), Japan is engaged in the most enormous industrial "retooling" for growth that the world has ever seen. It has identified new areas of very high added value (see Table 4) and is moving into them as swiftly as possible. It is constantly improving its own production methods and standards of quality control. Moreover, a great deal of the much-vaunted rise in imports comes from *Japanese* components factories overseas; and although they make global acquisitions to ensure that they are not excluded from critical world markets, its companies remain very Japanese in nature and opposed to a "hollowing out" of the home industrial base. Unlike Victorian Britain, Japan neither rests upon its laurels nor spends on Empire; and its steady increases in productivity, not only in manufacturing but also in services, means that its economic power is still expanding.[30]

In sum, this debate suggests that Japan and its people confront two very plain choices. The first is to make fundamental alterations in a system committed to the steady pursuit of economic growth over the past four decades. Succumbing to external pressures and domestic demand, the Japanese will spend more and save less, they will as a whole be richer and enjoy life's luxuries more, and society will be more cosmopolitan, less deferential and hierarchical, and to that extent less "Japanese." In James Fallows's phrase, Japan will be "more like us," that is, more like Americans.[31] On the other hand, its economy will have matured, its saving rates will be lower, its propensity to import manufactures will increase, its industrial base will give way to services,

Table 4. The Relative Added Value of Manufactures

Product	Added Value ($/lb)
Satellite	20,000
Jet fighter	2,500
Supercomputer	1,700
Aero-engine	900
Jumbo jet	350
Videocamera	280
Mainframe computer	160
Semiconductor	100
Submarine	45
Color television	16
NC machine tool	11
Luxury motor car	10
Standard motor car	5
Cargo ship	1

Source: *The Economist*, "Japanese Technology," 2 December 1989, p. 4

and its manufacturing culture will be somewhat eroded, with market shares reduced by Korea, Taiwan, and other late-developing nations. It will be an immensely wealthy people, perhaps the richest in the world; but, like the generations of successful Romans, Britons, or Americans before it, it will tend more and more to the consumption rather than the creation of wealth.

The alternative would see a relatively unchanged Japanese nation, committed to innovative wealth creation and to an expanding global market share in ever more profitable products. With certain modifications, the existing system would remain in place, emphasizing educational discipline, high savings, quality production, massive investments in research and development, and long-term planning orchestrated by company leaders (in conjunction with the bureaucracies), all attended by a retained high self-consciousness of "Japanness." While its corporations accumulated further wealth, much of it would be plowed back into investment. rather than released for general consumption; and while some of that growth would be the consequence of enhanced living standards at home, it would also be boosted by a relentless penetration of foreign markets, from East Asia to Southern Europe. Japan would thus remain essentially "one-dimensional," very different from America and other societies, with the exception of its Asian emulators. Moreover, simply because it appeared "less like us," its economic and technological eminence would produce international resentments that it would take enormous Japanese ingenuity to pacify. Even more than today, it would require the assistance of foreign lobbyists, partners, scholars, and publicists[32]—together with generous contributions to philanthropic endeavors, large amounts of foreign aid, and so on—to help mitigate international suspicions that its long-term intentions posed a threat.

It is with the latter meaning in mind that this chapter is entitled "The Japanese 'Plan' for a Post-2000 World." Because Japanese economic expansionism has been so purposeful and systematic, critics feel that there *must* exist a coherent strategy formulated—and regularly updated—by businessmen and bureaucrats in Tokyo, one which takes advantage of the Japanese corporation's capacity for long-term planning and, even more, of the fact that many other economies (especially the American) do not have an industrial or technology policy and still

naively rely upon laissez-faire.[33] While Japan experts caution that foreigners ought *not* to view MITI as a sort of economic equivalent to the
Prussian general staff,[34] the habit of various ministries and the Nomura
Research Institute of issuing "projections" and "visions" about the
future suggests that intense scheming is going on to ensure that whatever the next new trend, Japan will take advantage of it. An alternative
view, that Japan's long-term economic expansionism is not so much
orchestrated by officials in Tokyo as it is driven by the intense competitiveness of its major corporations, is not yet widely understood but
seems at least as plausible an explanation.[35] In that sense, references
to a "plan" have less to do with national strategy than with the long-
term ambitions of individual Japanese companies as they struggle for
global market shares.

The chief weakness in this debate upon Japan's future economic and
technological place in the world is that it has not paid much attention
to international politics or, indeed, to the sorts of global changes discussed earlier in this book. Presenting Japan either as a "rational actor"
which can always respond intelligently to new economic opportunities
or as a country about to undergo the same process of internal slowdown
as previous societies, the literature upon the future of Japan Inc.
devotes little attention to how the island state might be affected by
broad global transformations. What is generally assumed is a basic
continuity in present arrangements and tendencies: a reasonably open
trading system, allowing global capitalism to function normally; the
total disappearance of the Cold War; sporadic regional conflicts but
not ones in which Japan would be directly involved (although the
United States might well be); no resurgence of Russian imperialism;
touchy but not impossible relations between Tokyo and the European
Community; delicate relations with China, the mutual distrust to some
extent being ameliorated by Japanese credit; the intensification of
Japan's economic influence throughout Southeast Asia; and the preservation of the Japanese-American relationship despite occasional trade
and security differences, if only because the Japanese understand that
it is necessary to avoid an open break with Washington and, indeed,

to "prop up" American power in the Pacific over the next decade or so, until the outlines of the post–Cold War international order become much clearer.[36]

Should this relatively stable international order fail, however, things could look entirely different. Civil war in the former Soviet Union, the withdrawal of America's military deployments overseas, growing Chinese assertiveness, the emergence of India as a regional superpower, and greater rivalry between the world's "haves" and "have-nots" are all possibilities. In such circumstances, with new threats to security emerging just as the American strategic shield was becoming less reliable, a new generation of Japanese leaders might feel it necessary to increase defense capabilities. Whether the Japanese people would agree to that is difficult to say, but the country would be far more capable *economically* of creating modern armed forces than it was in the 1930s, when its total GNP was only one-tenth that of the United States. By around the year 2000, with a GNP perhaps close to that of the American total and with a formidable technological base, things would be different.[37]

Moreover, as will be discussed below, *non*military threats might be as great as if not greater than military dangers in an age of far-reaching demographic and technological change. Instead of the ever-increasing economic integration forecast by proponents of the "borderless world," there could be financial crashes, intensified commercial rivalries in agriculture, manufacturing, software, and services, and rising protectionism—all of which would clearly hurt Japan, so heavily dependent upon overseas markets and prosperity for its own well-being. In noneconomic spheres, from the global population explosion to the greenhouse effect, transnational impacts could also be serious, and perhaps even more difficult for the Japanese to control. Undeniably, Japan possesses considerable strengths when it comes to dealing with the global forces for change outlined in Part One above; to repeat an earlier point, it probably is better "prepared" for the twenty-first century than any other advanced industrial society.[38] But its many strengths, chiefly in the familiar fields of technology, production, and finance, may not be enough to keep it free of trouble.

Such strengths are evident, for example, in Japan's ability to handle the financial and communications revolution, the rise of multinational corporations, and, more generally, the challenge of remaining responsive to new technologies. Although globalization was chiefly American in origin, Japan has been remarkably quick to benefit from the new economic order. Despite declining share prices on the Tokyo stock market, seven out of ten of the world's largest banks in a September 1991 *Wall Street Journal* ranking were Japanese. "Overall, twenty-nine of the world's hundred largest banks are Japanese. Germany has twelve, France has ten, and the U.S. and Italy each have nine banks on the list." Much the same is true of the world's insurance companies (four out of the top five are Japanese) and securities firms (the top four are Japanese).[39] If the free flow of capital—for industrial investment, take-overs, purchases of property, bonds, and stock—is the driving force behind the emerging global economic order, then this society possesses great strength, at least for as long as it maintains high capital resources.

Japan has also distinguished itself by becoming the base for many of the world's largest public companies, the multinationals that now oc-cupy such an important place in the global economy: in 1991 Toyota, Hitachi, Toshiba, and another thirty-four of the world's hundred larg-est companies were Japanese.[40] Richer in capital assets than most of their American and European counterparts,* and less under share-holder pressure for short-term profits, most of Japan's companies are able to keep investing in the technologies of the future. Moreover, in what may be one of the most significant pointers to the technological "new world order" of the future, how many *influential* patents a coun-try owns, Japanese companies appear to be overtaking or eclipsing their rivals in field after field.[41]

If Japan's technological and manufacturing successes of the past decade are any guide to the years to come, then its breakthroughs into newer fields—aerospace, software, biotech—may come faster than its rivals are prepared for. Between 1980 and 1989 alone, for example, Japan's shares of global exports in certain high-technology products rose dramatically, in some cases literally from nowhere, as shown in Table 5.

Since many of these technologies (microelectronics, telecommunica-tions equipment) provide the physical means for the global financial

*In mid-1991, for example, Toyota Motor had a market value of $44.5 billion on profits (1990) of $3.2 billion, compared with General Motors' market value of $25 billion and a loss of $2 billion.

Table 5. Shares of Global Exports of High-Technology Products, 1980 and 1989[42]

Microelectronics		Computers	
1980	*1989*	*1980*	*1989*
1 U.S. (18.3%)	1 Japan (22.1%)	1 U.S. (38.6%)	1 U.S. (24%)
2 Japan (13.2%)	2 U.S. (21.9%)	2 W. Germany (11.5%)	2 Japan (17.5%)
3 Singapore (10.1%)	3 Malaysia (8.9%)	3 U.K. (10.4%)	3 U.K. (9%)
4 Malaysia (8.9%)	4 S. Korea (7.4%)	4 France (8.6%)	4 W. Germany (6.9%)
5 W. Germany (8.4%)	5 W. Germany (5.8%)	5 Italy (6.6%)	5 Taiwan (5.8%)

Aerospace		Telecommunications Equipment	
1980	*1989*	*1980*	*1989*
1 U.S. (47.6%)	1 U.S. (45.8%)	1 W. Germany (16.7%)	1 Japan (24.7%)
2 U.K. (19.7%)	2 W. Germany (12.5%)	2 Sweden (15.3%)	2 W. Germany (9.5%)
3 W. Germany (9.1%)	3 U.K. (10.9%)	3 U.S. (10.9%)	3 U.S. (8.8%)
4 France (6.0%)	4 France (10.2%)	4 Japan (10.3%)	4 Sweden (8.1%)
5 Canada (4.4%)	5 Canada (4.4%)	5 Netherlands (9.3%)	5 Hong Kong (6.3%)

Machine Tools & Robotics		Scientific/Precision Equipment	
1980	*1989*	*1980*	*1989*
1 W. Germany (25.8%)	1 Japan (23.3%)	1 U.S. (28.3%)	1 U.S. (25.2%)
2 U.S. (14.1%)	2 W. Germany (20.8%)	2 W. Germany (18.1%)	2 W. Germany (18.5%)
3 Japan (11.3%)	3 U.S. (12.1%)	3 U.K. (9.4%)	3 Japan (12.9%)
4 Sweden (9.1%)	4 Italy (10%)	4 France (8.0%)	4 U.K. (9.6%)
5 Italy (8.7%)	5 Switzerland (8.4%)	5 Japan (7.1%)	5 France (5.6%)

Medicine & Biologicals		Organic Chemicals	
1980	*1989*	*1980*	*1989*
1 W. Germany (16.7%)	1 W. Germany (15.6%)	1 W. Germany (19.1%)	1 W. Germany (17%)
2 Switzerland (12.5%)	2 Switzerland (12.2%)	2 U.S. (13.9%)	2 U.S. (15.5%)
3 U.K. (12.0%)	3 U.S. (12.2%)	3 Netherlands (10.9%)	3 France (8.7%)
4 France (11.9%)	4 U.K. (11.8%)	4 France (10.7%)	4 Netherlands (8.1%)
5 U.S. (11.4%)	5 France (10.3%)	5 U.K. (8.4%)	5 U.K. (8.4%)

and communications revolution, further advances of the latter provided another boost—a "feedback loop"—to Japanese industry.

While Japan looks to be in strong shape to handle today's technology explosion, it is less well placed with regard to its own demographic future, and still less with regard to global population trends. As many studies have noted, "Japan began its demographic transition from high to low fertility and mortality much later than the United States and other developed countries, but finished it with record speed."[43] In 1925, life expectancy at birth in Japan was about forty-five years and women had an average of 5.1 children. Nowadays, Japanese life expectancy is the highest in the world—seventy-six years for males and eighty-two years for females (1987)—but the total fertility rate has tumbled to well below the average 2.1 children per woman needed to maintain the overall population. In 1989, it fell to a record low of only 1.57 children per woman. Clearly, enhanced prosperity has contributed to this trend, as it has in every other industrialized society, but there seems to be something more at work in the Japanese case: in particular, Japanese women, educated to high levels, are reacting against the traditional expectations that after college they should concentrate upon rearing children—usually in cramped apartments—as their chief aim in life.

Few observers of Japanese society expect that this trend will be reversed. One prominent politician, rash enough in 1990 to moot the possibility that Japanese women should be discouraged from entering higher education, quickly disclaimed the idea after the ensuing uproar.[44] But if there is no demographic reversal, between now and 2025 Japan "will switch from having the lowest ratio of over-sixty-fives to its total population (one in eleven) to the highest (one in four) among the leading industrial countries."[45] This has caused economists to make gloomy predictions about Japan's long-term future: that with increasingly fewer workers supporting every retired person, payroll taxes and social security contributions will have to go up, so that Japan, which had been the most lightly taxed OECD country, will be one of the most heavily taxed; and that the 30 million or more over-sixty-fives in 2025 will draw upon their resources, cutting into the country's critically important savings rate, reducing the amount available for business investment, and weakening long-term economic growth. While lots of relatively prosperous Japanese pensioners are an attractive market in some areas (tourism, medical services), they will not help the country remain technologically competitive.[46] Once again, the specter of an end to the "Japanese miracle" is raised.

There is, of course, an obvious solution to the changing balance between the size of the Japanese work force and the numbers of elderly dependents: permit the immigration of the tens of thousands of Koreans, Filipinos, Pakistanis, Bangladeshis, and other peoples eager to gain employment there. Given Japan's exclusivist policies as well as its cramped geographical circumstances, this seems highly unlikely. While Japan's Immigration Bureau still welcomes foreign scientists, engineers, and other professionals, it has been cracking down on the 300,000 or so illegal immigrants, threatening them with deportation and their employers with fines or jail. Despite the pleas of the Japanese Food Service Association to secure more labor, or even the Tokyo Chamber of Commerce's proposed scheme for admitting up to 600,000 guest workers on two-year contracts, there seems little prospect that the Japanese will welcome this sort of "solution" to their growing labor shortages.[47] Tactless remarks by its politicians about the social weaknesses of America's multicultural, multiracial population reveal that concerns about preserving "Japanness" are always likely to outweigh merely utilitarian arguments in favor of increased immigration.

Still, while the change in Japan's demographic structure is important, it is by no means clear that it heralds economic stagnation. As many domestic critics have pointed out, the declining birth rate reflects the fact that the government's policies have so far failed to provide young Japanese couples with better amenities in life, like bigger and more affordable housing. Prevailing Japanese career norms underutilize women—female participation in the work force is much lower than in Britain and the United States, for example—and more positive policies in this realm could change things. Finally, since many fit over-sixty-fives are still capable of work and want to work, there is a case for rethinking retirement regulations.[48] By a combination of changes in these areas, both an increase in family size *and* a maintenance of the labor force are feasible.

In addition, Japan's larger companies are dealing with the labor shortage—and the high cost of Japanese labor—by going multinational. What was a limited number of overseas ventures a quarter century ago (chiefly assembly plants in Korea) has become a globally organized network of manufacturing plants, automobile factories, components producers, distribution centers, even research institutes, contributing to the parent company's plan. The benefits of this are both obvious and manifold. Not only have many companies found it cheaper to employ female labor in Thailand or Mexico to assemble electrical goods than to produce them in Japan itself, but the "out-sourcing" of components production helps to reduce the imbalance of merchandise trade with Japan's East Asian neighbors; indeed, Japanese ministers can point to these imported manufactures as evidence that the country is trying to reduce its overall trade surplus. Most important, the location of assembly and manufacturing plants abroad ensures access to key markets at a time of open or veiled protectionism: Mexican factories give Japan free access to the American and Canadian markets (and, again, disguise the U.S.-Japan trade gap), while automobile factories in England and Wales provide a European base for the EC market. At the end of the day, the profits go into the coffers of Toyota and Mitsubishi, boosting overall Japanese wealth.

Is this the way forward for Japan, for it to become ever more a *rentier* economy, its aging population reliant upon earnings from overseas investment and production to maintain its standard of living and allow it to purchase goods that can no longer be produced at home? Is this why the Japanese earnestly study the relative economic decline of late-Victorian Britain, and are fascinated by some similar possibilities in present-day America? Unquestionably, Japanese officials and businessmen worry that the unfavorable demographic trend, together with economic and social changes, could lead to Japan's own long-term economic decline. A people which once embraced Ezra Vogel's *Japan as Number One* is, twenty years later, now anxiously studying Bill Emmott's *The Sun Also Sets*.

In theory, of course, Japan *may* go the way of Holland and Britain, if it elects to abandon its manufacturing culture; but, as noted above, the indications from its own businessmen point in the opposite direction. The gloomier forecasts of the economic impact of an aging population all miss, *The Economist* has noted, "the effect of technological progress on productivity growth."[49] This refers not only to increased investments in new plant, machine tools, and high-tech steel mills and shipyards, but also to the fascination with automation and robotics noted earlier.* It is no coincidence that Japan now possesses close to three-quarters of the world's robots and more automated workplaces than anywhere else on earth. For, if their promise holds true, robots offer a wonderful escape from Japan's dilemma; they will keep the country at the forefront of manufacturing *and* compensate for any growing labor shortages, eliminating the need to import millions of foreign workers and their families. Technology thus provides a counter to demography. By initiating this further stage in the Industrial Revolution, Japanese industry thereby prepares itself for the twenty-first century.

By comparison, the challenges posed to Japan by the new agricultural revolution—biotech farming—appear less profound, although they are taken seriously.[50] A mountainous archipelago desperately short of flat, fertile land, yet with millions of full-time and part-time farmers traditionally working plots of one or two hectares, Japan is the least self-sufficient of the OECD nations in food supplies. Because of the enormous gap between industrial and agricultural productivity levels (and incomes), farm production is protected by large-scale subsidies and bureaucratic barriers—to the wrath of American agricultural export lobbies, and to the detriment of the Japanese consumer—yet Japan must still import more food than any other advanced economy. (Were it not for those imports, its current trade surplus would be much larger!) Finally, Japan has not traditionally possessed mighty chemical and agricultural corporations capable of moving into newer forms of food production like biotechnology. For many reasons, therefore, one might assume that the biotech revolution would be marginal to Japan's concerns.

Yet the signs are that this is altering fast. Japanese authorities are now seeking to reduce the number of inefficient farmers and are grudgingly making concessions to American demands to open the domestic food market. As millions of farmers retire or are bought out, Japan might seem even more likely to depend on foreign agricultural supplies.

* See Chapter 5.

In fact, a hard core of around 500,000 professional farmers is emerging, operating larger plots (their dairy farms are as big as those in the EC) and adopting mechanization, crop rotation, and other methods of enhancing productivity. Not only are improved types of cattle being bred at home, but Japanese agribusinesses are reaching out to purchase and manage beef farms in the United States. As Japanese agriculture modernizes itself, the authorities are also encouraging investments in biotechnology to make good Japan's inadequacies in this field. As has happened in other industries, the "catch-up" process frequently involves joint ventures with, or the purchase of, American companies that have the know-how.[51]

Although the biotech revolution in Japan is still in its infancy, the implications are clear enough. It would give the country a share in yet another leading industry of the twenty-first century, while reducing dependence upon foreign suppliers of agricultural goods and related raw materials. All this would play to Japan's existing strengths: easy access to Western technical literature, ample capital to purchase researchers, laboratories, and patents, support from large Japanese companies that want to broaden their product base, and assistance from the Japanese ministries. Perhaps the only objector would be the Foreign Ministry itself, as it tried to imagine explaining to U.S. farmers and congressmen why it needed to import ever less food from abroad.

This suggests that Japan has cleverly positioned itself both to take advantage of new technological trends and to reduce to a minimum the deleterious impacts of demographic change; and that, at least at first sight, the Japanese need feel less concern about global transformations than their competitors. Such a conclusion is probably accurate, *insofar as Japan can reconstruct itself internally to prepare for the future.* The real problems lie in the external realm, which is of course far less under Japanese control. The demographic challenge of preserving an adequate work force (through robots) is one thing; how to handle a China of 1.5 billion people—either increasingly prosperous and powerful *or* ridden with social and economic discontents—is quite another. How, indeed, is Japan to fare in an Asia forecast to surge in population from 3.0 to 4.9 billion over the next few decades (to 2025) while its own population is stagnant and aging? Can it really isolate itself from the impact of major global demographic shifts?

Similarly, how is it possible for a country so dependent upon exports to be assured of continued access to important global markets, especially if its own successes in industry, science, and technology threaten to make redundant the need for foreign produce? Automated assembly plants able to compete with cheap-labor factories in Southeast Asia appear on first encounter like a wonderful technological "fix," as does genetically engineered fruit, meat, and fish. But in practice would not their adoption provoke further resentments by other countries already convinced that Japan takes but rarely gives, and that "managed trade" is always managed in Tokyo's favor? Can the Japanese afford to give a further boost to protectionist sentiments in Europe and North America, especially if those markets become increasingly saturated and the global economy grows only moderately in the coming decades? Even if Asian markets become more important than Western ones, is not the problem—of Japan's unbalanced trade, and the ever-present threat of reprisals—simply transferred? In sum, global economic vulnerability has always been the price Japan has had to pay in achieving global commercial preeminence; and that vulnerability is, if anything, increasing.

The same paradox can be observed in relation to rising environmental challenges. Global warming, for example, presents Japan with a dilemma, although not an insuperable one. Because of its limited area and relatively small agricultural sector, Japan does not confront dire forecasts about a shift of grain-growing areas that faces (for example) Kansas. If, as some scientists predict, global warming leads to greater unpredictability and turbulence in the weather, then Japan may expect fiercer storms, flash floods, tornados; but that hardly seems a major or systemic threat to its well-being, and it could afford preventive and reactive measures. In the same way, while a rise in the sea level would affect low-lying areas, Japan is rich enough to strengthen its sea defenses. Perhaps it can even relocate its coastal settlements. For example, it has already allocated hundreds of millions of dollars to shore up and protect the tiny outlying island of Okinotorishima; if it should be permanently submerged under the rising seas, Japan could lose fishery and seabed rights.[52] Finally, if international agreements are made to reduce carbon emissions or improve energy efficiency, then Japan's record over the past two decades—the World Bank recently cited

Japan as "an environmental paragon" in those respects[53]—suggests it will have fewer problems in meeting new targets than most other countries. Global warming might be a nuisance, but an efficient and rich Japan can cope.

Still, if the next century were to see widespread environmentally induced disasters—interacting, as they probably would, with the global population explosion and massive social distress—one is bound to wonder whether Japan could remain an island unto itself. Could it preserve a technologically created "green" atmosphere adjacent to a continent where the uncontrolled industrialization of billions of people threatens the ecosystem? It is impossible to say at present, but it would surely be imprudent for the Japanese to conclude that deforestation and atmospheric pollution will only be *other* peoples' problems.

What the above suggests is that Japan can approach the twenty-first century with no more than guarded optimism. The best-selling writers predicting Japan's glorious future base their claims upon much valid evidence: the beneficial forces for change (capital, communications, robotics, biotech) are being exploited, the threatening ones (demographic chaos, global warming, financial collapse) either are distant or can probably be contained. Few other nations can feel as secure, especially in regard to technological change.

Nevertheless, there may be considerable dangers ahead for Japan as it prepares for the next century. We have noted the possibility of threatening external events, which are difficult to forecast in advance but—especially in the light of the many political revolutions of the past decade alone—cannot be dismissed. Nuclear proliferation in Asia, foreign-policy adventurism by regimes suffering from internal strains, a surge in Chinese power, confrontations on the Korean peninsula or in the South China sea . . . any of those would confirm Japan's strategic vulnerability. There could also be serious instabilities in its financial sector, which is much less securely founded than its manufacturing base.

Yet the greatest challenges may come, ironically, as a result of

Japan's own successes. If its economy continues to flourish as others stagnate, if it increases its demolition (say) of the American automobile industry and the European electronics industry, if it appears secure and comfortable, benefiting greatly from the international system but contributing little to its preservation, if it seems aloof and unhelpful in a world in which human disasters, regional conflicts, mass poverty, migratory waves, and the gap between "haves" and "have-nots" worsens, then foreign resentments might lead other nations to punish Japan economically—through tariffs, or other instruments—for what they believe to be its selfish policies.

To avoid such a prospect and contribute to the global order, Japan needs enlightened and courageous leadership to help it meet its internal transformations and make greater international contributions than it does at present. But it is in the quality of its political leadership that Japan suffers its greatest deficiency. Unlike its deficiencies in raw materials, this deficiency has not been countered; indeed, if studies of the "enigma" of Japanese power are correct, the political system virtually ensures that enlightened leaders will *not* emerge.[54] Instead, an "old boys' network" (graduates of Tokyo Law School, etc.) in the bureaucracies, big business, banks, and Liberal Party will continue to *share* power, with no one body or person permitted to assume the role of an American president or British prime minister. Thus there can be no "leadership" as Western societies understand it; and foreign observers should cease searching for a rising figure who could be the Japanese political equivalent of Helmut Schmidt or Margaret Thatcher.

This is ironic. Unlike most other societies, in which political leadership is regarded as a key element, if not *the* key element, in the nation's success, Japan appears to have constructed a machine that can go by itself. Rigorous, uniform educational standards, firm social codes regarding obedience, hierarchy, and deference, elite bureaucratic guidance, a commitment to savings and investment, fanatical attention to design and service, a team-spirit ethos determined to succeed against domestic and foreign rivals . . . all these have carried Japan from its 1945 nadir to where it stands now. They also are impressive elements of strength for the future. But as our increasingly complex world heads into the twenty-first century, they may not be enough to handle the nonmaterial political and moral tests which lie ahead, nor to deal with challenges outside Japan's borders. Sophisticated robots can overcome lots of problems. What they cannot do is provide vision, and political leadership, that will allow the Japanese people to operate successfully in the global society of today and tomorrow.[55]

9

INDIA AND CHINA

IN ANY DISCUSSION OF HOW JAPAN, THE
United States, or European countries might best prepare for the
twenty-first century, population size (although very important) is
merely one of several trends to be taken into account. In the case of
India and China, however, the demographic factor overshadows every
other, with critical implications not only for those two societies but also
for the world community. China and India are the two most populous
countries on earth. Their respective populations of 1.135 billion and
853 million people are now over 37 percent of the world total. If the
middle-range demographic projections are correct, each nation will
contain around 1.5 billion people by the year 2025, approximately 35
percent of the whole. The activities of this sheer mass of people will
affect global foodstuff demand, energy use, and the environment. For
example, China and India already are the world's fourth and fifth
largest contributors to the annual increase in the greenhouse effect,[1]
and the expected growth in their populations and rate of industrialization are likely to have even larger impacts upon the environment. On
the other hand, a marked expansion of their economies, raising standards of living, could greatly stimulate global trade, perhaps providing
large new markets for Japan and the NIEs as demand in the developed
world slowed. China and India are also important in foreign and mili-

tary affairs; what they may do in the future could affect regional security in East Asia and South Asia, as well as nuclear proliferation and global disarmament in general.

While already significant in world affairs, both Asian giants are limited by their relative poverty, with China's per capita GNP estimated at a mere $294 in 1987, and India's only $311. This means that India's total GNP is less than half of Italy's, and China's between one-sixth and one-seventh of Japan's.[2] Put another way, if both of them had managed to achieve South Korea's current per capita GNP of roughly $5,000, China would possess the world's largest economy and India's would be almost as big as America's.[3] Such an enormous increase in living standards—difficult to imagine, but theoretically possible—would bring not only much more purchasing power for China and India's citizens but also far greater resources for research and development, science and technology, and infrastructure and education, as well as for military power.

What, then, are the chances that these two nations can escape present low levels of average income and continue to enjoy the high rates of economic growth which, unlike Africa and Latin America, they achieved throughout the 1980s?

If average annual growth rates over the next few decades could be maintained at a reasonably high pace—say, 5 percent in real terms—progress would be assured. It might not fully compare with the much faster growth rates of the East Asian NIEs in recent years; but to the Chinese and Indian peoples the consequences would be positive. After all, although China is poor at present, it was far poorer a decade ago. An average annual GNP growth of 9 percent during the 1980s doubled real incomes, especially among the 800 million rural population, reduced poverty, cut infant and child mortality, and improved consumption levels.[4] Even if the average growth rates for the next twenty years

Table 6. Growth in the GDP of China and India, 1980–1989[5]

	1980–88 (average)	1988	1989
China	9.5	11.2	3.9
India	5.0	9.8	4.8

were less swift, a steady increase would be welcome—and might, in fact, be preferable to over-speedy growth, which often produces bottle-necks, inflation, and social turbulence.

But this escape from Malthus's trap is threatened by China's and India's twin population explosions, adding millions of new mouths each year. Indeed, were that eighteenth-century sage to return to our planet, he would witness in China and India conditions similar to those he described in his first *Essay*. Advances in medical care (especially vacci-nations) and initial rises in food supplies in the past few decades reduced infant mortality, and the populations surged, outstripping available resources and threatening a deterioration in conditions in-stead of hoped-for improvements.

This problem is so deep that regardless of their different political regimes—democratic and multiparty in India, a Communist Party monopoly of power in China—the respective leaderships have been struggling to persuade couples to limit family size. As in Africa, Central America, and other parts of the developing world, however, that cam-paign faces formidable obstacles: the belief, deep-rooted in peasant societies, that extra children add to the labor force and thus produce extra wealth; ancestor worship, fear of being unsupported in old age, preference for the extended family, and cultural assumptions about the role of women; and ignorance of and prejudice against contraceptive techniques, together with a resentment of government interference in family matters. Still, fearing demographic increases will outstrip re-sources and eat into the increases in output, Beijing and New Delhi have striven—often by clumsy and draconian means—to combat the population explosion.

Of the two, China has had the greater recent success, because of its more authoritarian and centralized structures of government. Mao himself had opposed population control, decrying fears that people would outstrip resources and arguing that a socialist economy could handle ever-larger numbers. Since the first decade or so of Communism saw a rise in living standards and the coming of near-universal (if basic) health care, these favorable trends interacted with the existing high levels of fertility to produce a surge in China's population. It was followed, however, by the eccentricities of the "Great Leap Forward" of 1957–61—dividing the population into groups of five thousand households on average, each group with its own land, communal kitchens, even backyard steel mills—which disrupted the economy, reduced food production and distribution, and caused widespread famine, exacerbated by poor harvests. The result was a disaster, with excess deaths estimated at about 30 million people in four years, "probably the largest number of famine deaths in modern times."[6] In reaction to such losses, Chinese families in the 1960s and 1970s were eager to have lots of babies, so that the birth rates leaped to pre-revolution levels of 33–43 births per thousand. The resultant population boom finally forced the government to institute some of the strictest family-planning rules in the world: couples had to marry late (i.e., in their mid-twenties) and were limited to one child, and all this was supervised and enforced by employers, officials, and health workers; those who flouted the single-child target were punished with fines, loss of job, and the withdrawal of social and educational privileges, while the wife was often browbeaten into an abortion.[7] The aim was that China's population should "level off" at 1.2 billion in 2000, and then fall to 700 million by 2050.

The sharp decrease in the number of births per family during the 1970s and 1980s, as well as the earlier dramatic fluctuations, can be seen in Chart 4.

While this plan was rigorously enforced in its early phase—almost 21 million people were reported to have been sterilized in accordance with the one-child policy in 1983 alone—the populace was increasingly resentful; another grisly consequence was a sharp rise in the number of baby girls murdered or abandoned by peasants desperate to ensure that if they could have only one child, it would be a son to look after them in old age.[8] By the mid-1980s, the authorities adopted a rather more conciliatory stance and exchanged their future population targets for less ambitious ones. At the same time, however, the "baby boom" children of the mid to late 1960s were reaching marriageable age. Not only were there more babies per family (especially in the countryside, where it was easier to avoid controls), but there were many more twenty-five-year-olds to have children. In consequence, China's swift

Chart 4. Total Fertility Rates, China, 1945–87[9]

population growth has resumed. The birth rate has increased from 17.8 per thousand in 1985 to 21.1 per thousand in 1987. In fact, 22 million Chinese babies were born in 1987, whereas only 7 million people died—a net increase almost as great as the entire population of Australia.[10] Yet had it not been for population control, officials estimate, 240 million *more* Chinese would have been born over the last two decades.[11]

All this confronts the Chinese government with an appalling dilemma, in the form of a growing mismatch between population and resources. Depending upon the estimates, China's land can sustain between 750 and 950 million people—figures surpassed some two to three decades ago. China contains one-fifth of the earth's population, with only 7 percent of its farmland, much of it of poor quality. Its population density is three times the world average, without a corresponding share of world resources. A Chinese scholar has observed of his country that the territory per capita is only one-third of the world average, farmland one-third, pasture land one-quarter, forest one-ninth, and water one-fourth. Compared with those of the United States, they are even lower. Per capita farmland in China is only one-eighth of the U.S. and forest only one-tenth. With China's present level of productivity and technology, excessive growth of population will surely increase the overstretched pressure on the environment and resources.[12]

For politicians and planners hoping that China will participate in the Pacific Rim "boom" then, the threat that economic gains will be swallowed up by population growth is a real one.

On the other hand, the leadership has to take into account that a strictly enforced policy of one child per family is very unpopular. Like the emperors before them—or the Russian czars—they would find a real "peasants' revolt" the most serious domestic challenge of all. In addition, China's demographic policy contradicts its aim of encouraging individual responsibility in agricultural and small-business enterprises. If an individual family is now responsible for developing its own parcel of land or operating a small firm, it will have an enormous incentive—and economic rationale—to produce a number of children, so that the business can expand. Limitations of births to one or two children per couple would inhibit enterprises of that sort.[13]

Finally, there are serious implications for the future demographic structure of China, which is likely to become *more unbalanced* than most. At present, many more children are being born than China's overstretched resources can sustain; but even if the government achieved zero population growth by the turn of the century—an unlikely prospect, admittedly—it would then confront an age profile distorted by the 1960s surge in births, *and* perhaps also by their hoped-for one-child-per-family policy in the 1990s. Zero growth by 2000, one demographer has pointed out, suggests that China's population in 2035 will contain "twice as many persons in their sixties as in their twenties, an age composition that even the most enthusiastic supporter of the virtues of the elderly could scarcely favor."[14]

Although India also has a rapidly growing elderly population,[15] its key problem remains the demographic explosion, simply because population growth rates are swifter. At independence, average life expectancy was 32.5 years for a male and 31.7 years for a female; by the late 1980s, it was about 58 years for both (and still rising), a result of improved health care, diet, sanitation, and general standards of living.[16] However, the fall in mortality rates has not been attended by a similar reduction in fertility rates as it was in China. The Indian government has considerably less power to reach into the villages and cajole peasant families to limit their size; and, with far greater localized poverty and much higher rates of illiteracy and child mortality than in China, the desire to bear children to enhance family income remains strong. It has been reinforced, negatively, by the powerful public reaction against Sanjay Gandhi's forced sterilization program in the late 1970s and by a general mistrust of officialdom, birth-control centers, and inefficient or dangerous contraceptive devices.[17] In any case, there is much greater cultural, religious, and regional diversity in India than in China, so that even if adequate birth-control facilities were available to all, there would probably be a different response from middle-class families in Gujarat than from the hill tribes of Manipur.

Whereas the total fertility rate in China had dropped to 2.4 by 1985–90, one of the lowest in Asia, in India it remained at a stubbornly high 4.3. While China's population increases by about 15 million each year, India's averaged 16.8 million each year in the 1985–90 period.[18] Even the forecast AIDS epidemic may hardly dent that sort of growth. Since India's infant mortality rate is twice China's, improvements in that domain would actually exacerbate the problem. In this respect, India's age structure, with almost 40 percent of the population under fifteen, is closer to that of countries in Africa and the Middle East. Moreover, because India's economy grew more slowly than China's and family income is less equitably distributed, its population surge has led to increases in the poverty level, both in rural and urban areas. At present, it is estimated that approximately half of India's 850 million people live in poverty.[19] Should these trends continue, India may have as large a population as China's by the year 2025, but its 1.5 billion inhabitants will contain a far higher number of the landless, underemployed, undernourished, functionally uneducated, and ill-sheltered already so evident across India today.[20]

· · · ·

If long-term growth is to continue and famine to be avoided, then—
just as in eighteenth-century Britain—agriculture will play a key role.
Farming alone contributes almost 30 percent of India's GNP, down
from the 40 percent share of 1965 but significantly more than Korea's
11 percent or Japan's 2.8 percent.[21] Moreover, agriculture accounts for
60 percent of India's employment. The agricultural sector of China's
economy is even more important; perhaps 80 percent of the population
is engaged in farming or related activities. The implication is obvious:
if agricultural productivity stagnates, it will be a drag upon the entire
economy (as it was in the USSR); if it surges, as happened in China
after the 1978 reforms, the enhanced purchasing power of hundreds
of millions of small farmers will provide a tremendous boost to the
economy, with "multiplier effects" upon the output of tractors, tools,
fertilizers, consumer goods, utility supplies, banking services, and so on.

India's rise in agricultural output since independence has also been
marked, although some observers believe it could have been more
impressive.[22] The most important gains were the result of the "green
revolution" from the 1960s onward, which greatly enhanced crop
yields. These improvements affected many crops, maize and millet for
example, but especially rice and wheat. By using "miracle rice" varieties, Indian farmers gained much greater yields in the irrigated semiarid
areas of the northwest. Even more important was the introduction of
dwarf wheats, which flourished in north-central and northwest India,
producing large increases in output. Overall, India's food supplies have
risen sharply over the past few decades, and it normally has sufficient
stocks in hand to meet drought and famine conditions; indeed, rice and
certain other foodstuffs have sometimes joined traditional crops such
as cotton, tea, and jute in the list of India's exports.

Although the increased output is welcome, the signs are that the
green revolution has largely spent itself. In any case, the successes of
Indian agriculture have not been uniform and the increases are significantly less than in China. The chief reason is that improved strains of
wheat and rice also need other important inputs such as fertilizers and
irrigation. In states with a hot-wet monsoon climate such as Bengal and

Orissa, traditional methods of rain-fed, intensive-labor rice cultivation continue, since there is no real incentive to adopt the newer seeds. In the drier states, much depends upon the availability of water supplies, which are affected by government irrigation schemes, political influence, and so on. Moreover, high-yielding varieties of wheat seeds require the systematic application of fertilizers and the use of tractors—so that poorer farmers find it hard to adopt the new methods.[23] Both central and state governments in India have been less concerned with countering the massive inequalities among the rural population—which would raise thorny issues of property rights, caste, privilege—than with encouraging agricultural output to rise as a whole.[24] In the same way, increases in milk production have tended to come from, and to benefit, powerful cooperatives with good connections to foreign aid donors, rather than the poorer farmers.[25] While agricultural development and national income rise, the *uneven* gains are probably insufficient to match the population increase.

In China, the rise in agricultural output has been greater, chiefly because the pre-1978 system of communal farming was abandoned. Admitting that the collectivized system had caused twenty years of stagnation in food output, the Deng regime introduced reforms that gave the peasant incentives; land itself remained in collective ownership, but individual families were permitted to farm it as they wished; after delivering a certain portion of their produce to the community, they could sell the rest on the open market; restrictions on hiring farm labor were lifted; and the prices paid for agricultural goods were raised, to provide a further incentive.[26] The result was a remarkable surge in Chinese agricultural output, especially grain, contrasting sharply with the stagnation in the Soviet Union, as shown in Chart 5.

On the other hand, by subsidizing basic food costs for consumers, the government ensured that the urban masses would not face large price increases. As a result, China's hundreds of millions of peasant farmers were better off than ever before,[27] stimulating the economy and more than doubling per capita income within a decade.

For a while, therefore, it looked as if China had achieved agricultural self-sufficiency, and might in fact become a major food exporter. By the end of the 1980s, however, optimism began to fade. While output of cash crops and vegetables continued to expand—peasants could make

Chart 5. Grain Production in the Soviet Union
and China, 1950–84[28]

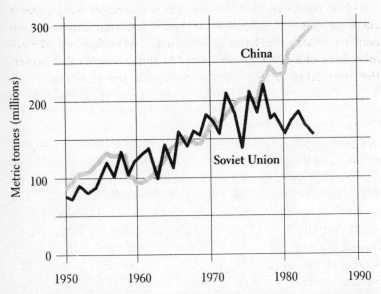

a higher profit on those—the critically important grain harvest did not always meet official targets, leading to large-scale imports of grain, which reduced China's hard-currency reserves. Governmental policy is to increase annual grain output from 400 million tons (the current level) to 500 million tons by the end of the century, to avoid dependence upon foreign supplies.[29] Yet many agricultural economists doubt that this can be achieved, at least not without considerable difficulties. There is little additional land suitable for crops, and as living standards rise, the people are consuming foods of a higher caliber (vegetables, poultry), further increasing demand. Meanwhile, the population steadily grows. For the regime to avoid the political and foreign-currency costs of depending on foreign imports, it will need to spend large sums on irrigation, fertilizers, farm equipment, better seeds, and improved processing, *and* to raise the prices paid to farmers even further.[30] This would favor grain producers over consumers—unless there were enhanced food subsidies, which would exacerbate the government deficit.

It would also take investment capital from other sectors and might hurt economic growth, the key to China's future.

This is not to say that Chinese agricultural policy has entered a cul-de-sac, but it is difficult to see how it can keep increasing crop output to match population growth—unless technology provides another form of agricultural revolution. As things now stand, however, the structural obstacles to such a revolution appear daunting.

While struggling to control population and increase food output, the Chinese and Indian governments must also move their economies into manufactures and services, to obtain higher per capita income and to absorb the tens of millions of new entrants into the work force each year. Industrialization is attractive, not just because it increases national wealth but also because it reduces population growth as the people become urbanized and undergo a demographic transition. This involves another race against time, for the drift of millions from rural areas like Sichuan is already creating enormous shanty cities of the São Paulo type.* Roughly speaking, only 200 million people are needed on China's farms, whereas the rural work force at present totals 400 million, leaving vast masses of peasants either to drift around the countryside—to the alarm of the authorities—or to exacerbate the pressures upon the cities. If economic growth falters or if industrialization fails to create enough jobs for the new urban masses, the future could be grim.

Creating their own industrial revolution, therefore, has always been central to India's and China's plans to prepare for the twenty-first century. Thus, despite a certain deference to Gandhi's notion of a peasant economy, India's leaders encouraged industrialization to strengthen the country's defense base, reduce dependence upon foreign manufacturers, and enhance national income. The route chosen was neither Japan's export-led growth nor the socialist model of the

---

*Because of this problem, the Chinese government forbids immigration into the larger cities, although families can move to designated medium-size towns.

USSR, but something in between—befitting, no doubt, the Fabian beliefs of many Indian politicians. Like Latin American nations, India chose to replace imports with its own heavy industrial products; iron and steel, cement, locomotives, automobiles, shipbuilding, defense-related production, engineering, and machine tools were all supported by the state. Transport, mining, and utilities were taken into the public sector. Others were given subsidies, very high tariff protection, and government orders. The result was the emergence of a number of publicly owned corporate giants in steel, aeronautics, engineering, and petrochemicals.[31] Where industrialization was not possible by internal means, foreign aid was encouraged—as, for example, Soviet help in building steel plants. By such devices, India planned to become an industrial giant.

Yet while the economy did grow between the 1950s and the 1980s, it hardly kept ahead of its own population increases. *Real income* per person rose by only 1.7 percent a year in the period 1950–65, and by 1 percent a year in the decade after that, causing some observers to joke at "the Hindu rate of growth."[32] In consequence, government economists kept scaling back their growth projections, from one Four-Year Plan to the next.[33] The most disappointing feature has been the pace of industrialization. In 1950, manufacturing accounted for 10.3 percent of the Gross Domestic Product, and crept up to 15.8 percent by 1978–79; it scarcely increased by 1989, when it totaled 16.1 percent (compared with 31.6 percent in Korea).[34] With industry as a whole (including manufacturing) employing only a small proportion of India's population,[35] the country slipped backward economically; in 1955, it was the world's tenth-biggest industrial power, but two decades later it ranked twentieth.[36] As late as 1965, the value of India's manufactured exports was eight times that of Korea's, yet by 1986 Korea's exports were 4.5 times the value of India's.

The reasons for this industrial stagnation are many, ranging from the lack of stimulus from the sluggish agricultural sector to pork-barrel politics which places steelworks or utility plants in inappropriate locations and blocks proposed economic reforms. The greatest cause, however, was probably India's decision to turn away from world markets and protect domestic industries. Without foreign markets and the stimulus of worldwide competition, India's public companies grew to rely upon state spending, saddling the economy with a large and over-manned public sector, while private industry had to contend with some of the most complex bureaucratic regulations in the world.[37] One might assume, theoretically, that such a large domestic economy could generate sustained growth without competing on world markets, but the evidence elsewhere (USSR, Argentina) suggests the contrary. Under prodding from the World Bank and IMF, and from many of their own frustrated entrepreneurs, recent Indian governments have acknowledged the need for trade liberalization and export-led growth, not least because of the large government deficit and external debt. As India turns to such policies, however, it will notice just how far it has fallen behind some of its Asian neighbors.

China's industrialization in the 1950s copied the Soviet emphasis upon central planning and heavy industry, and then was thrown into confusion during Mao's "Great Leap Forward" experiments. This changed, dramatically, with Deng Xiaoping's economic liberalization policies inaugurated in 1978–79. Although the largest transformations occurred in agriculture, progress was also made in manufacturing, commerce, consumer goods, and foreign trade. State industries were encouraged to respond to the commercial realities of quality, price, and market demand; privately run, small-scale enterprises were allowed; joint ventures with foreign firms were permitted, special enterprise zones were set up along the Chinese coastline, and an export-led drive was proclaimed. After ignoring East Asia's economic boom for decades, China relaxed its Marxist dogmas and appeared to be climbing on the free-market bandwagon. "To get rich is glorious," Mr. Deng urged his people, many of whom needed no convincing on that score.[38]

Statistically, the results were as impressive as the visual evidence of bustle and growth. Small-scale businesses sprang up—according to one source, by 1989 there were 225,000 privately run companies in the coastal provinces alone, employing many millions of people.[39] Provincial governments, eager to assert independence from Beijing and to earn additional income, negotiated joint ventures with the foreign entrepreneurs who swarmed into China during the 1980s. New enterprises rushed to fulfill the pent-up consumer demand for televisions, washing machines, and refrigerators; yet because that demand was only partly satisfied, there were still enormous private savings available for investment. While keeping a tight control upon what could be imported, China encouraged the export of textiles, household goods, toys, basic electrical equipment, and other low-tech products. Manufactured exports, worth a mere $9 billion in 1980, leaped to $37 billion by 1989, which was more than double the value of India's exports. In fact, since 1978 China's foreign trade has risen by an average of 13.5 percent a year and equals almost one-third of national income. It is now about the world's fourteenth-biggest trading nation.[40] All this caused optimistic observers to speculate that China might quadruple its GNP by early next century, boosting its already considerable power.[41]

Nevertheless, China's industrial drive has not been easy. To begin with, the helter-skelter growth exacerbated the gap in living standards between the well-placed coastal regions and the less developed inland provinces, where there is little foreign investment, traditional suspicions of capitalism abound, and the bureaucracy is still strong. While Guangdong, next to Hong Kong, saw industrial output soar 70 percent in 1987 and a further 30 percent in 1988 in response to foreign demand, inland neighbors like Hunan complained of the resultant inflation, diversion of foodstuffs and resources, blatant corruption and consumerism, and general unfairness of the new system.[42] Such complaints strengthened the hands of conservatives suspicious of a market economy and confirmed the resentments of groups whose fixed incomes were hurt by the high inflation accompanying modernization.[43]

The problem in China is not simply that of regional economic differentiation—as between northern and southern Italy—but the emergence of two entirely different systems of political economy, one based upon inward-oriented state enterprises and centralized controls, the other modeled upon the bustling, outward-oriented capitalism of Hong Kong and Korea.[44] In fact, much of China's industry still consists of state-owned companies, stagnating because they lack incentive to improve themselves and crippled by their inability to fix prices, dismiss inefficient workers, plan marketing and investment strategies, and acquire hard currencies. Because the government does not want to throw disgruntled workers out of a job, it has poured billions of dollars into state enterprises and permitted them to borrow large sums from state banks to cover their deficits. Despite the resources lavished upon those industries, their performance remains poor; in the partial economic recovery following the Tiananmen Square clamp-down, the state sector grew a mere 3 percent, collectives 9.4 percent, and private companies and joint ventures a remarkable 57.7 percent.[45]

With one part of the Chinese economy resembling Bulgaria and the other increasingly looking like Taiwan, it is not surprising that foreign companies are bewildered and reluctant to invest further. Clearly, this schizophrenic economic condition is related to the intense political struggle between Chinese conservatives and liberals in recent years. The Deng reforms were intended to encourage economic liberalization without conceding political liberalization. While that strategy may have worked for agriculture, it could not hold among businessmen, students, intellectuals, and officials in the coastal regions, who embraced economic freedoms, joint ventures, travel to (and study in) foreign democratic countries, and an increasing amount of Western media. Hence the rising protests in 1989—and the regime's heavy response. If the gap between the inland and coastal regions continues to widen, however, it is difficult to see how national unity can be preserved.

Even more than in India, therefore, leadership in China has sought to enjoy the benefits of trading in the global economy yet remains apprehensive of the larger consequences. There are, in addition, great technical difficulties in the way of abandoning older habits. For example, both countries require foreign technology, expertise, goods, and services to continue modernization, yet that worsens their current-account deficits—in India's case, to an alarming extent. Moreover, even as they seek to create an export-led boom, it is not at all clear that the developed world will permit the surge in imported manufactures that it allowed, in easier global circumstances, to Japan and the East Asian NIEs. Yet the greatest problem is social and political: how to transform ancient societies sufficiently to meet the challenges of the high-tech revolution of "the borderless world" *without* social strains, resentments, political unrest, and regional chaos—and that in countries already finding it hard to handle their population explosion.

Apart from sheer size, India and China differ from neighboring "trading states" in another critical respect: their ambition to be the regional superpower, in South Asia and East Asia respectively. There is little conviction in New Delhi and Beijing of the coming of a new international order; rather, both powers anticipate a "world of the future . . . very much like the world of the past, [where] those with real strength have the final say."[46] India remains in angry confrontation with Pakistan over Kashmir, worries about long-term Chinese policies along their shared border, and believes the "Indian" Ocean is not simply a geographical term but an expression of future strategical realities. The "Middle Kingdom" of China has quarreled with and fought against most of its neighbors (border disputes with Vietnam, India, and the former USSR), remains profoundly suspicious of Japan, dislikes the "hegemonism" and cultural influence of the United States, and still lays claim to Taiwan, not to mention more southerly territories like the Paracel Islands and Spratly Island.[47]

As a consequence, while China and India may appear relatively "less developed" in terms of per capita average income, literacy rates, and public health, they rank considerably higher in global military power. Each has numerous ground forces (China has 2.3 million regular soldiers, India 1.1 million), together with a large number of aircraft; in India's case, there is also a sizable surface fleet. China possesses land-based intercontinental ballistic missiles and continues to test nuclear devices and their delivery systems, and while India is not a full member of the nuclear club, it has the technological capacity to become one. Both are striving to keep defense costs under control, but, as rising powers conscious of regional challenges, neither is swayed by the argument that military force is anachronistic.

As in many countries in Africa and the Middle East, efforts to prepare Indian or Chinese society for the nonmilitary challenges of the early twenty-first century may therefore be stalled, diverted, or overwhelmed by the outbreak of border clashes, and perhaps further regional wars. Moreover, the concern with military strength and the belief that the country ought not to depend upon foreign suppliers have led India and China to allocate large resources—not just funds, but scientists, engineers, R&D institutions, industrial plants—to military-related production rather than to commercial export-led growth. How great a proportion of Chinese resources has been so allocated is impossible to say, but it could not have become the world's third-biggest nuclear power within a decade and a half* without a massive concentration of its limited scientific and technological talent.

In India's case, a powerful and technologically sophisticated military-industrial complex (with more than seventeen hundred research establishments) has been built up since independence. Supporters of this "indigenization" of defense production point to the stimulus given to Indian science and engineering, as well as to local subcontractors. Critics, of which there are an increasing number, retort that the system is not only expensive but also extremely inefficient; protected from external and internal competition, solely or heavily reliant upon state contracts, disinclined (and under no pressure) to sell abroad, its industry exists almost in isolation from the workings of the rest of the economy.[48]

Like the large powers in the developed world—or, for that matter, traditional Great Powers over centuries[49]—China and India today seek to enhance their prosperity within the economic order *and* to defend their interests in an anarchic international system. Whether one regards their pursuit of greater military security as anachronistic or realistic, the consequence is that neither Beijing nor New Delhi feels able to concentrate all national energies upon becoming rich; capital, material, and labor must also go to defense, implying a shift to "nonproductive" investment just when both need to invest as much as possible in long-term growth to catch up with their neighbors.

Despite such drawbacks, China and India possess a resource in which they are potentially very rich: human capital. But the existence of masses of people becomes more useful economically when a society provides quality education, encourages experimentation and entrepreneurship, and contains numerous skilled workers, engineers, scientists, technologists, and designers. As we have seen, a swift-growing population can hinder prosperity if the crush of numbers strains a

*China's first atomic bomb was exploded in 1964; by the late 1970s, it had overtaken France and Britain as nuclear powers.

nation's material resources and the people's talents are not developed. The equation is two-sided. One side, limiting demographic expansion, has already been discussed. It is the other side, the quality of the country's human capital, that requires consideration here.

In both societies, the educational deficits are large, in danger of getting worse, and probably more serious for their long-term prospects than problems like current-accounts deficits. Valiant attempts are being made by India and China to cater to education-hungry pupils. There have been improvements in recent years in public education, and certain scientific and scholarly achievements have won international recognition. Yet despite those positive signs, the educational system in both China and India is marred by sporadic and uneven levels of access, at virtually all levels, and by the very low ratio of skilled to unskilled people compared with those in the developed world.

Literacy—the basic educational statistic—shows the extent of the problem. China has a claimed adult literacy rate of 69 percent; still, that means that some 220 million are illiterate, almost three-quarters of them women—*the* key educational deficit throughout the developing world.[50] In India, the situation is worse. The adult literacy rate is a mere 43 percent of the population, but that again conceals a significant gender gap. More than half of the males are literate compared with only one-quarter of adult Indian females.[51] There are, therefore, over 200 million adult human beings in the country who cannot read or write. These figures will alter over time, since the number of children attending school is rising fast; in China, for example, about 90 percent of school-age children are taking lessons. But it remains an open question whether the schools, existing on threadbare resources, can cope with larger numbers or provide anything more than the most rudimentary coverage.[52] This is even more of a challenge in rural India, where the traditions of education are not strong—in 1981 less than half of the population aged fifteen to nineteen had been to school at all[53]—and the socioeconomic obstacles are enormous.

The statistics also show how the proportion of pupils continuing their education drops off swiftly after secondary school. In China, for example, there were 128 million pupils in primary school and a further 54 million in secondary school (1987 data), but—perhaps because graduates are so poorly paid—less than 2 million remained in higher education, a mere fraction of those in their twenties.[54] In India, although the proportion with *any* education at all is so much lower, there are more students in higher education—over 5 million by one account[55]—a discrepancy reflecting the country's large middle class and less egalitarian social structure.

Just what do these figures imply? Some development economists argue that India pours too large a share of its limited resources into higher education, with its British-imitative preferences (law, economics, humanities), and that those funds would be better employed in increasing primary and secondary education, and encouraging craft and technical subjects more in line with the country's basic needs.[56] On the other hand, planners wanting their country to catch up with Japan may feel that changes in the village are less important than developing manufacturing, design, science, and technology, by which criterion neither China nor India possesses enough skilled workers to compete. India, for example, with a population some seven times larger than Japan's, has fewer than one-quarter the number of scientific and technical personnel engaged in research and development.[57] Unless that gap—a thirty-to-one disparity in Japan's favor—is closed, how can they catch up?

In both China and India, education and science confront further obstacles. One is that, as in most developing countries, it is difficult for the state adequately to finance education. Whereas the United States, Japan, and European countries devote around 6 percent of their GNP to education, in China and India it is a strain to allocate 3 to 4 percent of their much smaller GNPs.[58] Secondly, neither state has used its existing funds very well. For national security reasons, India and China have allocated a large proportion of available capital, scientists, and industrial plant to support their military power. By contrast, the opportunities for commercial science and technology are still relatively small, with the ironic result that although only a minuscule share of the population experiences higher education, too many talented individuals are chasing too few suitable jobs. "In India more than half of the 3.3 million seeking work in 1972 had educational qualifications beyond matriculation level";[59] in consequence, large numbers of economists, engineers, and scientists emigrate to the developed world. In China, according to another report, "more than a third of scientific personnel are estimated to be idle for lack of suitable work."[60] Until a sufficiently large manufacturing sector emerges, much of this human talent will remain underused.

On the other hand, because of the absolute size of their economies and populations, the scientific endeavors of China and India are considerable in many fields. Even if too many science and technology personnel are concentrated in defense-related production, there exists a broad array of manufacturing activities which not only gives technological self-reliance, but permits the export of their products to different market niches.[61] In India's case, those markets are chiefly located in developing countries which require less sophisticated wares than (say) Germany, but it is also possible to find customers in the developed world. China, for its part, has developed a manufacturing base for intermediate-level technology, together with a small number of (chiefly defense-related) advanced products such as communications satellites, medium-ranged missiles, and the like. Most important of all, both countries have shown a keen interest in research and development—followed by production—in biotechnology, crop and earth sciences, forestry, and animal breeding and fisheries; that is, in fields where their indigenous resources can be preserved and expanded.

Because China and India have a technological edge over many developing societies, one might be sanguine about their future prospects—but for two major doubts. The first, the heart of the problem, is whether the potential for enhanced per capita standards of living will not be overwhelmed by the millions of newborn children each year. The second, related issue involves a cruel conundrum: is it actually wise for countries possessing half a billion to a billion peasants to attempt nowadays to follow "the stages of industrial growth" first established in the medium-sized nations of Western Europe 150 years ago, or to try to mimic the high-tech revolution emerging from the very different socioeconomic structures of California and Japan? And does that question imply that China and India should *not* attempt to catch up, a notion likely to be repudiated by politicians and planners for condemning their countries to remain forever behind the West?

Rejecting that notion in favor of technological-industrial growth does not settle the issue. Given their social structures, can India or China take the strain of creating world-competitive, high-tech enclaves (presumably enjoying the material benefits that would flow from their global successes) in the midst of hundreds of millions of their impoverished countrymen? Enhanced technology is supposed to have a "trickle-down effect," but does that work when the ratio of highly skilled to unskilled in the population is so disproportionately low? Might not the resources allocated to catching up with the developed world's computer, aerospace, and communications technology and the rest be more usefully diverted into appropriate technologies to expand productivity in the villages,[62] or into the "soft" investment of education, particularly among women?[63] No doubt the best solution would be to push forward at all levels, advanced, intermediate, in the schools and on the farm; but there is insufficient capital for that, which implies that the prospect of catching up remains limited.

This question of political choice raises yet another question concerning the futures of China and India: do they possess the national unity and purpose to meet the challenges thrown up by the fast-changing global scene, or will they be hindered by internal factionalism, regional tensions, and a general failure to carry the bulk of the population along with the leadership's aims? In China, this problem is fundamental; how can the government join the international economy while retaining a political and ideological monopoly at home? Tiananmen Square indicated that the leadership believes it can have one without the other; but far from settling the problem, Beijing's policies of force and censorship simply evade it. All subsequent reports about "the people's malaise" suggest that widely held feelings of betrayal, mistrust, and fear—especially in the urban population, the educated classes, perhaps also in the armed forces—may hamper economic recovery, and make it more difficult to strengthen China's fragile links with the world outside.[64]

The internal condition of India is altogether more complex, and every bit as serious. A country of 850 million people possessing twenty-five distinct ethnic identities, a stratified caste system, enormous income gaps between elites and poor, a bustling middle class of over 100 million people on the one hand and entrenched trade unions and

Marxist political parties on the other, and Muslim (75 million) and Sikh (13 million) minorities alongside the Hindu majority would be difficult to govern at the best of times. This has not been helped by the fact that India's relatively slow increases in real growth have benefited only some of the people. More important still, the excessive factionalism of Indian politics—hastily formed coalition governments, quarrels between the central government and the states, systematic corruption and favoritism, the subversion of bureaucratic decisions, demagogic appeals on issues of caste, race, and class—has raised in some observer's minds the spectacle of political anarchy.[65] But authoritarian rule by the Indian government—the "administration without politics" syndrome of the Emergency of 1975–77—would spell the end of the country's delicate if messy democracy. The present tendency toward weak central government and excessive political maneuvering has its own regrettable consequences. It plays into the hands of extremists, who, in setting caste against caste and Hindu against Muslim, have provoked bloody violence, worsening the political atmosphere in New Delhi and causing ethnic groups to defend their interests by force.[66] Secondly, it diverts attention from critical reforms of the Indian economy that could improve overall standards of living.[67] As with China, therefore, India's future prospects will be very heavily affected by the quality of the political leadership which will emerge as this decade unfolds—and that in turn depends on the Chinese and Indian peoples themselves.

Given the balance of strengths and weaknesses which these two countries possess, it is evident that their preparedness for twenty-first-century transformations is mixed, at best. With regard to the long-term shifts in the global military and economic power balances—the traditional way of measuring the relative "rise and fall of the Great Powers"—both nations are emerging as considerable regional leaders. However, the extent to which the transnational, *non*military challenges to China and India will affect their hope of becoming rich and strong is much less clear.

Take, for example, the implications of the robotics revolution. As

India modernizes, there could well emerge entrepreneurs, electronics firms, and other businesses possessing the technical know-how, financial capacity, and official support to adopt automated production. India has, after all, an existing machine-tool industry, which is the natural foundation for any serious move into robotics; it has many trained mathematicians and engineers; and it is now eager to emulate East Asia's venture into higher technologies. Provided that better infrastructure is in place and quality control assured, the automation of the workplace in India obviously looks much more feasible than in, say, Ethiopia. This is not to suggest that India would be a serious challenge to Japan's dominance in robotics, but that it can potentially be a medium-sized player like, for example, Italy or Britain.

On the other hand, it must be one of the chief aims of India's planners to create many *more* jobs in assembly and manufacturing as the rural population steadily moves into the cities, whereas FANUC-style production would mean the replacement of workers by machines. If robotic production spreads in other countries, or in India itself, the effect on supply and demand could lower wages and hurt standards of living. Having missed out on the original Industrial Revolution that brought workers into factories, perhaps the last thing Indian society needs over the next few decades is the spread of a technology which takes workers *out* of the factories—or becomes a disincentive for multinationals to establish such plants in the first place.

The rationale against fully automated production is, if anything, even greater in China's case. Its manufacturing boom of the 1980s was, as noted earlier, chiefly due to Beijing's liberalization of the coastal provinces, with "open cities" and "special economic zones" to tempt foreign investment and produce goods for export. The results have been spectacular, with Guangdong Province having enjoyed a *real* growth rate of 12 ½ percent a year since 1979—probably the highest in the world—and the single town of Shenzhen (next to Hong Kong) growing from less than 100,000 people to more than 2 million today. The key here, apart from the liberalization itself, is the low-cost, eager, hardworking labor. Because of its boom, Shenzhen's labor costs are ten times higher than elsewhere in Guangdong, but still only one-fifth of those in Hong Kong. In neighboring Fujian Province, the average factory wage in 1991 ($65 a month) was one-tenth the rate in Taiwan;* presumably, it was a mere one-thirtieth or one-fortieth of the average Japanese factory wage.[68]

Given such disparity in labor costs, the argument here is not that the robotics revolution in Japan (and, later, in Korea and Taiwan) poses an *immediate* threat to manufacturing employment in South China. Over the medium to longer term, however, China's situation will be affected by two developments. The first will be further breakthroughs in automated assembly and manufacturing, reducing the overall costs of employing robotic "serfs"; the second will be the rise in incomes, and thus in labor costs, in those provinces currently enjoying the boom—already Shenzhen has a per capita GDP close to $2,000 a year, while Hong Kong and Taiwan are becoming far too expensive for basic manufacturing.[69] In theory, this rise in labor costs along China's coastline could have a beneficial "ripple effect," spreading into the poorer country and inland provinces (always provided Beijing and the conservative regional authorities agree to extend the economic liberalization measures). Even so, one wonders if there would be enough foreign demand, and willingness to import, to turn hundreds of millions of Chinese peasants into assembly workers. The alternative is that, deterred by physical and political obstacles from investing in the cheap-labor inland provinces, Japanese and Taiwanese multinationals turn to robots to maintain their manufacturing competitiveness. If so, that would reduce China's chance of a steady, stage-by-stage transition toward a modern, high-per-capita-income economy.

On the face of it, the biotech revolution in agriculture appears to offer promise for both countries. With the productivity increases of the "green revolution" beginning to peter out, little suitable additional land available, and the threat of population growth eclipsing food output, the governments of China and India need to encourage all possible ways to improve agricultural yields. If biotechnology, including DNA-type genetic engineering, will permit "the power of the land" to stay ahead of population growth, then many of the feared outcomes— malnutrition, famine, increased mortality rates, social discontents—

---

*As a further contrast, it was reported in the *New York Times* (27 January 1992, p. A6) that per capita income in impoverished Anhui Province averaged "$74 a year in normal times." Is it any wonder that tens of millions of peasants are drifting into the towns and cities?

could be avoided, or at least mitigated. Creating crops that can grow in semiarid conditions, that are more resistant to disease, or simply that have a greater calorific yield is obviously beneficial. Thus, both countries are committing large resources to biotechnology research and application, from crop breeding, to animal embryo transfers, to producing biogas energy sources. The greater part of this activity plays to both countries' strengths: each possesses many scientists in these fields (unlike most sub-Saharan African nations), and this experimentation is not as capital-intensive as other high-tech ventures.

The dangers to China and India from the biotech revolution in agriculture do not, in the near term, outweigh these potential benefits—but they need to be taken seriously. The first might emerge, ironically, if there actually were to occur year-on-year increases in agricultural yields significantly higher than population growth. Because poor farmers cannot afford the new biotech applications, this may at present seem a remote possibility; but since scientific breakthroughs often occur at surprising speed, it cannot be discounted. In its early years such a productivity expansion would be welcome; over time, however, it could lead to a crisis of agricultural *over*productivity, such as has affected American farming on a number of occasions over the past century. Everything would depend upon the speed of the change: it took one hundred years of productivity increases, coupled with the lure of jobs elsewhere, to reduce American agriculture's share of the work force from a clear majority to the mere 3 percent that it constitutes today. Will India and China, whose agricultural sectors respectively employ nearly two-thirds and four-fifths of their work forces, have enough time to manage the transformation, especially given our present heightened pace of technological change? If not, then the rural discontents could be far more violent than those occurring among French or Korean farmers today.

The other danger might come not from biotech applications enhancing the power of the land but from the massive growth of *in vitro* experimentation and food output from the laboratories of Western agrochemical and pharmaceutical companies—that challenge to every sort of traditional farming discussed earlier.* Exactly how this might

*See Chapter 4.

affect China and India is difficult to estimate. Neither resembles those economies of Central America, the Caribbean, and sub-Saharan Africa that have traditionally earned foreign currency through the export of staples (cane sugar, vanilla, rubber) and now find those natural products rivaled by laboratory equivalents. For China and India, farming is vital to satisfy *domestic* needs, but it is industry and services that focus upon external markets. Still, both countries will want to avoid undue dependence upon Western biotech firms with their tendency toward high-profit, proprietary knowledge, for that would simply add to the current outflow of capital to pay for patents, technical fees, royalties, and the like. Finally, should major breakthroughs occur in laboratory-based food production at the same time as farm-based yields were creating huge surpluses, then the problem of sensibly reducing the agricultural sector would be exacerbated.

Similarity between China and India is far less evident when one considers the likely impact of the global financial and communications revolution. From the viewpoint of China's leadership, fanciful visions of the "borderless world" can only be regarded with suspicion, and not simply because of age-old cultural attitudes toward foreigners. Economically, a system of twenty-four-hour-a-day trading of capital and currencies benefits those companies and societies rich in funds, banks, and other financial services, together with service industries and professionals who "add value" to such transactions. Given the present state of China's political economy, little of this would appear attractive or, for that matter, relevant. To be sure, foreign bankers are needed to arrange funds for a joint venture with a major Western construction company or to handle the exchanges that flow from China's export boom—just as it is hoped that, with their low labor costs, the coastal provinces and enterprise zones will continue to offer an attractive location for the assembly plants of foreign multinationals. But that is not the same as if China itself—or, rather, its state-run banks and industries—were planning to be a major *independent* player on an international field where governments have become largely invisible, and where only shareholders and symbolic analysts count.

The other reason that China's leadership looks askance at the world of interactive electronic mail, satellite transmissions, the unhampered activities of free-market media giants, and the like is that such developments clearly threaten their authoritarian political system. Fax machines connecting students with their renegade brethren abroad, satellites transmitting American or Japanese programs onto Chinese television screens, newspapers and books investigating dangerous themes and questioning the Party's political monopoly, are all suspect—especially after the role they played in the convulsions of 1989. Economic modernization is worth supporting, if cautiously; the free play of ideas, with their tendency to challenge existing authority and traditional social norms, holds no attraction in Beijing.

In these respects, India offers different and intriguing possibilities. It contains, as mentioned, a large and burgeoning middle class. It possesses a considerable number of small to medium-sized businesses (in addition to the large public-sector companies), many of which are engaging in joint ventures. And its population is renowned for producing mathematicians, engineers, and economists. There is also the advantage of familiarity with English as the language of world finance, computers, communications, and international business. Already, high-tech "Silicon Valley" enterprises are clustering around cities like Bangalore in the south. Provided there can be further relaxation of the bureaucratic and legal obstacles that clog India's commercial system, a class of entrepreneurs, designers, software engineers, consultants, lawyers, and middlemen could emerge to play in the global marketplace and reap benefits from the borderless world.

But if that happens, the larger problem remains; as noted earlier, the emergence in developed economies of a class of "symbolic analysts" is already opening up a worrying gap between the minority who can take advantage of the new transnational trends and a great majority increasingly marginalized in the process. If that is going to hurt the social fabric of (say) the United States, how much greater would be the impacts in India, most of which has not yet undergone an industrial revolution, let alone prepared for the transnational provision of high-added-value professional services? Given the even greater gap in incomes and life-styles that would occur in India, how comfortable would it be to have islands of prosperity in a sea of poverty? Would such individuals, resented by the masses and with increasingly fewer local ties, be tempted to escape to overseas locations?

.   .   .   .

Ideally the best thing to happen would be for all China and India—entrepreneurs and peasants, technicians and laundry girls—to enjoy a steady rise in real standards of living. This would not bring per capita income up to Western levels, for the gap is simply too great; but it would surely be an immense improvement if the present, dreadfully low average annual income of $300–350 could be raised to that of Mexico (GNP per capita: $1,825) or possibly even Hungary ($2,237).[70]

Unfortunately, unless fresh technological breakthroughs occur in environmental controls and that technology is transferred wholesale to China and India, such rises in living standards would have appalling consequences for their environments. Already there is mounting evidence of the damage caused by population growth and modernization. China's headlong rush into industrialization after 1950 was undertaken without regard for the atmosphere, water supplies, or the countryside in general. As a result there now exist industrial regions whose air is so polluted that they cannot be seen (even in cloudless weather) by satellite reconnaissance for months at a time. Around 5 billion tons of topsoil are lost each year, about 1.1 million acres of farmland disappear annually as the cities and towns spread outward, thousands of miles of river are contaminated by industrial toxins, one-third of the coastal fishing grounds are ruined by pollution, and the air in Beijing is "sixteen times dirtier than it is in New York and an astonishing thirty-five times more contaminated than in London."[71] When great floods occur, as they do from time to time, the loss of topsoil is greater because of deforestation.* Despite a belated recognition of these problems by the Chinese authorities—the creation of natural conservation regions, pollution-control measures, tree-planting schemes—the overall situation continues to worsen.[72]

In India, the story is the same. Because of population growth, the area around New Delhi has lost a staggering 60 percent of its forest cover in the last decade alone, chiefly to firewood cutting. One recent

*And the damage caused by flooding is proportionately greater in recent times because, ironically, peasants now liberated to work on their own plots are more reluctant to be mobilized and sent away to join flood-control gangs.

analysis pointed out that because of poverty, continuing forest devasta-
tion, the negative impact of economic development, and sheer greed,
environmental pollution had assumed "threatening proportions":

> Of the country's 304 million hectares 50 percent are subject to ecological
> degradation. About 80 percent of the population lives under substandard
> conditions. The fourteen major rivers, including the Ganga, which provides
> nearly 85 percent of the country's drinking water, are all polluted. . . .
> Human diseases caused by contaminated or substandard food have doubled
> during the last thirty years. Over 80 percent of all [!] hospital patients are
> the victims of environmental pollution.[73]

Admittedly, there is increasing awareness of this damage, especially
by the middle classes in India, and plans exist to clean the rivers, halt
deforestation, preserve wildlife, check unregulated mining, and control
air pollution. Yet if, as former Prime Minister Rajiv Gandhi claimed,
"mass poverty was forcing the poor to degrade the environment on
which they depended for sheer survival," that process of erosion will
not be halted until poverty and population growth are themselves
checked.[74] The dilemma is acute, for if the only way to reduce poverty
is to increase industrialization on a large scale, the Indian environment
will suffer still more.

This environmental damage has, of course, profound implications for
the health of the Indian and Chinese peoples, as well as for the world's
atmosphere. As *The Economist* has noted, Deng Xiaoping's "decep-
tively simple goal" of raising China's GDP to $1,000 per head by the
year 2000 means that the economy has to triple in size:

> Of course that will not happen. But to try to make it happen the easy
> way—which is the one the Chinese will adopt—will be to build more power
> stations and factories. These will depend mainly on China's own coal, with
> its average ash content of 27 percent and sulfur content of up to 5 percent.
> Millions more Chinese will suffer from respiratory disorders, and a few more
> cities will disappear from satellite photographs.[75]

The greenhouse effect is also likely to increase if, for example, the
Chinese government carries through its well-meaning intention that
every home will boast a refrigerator by the year 2000.[76] Should hun-

dreds of millions of refrigerators all release CFCs into the atmosphere, the depletion of the earth's protective ozone layer would be immense. In one journalist's words, "China's industrial ambitions . . . pose a threat to the planet."[77] Presumably, the same is as true for India's industrial ambitions.

This leaves a mighty conundrum for China and India, and for the rest of the world. Both those nations are engaged in a race against time, for if their population explosion continues it will erode gains in agricultural and manufacturing output, reduce expectations of increases in real income, worsen regional imbalances, and damage the social peace. In sum, if they fail to escape from their Malthusian trap, a large proportion of the earth's inhabitants in the early twenty-first century will witness continued poverty and malnutrition. On the other hand, if China and India with their three *billion* people do happily manage to triple their average standard of living (to levels which the West would still find intolerably low), that would not only damage their local environment and public health, but also threaten the earth's overall atmosphere. Although this potential danger is beginning to ring alarm bells in the developed world, it would be inconceivable—and ridiculous—for the West to press China and India to abandon their plans for economic growth; it would also be hypocritical, since advanced societies (especially the United States) inflict much more damage per capita upon the earth's atmosphere.

The only logical solution remaining, therefore, is for the developed world to try to apply its capital, technology, and brainpower to help these two giant populations escape from poverty without harm to themselves and the planet, while at the same time embracing technological solutions, including alterations in energy use and life-style, to reduce its own, even larger damage to the global environment.

How likely this is needs to be discussed further; it is certainly not an issue that American and European politicians, campaigning for office on domestic, short-term issues, seem willing to confront. Yet it is already clear that unless rich and poor nations recognize that they inhabit the same biospace, the dilemmas facing China and India will intensify—and the results will not be merely local.

10

WINNERS AND LOSERS IN THE DEVELOPING WORLD

NOTHING BETTER ILLUSTRATES THE growing differences among developing countries than the fact that in the 1960s, South Korea had a per capita GNP exactly the same as Ghana's ($230) whereas today it is ten to twelve times more prosperous.[1] Both possessed a predominantly agrarian economy and had endured a half century or more of colonial rule. Upon independence, each faced innumerable handicaps in trying to "catch up" with the West, and although Korea possessed a greater historico-cultural coherence, its chances may have seemed less promising, since it had few natural resources (apart from tungsten) and suffered heavily during the 1950–53 fighting. Decades later, however, West African states remain among the most poverty-stricken countries in the world—the per capita GNPs of Niger, Sierra Leone, and Chad today, for example, are less than $500[2]—while Korea is entering the ranks of the high-income economies. Already the world's thirteenth-largest trading nation, Korea is planning to become one of the richest countries of all in the twenty-first century,[3] whereas the nations of West Africa face a future, at least in the near term, of chronic poverty, malnutrition, poor health, and underdevelopment. Finally, while Korea's rising prosperity is attended by a decrease in population growth, most African countries still face a demographic explosion that erodes any gains in national output.

This divergence is not new, for there have always been richer and poorer societies; the prosperity gap in the seventeenth century between, say, Amsterdam and the west coast of Ireland or between such bustling Indian ports as Surat and Calcutta[4] and the inhabitants of New Guinean hill villages must have been marked, although it probably did not equal the gulf between rich and poor nations today. The difference is that the twentieth-century global communications revolution has made such disparities widely known. This can breed resentments by poorer peoples against prosperous societies, but it can also provide a desire to emulate (as Korea emulated Japan). The key issue here is: what does it take to turn a "have-not" nation into a "have" nation? Does it simply require imitating economic techniques, or does it involve such intangibles as culture, social structure, and attitudes toward foreign practices?

This discrepancy in performance between East Asia and sub-Saharan Africa clearly makes redundant the term "Third World." However useful the expression might have been in the 1950s, when poor, non-aligned, and recently decolonized states were attempting to remain independent of the two superpower blocs,[5] the rise of super-rich oil-producing countries a decade later already made it questionable. Now that prosperous East Asian societies possess higher per capita GNPs than Russia, Eastern Europe, and even Western European states like Portugal, the word seems less suitable than ever. With Taiwanese and Korean corporations establishing assembly plants in the Philippines and creating distribution networks within the European Community, we need to recognize the differences that exist among non-Western economies. Some scholars now categorize *five* separate types of "developing" countries* to help assess the varied potential of societies in Asia, Africa, and Latin America.[6]

Relative national growth in the 1980s confirms these differences. Whereas East Asian economies grew on average at an impressive an-

---

*Ravenhill's divisions (see note 6 to this chapter) are high-income oil-exporting countries; industrializing economies with strong states and relatively low levels of indebtedness (Taiwan, etc.); industrializing economies with state apparatus under challenge and/or with debt problems (Argentina, Poland); potential newly industrializing countries (Malaysia, Thailand); and primary-commodity producers (in sub-Saharan Africa, Central America).

nual rate of 7.4 percent, those in Africa and Latin America gained only 1.8 and 1.7 percent respectively[7]—and since their populations grew faster, the net result was that they slipped backward, absolutely and relatively. Differences of economic structure also grew in this decade, with African and other primary-commodity-producing countries eager for higher raw-material prices whereas the export-oriented manufacturing nations of East Asia sought to keep commodity prices low. The most dramatic difference occurred in the shares of world trade in manufactures, a key indicator of economic competitiveness (see Chart 6).

Thus, while some scholars still refer to a *dual* world economy[8] of rich and poor countries, what is emerging is increasing differentiation. The rest of this chapter examines why that is so.

Chart 6. Shares of World Trade in Manufactures[9]

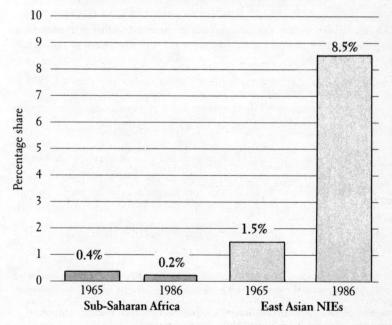

. . .

The developing countries most successfully catching up with the West are the trading states of the Pacific and East Asia. Except for Communist-controlled countries in the area, the Pacific Rim countries (including the western areas of Canada and the United States, and in part Australia) have enjoyed a lengthy boom in manufacturing, trade, and investment; but the center of that boom is on the *Asian* side of the Pacific, chiefly fueled by Japan's own spectacular growth and the stimulus given to neighboring economies and transpacific trade. According to one source:

> In 1962 the Western Pacific (notably East Asia) accounted for around 9 percent of world GNP, North America for 30 percent, and Western Europe for 31 percent. Twenty years later, the Western Pacific share had climbed to more than 15 percent, while North America's had fallen to 28 percent and Europe's to 27 percent. By the year 2000 it is likely that the Western Pacific will account for around one-quarter of world GNP, with the whole Pacific region increasing its share from just over 43 percent to around half of world GNP.[10]

East Asia's present boom is not, of course, uniform, and scholars distinguish between the different stages of economic and technological development in this vast region. Roughly speaking, the divisions would be as follows:

(a) Japan, now the world's largest financial center and, increasingly, the most innovative high-tech nation in the nonmilitary field;

(b) the four East Asian "tigers" or "dragons," the Newly Industrialized Economies (NIEs) of Singapore, Hong Kong, Taiwan, and South Korea, of which the latter two possess bigger populations and territorial size than the two port-city states, but all have enjoyed export-led growth in recent decades;

(c) the larger Southeast Asian states of Thailand, Malaysia, and Indonesia, which, stimulated by foreign (chiefly Japanese) investment, are becoming involved in manufacturing, assembly, and export (it is doubtful whether the Philippines should be included in this group);

(d) finally, the stunted and impoverished Communist societies of

Vietnam, Cambodia, and North Korea, as well as isolationist Myanmar pursuing its "Burmese Way to Socialism."

Because of this staggered level of development, economists in East Asia invoke the image of the "flying geese," with Japan the lead bird, followed by the East Asian NIEs, the larger Southeast Asian states, and so on. What Japan produced in one decade—relatively low-priced toys, kitchenware, electrical goods—will be imitated by the next wave of "geese" in the decade following, and by the third wave in the decade after that. However accurate the metaphor individually, the overall picture is clear: these birds are flying, purposefully and onward, to an attractive destination.

Of those states, it is the East Asian NIEs that have provided the clearest example of successful transformation. Although distant observers may regard them as similar, there are notable differences in size, population,* history, and political system. Even the economic structures are distinct; for example, Korea, which began its expansion at least a decade later than Taiwan (and democratized itself even more slowly) is heavily dependent upon a few enormous industrial conglomerates, or *chaebol,* of which the top four alone (Samsung, Hyundai, Lucky-Goldstar, and Daewoo) have sales equal to half the GNP. By contrast, Taiwan possesses many small companies, specializing in one or two product areas. While Taiwanese are concerned that their firms may lose out to foreign giants, Koreans worry that the *chaebol* will find it increasingly difficult to compete in large-scale industries like petrochemicals and semiconductors and shipbuilding at the same time.[11]

Despite such structural differences, these societies each contain certain basic characteristics, which, *taken together,* help to explain their decade-upon-decade growth. The first, and perhaps the most important, is the emphasis upon education. This derives from Confucian traditions of competitive examinations and respect for learning, reinforced daily by the mother of the family, who complements what is taught at school. To Western eyes, this process—like Japan's—appears to concentrate on rote learning, acquiring technical skills, and emphasizing harmony, rather than encouraging individual talent and the

*While Korea has a population of around 43 million and Taiwan about 20 million, Hong Kong possesses 5.7 million and Singapore only 2.7 million.

habit of questioning authority. Even if some East Asian educators would nowadays admit that criticism, most believe that their own educational mores create social harmony and a well-trained work force. Moreover, the uniformity of the system does not exclude an intense individual competitiveness; in Taiwan (where, incidentally, twelve members of the fourteen-member cabinet of 1989 had acquired Ph.D.s abroad), only the top third of each year's 110,000 students taking the national university entrance examinations are selected, to emphasize the importance of college education.[12] Perhaps nothing better illustrates this stress upon learning than the fact that Korea (43 million population) has around 1.4 million students in higher education, compared with 145,000 in Iran (54 million), 15,000 in Ethiopia (46 million), and 159,000 in Vietnam (64 million); or the further fact that already by 1980 "as many engineering students were graduating from Korean institutions as in the United Kingdom, West Germany, and Sweden combined."[13]

The second common factor is a high level of national savings. By employing fiscal measures, taxes, and import controls to encourage personal savings, large amounts of low-interest capital were made available for investment in manufacture and commerce. During the first few decades of growth, personal consumption and living standards were controlled—by restrictions upon moving capital abroad and importing foreign luxury goods—in order to funnel resources into industrial growth. While average prosperity rose, most of the fruits of economic success were plowed back into further expansion. Only when economic "takeoff" was well under way has the system begun to alter; increased consumption, foreign purchases, and capital investment in new homes all allow internal demand to play a larger role in the country's growth. In such circumstances, one would expect to see overall savings ratios decline. Even in the late 1980s, however, the East Asian NIEs still had high national savings rates, as shown in Table 7.

The third feature has been a strong political framework within which economic growth is fostered. While entrepreneurship and private property are encouraged, the "tigers" never followed a laissez-faire model. Industries targeted for growth were given a variety of supports—export subsidies, training grants, tariff protection from foreign competitors. As noted above, the fiscal system was arranged to produce high savings

Table 7. Comparative Savings Ratios, 1987[14]

Taiwan	38.8%
Malaysia	37.8%
Korea	37.0%
Japan	32.3%
Indonesia	29.1%
U.S.	12.7%

ratios. Taxes assisted the business sector, as did energy policy. Trade unions operated under restrictions. Democracy was constrained, by the governor of Hong Kong, *dirigiste* administrations in Singapore, and the military regimes in Taiwan and Korea. Only lately have free elections and party politics been permitted. Defenders of this system argued that it was necessary to restrain libertarian impulses while concentrating on economic growth, and that democratic reforms are a "reward" for the people's patience. The point is that domestic politics were unlike those in the West, yet did not hurt commercial expansion.

The fourth feature was the commitment to exports, in contrast to the import-substitution policies of India and the consumer-driven policies of the United States. This was traditional for a small, bustling trading state like Hong Kong, but it involved substantial restructuring in Taiwan and Korea, where managers and work force had to be trained to produce what foreign customers wanted. In all cases, the value of the currency was kept low, to increase exports and decrease imports. Moreover, the East Asian NIEs took advantage of favorable global circumstances; labor costs were much lower than in North America and Europe, and they benefited from an open international trading order, created and protected by the United States, while shielding their own industries from foreign competition. Over time, this led to large trade surpluses, and to threats of retaliation from European and American governments, which is a reminder of the NIEs' heavy dependence upon the current international economic system. The important thing, however, is that they targeted export-led growth in manufactures whereas other developing nations continued to rely upon commodity exports and made little effort to cater to foreign consumers' tastes.[15] Given this focus upon trade, it is not surprising to learn that Asia now contains seven of the world's twelve largest ports.

Finally, the East Asian NIEs possess a local model, namely, Japan, which Yemen, Guatemala, and Burkina Faso simply do not have. For four decades East Asian peoples have observed the dramatic success of a non-Western neighbor, based upon its educational and technical skills, high savings ratios, long-term state-guided targeting of industries and markets, and determination to compete on world markets, though this admiration of Japan is nowadays mixed with a certain alarm at becoming members of a yen bloc dominated by Tokyo. While the Japanese domestic market is extremely important for the East Asian NIEs, and they benefit from Japanese investments, assembly plants, engineers, and expertise, they have little enthusiasm for a new Greater East Asia Co-Prosperity Sphere.[16]

The benefits of economic success are not merely seen in East Asia's steadily rising standards of living. Children are on average four or five inches taller than they were in the 1940s, and grow up in countries that are among the world's healthiest:

> A Taiwanese child born in 1988 could expect to live seventy-four years, only a year less than an American or a West German, and fifteen years longer than a Taiwanese born in 1952; a South Korean born in 1988 could expect seventy years on earth, up from fifty-eight in 1965. In 1988 the Taiwanese took in 50 percent more calories each day than they had done thirty-five years earlier. They had two hundred times as many televisions, telephones and cars per household; in Korea the rise in the possession of these goods was even higher.[17]

In addition, the East Asian NIEs enjoy high literacy rates, once again confirming that they are altogether closer to "First" World nations than to poor, developing countries.

Will this progress last into the twenty-first century? Politically, Hong Kong's future is completely uncertain, and many companies are relocating their headquarters elsewhere; Taiwan remains a diplomatic pariah state, because of Beijing's traditional claims; and South Korea still feels threatened by the unpredictable militarized regime in the north. The future of China—and of Siberia—is uncertain, and causes concern. The 1980s rise in Asian stock-market prices (driven by vast increases in the money supply) was excessive and speculative, and destined to tumble. Protectionist tendencies in the developed world threaten the

Table 8. Comparative Living Standards[18]

	Life Expectancy at Birth, 1987 (years)	Adult Literacy Rate, 1985 (%)	GNP per capita, 1988 (U.S.$)
Niger	45	14	300
Togo	54	41	310
India	59	43	340
SINGAPORE	73	86	9,070
SOUTH KOREA	70	95	5,000
Spain	77	95	7,740
New Zealand	75	99	10,000

trading states even more than external pressures to abandon price supports for local farmers. A rise in the value of the Korean and Taiwanese currencies has cut export earnings and reduced overall rate of growth. Some Japanese competitors have moved production to neighboring low-cost countries such as Thailand and southern China. Sharp rises in oil prices increase the import bills. Higher wages (in Korea they increased by an average 14 percent in 1988, and by 17 percent in 1989) affect labor costs and competitiveness. The social peace, precarious in these recent democracies, is damaged by bouts of student and industrial unrest.[19]

On the other hand, these may simply be growing pains. Savings ratios are still extremely high. Large numbers of new engineers and technicians pour out of college each year. The workers' enhanced purchasing power has created a booming domestic market, and governments are investing more in housing, infrastructure, and public facilities. The labor force will not grow as swiftly as before, because of the demographic slowdown, but it will be better educated and spend more.[20] A surge in overseas investments is assisting the long-term balance of payments. As the populous markets of Indonesia, Thailand, and Malaysia grow at double-digit rates, there is plenty of work for the trading states. A hardening of the currency can be met by greater commitment to quality exports, high rates of industrial investment, and a move into newer, high-technology manufacture—in imitation of the 1980s retooling of Japanese industry when its currency hardened swiftly. Nowhere else in the world would growth rates of "only" 5 or

6 percent be considered as worrying, or a harbinger of decline. Barring a war in East Asia or a massive global slump, the signs are that the four "tigers" are better structured than most to grow in wealth and health.

For confirmation of that remark, one need only consider the present difficult condition of Latin America, which lost ground in the 1980s just as East Asia was gaining it. Here again, distinctions have to be made between various countries within the continent, with its more than 400 million people in an area of almost 7 million square miles stretching from the Rio Grande to Antarctica, and with a range of political cultures and socioeconomic structures. Argentina, which around 1900 had a standard of living suggesting it was a "developed" economy, is very different from Honduras and Guyana. Similarly, population change in Latin America occurs in *three* distinct forms: such nations as Bolivia, the Dominican Republic, and Haiti have high fertility rates and lower life expectancies; a middle group—Brazil, Colombia, Mexico, Venezuela, Costa Rica, and Panama—are beginning to experience declines in fertility and longer life expectancy; and the temperate-zone countries of Argentina, Chile, and Uruguay have the demographic characteristics of developed countries.[21]

Despite this diversity, there are reasons for considering Latin America's prospects as a whole: the economic challenges confronting the region are similar, as are its countries' domestic politics—in particular, the fragility of its recently emerged democracies—and all its countries are affected by their relationship with the developed world, especially the United States.

Several decades ago, Latin America's future appeared encouraging. Sharing in the post-1950 global boom, benefiting from demand for its coffee, timber, beef, oil, and minerals, and enjoying foreign investments in its agriculture, industry, and infrastructure, the region was moving upward. In the thirty years after 1945, its production of steel multiplied twenty times and its output of electric energy, metals, and machinery more than tenfold.[22] Real GDP per person rose at an annual average of 2.8 percent during the 1960s and spurted to an annual average increase of 3.4 percent in the 1970s. Unfortunately, the growth then reversed itself, and between 1980 and 1988 Latin America's real GDP per person steadily fell by an annual average of 0.9 percent.[23] In some states, such as Peru and Argentina, real income dropped by as much as one-quarter during the 1980s. With very few exceptions (Chile, Colombia, Dominican Republic, Barbados, Bahamas), most countries now have per capita GDPs lower than those a decade earlier, or even two decades earlier:

The reasons for this reversal offer a striking contrast to the East Asian NIEs. Instead of encouraging industrialists to target foreign markets and stimulate the economy through export-led growth, many Latin American governments pursued a policy of import substitution, creating their own steel, cement, paper, automobiles, and electronics-goods industries, which were given protective tariffs, government subsi-

Table 9. Per Capita GDP of Latin American Countries[24]
(U.S. $)

Country	1960	1970	1980	1988
Chile	1,845	2,236	2,448	2,518
Argentina	2,384	3,075	3,359	2,862
Uruguay	2,352	2,478	3,221	2,989
Brazil	1,013	1,372	2,481	2,449
Paraguay	779	931	1,612	1,557
Bolivia	634	818	983	724
Peru	1,233	1,554	1,716	1,503
Ecuador	771	904	1,581	1,477
Colombia	927	1,157	1,595	1,739
Venezuela	3,879	4,941	5,225	4,544
Guyana	1,008	1,111	1,215	995
Surinam	887	2,337	3,722	3,420
Mexico	1,425	2,022	2,872	2,588
Guatemala	1,100	1,420	1,866	1,502
Honduras	619	782	954	851
El Salvador	832	1,032	1,125	995
Nicaragua	1,055	1,495	1,147	819
Costa Rica	1,435	1,825	2,394	2,235
Panama	1,264	2,017	2,622	2,229
Dominican Republic	823	987	1,497	1,509
Haiti	331	292	386	319
Jamaica	1,610	2,364	1,880	1,843
Trinidad & Tobago	3,848	4,927	8,116	5,510
Barbados	2,000	3,530	3,994	4,233
Bahamas	8,448	10,737	10,631	11,317

dies, and tax breaks to insulate them from international competition. As a result, their products became less attractive abroad.* Moreover, while it was relatively easy to create a basic iron and steel industry, it proved harder to establish high-tech industries like computers, aerospace, machine tools, and pharmaceuticals—so most of these states depend on imported manufactured goods, whereas exports still chiefly consist of raw materials like oil, coffee, and soybeans.[25]

Secondly, economic growth was accompanied by lax financial policies and an increasing reliance upon foreign borrowings. Governments poured money not only into infrastructure and schools but also into state-owned enterprises, large bureaucracies, and oversized armed forces, paying for them by printing money and raising loans from Western (chiefly U.S.) banks and international agencies. The result was that public spending's share of GDP soared, and price inflation accelerated and was further increased by index-linked rises in salaries and wages. Inflation became so large that it was difficult to comprehend, let alone to combat. "In 1989, for example, annual inflation in Nicaragua was more than 3,400 percent; in Argentina inflation reached 3,700 percent, in Brazil almost 1,500 percent, and in Peru nearly 3,000 percent. Ecuador, with only 60 percent inflation, did comparatively well."[26] In such circumstances the currency becomes worthless, as does the idea of seeking to raise national savings rates for long-term capital investment.

Another result was that some Latin American countries found themselves among the most indebted in the world, as shown in Table 10.

In consequence, total Latin American indebtedness now equals about $1,000 for every man, woman, and child. But instead of being directed into productive investment, that money was wasted domestically or disappeared as "capital flight" to private accounts in U.S. and European banks. This left most countries incapable of repaying even the interest on their loans. Defaults on loans (or suspension of interest payments) then produced a drying-up of capital from indignant Western banks and a net capital *outflow* from Latin America just when it

---

*As mentioned earlier, Japan and its East Asian emulators also sought to protect fledgling domestic industries, but that was in order to create a strong base from which to mount an export offensive—*not* to establish an economic bastion within which their industries would be content to remain.

Table 10. Growth of Latin American Indebtedness, Selected Countries[27]

Country	Total External Debt (billion U.S.$)			Long-Term Public Debt As A Percentage of GNP		
	1977	1982	1987	1977	1982	1987
Argentina	8.1	32.4	53.9	10	31	62
Brazil	28.3	68.7	109.4	13	20	29
Chile	4.9	8.5	18.7	28	23	89
Guyana	0.4	0.9	1.2	100	158	353
Honduras	0.6	1.6	3.1	29	53	71
Jamaica	1.1	2.7	4.3	31	69	139
Mexico	26.6	78.0	93.7	25	32	59
Venezuela	9.8	27.0	29.0	10	16	52

needed capital to aid economic growth.* Starved of foreign funds and with currencies made worthless by hyperinflation, many countries are in a far worse position than could have been imagined twenty-five years ago.[28] For a while, it was even feared that the region's financial problems might undermine parts of the international banking system. It now appears that the chief damage will be in the continent itself, where 180 million people (40 percent) are living in poverty—a rise of 50 million alone in the 1980s.

Given such profligacy, and the conservative, "anti-big-government" incumbents in the White House during the 1980s, it was predictable that Latin America would come under pressure—from the World Bank, the IMF, private bankers, Washington itself—to slash public spending, control inflation, and repay debts. Such recipes were easier said than done in the existing circumstances. Islands of democracy (e.g., Costa Rica) did exist, but many states were ruled by right-wing military dictatorships or social revolutionaries; internal guerrilla wars, military coups d'état, and labor unrest were common. Even as democracy began to reassert itself in the 1980s, the new leaders found themselves in a near-impossible situation: inheritors of the massive external debts contracted by the outgoing regimes, legatees in many cases of inflationary index-linked wage systems, targets of landowner resentment and/or of guerrilla attacks, frustrated by elaborate and often corrupt bureaucracies, and deficient in trained personnel. While grap-

---

*In 1989, the net transfer of capital leaving Latin America was around $25 billion.

pling with these weaknesses, they discovered that the Western world which applauded the return to democracy was unsympathetic to fresh lending, increasingly inclined to protectionism, and insistent on unilateral measures (e.g. in the Amazon rain forests) to stop global warming.

Two other weaknesses also slow any hoped-for recovery. One is the unimpressive accomplishments of the educational systems. This is not due to an absence of schools and universities, as in parts of Africa. Many Latin American countries have extensive public education, dozens of universities, and high adult literacy rates; Brazil, for example, has sixty-eight universities, Argentina forty-one.[29] The real problem is neglect and underinvestment. One citizen recently bemoaned the collapse in Argentina as follows:

> Education, which kept illiteracy at bay for more than a century, lies in ruins. The universities are unheated and many public schools lack panes for their window frames. Last summer [1990] an elementary school teacher with ten years' experience earned less than $110 a month. An associate professor at the Universidad de Buenos Aires, teaching ten hours a week, was paid $37 a month. A doctor's salary at a municipal hospital was $120 a month. . . . At times, teachers took turns teaching, or cut their class hours, because they and their students could not afford transportation.[30]

Presumably, if resources were available, those decaying educational and health-care structures could be resuscitated, helping national recovery; but where the capital can be raised in present circumstances is difficult to see. Moreover, in the strife-torn countries of Central America there is little education to begin with; in Guatemala, the latest census estimated that 63 percent of those ten years of age and older were illiterate, while in Honduras the illiteracy rate was 40 percent.[31] Unfortunately, it is in the most educationally deprived Latin American countries that resources are being eroded by swift population increases.

Despite these disadvantages, recent reports on Latin America have suggested that the "lost decade" of the 1980s will be followed by a period of recovery. The coming of democratic regimes, the compromises emerging from protracted debt-recycling talks, the stiff economic reforms (cutting public spending, abandoning indexation) to reduce inflation rates, the replacement of "state protectionism with import liberalization and privatization,"[32] the conversion of budget deficits into surpluses . . . all these have caused the Inter-American Development Bank to argue that "a decisive and genuine takeoff" is at hand, provided the new policies are sustained.[33] Growth began to resume in Argentina, Mexico, and Venezuela. Even investment bankers are reported to be returning to the continent. Whether these changes are going to be enough remains uncertain, especially since the newly elected governments face widespread resentment at the proposed reforms. As one commentator put it, "Much of Latin America is entering the 1990s in a race between economic deterioration and political progress."[34] Whereas Spain, Portugal, and Greece moved to democracy while enjoying reasonable prosperity, Latin America (like Eastern Europe) has to make that change as its economies flounder—which places immense responsibilities upon the political leadership.

Although it can be argued that the region's future is in its own hands, it will also be heavily influenced by the United States. In many ways, the U.S.–Latin America relationship is similar to that between Japan and the East Asian NIEs, which are heavily dependent upon Japan as their major market and source of capital.[35] Yet there is more to this relationship than Latin America's economic dependence upon the United States, whose banking system has also suffered because of Latin American indebtedness. U.S. exports, which are fifty times larger to this region than to Eastern Europe, were badly hurt by Latin America's economic difficulties and would benefit greatly from a resumption of growth. The United States' own environment may now be threatened by the diminution of the Amazon and Central American rain forests. Its awful drug problem, driven by domestic demand, is fueled by Latin American supplies—more than 80 percent of the cocaine and 90 percent of the marijuana entering the United States are produced or move through this region. Finally, the population of the United States is being altered by migration from Mexico, the Caribbean, and Central America; if there should be a widespread socioeconomic collapse south of the Rio Grande, the "spillover" effects will be felt across the United States. Instead of being marginalized by the end of the Cold War, Latin America may present Washington with a set of awesome challenges—social, environmental, financial, and ultimately political.[36]

Thus, while the region's own politicians and publics have to bear the major responsibility for recovery, richer nations—especially the United States—may find it in their own best interest to lend a hand.

If these remarks disappoint readers in Brazil or Peru, they may care to glance, in grim consolation, at the world of Islam. It is one thing to face population pressures, shortage of resources, educational/techno-logical deficiencies, and regional conflicts which would challenge the wisest governments. But it is another when the regimes themselves stand in angry resentment of global forces for change instead of (as in East Asia) selectively responding to such trends. Far from preparing for the twenty-first century, much of the Arab and Muslim world appears to have difficulty in coming to terms with the nineteenth century, with its composite legacy of secularization, democracy, laissez-faire econom-ics, transnational industrial and commercial linkages, social change, and intellectual questioning. If one needed an example of the impor-tance of cultural attitudes in explaining a society's response to change, contemporary Islam provides it.

Before analyzing the distinctive role of Islamic culture, one should note the danger of generalizing about an area that contains such vari-ety. After all, it is not even clear what *name* should be used to describe this part of the earth. To term it "the Middle East"[37] is, apart from revealing an Atlantic-centered bias, to leave out such North African states as Libya, Tunisia, Algeria, and Morocco. To term it "the Arab World"[38] is to exclude Iran (and, of course, Israel), the Kurds, and the non-Muslim tribes of southern Sudan and Mauretania. Even the no-menclature "Islam," or "the Muslim world," disguises the fact that many millions in the region are Christian, Copts, and Jews, and that Islamic societies extend from West Africa to Indonesia.[39]

In addition, the uneven location of oil in the Middle East has created a dichotomy between super-rich and dreadfully poor societies that has no equivalent in Central America or sub-Saharan Africa.* Countries

---

*The few oil-producing countries in Africa, such as Gabon and Nigeria, still have low per capita GNPs compared with the Arab Gulf states.

like Kuwait (2 million), the United Arab Emirates (1.3 million), and Saudi Arabia (11.5 million) enjoy some of the world's highest incomes, but exist alongside populous neighbors one-third (Jordan, Iran, Iraq) or even one-tenth as rich (Egypt, Yemen). The gap is accentuated by different political systems: conservative, antidemocratic, traditionalist in the Gulf sheikhdoms; demagogic, populist, militarized in countries such as Libya, Syria, Iraq, and Iran. The 1990 Iraqi attack upon Kuwait and the different responses of the Saudi elites on the one hand and the street masses in Amman or Rabat on the other illustrated this divide between "haves" and "have-nots" in the Muslim world. The presence of millions of Egyptian, Yemeni, Jordanian, and Palestinian guest workers in the oil-rich states simply increased the mutual resentments, while the Saudi and Emirate habit of giving massive aid to Iraq during its war against Iran or to Egypt to assist its economic needs reinforces the impression of wealthy but precarious regimes seeking to achieve security by bribing their larger, jealous neighbors.[40] Is it any wonder that the unemployed, badly housed urban masses, despairing of their own secular advancement, are attracted to religious leaders or "strongmen" appealing to Islamic pride, a sense of identity, and resistance to foreign powers and their local lackeys?

More than in any other developing region, then, the future of the Middle East and North Africa is affected by issues of war and conflict. The area probably contains more soldiers, aircraft, missiles, and other weaponry than anywhere else in the world, with billions of dollars of armaments having been supplied by Western, Soviet, and Chinese producers during the past few decades. Given the range and destructiveness of these weapons, another Arab-Israeli war would be a nightmare, yet many Muslim states still regard Israel with acute hostility. Even if the Arab-Israeli antagonism did not exist, the region is full of other rivalries, between Syria and Iraq, Libya and Egypt, Iran and Iraq, and so on. Vicious one-man dictatorships glare threateningly at archconservative, antidemocratic, feudal sheikhdoms. Fundamentalist regimes exist from Iran to the Sudan. Terrorist groups in exile threaten to eliminate their foes. Unrest among the masses puts a question over the future of Egypt, Algeria, Morocco, Jordan.[41] The recent fate of Lebanon, instead of serving as a warning against sectarian fanaticism, is more often viewed as a lesson in power politics, that the strong will devour the weak.

To the Western observer brought up in Enlightenment traditions— or, for that matter, to economic rationalists preaching the virtues of the borderless world—the answer to the Muslim nations' problems would appear to be a massive program of *education,* not simply in the techni- cal, skills-acquiring sense but also to advance parliamentary discourse, pluralism, and a secular civic culture. Is that not the reason, after all, for the political stability and economic success of Scandinavia or Japan today?

If that argument is correct, then such an observer would find few of those features in contemporary Islam. In countries where fundamental- ism is strong, there is little or no prospect of education or advancement for the female half of the population.* Where engineers and techni- cians exist, their expertise has all too often been mobilized for war purposes, as in Iraq. Tragically, Egypt possesses a large and bustling university system but a totally inadequate number of jobs for graduates and skilled workers, so that millions of both are underemployed. In Yemen, the overall state of education is dismal. By contrast, the oil-rich states have poured massive resources into schools, technical institutes, and universities, but that alone is insufficient to create an "enterprise culture" that would produce export-led manufacturing along East Asian lines. Ironically, possession of vast oil reserves could be a *disad- vantage,* since it reduces the incentive to rely upon the skills and quality of the people, as occurs in countries (Japan, Switzerland) with few natural resources. Such discouraging circumstances may also explain why many educated and entrepreneurial Arabs, who passionately wanted their societies to borrow from the West, have emigrated.

It is difficult to know whether the reason for the Muslim world's troubled condition is cultural or historical. Western critics who point to the region's religious intolerance, technological backwardness, and a feudal cast of mind often forget that centuries before the Reforma- tion, Islam led the world in mathematics, cartography, medicine, and

*In 1985, adult female literacy in the Yemen Arab Republic was a mere 3 percent, in Saudi Arabia 12 percent, in Iran 39 percent. On the other hand, many women from the middle and upper middle classes in Muslim countries are educated, which suggests that poverty, as much as culture, plays a role.

many other aspects of science and industry, and contained libraries, universities, and observatories when Japan and America possessed none and Europe only a few. These assets were later sacrificed to a revival of traditionalist thought and the sectarian split between Shi'ite and Sunni Muslims, but Islam's retreat into itself—its being "out of step with History," as one author termed it[42]—was probably also a response to the rise of a successful, expansionist Europe. Sailing along the Arab littoral, assisting in the demise of the Mughal Empire, penetrating strategic points with railways, canals, and ports, steadily moving into North Africa, the Nile Valley, the Persian Gulf, the Levant, and then Arabia itself, dividing the Middle East along unnatural boundaries as part of a post–World War I diplomatic bargain, developing American power to buttress and then replace European influences, inserting an Israeli state in the midst of Arab peoples, instigating coups against local popular leaders, and usually indicating that this part of the globe was important only for its oil, the West may have played more of a role in turning the Muslim world into what it is today than outside commentators are willing to recognize.[43] Clearly, Islam suffers many self-inflicted problems. But if much of its angry, confrontational stance toward the international order today *is* due to a long-held fear of being swallowed up by the West, not much in the way of change can be expected until that fear is dissipated.

The condition of sub-Saharan Africa—"the Third World's Third World," as it has been described—is even more desperate.[44] When one considers recent developments such as *perestroika* in the former Soviet Union, the coming integration of Europe, and the economic miracle of Japan and the East Asian NIEs, remarked a former president of Nigeria, General Olusegun Obasanjo, "contrasting all this with what is taking place in Africa, it is difficult to believe that we inhabit the same historical time."[45] Recent reports upon the continent's plight are extraordinarily gloomy, describing Africa as "a human and environmental disaster area," as "moribund," "marginalized," and "peripheral to the rest of the world," and as having so many intractable problems that some foreign development experts are abandoning it to work elsewhere. In the view of the World Bank, virtually everywhere else in the world is likely to experience a decline in poverty by the year 2000 *except* Africa, where things will only get worse.[46] "Sub-Saharan Africa," concludes one economist, "suffers from a combination of economic, social, political, institutional, and environmental handicaps which have so far largely defied development efforts by the African countries and their donors."[47] How, an empathetic study asks, can Africa survive?[48]

The unanimity of views is remarkable, given the enormous variety among the forty-five states that compose sub-Saharan Africa.* Nine of them have less than 1 million people each, whereas Nigeria contains about 110 million. Some lie in the desert, some in tropical rain forests. Many are rich in mineral deposits, others have only scrubland. While a number (Botswana, Cameroon, Congo, Gabon, Kenya) have seen significant increases in living standards since independence, they are the exception—suggesting that the obstacles to growth on East Asian lines are so deep-rooted and resistant to the "development strategies" of foreign experts and/or their own leaders that it may require profound attitudinal changes to achieve recovery.

This was not the mood thirty years ago, when the peoples of Africa were gaining their independence. True, there was economic backwardness, but this was assumed to have been caused by decades of foreign rule, leading to dependency upon a single metropolitan market, monoculture, lack of access to capital, and so on. Now that Africans had control of their destinies, they could build industries, develop cities, airports, and infrastructure, and attract foreign investment and aid from either Western powers or the USSR and its partners. The 1950s–1960s boom in world trade and demand for commodities strengthened this optimism. Although there were individual areas of need, Africa as a whole was self-sufficient in food and, in fact, a net food exporter. Externally, African states were of increasing importance at the United Nations and other world bodies.

What went wrong? The unhappy answer is "lots of things." The first, and perhaps most serious, was that over the following three decades the population mushroomed as imported medical techniques

*As will be clear from the text, this discussion excludes the Republic of South Africa.

and a reduction in malaria-borne mosquitoes drastically curtailed infant mortality. Africa's population was already increasing at an average annual rate of 2.6 percent in the 1960s, jumped to 2.9 percent during the 1970s, and increased to over 3.0 percent by the late 1980s, implying a doubling in size every twenty-two years; this was, therefore, the highest rate for any region in the world.[49] In certain countries, the increases were staggering. Between 1960 and 1990, Kenya's population quadrupled, from 6.3 million to 25.1 million, and Côte d'Ivoire's jumped from 3.8 million to 12.6 million. Altogether, Africa's population—including the North African states—leaped from 281 to 647 million in three decades.[50] Moreover, while the majority of Africans inhabit rural settlements, the continent has been urbanizing at dizzying speed. Vast shanty cities have already emerged on the edges of national capitals (Accra, Monrovia, Lilongwe). By 2025, urban dwellers are forecast to make up 55 percent of Africa's total population.

The worst news is that the increase is unlikely to diminish in the near future. Although most African countries spend less than 1 percent of GNP on health care and consequently have the highest infant mortality rates in the world—in Mali, for example, there are 169 infant deaths for every thousand live births—those rates are substantially less than they were a quarter century ago and will tumble further in the future, which is why demographers forecast that Africa's population in 2025 could be nearly three times that of today.[51] Another reason that this demographic boom will not be halted swiftly is traditional African belief systems concerning fecundity, children, ancestors, and the role of women. Acutely aware of the invisible but pervasive presence of their ancestors, determined to expand their lineage, regarding childlessness or small families as the work of evil spirits, most Africans seek to have as many children as possible; a woman's virtue and usefulness are measured by the number of offspring she can bear. "Desired family size," according to polls of African women, ranges from five to nine children. The social attitudes that lead women in North America, Europe, and Japan to delay childbearing—education, career ambitions, desire for independence—scarcely exist in African societies; where such emerge, they are swiftly suppressed by familial pressures.[52]

This population growth has not been accompanied by equal or larger increases in Africa's productivity, which would of course transform the picture. During the 1960s, farm output was rising by around 3 percent each year, keeping pace with the population, but since 1970, agricultural production has grown at only half that rate. Part of this decline was due to the drought, hitting most countries south of the Sahara. Furthermore, existing agricultural resources have been badly eroded by overgrazing—caused by the sharp rise in the number of cattle and goats—as well as by deforestation—to provide fuel and shelter for the growing population. When rain falls, the water runs off the denuded fields, taking the topsoil with it. None of this was helped by changes in agricultural production, with farmers encouraged to grow tea, coffee, cocoa, palm oil, and rubber for export rather than food for domestic consumption. After benefiting from high commodity prices in the early stages, producers suffered a number of blows; heavy taxation on cash crops, plus mandatory governmental marketing, reduced the incentives to increase output; competition grew from Asian and Latin American producers; many African currencies were overvalued, which hurt exports; and in the mid-1970s world commodity prices tumbled. Yet the cost of imported manufactures and foodstuffs remained high, and sub-Saharan Africa was badly hurt by the quadrupling of oil prices.[53]

These blows increased Africa's indebtedness, in a qualitatively different way. Early, postcolonial borrowings were driven by the desire for modernity, as money was poured into cement works, steel plants, airports, harbors, national airlines, electrification schemes, and telephone networks. Much of it suffered from bureaucratic interference, a lack of skilled personnel, unrealistic planning, and inadequate basic facilities, and now lies half finished or (where completed) suffers from lack of upkeep. But borrowing to pay for imported oil, or to feed half the nation's population, means that indebtedness rises without any possible return upon funds. In consequence, Africa's total debt expanded from $14 billion in 1973 to $125 billion in 1987, when its capacity to repay was dropping fast; by the mid-1980s, payments on loans consumed about half of Africa's export earnings, a proportion even greater than for Latin American debtor nations. Following repeated debt reschedulings, Western bankers—never enthusiastic to begin with—virtually abandoned private loans to Africa.[54]

As a result, Africa's economy is in a far worse condition now than at Independence, apart from a few countries like Botswana and

Mauritius. Perhaps the most startling illustration of its plight is the fact that "excluding South Africa, the nations of sub-Saharan Africa with their 450 million people have a total GDP less than that of Belgium's 11 million people"; in fact, the entire continent generates roughly 1 percent of world GDP.[55] Its share of world markets has shriveled just as East Asia's share has risen fast. Plans for modernization lie unrealized. Manufacturing still represents only 11 percent of Africa's economic activity—scarcely up from the 9 percent share in 1965; and only 12 percent of the continent's exports is composed of manufactures (compared with Korea's 90 percent). There is a marked increase in the signs of decay: crumbling infrastructure, power failures, broken-down communications, abandoned projects, and everywhere the pressure of providing for increasing populations. Already Africa needs to import 15 million tonnes of maize a year to achieve minimal levels of food consumption, but with population increasing faster than agricultural output, that total could multiply over the next decade—implying an even greater diversion of funds from investment and infrastructure.[56]

Two further characteristics worsen Africa's condition. The first is the prevalence of wars, coups d'état, and political instability. This is partly the legacy of the European "carve-up" of Africa, when colonial boundaries were drawn without regard for the differing tribes and ethnic groups,* or even of earlier conquests by successful tribes of neighboring lands and peoples; Ethiopia, for example, is said to contain seventy-six ethnic groups and 286 languages.[57] While it is generally accepted that those boundaries cannot be unscrambled, most of them are clearly artificial. Governments are not a focus of loyalty (except perhaps to kinsmen of the group in power), and ethnic tensions have produced innumerable civil wars—from Biafra's attempt to secede from Nigeria, to the conflict between Arab north and African south in the Sudan, to Eritrean struggles to escape from Ethiopia, to the Tutsi-Hutu struggle in Burundi, to clashes and suppressions and guerrilla campaigns from Uganda to the western Sahara, from Angola to Mozambique.[58]

These antagonisms have often been worsened by struggles over ideology and government authority. The rulers of many new African states

---

*In this regard, East Asian nations like Taiwan and Korea, possessing coherent indigenous populations, are once again more favorably situated.

rapidly switched to either a personal dictatorship or single-party rule. They also embraced a Soviet or Maoist political economy, instituting price controls, production targets, forced industrialization, the takeover of private enterprises, and other features of "scientific socialism" that—unbeknownst to them—were destroying the Soviet economy. Agriculture was neglected, while bureaucracy flourished. The result was the disappearance of agricultural surpluses, inattention to manufacturing for the world market, and the expansion of party and government bureaucracies, exacerbating the region's problems.

The second weakness was the totally inadequate investment in human resources and in developing a culture of entrepreneurship, scientific inquiry, and technical prowess. According to one survey, Africa has been spending less than $1 each year on research and development per head of population, whereas the United States was spending $200 per head. Consequently, Africa's scientific population has always trailed the rest of the world.

In many African countries—Malawi, Zambia, Lesotho, Somalia— government spending on education has fallen, so that after some decades of advance, a smaller share of children are now in school. While there is a hunger for learning, it cannot be satisfied beyond the secondary level except for a small minority. Angola, for example, had 2.4 million pupils in primary schools in 1982–83, but only 153,000 in secondary schools and a mere 4,700 in higher education.[59] By contrast, Sweden, with a slightly smaller total population, had 570,000 in secondary education and 179,000 in higher education.[60] Among the 5 million inhabitants of Burundi in 1984, only 218 were scientists and engineers. While African scientists urgently call for leadership that "personally

Table 11. Numbers of Scientists and Engineers
per Million of Population[61]

Japan	3,548
U.S.	2,685
Europe	1,632
Latin America	209
Arab states	202
Asia (minus Japan)	99
Africa	53

takes science and technology as the key element for the transformation of society,"[62] the circumstances by which so many African leaders rose to power (e.g., military coups d'état) and the struggle to hold their countries together make a science-led strategy highly unlikely.

Despite these relative weaknesses, some observers claim to have detected signs of a turnaround. With the exception of dyed-in-the-wool African socialists,[63] many leaders are now attempting to institute reforms. In return for "structural adjustments," that is, measures to encourage free enterprise, certain African societies have secured additional loans from Western nations and the World Bank. The latter organization has identified past errors (many of them urged upon African governments and funded by itself) and encouraged economic reforms. Mozambique, Ghana, and Zambia have all claimed recent successes in reversing negative growth, albeit at considerable social cost. Democratic principles are also returning to the continent: the dismantling of apartheid in South Africa, the cease-fire in Angola, the independence of Namibia, the success of Botswana's record of democracy and prosperity, the cries for reforms in Gabon, Kenya, and Zaire, the rising awareness among African intellectuals of the transformations in East Asia, may all help—so the argument goes—to change attitudes, which is the prerequisite for recovery.[64] Moreover, at the grass-roots level, there are examples of economic self-improvement, cooperative ventures to halt erosion and improve yields, and village-based schemes of improvement.[65] This is, after all, a continent of enormous agricultural and mineral resources, provided they can be sensibly exploited.

Despite such signs of promise, conditions are likely to stay bad. Population increases, the diminution of grazing lands and food supplies, the burdens of indebtedness, the decay of infrastructures, the reduction of spending upon health care and education, the residual strength of animist religions and traditional belief systems, the powerful hold of corrupt bureaucracies and ethnic loyalties . . . all those tilt against the relatively few African political leaders, educators, scientists, and economists who perceive the need for changes. As Africa struggles to stay connected with the rest of the world, the indications—declining amounts of aid, shrinking trade and investment flows, reduction in media coverage, diminished superpower involvement—are that it is becoming more peripheral. Some experts argue that disengagement by developed countries might have the positive effect of compelling Africans to begin a *self-driven* recovery, as well as ending the misuse of aid monies.[66] Others feel that Africa cannot live without the West, although its leaders and publics will have to abandon existing habits, and development aid must be more intelligently applied.[67] Whichever view is correct, the coming decade will be critical for Africa. Even a partial recovery would give grounds for hope; on the other hand, a second decade of decline, together with a further surge in population, would result in catastrophe.

The developing countries' response to the broad forces for global change is, clearly, going to be uneven. While some are in distress, others are booming—but what else ought one to expect when analyzing nations ranging from Singapore to Burkina Faso? Furthermore, the signs are that the gap will widen; one group enjoys interacting beneficial trends, while others suffer from linked weaknesses and deficiencies.[68]

This is most clearly the case in respect to demography. As noted earlier, the commitment of East Asian trading states to education, manufacturing, *and* export-led growth produced a steady rise in living standards and allowed those societies to make the demographic transition to smaller family sizes. This was in marked contrast to sub-Saharan Africa, where different cultural attitudes and social structures, improved health care, and rising incomes led not to a drop in population growth but to the opposite. Just before independence in 1960, for example, the average Kenyan woman had 6.2 children, whereas by 1980 she had 8.2[69]—and that in a period when Africa's economic prospects were fading.

In Africa's case the "global trend" which influences all others is the demographic explosion. It spills into every domain—overgrazing, local conflicts over water and wood supplies, massive unplanned urbanization, strains upon the educational and social structures, reliance upon imported food supplies (at the cost of increasing indebtedness), ethnic tensions, domestic unrest, border wars. Only belatedly are some African governments working to persuade families to limit their size as people become aware that access to family planning and improved educational opportunities for women produce significant declines in birth rates. Against such promising indications stand the many cultural, gender-related, and economic forces described above that encourage large families. This resistance to change is aided by Africa's general lack of resources. Raising Somalia's female literacy rate (6 percent) to South Korea's (88 percent) to produce a demographic transition sounds fine until one considers how that massive reform could be implemented and paid for. Unfortunately, the projections suggest that as Africa's population almost trebles over the next few decades, the only development curtailing it could be the rapid growth of AIDS.*[70]

In many parts of Latin America, the demographic explosion will also affect the capacity to handle globally driven forces for change. While wide differences in total fertility rates exist between the moderate-climate countries and those in the tropics, the overall picture is that Latin America's population, which was roughly equal to the United States and Canada's in 1960, is increasing so swiftly that it will be more than double the latter in 2025.†[71] Even if birth rates are now declining in the larger countries, there will still be enormous increases; Mexico's population will leap to 150 million by 2025 and Brazil's to 245 million.[72] This implies a massive incidence of child poverty and malnutrition, further strain upon already inadequate health-care and educational services, the crowding of millions of human beings into a dozen or more "megacities," pollution, and the degradation of grazing land, forests, and other natural resources. In Mexico, for example, 44 million are without sewers and 21 million without potable water, which means that when disease (e.g., cholera) strikes, it spreads swiftly.[73] These are not strong foundations upon which to improve the region's relative standing in an increasingly competitive international economic order.

In this regard, many Muslim states are in a similar or worse position; in no Arab country is the population increasing by less than 2 percent a year,[74] and in most the rate is considerably higher. The region's total population of more than 200 million will double in less than twenty-five years, and city populations are growing twice as fast as national aver-

---

*Discussed above on pp. 27–29.

†The U.S./Canada total in 1960 was 217 million, to Latin America's 210 million; by 2025, it is estimated, the figures will be 332 million and 762 million.

ages. This puts enormous pressures upon scarce food, water, and land resources and produces unbalanced populations. Already, in most Arab countries at least four out of every ten people are under the age of fifteen—the classic recipe for subsequent social unrest and political revolution. "Walk along Avenue Habib Bourgiuba, the main street of Tunis, on any working day and you will see cafés brimming with bored young men; up to 40 percent of Tunisians are unemployed. Sleepy Casablanca has become a city of 3 million souls, with a swelling penumbra of slums. Food riots broke out in Morocco's northern cities in 1984. Greater Cairo is home to 13 million people, hundreds of thousands of whom make their homes in cemeteries, cardboard shanties, alleys, and doorways. . . ." One in five Egyptian workers is jobless, as is one in four Algerian workers.[75] In what is widely regarded as the most turbulent part of the world, therefore, demography is contributing to the prospects of future unrest year by year. Even the Israeli-Palestine quarrel has become an issue of demography, with the influx of Soviet Jews intended to counter the greater fertility of the Palestinians.

There is, moreover, little likelihood that population growth will fall in the near future, since infant mortality rates in many Muslim countries are still high, which means that further improvements in prenatal and postnatal care will produce rises in the birth rate, as is happening in the Gulf states and Saudi Arabia.

As elsewhere, politics intrudes; many regimes are deliberately encouraging women to have large families, arguing that this adds to the

Table 12. Comparative Infant Mortality Rates[76]
(infant deaths per 1,000 live births)

	1965–70	*1985–90*
Algeria	150	74
Egypt	170	85
Sudan	156	108
Yemen Arab Republic	186	116
Saudi Arabia	140	71
Kuwait	55	19
Iraq	111	69
Japan	16	5
U.S.	22	10
Sweden	13	6

country's military strength. "Bear a child," posters in Iraq proclaim, "and you pierce an arrow in the enemy's eye."[77] Countries such as Iraq and Libya offer many incentives for larger families, as do the Gulf states and Saudi Arabia, anxious to fill their oil-rich lands with native-born rather than foreign workers. Only in Egypt are propaganda campaigns launched to curb family size, but even if that is successful—despite resistance from the Muslim Brotherhood—present numbers are disturbing. With a current population of over 55 million Egyptians, six out of ten of whom are under twenty, and with an additional million being born every eight months, the country is in danger of bursting at the seams during the next few decades.

For much the same reasons, we ought to expect a differentiated success rate among developing countries in handling environmental challenges, with the East Asian NIEs way ahead of the others. This is not to ignore significant local schemes to improve the ecology that are springing up in Africa and the interesting proposals for "sustainable development" elsewhere in the developing world,[78] or to forget that industrialization has caused environmental damage in East Asia, from choked roads to diminished forests. Yet the fact is that nations with lots of resources (capital, scientists, engineers, technology, a per capita GNP of over $4,000) are better able to deal with environmental threats than those without monies, tools, and personnel. There is also a "feedback loop" between high educational levels, enhanced ecological consciousness, and a willingness to prevent environmental damage, which suggests that East Asia will be more responsive in this field. By contrast, it is the poorer societies (Egypt, Bangladesh, Ethiopia) which, lacking financial and personnel resources, find it difficult to respond to cyclones, floods, drought, and other natural disasters—with their devastated populations augmenting the millions of refugees and migrants. Should global warming produce sea-level rises and heightened storm surges, teeming island populations from the Caribbean to the Pacific are in danger of being washed away.[79]

Finally, it is Latin America's, South Asia's, and Africa's population explosion that is the major cause for the overgrazing, soil erosion, salinization, and clearing of the tropical rain forests, which, while contributing to global warming, also hurt the local populations and exacerbate regional struggles for power. Elsewhere, in the Middle East for example, supplies of water are the greatest concern, especially in view of growing demographic pressures. Already, the average Jordanian uses only one-third the amount of domestic water consumed in Israel and has little hope of increasing the supply, yet Jordan's population is expected to double during the next twenty years.[80] With all governments in the area striving to boost agricultural output, and highly sensitive to famine and unrest among their peasant farmers, the search for secure water influences domestic politics, international relations, and spending priorities. Egypt worries that either the Sudan or Ethiopia might dam the Nile in order to increase irrigation. Syria and Iraq have taken alarm at Turkey's new Ataturk Dam, which can interrupt the flow of the Euphrates. Jordan, Syria, and Israel quarrel over water rights in the Litani, Yarmuk, and Jordan river valleys, as do Arabs and Jews over well supplies in the occupied West Bank. Saudi Arabia's ambition to grow wheat is draining its aquifers, and the same will occur with Libya's gigantic scheme to tap water from under the Sahara.[81] As more and more people struggle for the same—or diminishing— amounts of water, grand ideas about preparing for the twenty-first century look increasingly irrelevant; surviving *this* century becomes the issue.

On the other hand, the revolution in biotech farming is of great relevance to developing countries, even if the consequences will be mixed. Improved strains of plants and more sophisticated pesticides and fertilizers could, potentially, enhance yields in the developing world, reduce pressures upon marginal lands, restore agricultural self-sufficiency, improve the balance of payments, and raise standards of living. Since much biotech does not involve expensive enterprise, we could witness farmers' groups experimenting with new seeds, improved breeding techniques, cultivation of gene tissue, regional gene banks, and other developments. On the other hand, it is also possible that giant pharmaceutical and agrochemical firms in the "First" World may monopolize much of the knowledge—and the profit—that this transformation implies. Global foodstuff surpluses caused by the biotech revolution could be used to counter malnutrition. They could also undermine commodity prices and hurt societies in which most inhabitants are employed in agriculture. Dematerializing food production would undercut agrarian societies, which is why some biotech experts in the development field call for serious planning in "agricultural conversion," that is, conversion into other economic activities.[82]

As noted earlier,* all this depends on whether the new technology is employed chiefly to enhance traditional ways of growing food and made accessible (through international agencies, technology transfer, etc.) to farmers in the developing world, or is directed toward *in vitro* food production and processing in the laboratories of proprietary multinationals, rendering traditional agriculture obsolete. Should the latter trend prevail, a high-tech manufacturing country with a diminishing agricultural sector (e.g., Korea) will find it easier to adjust than a society reliant upon commodity exports (e.g., Gambia, Ivory Coast, Costa Rica).

While the uses of biotechnology are relatively diverse, that is not the case with robotics and automated manufacture. The requirements for an indigenous robotics industry—capital, an advanced electronics sector, design engineers, a dearth of skilled labor—suggest that countries like Taiwan and Korea may follow Japan's example out of concern that its automation will make their own products uncompetitive. On the other hand, automated factories assembling goods more swiftly, regularly, and economically than human beings poses a challenge to *middle-income* economies (Malaysia, Mexico) whose comparative advantage would be undercut. As for countries without a manufacturing base, it is difficult to see how the robotics revolution would have any meaning—except to further devalue the resource which they possess in abundance, masses of impoverished and undereducated human beings.

Finally, the global financial and communications revolution and the emergence of multinational corporations threaten to increase the gap between richer and poorer countries, even in the developing world. The industrial conglomerates of Korea are now positioning themselves to become multinational, and the East Asian NIEs in general are able to exploit the world economy (as can be seen in their trade balances, stock markets, electronics industries, strategic marketing alliances, and so on). Furthermore, if the borderless world rewards entrepreneurs, designers, brokers, patent owners, lawyers, and dealers in high-value-added services, then East Asia's commitment to education, science,

*See Chapter 4.

and technology can only increase its lead over other developing economies. By contrast, their relative lack of capital, high technology, scientists and skilled workers, and export-oriented industry makes it difficult
for poorer countries to partake in the communications and financial
revolution, although several states (Brazil, India) clearly hope to do so.
Some grimmer forecasts suggest the developing world may become
more marginalized, partly because of the dematerialization of labor,
raw materials, and foodstuffs, partly because the advanced economies
may concentrate upon greater knowledge-based commerce among
themselves.

Is there any way of turning this around? Obviously, a society strongly
influenced by fundamentalist mullahs with a dislike of "modernization" is unlikely to join the international economy; and it does not *have*
to enter the borderless world if its people believe that it would be
healthier, spiritually if not economically, to remain outside. Nor ought
we to expect that countries dominated by selfish, authoritarian elites
bent upon enhancing their military power—developing world countries
spent almost $150 billion on weapons and armies in 1988 alone—will
rush to imitate Japan and Singapore.

But what about those societies that wish to improve themselves yet
find that they are hampered by circumstances? There are, after all, *so*
many developing countries, the vast majority of which depend upon
exporting food and raw materials. With dozens of poor countries seeking desperately to sell their cane sugar or bananas or timber or coffee
in the global market, prices fall, and they are made more desperate.[83]
Moreover, although much international aid goes to the developing
world, in fact far more money flows *out of* impoverished countries of
Africa, Asia, and Latin America and *into* the richer economies of
Europe, North America, and Japan—to the tune of at least $43 billion
each year.[84] This outward flow of interest repayments, repatriated
profits, capital flight, royalties, and fees for patents and information
services makes it difficult for poorer countries to get to their feet; and
even if they were able to increase their industrial output, the result
might be a massive rise in "the costs of technological dependence."[85]
Like their increasing reliance upon Northern suppliers for food and
medical aid, this has created another dependency relationship for
poorer nations.

This structural underdevelopment also extends to communications. Many developing countries have accused richer nations of cultural domination by control of the major news-collecting resources, by the unstinted flow of their cultural products, by the power of advertising agencies, international newspaper chains, and newsprint companies, and by their hold over broadcasting, navigation, and much else.[86] While it is true that *no* government nowadays can control the communications revolution, it remains important politically whose viewpoints (on free enterprise, North-South relations, cultural and religious issues) the new global media will favor. How, it is asked, can poorer countries be expected to benefit from the communications and financial revolution when they suffer from "the swamping effect of this vast machinery" which represses traditional cultures and gives them no voice on the world stage?[87]

In sum, as we move into the next century the developed economies appear to have all the trump cards in their hands—capital, technology, control of communications, surplus foodstuffs, powerful multinational companies[88]—and, if anything, their advantages are *growing* because technology is eroding the value of labor and materials, the chief assets of developing countries. Although nominally independent since decolonization, these countries are probably more dependent upon Europe and the United States than a century ago. Ironically, three or four decades of efforts by developing countries to gain control of their own destinies—by nationalizing Western companies, setting up commodity-exporting cartels, subsidizing indigenous manufacturing to achieve import substitution, campaigning for a new world order based upon redistribution of the existing imbalances of wealth—have all failed. The "market," backed by governments of the developed economies, has proved too strong, and the struggle against it has weakened developing economies still further—except those (like Korea and Taiwan) which decided to join.

While the gap between rich and poor in today's world is disturbing, those arguing this structuralist viewpoint have all too often supported heavy-handed state interventionism and a retreat from open competition, which preserved indigenous production in the short term but rendered it less efficient against those stimulated by market forces. "Scientific socialism for Africa" may still appeal to some intellectuals,[89] but by encouraging societies to look inward it made them less well equipped to move to ever-higher-value-added manufacturing. And a new "world communications order," as proposed a few years ago by UNESCO to balance the West's dominance, sounds superficially attractive but would in all likelihood become the pawn of bureaucratic and ideological interests rather than function as an objective source of news reporting. On the other hand, the advocates of free-market forces often ignore the massive political difficulties which governments in developing countries would encounter in abolishing price controls, selling off national industries, and reducing food subsidies. They also forget that the spectacular commercial expansion of Japan and the East Asian NIEs was carried out by strong states which eschewed laissez-faire. Instead of copying either socialist or free-market systems, therefore, the developing countries might imitate East Asia's "mixed strategies" which combine official controls and private enterprise.[90]

Although the idea of a mixed strategy is intriguing, how can West or Central African countries imitate East Asia without a "strong state" apparatus, and with a weak tradition of cooperation between government and firms, far lower educational achievements, and a different set of cultural attitudes toward family size and international economics? With the global scene less welcoming to industrializing newcomers, how likely are they to achieve the same degree of success as the East Asian NIEs did, when they took off a quarter century ago?[91] Even if, by an economic miracle, the world's poorest fifty nations *did* adopt the Korean style of export-led growth in manufactures, would they not create the same crisis of industrial overproduction as exists in the commodity markets today?

How many developing nations will be able to follow East Asia's growth is impossible to tell. The 1991 *World Development Report* optimistically forecast significant progress across the globe, provided poorer nations adopt "market friendly" policies and richer nations eschew protectionism.[92] Were Taiwan and Korea to be followed by the larger states of Southeast Asia, then by South Asia and a number of Latin American countries, that would blur the North-South divide and make international economic alignments altogether more variegated. Moreover, sustained manufacturing success among developing countries *outside* East Asia might stimulate imitation elsewhere. At the moment, however, the usual cluster of factors influencing relative economic performance—cultural attitudes, education, political stability, capacity to carry out long-term plans—suggests that while a small but growing number of countries is moving from a "have-not" to a "have" status, many more remain behind. The story of winners and losers will continue, therefore, only this time modern communications will remind us all of the growing disparity.

11

THE ERSTWHILE USSR AND
ITS CRUMBLED EMPIRE

WHEN WRITING ABOUT THE PROSPECTS
for the states of the former Soviet Union, observers confront the same
problem that baffled them in 1918: not only is it hard to guess where
the region is headed, it is also unclear how far the disintegration from
unified empire to splintered subparts will go. So severe and complex is
the crisis that the only certain fact is the existence of innumerable
uncertainties. This makes it inordinately difficult to estimate the region's ability to prepare for the twenty-first century, since its leadership
is primarily concerned with surviving the present chaos and its people
are overwhelmed by the daily need to make ends meet. In such circumstances little energy is left to consider global trends, let alone adjust to
newer challenges.

Despite its current sociopolitical crisis, the successors to the USSR
possess a multitude of material resources. The Soviet Union consisted
of 22.4 million square kilometers or 8.6 million square miles, one-sixth
of the land surface of the globe. Strategically, that made it remarkably
invulnerable to external attack, as foreign warlords from Charles XII
of Sweden to Hitler discovered to their cost. Economically, it provided
a large internal market and a below-average dependency upon foreign
trade, advantages shared by such other extensive countries as China
and the United States. It also has, potentially, an enormous agricultural

base, with an arable area equal to that of the United States and Canada combined. Its 6,500-mile-wide landmass contains the world's largest array of raw materials; before its collapse, it was the biggest producer of iron, nickel, lead, oil, and natural gas, and the third-biggest producer of coal. It was the world's second-largest source of gold and chromium, and a leading producer of silver, copper, and zinc. Soviet scientists proudly claimed that the country contained "58 percent of the world's coal deposits, 58.7 percent of its oil, 41 percent of its iron ore, 76.7 percent of its apatite, 25 percent of all timberland, 88 percent of its manganese, 54 percent of its potassium salts, and nearly one-third of its phosphates."[1] While such statistical precision seems dubious, these lands are extraordinarily gifted in natural resources.

The exploitation of such resources from the late 1920s onward produced a massive industrial and manufacturing base. By the middle of World War II, and despite huge territorial losses, its economy became the second largest in the world, after America's. A few years ago Moscow boasted that it was first in the production of steel, pig iron, coke, oil, machine tools, diesel and electric trains, cement, mineral fertilizers, tractors, textiles, shoes, and prefabricated concrete structures.[2] In addition to its extensive rail and airline networks, it had a very considerable mercantile marine and the world's largest long-range fishing fleet.

This enormous territory is occupied by 288 million people (1989), with what was claimed to be one of the most comprehensive educational systems in the world. Education was free from seven to seventeen, but millions of children were in kindergarten and many part-time, correspondence, and vocational courses existed for those not in full-time higher education. According to the official statistics, about 100 million people were studying at schools, colleges, and training and correspondence courses in the early 1980s, including over 44 million pupils in 145,000 primary and secondary schools, 4.6 million students in the 4,380 technical colleges, and 5.2 million students in the nation's 883 universities and institutes.[3] The educational system was geared toward economic utility rather than the pursuit of knowledge for its own sake; this was reflected in the huge number of engineers in the Soviet Union—about 40 percent of higher-education graduates—and in the many technological and scientific institutions. Overall, the country claimed to possess about 14.9 million "economically active scientists and engineers" in 1985, supported by a further 17.4 million "economically active technicians."[4] The USSR also possessed 70,000 medical research staff, along with 960,000 doctors and dentists—more active physicians, in other words, than any other country in the world.[5] Given the numbers in science, technology, and engineering, and its achievements in mathematics and science, it is not surprising that the Soviet Union claimed great strengths in many fields, from low-temperature physics to plant research.[6]

In the view of its own leaders, at least until recently, the Soviet Union's greatest achievement was to become one of the world's two military superpowers, equaled only by the far wealthier United States. While the social and economic costs were great, Stalin and his successors never doubted the importance of massive armed forces, both to deter capitalist countries from aggression and, in the second stage, to exert influence upon world affairs.[7] Consequently, the Soviet Union possessed a staggering array of weapons, nuclear and conventional, and a vast force of personnel to use them, if necessary.[8] Even when the Gorbachev initiatives led to considerable reductions in weapons and manpower, the USSR still had the world's largest rocket forces, the second-largest army (after China), the second-largest navy (after the United States), and the largest air force and armored forces. If military power *does* count in the early twenty-first century, a federated successor state to the USSR—or even subparts such as Russia and the Ukraine—will possess plenty of it.

Given such material advantages, the region ought in theory to be better prepared than many less well endowed nations to meet the challenges of the coming century. Yet all this potential is weakened by profound and interconnected flaws that threaten the prospects for survival. As with large empires in the past, territorial size and resources alone will not prevent collapse if the system becomes inoperable.

At the heart of the Soviet problem there lay a triple crisis, each part feeding upon the other and accelerating the collapse. A crisis in the *political legitimacy* of the Soviet system interacted with a crisis in *economic production and social provision,* and both were exacerbated by a crisis in *ethnic and cultural relationships.* The result was an unsurmountable mix of challenges.

The sheer extent of the economic collapse was not realized until recently, partly because of the Kremlin's secrecy, partly because the West overestimated the efficiency of the Soviet economy. It is now evident that there was a long-term slowdown in growth even before the present crisis, as shown in Chart 7.

In all probability, these figures understate the real decline;[9] but the chief point is that while the Soviet economy was expanding throughout the middle third of the twentieth century, it has been stagnating in the final third. The earlier growth was due to massive "inputs" such as

Chart 7. The Decline in the Rate of Growth of Soviet GNP[10]

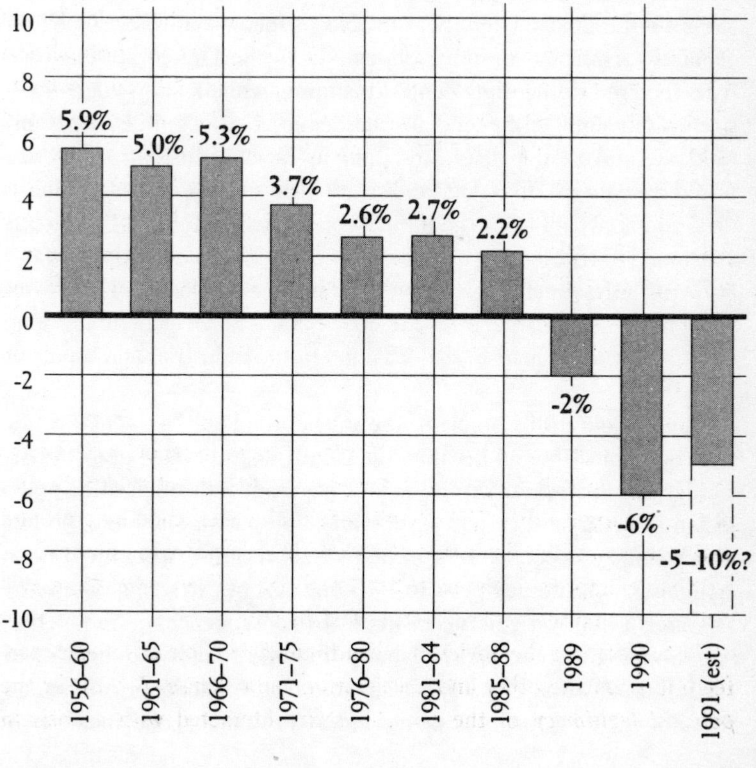

labor, cheap energy, and plentiful raw materials, ideal for building a heavy-industry economy of the 1930s and the postwar construction of the late 1940s and 1950s. Thus, iron and steel, cement, locomotives, machine tools, tractors, textiles, and prefabricated buildings were produced in large numbers according to a central plan. So long as targets were met, this tight socialist planning paid little attention to cost, sheltered management from competition and workers from unemployment, and was unconcerned about the consumer. Indeed, the only "consumers" to get what they wanted were the Soviet armed services, which enjoyed a preferential allocation of factories, machine tools, and skilled workers for military production.

When, from the 1960s onward, world manufacturing began to shift away from traditional heavy goods toward high-value-added, knowledge-intensive, and consumer-driven industries—computers, software electronics, automobiles, civilian aircraft, pharmaceuticals, communications—the Soviet Union was unable to follow suit. Developing an economy driven by consumer demand as in the United States would have required dismantling central planning, while a knowledge-intensive society implied an end to censorship, tight controls, party orthodoxy, and monopoly.[11] Investing in new manufacturing sectors would have meant diverting funds from farm support, from food subsidies, and above all from the military; in fact, spending on those areas continued to rise, leaving nothing for modernizing older industries and decaying infrastructure, let alone for new technologies. The Soviet economy thus became trapped, deep-frozen in an economic "long cycle," shown in Chart 8, that was tied to the industries and inputs of the 1930s.[12]

To compound this problem, the classic inputs of land, energy, raw materials, and labor all became less plentiful, and costs began to rise. Earlier, cheap stocks of oil and natural gas made industrialization possible and earned hard currency; yet while large supplies remain, most of it is at much deeper levels or in permafrost regions. According to one estimate, in the decade prior to 1985 the cost of extracting oil rose by 70 percent and was still increasing.[13] In consequence, oil production was dropping even before the labor unrest and transport difficulties of the following years. This was exacerbated by the systematic misuse and waste of energy throughout Soviet industry, by managerial inefficiency

Chart 8. The Soviet Economy's Long Cycle[14]

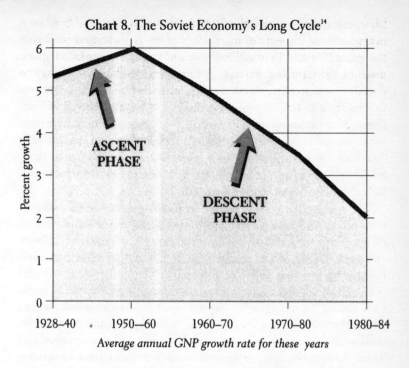

Average annual GNP growth rate for these years

and worker carelessness. Soviet planners had hoped to ease this situation by building nuclear power plants, but the Chernobyl disaster and the public mistrust of nuclear power dashed those hopes. Enormous amounts of capital are needed for the energy sector—to modernize existing plants, to decontaminate the nuclear stations, and to build new natural-gas pipelines—but there are insufficient resources to do this.[15] At the same time, as we shall see below, this drying-up of cheap sources of additional energy is paralleled by a similar trend in the supply of labor.

Since the former USSR can no longer rely upon cheap raw materials and an increasing work force, it logically needs to improve the use of available materials and raise the productivity of existing labor. Such an emphasis upon *quality* over *quantity* is contrary to the Russian practice, which, since the time of Peter the Great, has favored *more* of everything (cavalry, tanks, steel, cement). How does a society now shackled

by a badly functioning and inefficient industrial system switch to quality production? Seventy years of experience have demonstrated that
centralized "scientific socialism" does not work. Responsibility and
decision-making gravitated toward enormous bureaucracies under the
ultimate control of the Politburo. New ideas and proposals had to pass
the constant test of ideological orthodoxy. Obeying the rules of the
system was the most prudent thing to do. As public morale plummeted,
inefficiencies multiplied. The Soviet economy became riddled with
"contradictions," a gigantic irony given Marx's use of that word to
predict capitalism's eventual collapse. As another irony, both Japan and
Germany—the losers in 1945—came to possess larger GNPs than the
USSR, which slipped from second to fourth place in world rankings
even before its economic and constitutional disintegration. Indeed, a
recent survey estimates per capita annual income in the region at large
at a mere $1,780, which would imply a total output of around $500
billion—far less than Italy's or Britain's.[16]

In agriculture, decades of collectivized farming destroyed all incentives among the work force; vast subsidies kept food prices low but
distorted the laws of supply and demand; and bureaucrats, rather than
farmers or peasants themselves, decided what was to be grown and
when. Admittedly, other difficulties faced Soviet agriculture, from the
severe climate to a public infrastructure so bad that much of the harvest
never moved or rotted on the way to market. Yet while most farming
was collectivized, bureaucratized, and constantly interfered with, private plots (occupying 4 percent of Russia's arable land) produced the
remarkable total of around 25 percent of total crop output. Before the
Bolshevik Revolution, the country had been one of the greatest food
exporters in the world; at present, it is the world's greatest importer of
foodstuffs, at enormous cost in hard currency and gold.[17] Finally, the
fewer food supplies that reach the shops, the greater the hoarding and
the tensions between town and countryside, producing a further turn
toward paralysis. This may be mitigated in the future by granting long
land leases to peasants, but it is likely that they will grow profitable
items such as fruit and vegetables, *not* the critically important grains
which are the responsibility of the collective farms.[18]

Much the same is true of the present dilapidated state of industry.
Suffering from energy and labor shortages, handicapped by bureau-

cratic planning and an overheavy concentration upon traditional industries, unresponsive to consumer choice, and protected from international and internal competition, it has steadily ossified. Producing more steel or cement than any other nation was no help when a great proportion rusted or crumbled away in railway sidings. Possessing more engineers than any other country was a dubious distinction when their talents were chiefly wasted. Management itself was a contradiction in a Soviet factory, where production targets were prescribed elsewhere and no deviation from the plan was permitted.

It is easy to list the other problems that brought about the present crisis. *Infrastructure* was poor, reducing the prospect of getting food to market, cement to building sites, felled logs to timber factories, and so on. The *currency* was in an even worse condition; with few consumer goods to be purchased, there were "forced savings" of billions of near-worthless rubles, a massive black market, and a steady return to a barter system—leaving the people unready for any future convertibility of the ruble, without which they will remain on the margins of international commerce, investment, and production. The state of *public health* was deteriorating, because of poor standards of sanitation and public hygiene, the erosion in hospital care, crammed housing, and high levels of alcoholism. In contrast to health trends in other industrialized economies, infant mortality has been rising and average male life expectancy falling in recent years.[19] In this situation, the large numbers of doctors claimed by Soviet statistics became meaningless. Overall, the economy and society were showing ever more signs of joining the so-called Third World than of catching up with the First.

This economic distress would have been bad enough without the other two elements that made the Soviet triple crisis, the lack of political legitimacy and the reemergence of the nationalities problem. Clearly, these elements exacerbated each other; had the economy been working properly, for example, there would have been far less criticism of the Soviet leadership. As it was, the daily evidence of shoddy consumer goods, terrible housing, and mediocre health care stood in contrast to the regime's claims that its system was superior. The emptiness of such claims produced a widespread alienation, not only from the daily drudgery but also from the Marxist rhetoric of the mind-stultifying official media. Given rigorous KGB actions against dissidents, this alienation did not assume a revolutionary form as the 1970s and 1980s unfolded; but it produced cynicism about politics, withdrawal into one's own thoughts, lack of motivation in the factory and office, disregard for getting things right, and lack of pride in what one was producing or farming or manufacturing. A shabby economy and an equally shabby political ideology thus helped to create their own self-destruct mechanism, an ever-shabbier social and economic product, and a general malaise which each year reduced the Soviet Union's relative position in the world.[20]

Perestroika was the recognition that this decay had to be reversed, in both its economic and its political dimensions. Given the present chaos, there is no guarantee that a recovery will in fact occur. Satirists in Russia have joked that while it is relatively easy to turn a fish into a fish stew (that is, to convert a free-market economy into a socialist economy), no one really knows how to reverse the process. There is also the difficulty of converting an authoritarian system into a liberal democracy abiding by the rule of law. It was done earlier when the Allied victors reformed the Axis states after 1945; but whether that transformation can be carried out successfully by the national leadership and general public, and in the midst of economic chaos, is altogether uncertain. Other examples of such returns have taken place in countries very different from the collapsed Soviet Union.* It is not enough to allow free parliamentary elections and independent parties; steps also have to be taken to dismantle the instruments of centralized control, from the state's running of the media to a judiciary trained to observe socialist law. All of that is easier said than done, even if the failure of the August 1991 right-wing coup further discredited the old system.

The danger is, of course, that the former political, constitutional, and governmental structures will disintegrate before newer ones, able to command public loyalties, take their place. With radicals protesting

---

*In Poland, Czechoslovakia, and Hungary, for example, recent democratization was a return to their interwar condition, and the Communist dictatorship could be described as an "unnatural" imposition from outside. The democratization of Portugal, Spain, and Greece, by contrast, occurred in societies without a Communist economy.

that the reforms are too slow and conservatives that they are too hasty, with constitutional and political changes entangled in debates over controversial economic proposals (e.g., price reform), even the most intelligent reform leadership can become beleaguered. The idea of creating a prosperous, democratic, free-market (or social-market) economy may exist, but it is not possible to achieve it in one short leap. The certainties of the old system (guaranteed employment, food subsidies) have to be surrendered before the arrival of the material benefits of the new (the promised higher standard of living). Lost between the disintegration of what was familiar and the uncertainty of what is to come, people grow fearful. Although intellectuals and speculators thrive in such circumstances, housewives, factory workers, peasants, and ex-servicemen are more likely to become disaffected.[21]

The third, interlinked dimension of the Soviet triple crisis, perhaps the most serious and intractable of all, is the strength of ethnic differences and nationalisms. The Russian and Soviet state formed one of the world's most heterogenous multinational empires. Constitutionally, this was recognized in a federation of fifteen nominally independent republics, each the homeland of a major national group; but within those republics there were many ethnic subgroups, often with their own lower-level administrations. Officially, there were fifty-three ethnically defined political-administrative units in the Soviet Union, but since there are about one hundred separate ethnic groups in the country, half of the nationalities lacked their own unit.[22] Many of these groups are small, known outside their area only to linguistic specialists—Udmerts, Ossetians, Buryats, Karakalpaks, Ingush, Laks, and so on;[23] others, like the Belorussians, Uzbeks, and Kazakhs, have sizable populations, while the Ukraine has over 50 million inhabitants—more than Spain or Poland. Every republic contains ethnic minorities, including Russia itself with its Tartars, Bashkirs, and thirty other different nationalities; as the Russian expert Edward Keenan recently put it, "Only a few of the fifteen Soviet republics are nearly as homogenous as Northern Ireland or Yugoslavia. . . ."[24]

The critical fact was not the rich tapestry of languages and cultures, but that so many were in tension with their neighbors and the metropole. Hundreds of years of rivalry between different groups of nomads, hillfolks, and plainsmen and successive waves of migration and conquest proved stronger than scientific socialism. Differences of race and language were often joined by those of religion, as in Nagorno-Karabakh.[25] In certain areas, the rivalry was caused by population transfers (Volga Germans, Tartars, Don Cossacks) and border adjustments (Moldava) under Stalin.[26] For decades, inter-ethnic tensions were held in check by the Soviet police state. The official propaganda that the Soviet peoples had to stand united against the Fascist and capitalist foe also helped to paper over ethnic divisions. But with the German threat gone, the Cold War evaporating, socialist ideology discredited, and Moscow talking of *glasnost* and *perestroika* at home as well as actually restoring the liberties of the Eastern European peoples, the "cement" holding together the different races of the Soviet Union crumbled.

The tension between center and periphery is also easy to comprehend as the natural result of four hundred years of Russian expansion from the Muscovite heartland. Although many million Russians were moved elsewhere, to the Baltic states, the southern republics, and the Pacific provinces, the basic dichotomy remained; the periphery of the Soviet Union was ethnically non-Russian territory, often far from the Russian heartland:

Non-Russian lands extend in a vast arc from the shores of the Baltic Sea in the northwest (Estonia, Latvia, and Lithuania); south along the western border (Belorussia, Ukraine, and Moldavia); east across the Caucasus (Armenia, Georgia, and Azerbaidzhan); on to Central Asia (the areas inhabited by Turkmen, Uzbeks, Tadzhiks, and Kirgiz) and the Kazakh steppe; and, finally, across Asia to the Pacific Ocean (homelands of the Buryats, Tuvinians, Altays, Khakas, and other peoples).[27]

These ethnic minorities straining to be independent now clash with the 25 to 28 million relocated Russian settlers who—like the French *colons* in Algeria in the 1950s—desperately want to keep a relationship with the center. To their dismay, *glasnost* and *perestroika* have raised, for the first time since 1917–20, the prospect that they will be submerged by their more populous non-Russian neighbors intent upon changing the official language, public education, and the rest. According to some experts, we ought not to be surprised if these minority-majority tensions produce the sort of conflicts which our present century has seen all too often, when populations, resettled under an imperial regime, were left behind after decolonization.[28]

Inevitably, the rise of such centrifugal forces produced a reaction in the "center." Conservative voices in the military, the KGB, and the rump of the Communist Party called for the reestablishment of law and order, and accused the reformers of bringing the USSR to a state of collapse. There were, for example, warnings to the Ukraine not to discriminate against its 12 million Russian minority. There was also some old-Russian nationalism, fed by decades of resentments of subsidizing the republics, as well as by cultural dislike. According to this viewpoint, the non-Russian areas are encumbrances and should be decolonized, possibly with some border adjustments; since Russia itself possesses so much natural wealth (oil, natural gas, minerals, timber, diamonds), it is the ungrateful Balts and Muslims who would be the losers. A modified version of this attitude would be that all the republics should form a loose association, negotiate commercial relationships on a bilateral basis, and have much more control over their own budgets (including contributions to the confederation).[29] After the failure of the conservatives' 1991 coup, some republics moved in this direction, while others looked on, hoarding their newfound sovereignty. Yet complete independence itself brings its own difficulties, especially economic, since Stalinist planning deliberately ensured that no republic was self-sufficient. (Radios manufactured in the Baltics, for example, rely on parts made in Nagorno-Karabakh, the Armenian enclave in Azerbaijan).[30] Each republic thus has the power to damage others, albeit by hurting itself in the process.

Where these pressures will carry the republics is impossible to forecast. Independence for the Baltic states and some Muslim republics in the south might not mean much, for those border regions would still need to negotiate a workable commercial relationship with Moscow. However, total independence for the larger, resource-rich republics like Kazakhstan—not to mention the Ukraine, the USSR's former breadbasket and a major source of coal and industrial products—would be a heavy and probably fatal blow to any hopes of a reformed union.

Because of the existence of ethnic minorities, independence might also produce convulsions like those which occurred across the Indian subcontinent in 1947. Indeed, in Kazahkstan and Kirgizia, indigenous ethnic groups are only a bare majority, while in the Ukraine millions of Russians are likely to lose their jobs if "modernization" takes place in the mines and factories—which is probably what the IMF and other world economic bodies will demand as the Ukraine's price of membership. As the British discovered earlier this century, once agreement is reached to transform a multinational empire into a commonwealth, it is increasingly difficult to control the process, with results more dramatic and far-reaching than originally planned.[31]

As evidence of Soviet weakness grew during the 1980s, it was often pointed out by conservatives in the West that the USSR still possessed an enormous amount of military force, which would ultimately count in the world of power politics.[32] Yet even these vaunted military capacities were affected—deleteriously—by the nonmilitary developments discussed above. The failure to match the West and Japan in advanced technologies diminished Soviet military power, making it less capable of dealing with sophisticated weapons produced elsewhere. To pour more resources into the military would have been economically counterproductive, however, as well as unpopular with most of the people. Demographic trends also impacted upon the Soviet armed forces, since an increasing proportion of army recruits had to be gathered from ethnic groups who were mistrustful of Russia and did not even speak its language. Well before the dissolution of the USSR, there were widespread refusals in the Baltic and southern republics to enlist, and the Ukraine was insisting that "its" troops not be used to suppress nationalist movements. Even the Red Army, it appeared, could not withstand the fissiparous tendencies.[33] Finally, whatever military power exists after current arms-control agreements and voluntary cutbacks, it is unclear how useful the military will be in dealing with threats that are essentially economic, social, and environmental.

On the other hand, the fate of the armed forces and the weapons of the former USSR is of great importance, not only to the successor states themselves but also to their neighbors, Europe, and the United States. With Russia and the Ukraine spasmodically quarreling over the disposal of the Soviet navy; the Ukraine and Kazakhstan declining to demobilize their strategic nuclear weapons systems; military command-ers, republics, and even cities selling off tanks, aircraft, and missiles—the latter being acquired by smaller republic armies and related paramilitary groups (the army of the Dnestr republic, for example); and millions of unpaid and dissatisfied ex-servicemen losing their housing, pay, career, there is good reason for the West to be concerned lest the implosion of Soviet power and the existence of all this military hard-ware lead to catastrophe.

While all agree that the present crisis cannot go on forever, these structural problems are so deep-rooted that any proposed solution, whether liberal or conservative, provokes counterarguments. Liberaliz-ing the links with the non-Russian republics may ease that aspect of the crisis but could also lead to wars of ethnic succession. Loosening central controls on the ailing economy could stimulate production and food supplies and encourage entrepreneurship; it could also lead to violent public outrage at higher costs, large-scale unemployment, re-gional differences, and the breakdown of inter-republican trade. Yet to return to a command economy and the principles of scientific socialism would be to worsen the region's relative economic position in the world. A suppression of *glasnost* in any of the republics could cause a collapse in public morale, a decline in creativity, and internal ferment, especially between nationalists and resident Russians. A *Putsch* against the lead-ership of any republic would probably split it in half, as occurred in Georgia in 1991.

Because of these uncertainties, Western planners have now begun to anticipate a whole spectrum of possible outcomes.[34] Few nowadays expect that there would be a "good" solution to the triple crisis, with the economy reviving smartly, political legitimacy flourishing, and eth-nic rivalries subsiding. In a moderately optimistic view, the "Common-wealth" would stay together, and Moscow's controls over the republics would loosen. Economic reforms to encourage free-market activities would lead to mixed results but avoid a total collapse, while political and party ferment would continue but without great violence. This would hardly allow the region to catch up with East Asia, but it would still remain afloat. One can also think of less optimistic outcomes, from a collapse into civil war and internal disintegration to further conservative attempts at a coup d'état. Some scholars use the term "Weimar Russia," suggesting that a bitter and divided populace will increasingly favor extreme policies against internal foes and different ethnic groups.[35]

However the successor states to the Soviet Union fare, they clearly are unprepared for the newer forces for global change. On the contrary, every development discussed in Part One of this study is likely to bring fresh challenges to already troubled societies.

For example, the earth's lopsided demographic future, with all its potential social and political consequences, is mirrored here simply because the USSR's territorial extent made it both "North" and "South." Even by the early 1980s the country's demographic future contained such a compound of problems that experts were increasingly describing it in terms of unrelieved gloom. As one put it:

> On any basis, short-term or long-term, the prospects for the development of Soviet population and manpower resources until the end of the century are quite dismal. From the reduction in the country's birth rate to the incredible increase in the death rates beyond all reasonable past projections; from the decrease in the supply of new entrants to the labor force, compounded by its unequal regional distribution, to the relative aging of the population, not much hope lies before the Soviet government in these trends.[36]

The biggest impact upon the economy was that net additions to the labor force—a key "input" to the earlier expansion—drastically fell as increased numbers retired (or died before retirement age) and the overall birth rate declined. During the 1970s, for example, 22 million people were added to the labor force. In the 1980s, that figure plunged to 7.7 million; and in the 1990s it is forecast to drop further, to 5.7 million.[37] Should social and economic conditions worsen—thus increasing the disincentives to have children—or mass emigration be tolerated, the decline could intensify.

This demographic slowdown is by no means uniform, but disproportionately affects the Slavic peoples in the North. What is happening at present and is projected to continue into the future is a sort of "demographic revenge" by the colonized peoples, especially in the southern Muslim republics, whose birth rates are similar to those in the Middle East. The average annual population growth rates of those republics range from 2.5 to 3.5 percent, which is *three to five times larger* than the 0.7 percent average annual increases in the Russian population.[38] Already, according to one calculation,* Russians represent less than half of the total population, for the first time since the establishment of Bolshevik rule. The same calculation estimates that the Russian share will be 46.4 percent in the year 2000, and then fall relentlessly throughout the twenty-first century, as shown in Chart 9, as the population share of the nonwhite peoples of the Asian republics increases.

These are, the author warns, "only projections"; but the overall pattern was clear some time ago: "already in the early twenty-first century the country will be transformed from a one majority/many minorities structure to a many minorities structure."[39] Even before Gorbachev, Moscow's rule was being demographically undermined from one decade to the next. This may seem less important now that the republics are independent, but constitutional changes alone will not obviate the likely consequences of these demographic trends: population drift from the crowded republics of the South into southern Russia and the Ukraine, minority ethnic groups growing faster than the resident majority, resource disputes, heightened religious feuds, and the rest.

Given the geography of this region, it would naturally be affected in all manner of ways by changes in the environment. For example, global warming, were it to be significant, could make growing crops in semiarid regions even more difficult and shift the zone of cultivation northward—serious enough in itself without the new complication that such a movement might be from one independent republic's border (say, the

---

*In the 1979 census, the Russians constituted 52.4 percent of the total USSR population, but according to Bernstam, "Trends in the Soviet Population," p. 209, that included members of ethnic minorities living in the Russian republic, and the real figure was 50.9 percent. By 1984, the Russian share had shrunk to 49.9 percent.

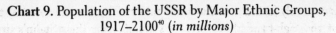

Chart 9. Population of the USSR by Major Ethnic Groups, 1917–2100[40] (*in millions*)

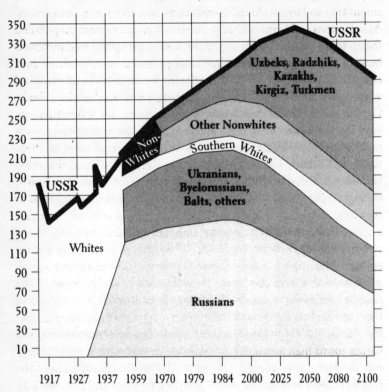

Ukraine) into another's (Russia). Low-lying regions, of which there are many, would be hit by any rise in sea levels. Yet the most serious consequence of higher temperatures could well be the unfreezing of the permafrost zone, releasing methane and increasing flooding. Moreover, such transformations would occur in regions ill equipped financially to provide adequate responses.

At present, with the full extent and consequences of the greenhouse effect still being disputed by scientists, these dangers may appear theoretical—and far less urgent than the immediate environmental problems currently facing politicians and publics. These were caused by the inept and high-handed decisions of state planners since Stalin's time, committed to large-scale industrialization regardless of consequences. As in Eastern and Central Europe, carbon and other emissions polluted the atmosphere, severely damaged the woods and forests, and increased health hazards among local inhabitants powerless to stop official policies. Rivers and lakes have been affected by industrial and chemical wastes, the dumping of oil, and leaching from overfertilized fields. Grandiose schemes to dam or divert water supplies for hydroelectricity have led to erosion or (as near St. Petersburg) dangerous silting. Such problems exist across the erstwhile Soviet Union, and many of them have only recently been made public. By contrast, most of the world knows of the dreadful effects of the Chernobyl disaster: the deaths through radiation of hundreds of adults and children, the pollution of the rivers and lakes, the blow dealt to local agriculture—all damaging a society already bowed low by nonenvironmental disasters.[41]

These newer challenges also exacerbate the demographic, ethnic, political, and economic elements of the Soviet triple crisis. For a good example of this, one need look no further than the drying up of the Aral Sea discussed earlier.* The environmental point is that because the rivers feeding into the sea have been tapped so heavily for irrigation, the decline in the water level has caused massive salinization, left harbor towns high and dry, and increased desertification; and the only way to reverse this would be to cease all water usage throughout the vast watershed area *for the next three decades.* But Central Asia's 33 million people (excluding Kazakhstan) depend upon tapping that river water for their livelihood; Uzbekistan's cotton production, its main cash crop, is grown on irrigated land that is already becoming salinated, but to cease irrigation would be a deathblow. The scarcity of water is already the chief natural reason that the region is so poor—the standard of living in Central Asia is half the national average and many babies starve to death—yet ironically this is where the population is growing the fastest. About 40 percent of the people are under eighteen, and within the next two decades the population will have nearly doubled

*See pp. 101–2 above.

to around 60 million, chiefly Muslim. As in North Africa and the Middle East, therefore, it is easy to foresee future conflicts as water supplies and agricultural output shrink while population booms.

Until recently, a Ministry of Water in Moscow allocated shares of available water to each Central Asian republic and also required each to ensure that a certain amount (clearly not enough) reached the Aral Sea. With the collapse of the Soviet state and the abolition of the Ministry of Water, these agreements have broken down. Desperate to preserve their way of life, farmers in the upstream valleys are taking more water, which means less for those downstream, in Uzbekistan. And all the time the Aral Sea continues to shrink.[42]

Could the biotech revolution in agriculture come to the rescue here? At first sight, this appears an attractive option; genetically altered crops capable of withstanding arid conditions, *in vitro* production and processing of food to relieve the pressures upon the land, enhanced biomass yields to meet energy demand, and a general expansion in agricultural output sound like answers to a prayer. Nor is there a lack of Russian scientists and technicians in plant breeding and related disciplines. However, it would be difficult for poverty-stricken southern republics to pay for the patents and other fees, not to mention the establishment of modern laboratories, factories, and processing plants for large-scale production. Who would fund these enterprises, and the associated investment in education and infrastructure? Certainly not an impoverished government in Moscow, grappling with its own problems and possessing increasingly fewer ties with the Asian republics. Even if a brave Western company undertook to develop biotech agriculture in, say, Uzbekistan and overcame all the other obstacles, that still would not solve the crisis over water supplies.

More generally, while it is conceivable that some parts of agriculture could be improved by the adoption of biotech,* the sorry condition of Soviet farming suggests that its real need is for structural reforms (decollectivization, realistic food prices, improved infrastructure). Yet if these reforms occurred, with farm output increasing at the pace it did in China and standards of living improving smartly, there would

---

*For example, using bovine growth-hormone techniques to increase milk yields in the Baltic states.

still remain a major disincentive to turn to genetically altered beef and milk; and the global adoption of technologies which "dematerialized" agriculture could have tremendous economic and social consequences in areas where so large a percentage of the labor force is engaged in farming and few alternative jobs beckon.

Much the same may be said about the readiness of the states of the former USSR to confront the automation revolution coming out of East Asia. Despite its innumerable engineers and technicians and the use of simpler robots in certain state-owned industries, it is hard to see how Russia would gain the economic advantages which Japan enjoys from robotics. Whereas the latter moved into automation because of labor shortages and its companies willingly retrain or redeploy workers made redundant by new machines, Russia and the other republics at present possess a chronic system of *under*employment, which widespread automation would only exacerbate.

Furthermore, transforming the republics' economies to embrace the brave new world of robotics, biotechnology, lasers, optics, telecommunications, and the like heavily depends upon the possession of a flourishing computer industry. In fact, that industry is so undeveloped and the number of machines so few—in 1987 there were only 100,000 personal computers in the USSR, compared with the *annual* U.S. production of more than 5 million[43]—that enormous amounts of capital would be needed to create an information society. Such a change involves reliance upon foreign machines and technological expertise which would have to be paid for, and it requires the extensive retraining of the work force, *plus* the appropriate software information, *plus* an efficient servicing network in order to use the machines properly in the first place. Even as Russian planners and foreign advisers grapple with the problem of how and where to commence this process, on either side of the Pacific a flood of new inventions widens the gap between high-tech societies and the rest, making it ever more difficult to catch up.

Finally, any move toward a high-tech economy has to confront the cluster of problems that brought about the USSR's collapse in the first place. The Russian academician Andrei Ershev, who enthusiastically proposes turning his country into an information society by the early twenty-first century, also admits the "apparent absurdity" of such a scheme at present:

> The mediocre living conditions produced by primitive wage-leveling, the difficulties of providing food and shelter, the overloading and alarming degradation of our energy and transportation structures, and the exorbitantly high share of low-skill and manual labor in our economy—all of these things are "real life" and they demand urgent action as well as the immediate concentration of all available resources.[44]

In such circumstances, he concludes, talk of a long-term program to produce a Russian equivalent of (say) California appears to be mere philosophizing, remote from the existing turmoil and backwardness.[45]

Until their economies are restructured, the republics can also play little part in the financial and communications revolution, or in the concomitant rise of the multinational corporation—except perhaps as providers of cheap factory labor, like Mexico and Thailand. It was the Soviet regime's inability to handle—or prevent—the spread of ideas and images via the newer forms of communication which, in part at least, contributed to its collapse. Authoritarian successor regimes set up in certain republics (e.g., Georgia) may also find it difficult to control information, however hard they try. But even where *glasnost* prevails, it is difficult to envisage the emergence of a Kazakhstani equivalent to CNN or the BBC, or a Ukrainian rival to McKinsey. Since the republics lack a convertible currency, international banks, stockholders, and electronic trading institutions, the borderless world of twenty-four-hour-a-day financial flows must appear irrelevant to current concerns.

Some years ago, *The Economist* tartly observed that in 1913 "Imperial Russia had a real product per man-hour three times greater than Japan's [but it] has spent its nigh seventy socialist years slipping relatively backwards, to maybe a quarter of Japan's rate now."[46] In so many ways, the collapsing Soviet Union became the antithesis of Japan: vast in size and rich in resources, compared with the cramped, resource-weak island state; a medley of peoples, compared with one of the world's most self-consciously homogeneous races; socially disintegrating, compared with the coherent, deferential, and group-conscious

Japanese citizenry; disadvantaged by high technology and the "dematerialization" of production, just as Japan is advantaged by the very same; unable, ironically, despite the socialist emphasis on planning, to prepare for the future, compared with Tokyo's apparently purposeful march toward the twenty-first century. As many observers have noted, the untidy, industrially backward, heterogeneous Russian Empire was one of the least suitable places in which to create a Marxist society, assuming such a society was possible *anywhere*. [47] For the very same reasons, its successors do not seem well prepared to deal with contemporary global forces for change—which suggests that in whatever form the republics enter the twenty-first century, they will continue to grapple with their relative backwardness.

These conclusions could, of course, turn out to be too pessimistic. At present, all we see is chaos, struggle, economic collapse, ethnic disintegration—just as the observers of 1918 did. How could they have foreseen then that a decade or so later the USSR would have begun to produce chemicals, aircraft, trucks, tanks, and machine tools and be growing faster than any other industrialized society?[48] By extension, how could Western admirers of Stalin's centralized economy in the 1930s know that the very system contained the seeds of its own collapse? Like any other society on earth, the former Soviet republics could theoretically make harmonious progress instead of suffering serious decline and convulsions. Nevertheless, in view of their existing stricken condition and of the newer challenges that are emerging, it is hard to believe that the future is a rosy one. And since the region's troubles could very easily have consequences elsewhere—from the illegal disposal of nuclear weapons to an enormous increase in opium exports from the southern republics (to gain hard currency)—the Western democracies might be unwise to assume that the collapse of the "evil empire" is going to be an unqualified advantage to themselves.

EASTERN AND CENTRAL EUROPE

Whatever happens to the successor states of the USSR, the policies of *glasnost* and *perestroika* have had enormous consequences for the former Soviet satellites in Eastern and Central Europe. Free elections, the demise of most Communist parties (or, at the very least, their loss of monopoly), the move toward free-market economic policies, the dismantling of the Iron Curtain, the collapse of the Warsaw Pact, the incorporation of the German Democratic Republic into its larger West German neighbor, the beginnings of talks about Hungarian or Czech membership in the European Community—all of these extraordinary developments, scarcely imaginable a few years ago, were possible only because the Gorbachev regime in Moscow was willing to loosen its grip.[49] Whatever the original motives for that liberalization, the political and strategic geography of Europe from the Thuringian Forest to the mouth of the Danube has been transformed as a result—leaving a half-dozen successor governments and their publics to grapple with the new conditions.

Of the populations affected by this change, those in the former East German state enjoy a different status from the rest. Although they face problems of unemployment in adjusting to the capitalist way of life and their infrastructure, environment, and industrial base are so decayed that enormous amounts of capital are needed to bring them up to "west" German levels, these are difficulties of a medium-term nature. Fortunately for the people themselves, they were merged into a state with the world's largest merchandise-trade and current-account balances.[50] Moreover, reconstruction provides a massive Keynesian-type "boost" to utilities companies, road-construction firms, and manufacturing in general. The German budget deficit may soar, but much of this is because of enhanced *capital* spending which is economically beneficial.

While the "east" Germans have been given a free ticket into the prosperous Western community, their neighbors will have to struggle to pay the fare.* Obviously, some have better prospects than others; there is a world of difference between Hungary, which for years experimented cautiously with Westernization, and Romania, which suffered from the economic distortions of the totalitarian Ceausescu regime.

---

*"It is not fair," a Polish journalist told a Western visitor in early 1991. "Why can't there be a West Poland to come to the rescue of poor East Poland? Why is there no West Poland to take away the bad zlotys, the bad cars, the bad passports, and give us the good ones?" Cited in W. R. Mead, "Dark Continent," *Harper's Magazine* (April 1991), p. 52.

Yet whatever the dissimilarities, each has to move its economy and society from one system to another without collapsing in the effort.

The establishment of secure and politically legitimate democratic governments will be more easily achieved in some of these nations than in others. Because of its cultural and religious unity and its deep sense of self-identity, Poland is the most favorably placed in this respect. The same strengths also assist Hungary. Yet even where democracy flourishes, it could be messy and painful, with coalitions forming and breaking up, angry debates over church policy or economic policy, latent authoritarianism, social radicals being denounced by farmers' parties or leagues of former Communists—in other words, the messy and painful politics of, say, France and Italy in the late 1940s and 1950s as they emerged from their wartime regimes and struggled to modernize. Nevertheless, the Central European states have better prospects of achieving political legitimacy than Romania and Bulgaria, where democratic traditions are much weaker, large numbers of "ex- and not-so-ex-Communists"[51] retain influence, and economic conditions are grim.

Securing political legitimacy will be more difficult if, as in the collapsed USSR, ethnic divisions reemerge. Here again Poland is favorably placed, because of the homogeneity of its population and Germany's renunciation of claims to Polish-held territory. The same is true of Hungary, which is 93 percent Magyar; the problem, from Budapest's viewpoint, is the many Hungarian minorities *outside* the border—600,000 in southern Slovakia, over 400,000 in Yugoslavia, and as many as 2 million in Romania, the last locked in angry confrontation with the Romanian majority.[52] By contrast, the country suffering from the most severe ethnic divisions is undoubtedly the former Yugoslavia, which has never overcome its sixty-year-long history as a confederation of rival cultures, languages, and religions. Apart from the central struggle between Serbs and non-Serbs over Belgrade's "hegemonism,"[53] which has already led to extensive civil war, there also exist enormous problems over the future of Macedonia and Kosovo which could explode at any time.

Although tensions elsewhere are not as severe, most neighboring countries have inherited deep-rooted "majority vs. minority" problems. Since independence the government in Prague has negotiated with the

Slovaks over issues ranging from the country's name to demands for greater Slovak autonomy, but without stemming the move to independence.[54] Romanians resent the agitations of the Hungarian minority, while the latter chafe at Romanian dominance.[55] Turkey complains of harsh Bulgarian treatment of its Turkish-speaking minority, while Greece cannot forgive Turkey's occupation of northern Cyprus. All are carefully watching Macedonia. In the first decades of this century, observers worried whether rivalries in the Balkans would lead to instability and war, dragging in other nations. It would be a sad comment upon how little human beings learn if in the final decade the fears returned—and were justified.

These tensions could be ameliorated by prosperity, but the productivity and living standards of the region are well behind those of the West. According to one calculation, Czechoslovakia's per capita income was 10 percent above Austria's in 1939, but now is about 35 percent *below*;[56] the latter calculation is probably too optimistic, yet Czech living standards are far ahead of those further east, from Ruthenia to Macedonia. Given their industrial decay, inefficient infrastructure, lack of technical and marketing expertise, nontransferable (and increasingly worthless) currencies, and massive ecological damage, some of these societies will find it hard to move to a free-market economy, especially in a decade of increasing capital shortages worldwide. In removing price subsidies, cutting support for state-run enterprises, and reducing bureaucracies as recommended by the IMF and World Bank, even such potentially fast adjusters as Hungary and Poland will endure high unemployment, bankruptcies, and popular agitation against price increases and foreign interference. Many may see their already declining GNPs plunge by another 10 percent before the reforms work and the hoped-for recovery takes place (see Chart 10).

This recovery is made more problematic by the chaos within the former Soviet Union itself. For decades, these countries relied on Soviet oil purchased at below-world-market prices, and on barter. Eastern and Central Europe now confront massive shortfalls in fuel, and have to pay for oil imports in dollars. Shortages in hard currency could be helped by increased exports to Russia—but that presumes that Russia can pay for such goods, and complicates the task of orienting these economies to *Western* markets.[57] Moreover, the worsening con-

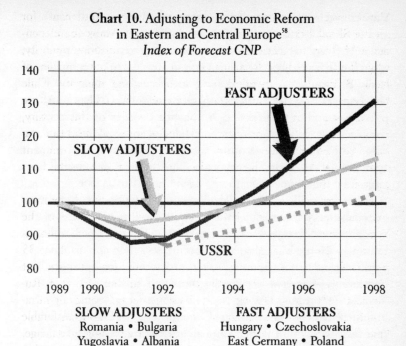

Chart 10. Adjusting to Economic Reform
in Eastern and Central Europe[58]
Index of Forecast GNP

SLOW ADJUSTERS	FAST ADJUSTERS
Romania • Bulgaria	Hungary • Czechoslovakia
Yugoslavia • Albania	East Germany • Poland

ditions in the erstwhile USSR and Romania, together with the Yugoslav civil war, raise fears of a mass exodus westward, placing further strains upon already creaking social services. Already the fighting in Bosnia has displaced millions of people, perhaps permanently. Hence the erection of barriers along the eastern and southern borders of Central European states, creating a new iron curtain to separate the former Soviet satellites from their strife-torn neighbors.[59] Of all the ironies in this region, that could be the greatest.

In sum, the societies of Eastern and Central Europe already have enough to do without having to worry about global changes driven by technology, environmental trends, and demographic change.[60] As they are already aware, ecological damage has badly affected their health and standards of living, and it will take immense sums to repair that damage *and* to adopt alternative fuels, life-styles, and so on. Many of them rely for energy upon Soviet-designed nuclear power stations, which are hazardous but could be shut down only at the cost of immense disruptions. Environmental worries, along with economic uncertainty, are apparently causing the birth rates in all Eastern and Central European countries—and in the Ukraine—to plummet well below replacement fertility rates.[61] On the other hand, demographic change can also exacerbate ethnic tensions within countries (Albanians with far higher birth rates than Serbs, for example) and increase the possibility of large-scale transborder migrations. Again, as in Russia, the farmers of these regions really need decollectivization and capital investment, *not* the challenge of biotech-altered beef and grain; they also need prosperous and accessible export markets, in Western Europe, which will cause tensions with the EC's farmers.[62] Lacking national stock markets, and with their industries requiring basic restructuring, they also have little opportunity at present to enjoy the purported benefits of twenty-four-hour-a-day "futures" trading or of all-automated factories.

But the nations of Eastern and Central Europe *do* have some important resources: lots of talented and ambitious people, a basically sound educational infrastructure, long traditions of excellence in manufacturing (Czechoslovakia) or mathematics and science (Hungary), plus—for the first time in half a century—access to new ideas, ventures, stimuli. Given the tasks ahead of them, particularly in the short to medium term, such native talents may be insufficient to allow the societies of the region to catch up, let alone prepare them for the twenty-first century. But at least they are out of jail, and are free to decide in what direction they wish to travel.

12

EUROPE AND THE FUTURE

COMPARED WITH THE PROBLEMS THAT confront the countries of Central Asia and North Africa, the European Community (EC) nations must appear relatively comfortable as they seek to respond to global trends. Rich in such resources as capital, infrastructure, and (especially) scientific and skilled personnel, and enjoying standards of living among the highest in the world, Europeans have innumerable advantages over the struggling peoples to the east and the south. With Japan and North America, the EC has emerged as one of the three great centers of economic, technological, and political power in an otherwise fractured world. Undoubtedly, it faces problems in redefining its foreign and defense policies in a post–Cold War world and more especially in finding ways to further its unity; but while difficult they are probably not insuperable.

What is much less certain, however, is whether Europeans will be able to enjoy their comfortable way of life *unaffected* by today's global developments. Can Europe's relatively rich societies insulate themselves from the demographic pressures building up elsewhere, or from profound climate changes? Can the EC handle globalization, even as it seeks further to integrate itself? Can it deal with fissiparous political tendencies, the growing resentments against ethnic neighbors and recent immigrants, the new tribalisms? In some parts of the world, the journalist Thomas Friedman has recently observed, robots are assembling luxury sedans. In other parts (Sarajevo), children are being killed by tank fire because they are of another culture and religion.[1] The effects of both technological changes and historical antagonisms "spill over" national boundaries, to be felt some distance away; and the same is true of other transnational forces. If it is unlikely that even Japan will remain a privileged enclave amid the rest of the world's problems, how could Europe—much more closely linked to the regions of turbulence, and more fissured within—expect to go unscathed? And will the continent's political leaders be capable of settling the "old" agenda (future of NATO, the Common Agricultural Policy) while having to respond to newer, less familiar issues as well?

All this is the more difficult to answer because, unlike unified countries such as Japan or the United States or Australia, Europe is at present trying to hammer out its own constitutional form, a process that consumes most of its political energies. To that extent at least, EC politicians and those of the nations of the erstwhile USSR have something in common. While one region struggles toward integration, the other strives to manage disintegration; and neither leadership has much time to spare for what must surely appear to them less urgent issues. In the minds of the Brussels planners, and perhaps also of the twelve member-states that now compose the EC,* the debate over future European unity takes precedence over such matters as global population change, robotics, and the greenhouse effect.

Yet, while the politics of European integration overshadow those broader global trends, the latter cannot simply be ignored. As it is, the governments and peoples of Europe confront the *twin* challenges of hammering out the continent's future shape at the same time as they respond (or fail to respond) to the forces for global change. Because of that, the title of this chapter, "Europe and the Future," implies a double meaning, namely:

(a) what organizational *form* Europe will assume as it moves into the twenty-first century; and

---

*Germany, France, Italy, the Netherlands, Belgium, Luxembourg, Britain, Denmark, Ireland, Spain, Portugal, Greece.

(b) whatever its shape, how the region will *fare* as it grapples with the transnational changes described in Part One of this book.

While these two questions about Europe's future are distinct, each affects the other. If the Europeans unite, they have a better chance of producing common policies on global warming, immigration, North-South relations, and security; they can also collectively fund technological projects (e.g., the Airbus) beyond the resources of a single European state. Indeed, the fact that the world is altering—shifting strategical balances, differentiated economic growth patterns, the rise of East Asia, and the altered position of the post-1945 superpowers—has always fueled the argument for greater European unification. From the early ideas of Jean Monnet and Robert Schuman to today's proponents of a more tightly knit EC, the motive is plain: if Europe is to recover the relative importance in the world it possessed around 1900, it must avoid wars among its member states, harmonize economic practices, and evolve common policies, including foreign and defense policies. Much as they have tried, individual European nations have not been able to recover their former international position. Only by coming together can they create a bloc of European peoples, more prosperous and perhaps even more powerful than any other state in the world.[2]

At present Europe is a long way from such a vision, although it has come far from its fractured condition of 1945. Since the late 1940s its defense has rested in the North Atlantic Treaty Organization (NATO), with U.S. contributions providing both nuclear-strategic and conventional-force support to deter attacks. In the economic sphere, there exists the loosely structured European Free Trade Association (EFTA), chiefly of smaller neutral states engaged in free trade in industrial products. Altogether more important, however, is the European Community itself, which is usually what is meant when commentators use the term "Europe." Established by the Treaty of Rome in 1957 to create a common customs union as the foundation upon which greater European unity (including political unity) might be developed, the EC possesses a European Commission to act as a central planning executive, a European Parliament, and even a European Court of Justice. As such, it contains the constitutional "skeleton" for a federal state.

However, none of these organizations integrates all European countries. NATO contains the non-European countries Canada and the United States, but not (obviously) European neutrals. EFTA was devised as an EC alternative by states opposed to the harmonization of agricultural, social, and fiscal policies, not to mention political-constitutional integration. As the EC has grown in importance, EFTA's position is in doubt; with the Warsaw Pact dissolved and NATO's future uncertain, some EFTA nations (Austria, Sweden, Switzerland) are reconsidering their assumption that EC membership would conflict with their neutrality. One possibility is to extend the EC's frontier-free single market to all EFTA nations*—such a provisional arrangement was concluded in October 1991—but that is disliked by centralists who fear the bad example of "less-than-full" membership. At present, there is a confusion of memberships: Turkey is in NATO but not the EC (though it has applied to the latter body); Eire is in the EC but not NATO; Norway is in NATO and still wonders about its 1972 decision, by referendum, to decline membership in the EC. The changes in Central Europe and the former USSR have led some of those countries, including Russia, to proclaim a wish to join the EC, and even NATO!

Despite such complications, Europe could become much more important in world affairs. A few years ago, Professor Samuel Huntington suggested that "the baton of world leadership" next century may pass from America not to Japan, or China, or Russia, but to a European federation:

> The European Community, if it were to become politically cohesive, would have the population, resources, economic wealth, technology, and actual and potential military strength to be the preeminent power of the twenty-first century. Japan, the United States, and the Soviet Union have specialized respectively in investment, consumption, and arms. Europe balances all three. It invests less of its GNP than Japan but more than the United States and possibly more than the Soviet Union. It consumes less of its GNP than the United States but more than Japan and the Soviet Union. It arms less than the United States and the Soviet Union but more than Japan.
>
> It is also possible to conceive of a European ideological appeal comparable to the American one. Throughout the world, people line up at the doors

---

*This would establish a market of 380 million consumers, accounting for over 40 percent of world trade.

of American consulates seeking immigration visas. In Brussels, countries line up at the door of the Community seeking admission. A federation of democratic, wealthy, socially diverse, mixed-economy societies would be a powerful force on the world scene. If the next century is not the American century it is most likely to be the European century.[3]

This may strike the reader as heady stuff, ignoring Europe's past quarrels and present difficulties. Even a quarter century after the Treaty of Rome the EC remained, in one critic's words, "a maze of border controls, government subsidies to national industries, closed national systems of procurement in military and other key public sectors, and national regulation of industrial standards, copyrights, transportation, banking, insurance and health requirements for the entry of goods."[4] How will it fare, therefore, in the trickier and more critical realms of common immigration rules, a common currency and central bank, integrated (or at least federated) armed forces, and unified foreign and defense policies? Is it not utopian to imagine twelve or fifteen nations, each with a tradition of acting as a sovereign unit, ever becoming a United States of Europe as the early federalists once hoped? Is it not more practicable to undertake modest reform measures (e.g., harmonizing of patents and weights and measures) and be content with a loose federation of peoples possessing close cultural ties and more consistent industrial practices, without wasting energies pursuing the chimera of turning Europe into an integrated world-political player? After all, won't Europe find it hard enough simply to avoid being hurt by *existing* difficulties?

Those desiring a "strong" Europe would probably concede that full unity is impossible at present, but argue that there is a compelling need for economic harmony, as well as encouraging the habit of thinking and acting politically as one. By contrast, those preferring a "weak" institutional center support an enlarged common market for goods and services but abhor bureaucratic controls over business, the distortions of the Common Agricultural Policy (CAP), the costs of harmonizing social-welfare policies, the loss of fiscal sovereignty implied in a common currency and a European central bank, and the transfer of parliamentary and governmental powers to pan-European bodies. Between these poles is a variety of middle positions, depending upon the member state in question: some want to boost the powers of the European Parliament, others to enhance the influence of the Council of Ministers; some want defense integration, others fear it will undermine NATO, and yet others wish to remain neutral.[5] Even voices favoring integration have very different motivations, from Italian automobile bosses wanting a single continental market to German intellectuals eager to "embed" their newly united country within European structures.[6]

Any investigation of the possibilities of an integrated Europe will need to focus not only on the agreed-upon removal of all internal barriers for the exchange of goods and services, but also on more controversial measures like a common currency, enhanced powers for the European Parliament, and coordinated defense policies. It is in those realms that there lie both the greatest potential for transforming "Europe" into something very different from today's geographical expression *and* the greatest cluster of obstacles to changing the existing structure of a continent of nation-states. If these obstacles are overcome, the EC might well develop the place in global affairs which federationists envision for it; if they are not, it could remain what one disgusted Belgian minister called it during the 1991 Gulf War—"an economic giant, a political dwarf, and a military worm."[7]

Although organizations to promote regional cooperation exist elsewhere in the world, none possesses the commercial importance or attracts the intellectual and political interest of the EC. It conducts one-third of world trade. Collectively, its financial resources are enormous, since it possesses many of the world's largest banks, insurance companies, and finance houses. Of the globe's top ten trading nations, seven are European.[8] In industries such as automobiles, pharmaceuticals, machine tools, and engineering goods generally, the EC countries together produce more than any other country in the world.[9] Until the North American free-trade bloc of Mexico, the United States, and Canada is fully in place, it is the largest market in the world. Galvanized by Japanese and American competition, it is pouring large amounts of money into high-tech industries such as aerospace, supercomputers, maglev trains, and the like. All this industrial and commercial activity is aided by, and in turn helps to aid, an enormous array of cultural institutions, research libraries, scientific centers, hundreds of universities, and millions of college-level students and highly skilled workers.*

Europe's resources are divided, however, into twenty-six sovereign nation-states, ranging from Greece to Norway and from Finland to Portugal. The economic rationale for a harmonization of the tariffs, commercial practice, taxes, traffic legislation, and associated activities of these countries is simply overwhelming. A truck that could travel 750 miles from the north to the south of the United Kingdom in thirty-six hours would, upon crossing the English Channel, need fifty-eight hours to cover the same distance from Calais to Milan—because of all the border stops. A citizen of "Europe," touring from one country to the next and changing his money at each resting place into and out of the local currency, would find that about *half* of his original sum was swallowed up in exchange transactions.[10] Add to this the sheer variety of different national standards—from the type of electrical plugs to entire telecommunications systems—and it is easy to understand why businessmen have been pressing for a genuinely common market in goods and services. Such standardization would, it is claimed, give an additional "one-time boost" to Europe's growth as well as ensuring that it possessed more flexible and efficient economic structures to compete in the early twenty-first century.[11] According to the recent Cecchini Report, "the cost of non-Europe," that is, the burden upon the EC economies if they do *not* unify, is horrendous; on the other hand, implementing a common market could result in savings of $200–300 billion and add 4 to 7 percent to the EC's overall product.[12] Europe can either seize this opportunity, the report argued, or fall behind Japan and America.

Following those and other arguments of the European Commission, the free movement of goods, services, capital, and people throughout the Community was agreed upon, that measure taking effect after 31 December 1992. Since that was the original intent of the Treaty of Rome, it was not so controversial as, for example, a scheme for a European central bank or a common defense policy. But it said much for the gap between theory and reality that when, in 1985, the EC commissioner for the internal market (Lord Cockfield) offered his

---

*Admittedly, there are major resource differences between countries such as Germany and Portugal—in 1984, the former had seven times the number of R&D scientists and engineers per million inhabitants as the latter—but the remarks here are about the EC as a whole.

White Paper on the measures required to achieve a single common market, over three hundred areas for action were identified, ranging from banking licenses to capital controls, civil aviation to tax laws, environmental issues to consumer safety.[13]

With many of these measures implemented and others to come, the prospect of a Common Market galvanized a surge in business mergers, cross-border investments, takeovers, and marketing agreements, as European manufacturers, financial houses, service industries, and media giants prepared themselves for the more open but also much more competitive circumstances of the 1990s. Deutsche Bank and Morgan Grenfell, Siemens and Plessey, Hennessy and Guinness, Volvo and Renault . . . by the late 1980s, reports of such alliances gave the impression that virtually every company was restructuring itself to survive within this colossal market. This burst of acquisitions—together with journalistic talk of a "Fortress Europe"—in turn stimulated American and Japanese multinational corporations into expanding *their* presence within the EC. Once again, household names were involved—Ford and Jaguar, Philip Morris and Suchard, IBM and Siemens, Fujitsu and ICL, Honda and Rover, Mitsubishi and Daimler-Benz; no one, it appeared, wanted to be left out.[14]

Despite this, a completely free EC market is still not at hand, chiefly because of the rearguard action of vested interests that would be damaged by unfettered laissez-faire. Allowing the same accountancy firm to operate in London, Frankfurt, and Milan is one thing; but open competition among, say, airlines is much harder to achieve, because individual European governments want to protect their "national" carriers. Similarly, influential automobile producers like Peugeot and Fiat, which had been able to persuade their governments to restrict Japanese automobile imports, are now concerned at the establishment of Japanese car factories within the EC (chiefly in Britain) and are fighting hard for a period of continued import quotas. At first sight this is a blatant denial of the single-market principle in favor of less efficient producers. To French and Italian manufacturers, things look different; European economic unity was supposed to benefit *European* companies and their workers, not multinationals from a country that has maintained the most sophisticated import controls for the past forty years.

In addition, this frenzy of mergers and acquisitions across Europe struck many critics as socially unbalanced, benefiting the chairmen, stockholders, lawyers, and others in those businesses, but offering little to people as a whole. Given the deep-rooted European cultural conviction that it does *not* want to become like the United States, there is a strong social-policy element to the plans concerning Europe's future. As everyone can see, the previous structure of national boundaries, tariffs, and commercial/legal systems encouraged country-specific industries—airlines, telephone companies, automobile producers, computer manufacturers, banks, armaments works—in each member state. Compared with the roughly similar market size of the United States, Europe will clearly have *too many* airlines, electrical companies, and automakers when the barriers come down; and the less efficient ones will either collapse or (more likely) be taken over—unless home governments, rejecting the spirit of integration, continue to protect them. The "harmonization" of Europe's economies is likely, therefore, to create pockets of local high unemployment, even within the overall stimulus given to growth.

Moreover, this economic unification is happening in a continent with very different levels of income and social welfare: the per capita GNP in Germany, for example, is three to four times that in Portugal and Greece,[15] and the gap in welfare provisions probably even greater. Since a true common market would permit a manufacturer to produce goods anywhere within the Community's boundaries, there is a temptation to direct new investment—or relocate existing production—to the poorer regions with their lower wages and other costs; which, after all, is why a U.S. company moves from Connecticut to Mississippi, or a Japanese firm establishes a factory in Thailand. Here again, because of Europe's different political culture, with its emphasis upon social welfare and the power of trade unions (especially in Germany), such laissez-faire policies are being resisted. Instead, political pressure is mounting to ensure that wages in poorer regions are brought closer to those in prosperous countries, and that there be a uniformity of welfare provisions, in line with those in richer societies. Despite protests from businessmen (and the British government) at the costs involved, the EC seems intent upon enlarging its "social charter." In sum, the European "common market" idea involves not just a free-trade zone (as in a Mexican-U.S.-Canadian trading bloc), but the harmonization of much else besides; and it is precisely in these *non*business spheres of unification that the greater political problems will lie.

In the same way, the Common Agricultural Policy (CAP) does not accord with the logic of the global marketplace and seems, indeed, to be a substantial drag upon overall world trade and growth. By establishing a common tariff to give Community farmers protection against lower-cost non-EC producers, by fixing minimum support prices in key foodstuffs and guaranteeing to purchase farm produce if prices fall to those levels, and by providing generous export subsidies so that surpluses can be sold abroad, the CAP has distorted world agricultural supply and demand.* It also drives food prices higher. Over 70 percent of the EC's spending is taken by agriculture and fisheries, leaving little for social and regional development that could benefit far larger numbers;[16] and the monies go disproportionately to the larger farmers of northern France or East Anglia, instead of the peasants and smallholders of the Apennines. Externally, it has turned the EC into a major exporter of foodstuffs, taking third markets from other farm-exporting nations, producing an upward spiral in world agricultural subsidies, and straining relations with the United States, Canada, Argentina, and Australia. In 1990, support for farmers cost EC governments and consumers $133.4 billion, compared with $74.1 billion in the United States and $59 billion in Japan.[17]

To the supporters of European unity, the CAP nonetheless remains necessary. In their view, a European common market is not just for the benefit of industry. It also has to compensate for the growing gap in living standards between industry-heavy economies on the one hand (Germany) and agriculture-heavy economies on the other (Greece, Portugal), as well as for the differences in income *within* one nation's regions and sectors. If agriculture does consume most of the EC budget, this is a way of transferring resources from the richer nations to Community members containing large numbers of peasant families with low per capita income. To expose farming to unrestricted free

---

*The industrial equivalent might be for the U.S. government to guarantee to purchase all *unsold* American-made cars and trucks at a fixed price, and then to subsidize the sale of those vehicles abroad. This would no doubt benefit the U.S. automobile companies and workers, but one can imagine the distortions it would create in the global automobile market.

trade would be to create—or exacerbate—regional social problems everywhere from Sicily to Galway; besides, too many powerful parties (such as the CDU in Germany) feel heavily dependent upon the farmers' vote. Finally, there is the aesthetic, emotional, and cultural point: far too many regions and towns, of stunning beauty and outstanding historical importance, have already suffered from population drift.[18] Some form of support for agriculture will be needed as long as it is wished to preserve thriving communities in such areas as the Auvergne, Calabria, and Castile.

Equally tricky is the intention, announced at the 1991 Maastricht meeting of EC leaders, to create a common European currency,* with a European federal bank to control the money supply. After all, a customs union within which twelve or more currencies operate is something of a contradiction. Except for currency dealers themselves, it is claimed that every business—and traveler—would benefit from a common currency, which would also stimulate further cross-border investment. Moreover, given the volatility of the U.S. dollar in recent decades, the international financial system as a whole might gain from a much more broadly based world currency. Since the EC countries have already agreed to coordinate currency fluctuations within a relatively narrow range established by the Exchange Rate Mechanism (ERM), why not take the next step and merge the currencies into one?

The answer is, of course, that currency union would involve a far more substantial assault upon sovereignty—that is, upon the freedom of governments and parliaments to alter interest rates, print money, and run deficits—than schemes for harmonizing professional standards or protecting agricultural incomes. If every national bank were free to print ECUs and if every government (including fiscally lax administrations in Athens and Rome) could run massive budgetary deficits in this new currency and expand their national debts at the rate they did during the 1980s, the result would be a fiasco—which is why, of course, the fiscally conservative Bundesbank is insisting that the only issuer of the new currency be a European Federal Bank, one as independent of

*A European Currency Unit (ECU) already exists. This is simply an accounting device by which EC revenues and expenditures are calculated, with its rates being occasionally adjusted to reflect the relative strength of the member economies. As a notional currency, it cannot be used for everyday exchanges.

political controls as the Bundesbank itself. In fact, because of the strong German economy and the degree to which its neighbors have tied their exchange and interest rates to Germany's, the Bundesbank has already become a sort of European central bank, and these existing tacit arrangements could be formalized in the future, with a Eurofed Bank issuing ECUs in the way that the Bundesbank now issues DMs.

It was for this reason that Mrs. Thatcher told the House of Commons in late 1990, "If you hand over your sterling, you hand over the powers of this parliament to Europe."[19] With monetary unification, it becomes impossible for a single country to "steer" its economy by altering interest rates. What could it possibly mean, for example, for the Bank of France to increase the discount rate by 2 percent if banks and businesses could obtain the same currency at the old rate outside France? In September 1992, unable to bear the costs of keeping their currencies within the narrow exchange-rate bonds of the existing European monetary system, Britain and Italy left that system, dealing a heavy blow to earlier hopes of fiscal union by 1995. But would they even have had the independence to do such a thing had the EC states possessed a common currency? Since a European Federal Bank acting in the same way as the Bundesbank would be an extremely conservative body in its anti-inflationary policies, may not continued membership of the European monetary union eventually produce greater difficulties for France (where the Bank of France has little independence of the Treasury) or other countries which run large deficits?

In its noneconomic aspects also, the trend toward European unity is eroding national sovereignty, despite attempts by various political groups to prevent it. In the European Commission's view, economic integration is occurring so swiftly that it would be "very dangerous for the coherence of the Community" if the political relationships remained backward and immature.[20] This does not mean that agreement over political union will be smooth and steady. The way in which the Kuwait-Iraq crisis exposed Europe's fragmented stance on foreign-policy issues and Denmark and France's 1992 referenda on the Maastricht agreements revealed the strength of public unease at the further loss of national sovereignty were reminders of the difficulties in the way of an advance to a more federated Europe.

If further harmonization is to come, however, changes may be necessary in the functions and powers of existing EC institutions. At present the driving force toward integration is the European Commission, whose seventeen members are required to act independently of national concerns and consider the interests of the Community as a whole. While each commissioner has a department and portfolio—agriculture, competition policy, internal market and industry, regional policy, etc.—they all work toward implementing the various EC treaties on the harmonization of national procedures.

Nevertheless, the European Commission is not the *political* decision-making center of the EC, for that resides in the Council of Ministers—the ministers, that is, of the national states themselves. To several EC countries, in particular France, this is exactly where political power should lie, since those leaders have been democratically elected (whereas the commissioners have not) and Europe will progress only if its member states agree on the agenda together. Perhaps there could be a further watering-down of the unanimity principle—to prevent one or two members from blocking what the others want to do—but the French conception of enhanced political harmonization for Europe consists essentially of the heads of state (and other ministers) meeting more often and making the big decisions.

Such ideas reflect Paris's desire to turn Europe into a factor in world affairs *without* surrendering France's cherished national identity; but this emphasis upon policymaking by doing deals within the Council of Ministers causes concern among the genuine European federalists, who want instead to enhance the powers of the European Parliament, a deliberating assembly of 518 members directly elected for five-year terms with numbers apportioned by population size.[21] Federalists believe this body may become the equivalent of the U.S. House of Representatives, with the power of the purse, ability to vote on policies proposed by the executive, etc. At present, however, it is held in check by more powerful and jealous authorities: the European Commission, fearing that its own pan-European agenda might be blocked by a parliamentary coalition of local interests; the heads of state/Council of Ministers, many of whom dislike the idea of conceding powers to a

parliament in which their nationals would be in a distinct minority;*
and, finally, the national parliaments and assemblies themselves, most
of whom oppose the transfer abroad of their powers. Only slowly have
the European Parliament's rights been extended, therefore, and the
Strasbourg assembly still possesses "only feeble powers of amendment."[22] It can dismiss the European Commission and reject the
budget, but those are dramatic and in a way emergency powers; in
practice, many of its decisions bind neither the council nor the commission.

As the EC approaches the twenty-first century, then, fresh proposals
for greater integration keep cropping up. Ideas are afoot to establish
a second chamber or a "senate" at Strasbourg, or a committee of
national MPs to scrutinize EC legislation; and, as noted earlier, rival
schemes are under way to strengthen either the Council of Ministers
(the French preference) or the European Parliament (the German
preference), while other countries (Britain and Denmark especially)
appear suspicious of all such ideas. Despite the early media excitement
about "Europe 1992," the public mood is much more uncertain, suggesting that political unity will not be achieved easily.

Yet, for all the unevenness and messiness, there actually has been a sort
of dialectical advance, so that the "Europe" of 1992 is different from
that of 1980, just as the Europe of 1973 was different from that of
1957. Whether driven by business pressures for a full common market
or by such external trends as the rise of Japan, the movement toward
integration rarely slows down for long. Disagreement in one area (agriculture, or currency reform) has not prevented agreement elsewhere
(regional policy, or overseas aid), for there are simply too many forces
at work for everything to come to a halt. Slowly but surely, it is argued,
"the Community is becoming rather less a collection of nation-states
and rather more a coherent entity which the rest of the world recog-
nizes as a power in itself."[23]

*Even the larger EC countries can send only eighty-one members to the 518-strong European
Parliament.

But if this is true, then Europe must also become a "coherent entity" in the difficult areas of foreign and defense policy. For many reasons, Europe could not develop an independent stance on diplomatic and strategic issues after World War II. Traditions of national rivalry, the shattered state of its economy, the uncertainty about how to deal with Germany, and the mounting pressures on its eastern borders from the USSR all meant that Western Europe's security could be preserved only within a "North Atlantic" foreign- and defense-policy structure dominated by Washington. Several decades later, however, things began to change. Europe not only approached the United States in overall wealth but was also becoming much stronger economically than the languishing Soviet Union. America's productivity and growth rates were slowing, and its increasingly large federal deficits were troubling bankers and congressmen alike. On both sides of the Atlantic, therefore, voices began to call for change, and in particular for Europe to assume an ever-increasing share of its own defense, perhaps even to develop its own defense policies.[24]

In theory, of course, there was a lot to be said for the creation of a common European defense. Europe was rich enough to allocate 4 to 5 percent of its total GNP to defense, sufficient to provide an array of strategic and conventional forces similar to those possessed by the post-1945 superpowers. The scientific and manufacturing structures— and the military-industrial complex—were in place; and if the ground forces of Germany, France, Britain, and Italy alone were merged, there would exist one of the largest and best-equipped armies in the world, albeit one with communications problems. Since this solution was and is feasible, why shouldn't Europe "grow up" and rely increasingly less on the United States for its defense? After all, the transatlantic relationship could remain—because of economic, cultural, and other ties— even after the gradual dissolution of NATO.

With the collapse of the Soviet Union, the debate upon Europe's future defense has entered upon an entirely new course. To be sure, the Cold War's end produced immense relief at the fading of the threat of nuclear obliteration and at the transformation of the political and strategical landscape; amazingly, there had taken place "a deep, multidimensional shift in power to the West,"[25] and a redrawing of the map of Europe, yet without major war. But if that eased the pressures upon Western defense forces—and led to considerable cuts in defense spending—it also threw the planners into confusion as they considered the uncertainties which the vastly altered international conditions might produce. Naturally, the first concern was to demilitarize the great arsenals of the European continent as swiftly as possible, through a series of linked East-West negotiations: the Conference on Security and Cooperation in Europe (CSCE), an outgrowth of the 1975 Helsinki Accords, which brought together all thirty-five states in Europe and North America to work upon further "confidence and security building measures"; the Vienna negotiations on Conventional Forces in Europe (CFE) to establish conventional-force reductions and impose operational constraints on armed forces across the entire continent; and other talks on mutual aerial surveillance (the "Open Skies Agreement"), on the reduction and eventual elimination of chemical weapons, and on crisis prevention.[26]

Assuming that this complex process is not disrupted, policymakers in the West will have to address the longer-term issue of whether NATO itself should continue. Created to meet the extraordinary circumstances of the late 1940s, the alliance served its task admirably, but with the Cold War "over"—indeed, with Russian and Ukrainian leaders occasionally declaring that they hope their states can join—it is not surprising that calls have arisen to replace NATO by something else, more general, more political, less American. In such a period of flux, an entire *à la carte* menu of options could be considered. The nineteenth-century Concert of Europe, that is, a big-powers "club" to keep the others in order, has been proposed as one possible model. The Conference on Security and Cooperation in Europe is another favored forum, partly because no one in Europe is excluded (San Marino, the Holy See, and Liechtenstein are all members) and it possesses a broad political agenda as well as dealing with disarmament and peacekeeping issues.[27]

This search for newer structures to provide for Europe's future security has been further complicated by the reemergence of the "German question," that is, how to achieve a harmonious relationship between the most populous, economically productive, technologically advanced, and (in past experience) militarily efficient nation in Europe and its smaller, less powerful neighbors. This question has deep historical overtones, going back to before Bismarck's time;[28] and while the German question appeared to be "answered" by the post-1945 division of Europe, it proved only a temporary solution. Anti-German circles in Europe and the United States remain suspicious that this large nation, enhanced in size and population, will be tempted to throw its weight around politically, even perhaps militarily.[29] Given the thoroughness of the "denazification" process and Berlin's embarrassment at being drawn into armed conflicts, it is difficult to see how apprehensions about German aggressiveness have any current validity, although so many changes have occurred in European politics recently that it is not surprising such fears exist.

What is more plausible is that Germany's economic importance will give it increasing weight within the EC and toward Central and Eastern Europe; and that the Franco-German "duopoly," which set the pace for EC policies over previous decades, might no longer operate as before. If there is to be a European currency union and a European federal bank, few doubt who will have the largest say in how the new system operates. Diplomatically, if Germany is bent upon an action (e.g., the recognition of an independent Croatia), its neighbors find they can do little but follow suit. It is also possible to imagine German dominance of a future European defense organization, especially in the procurement of tanks, fighters, and the like. Meanwhile, a German commercial and financial *pénétration pacifique* into Central and Eastern Europe is probably inevitable, for geographical reasons and the complementarity of trade relations with countries like Hungary and Romania; indeed, once the Iron Curtain was lifted, a resumption of those links was virtually certain to follow. Although anxious Poles might hint that it is "bad" if foreign investment in Poland is "majority German,"[30] that ratio will change only if other Western countries direct large funds there; if they do not, then German investments are surely better than none.

Whether this unease about Germany's future is anachronistic or not, it exists in some quarters and has caused the German leadership to call for Germany to be more firmly embedded in pan-European structures and for the EC to move as swiftly as possible toward the "strong," integrated European solution. Far from disengaging from its western neighbors, Germany stressed its wish for closer relationships to ensure, in Thomas Mann's words, "not a German Europe, but a European Germany."[31] No doubt this was meant genuinely, but does it address the problem of uneven national sizes (and thus uneven influences) in a united Europe? Before 1989 the EC had enough difficulty in reaching accords when it consisted of four medium-sized nations and another eight medium-to-very-small nations. Will it be more coherent in the future, if it consists of one large nation (Germany), three or four medium-sized ones (France, Britain, Italy, Spain), and, say, ten to fifteen countries of varying smaller sizes? Admittedly, such territorial disproportions exist between California and Delaware and Rhode Island; but this is the "old" world, not the "new," and it remains to be seen whether centuries of European nationalism can be subsumed without rancor into the proposed new structures.

In sum, whether one considers currency issues or defense issues, the EC's dilemma is the same. The "strong" and integrated European solution is extremely attractive in theory, at least to the committed federalists, but it contains innumerable problems in practice. If, however, Europe retains the "weak" and loosely organized solution, it also faces problems. It will remain marginal in world affairs except in economic terms, and even there its massive potential may be hampered by continuing disunity. Far from having settled things by preferring merely a limited amount of commercial harmonization, the EC could find itself facing a contradiction between increasingly integrated, pan-European economic practices on the one hand and increasingly inadequate political structures on the other. For this reason some Community members eager to deepen their unity (the Benelux countries, Germany, Italy) occasionally suggest a "twin-speed" solution, in which they go on ahead, leaving less enthusiastic members (Britain, Greece, and others) to follow suit when they will. Yet that itself, others suspect, brings a fresh batch of problems once the practical consequences are examined.[32]

Will these now-familiar questions—currency harmonization, modifying the CAP, giving more powers to the European Parliament, improving defense coordination, negotiating the admission into the EC of such well-qualified candidates as Austria and Switzerland, hand-wringing over the Community's inability to achieve a unified foreign policy toward (say) the Middle East—also be the sole or main agenda items for European politicians as they and their publics move into the next century? In particular, will Europe be allowed the luxury of concentrating on its own special debate—how far to unify—aloof from the global trends, and possible global turbulences, discussed in Part One of this book? The answer must surely be no. In fact, as will be discussed below, member states of the EC and their citizens are already being affected by demographic trends, migration, environmental issues, the globalization of industry, and the coming of new technologies—and are likely to be further affected in the next few decades. Although undoubtedly prosperous and well equipped compared with much of the rest of the world—and in that sense "winners" rather than "losers"—Europeans would be foolish to assume that they can remain untouched by the broader impacts of demography and technology upon our planet.

This, then, is the "double agenda" for European policymakers: to hammer out the future shape of the EC *at the same time* as they face the broad trends affecting all societies on this planet. Whether the internal controversies will hinder preparations for transnational changes or these changes will stimulate European unity so that an integrated Community will better be able to deal with global forces is the key question.

Demographic trends will clearly be an increasingly important issue for Europe's leaders and their planners. Until recently, the focus was upon "the graying of Europe"; for example, the 10 million out of France's 55 million people aged over sixty will have risen to 15 million by 2020.[33] Because of the plunge in European population replacement rates—especially in Germany and Italy but also in most other countries of Europe—most populations appear indeed headed for absolute decline. In fact, only Ireland had a fertility rate over 2.1 children per mother, the natural replacement level. West Germany, whose population was forecast (in early 1989) to fall from 61 million to 45 million by 2030, was said to be "committing suicide"; if present trends persisted, the same forecast reported, "Europe's vaunted market of 320 million people will peak in 2000—and fall to less than 300 million by 2100."[34] Economists, demographers, and other planners pointed to the

economic and social implications of this decline—the closing of schools
in rural and inner-city areas, shortages of skilled labor, the need to
increase job mobility throughout the EC and to invest much more in
training, and the pressures upon social and health-care services as a
larger proportion of the population becomes over sixty-five.[35] Perhaps
this demographic pattern will reverse itself, as it has done in Sweden
and certain other Northern European states in recent years;* but the
general tendency is toward a smaller population.

In the special case of West Germany, this declining population trend
altered in the late 1980s because the political thaw in the Soviet Union
and Eastern Europe allowed an increasing migration of ethnic Germans, from 50,000 (1986) to 200,000 (1987) and an enormous 380,000
as the DDR disintegrated (1989); most of these immigrants were
younger people who could be trained.[36] German unification altered the
situation again, by incorporating lots of elderly "East" Germans, so the
Berlin government now confronts its former long-term demographic
challenge—this time with a population of 78 million, not 61 million.

Still, if this were the extent of the EC's demographic problems, they
would probably be capable of solution, through better support for
young married couples (to increase the birth rate) and—in Germany's
case—measures to retrain newly arrived ethnic Germans from Hungary
and elsewhere so that they could enter the work force. But the entire
situation could be altered by circumstances *outside* the EC's borders
and, to some extent, outside its control. The disintegration of both the
USSR and of its enforced order over former Warsaw Pact countries
opens up the possibility of ethnic tensions, border wars, social turbulence, and the mass migration of refugees.† The horrible example of
"ethnic cleansing" in Bosnia and large parts of Croatia in the summer
of 1992 drove millions of homeless, desperate people onto the roads,
heading north and west. Moreover, economic dislocations across Eastern Europe and the former Soviet Union are adding to the flood of
those seeking jobs, shelter, and security. If a full-scale economic collapse occurs—or, on the other hand, a significant reconstruction of
industry and agriculture is pushed through, causing the loss of millions

---

*For further discussion of this reversal, see below, p. 343.
†See the discussion in Chapter 11.

of jobs from inefficient factories and collective farms in the former USSR and Eastern Europe—the temptation for millions to migrate to the EC will be increased. Already, Germany, Austria, and Hungary feel besieged by refugee families.[37]

For France, Spain, and Italy, by contrast, the larger demographic problem lies to the south, in the fast-growing populations of the states of North Africa. Already France contains several million immigrants, chiefly from its former African colonies, and about a million are working in Italy (given illegal immigration, the number could be considerably higher).[38] These newcomers carry out the tasks—fruit-picking, factory work, transport services, cleaning—that Europeans are not eager to do themselves; but their presence has provoked a rise in native resentments, leading to occasional riots, a surge in right-wing political parties calling for repatriation, and worried official discussions about how to handle the problem. The greatest apprehension is that this is only the beginning, and that population and economic trends in Africa will produce a mass future migration unless it is forcibly prevented. As Algeria's population doubles from 25 to 50 million between now and 2025 and Egypt's soars from 55 to 95 million, how else will so many of these new entrants to the global work force find jobs *except* by joining their cousins already on the other side of the Mediterranean? Simply because of numbers and geography, the former Italian minister Gianni De Michelis recently predicted "terrible demographic pressure in the next ten to fifteen years."[39]

Inevitably, these fears make it more difficult for European federalists to push for unimpeded movement of people within the EC borders (and help to explain why the European Commission has been lukewarm to Turkey's membership application and worries about admitting Austria, Hungary, and their neighbors). If some EC governments are opposed to relaxing immigration and customs procedures at airports and ports—pleading the need to check terrorists, drug dealers, and illegal immigrants—how much more worried will they be if an enlarged Community becomes the destination of millions and millions of Eastern European, Russian, Middle Eastern, and African refugees? Unlike the continent-wide United States, European states do not see themselves as melting-pot societies, so the argument that Europe *needs* immigrants to forestall future labor shortages—again, because of the "graying" of its indigenous population—is not a popular one. Even those supporting the liberal Schengen Accord, by which Belgium, France, the Netherlands, Luxembourg, and West Germany agreed to abolish all formalities at their shared frontiers, found their plans suspended, for a while, because of the DDR's economic collapse and concern about a flood of East German immigrants; if nothing else, it was a warning that abolishing frontiers within the EC could produce major difficulties.[40]

In other words, far from being something that Europe can safely ignore, global demographic trends can affect the social order, delay (or reverse) the opening of the EC's internal barriers, and even influence its foreign policy. Over the next few decades, migration may become the single most important aspect of relations between the EC and the Muslim world; and if certain European states eventually contain large numbers of Arabs, will that not affect Europe's stance on Near Eastern conflicts, should any occur in the future? If the nations of Europe have difficulty in forging a common foreign policy toward the neighboring civil war in Bosnia, how likely are they to adopt a united stance over future convulsions in the Ukraine or North Africa? How can European politicians control the surge in nativist reactions against immigrants from Africa and Asia when fresh incidents of unrest in, say, Algiers cause increasing numbers of secular, middle-class Algerians to consider moving to France—while the same reports provoke a surge in popularity of right-wing nationalist leaders like Le Pen? How will European cities retain their character and appeal if, over the next few decades, large numbers of poor immigrants form mass ghettoes of underprivilege; and will the EC's social funds bear the strain? Finally, if strict "Fortress Europe" policies are adopted—essentially, using the armed forces to prevent illegal migration by land, sea, or air—does that really address the larger problem, that Europe's overall population is stagnating while those of neighboring continents are forecast to double and treble by early next century?

The same conclusion—about Europe's vulnerability to events *elsewhere*—may also be true with regard to other transnational trends. In dealing with environmental issues, for example, Europe has encountered the same experiences as other developed areas. Growing population and industrialization during this century led to atmospheric pollution, contaminated rivers and seas, and a damaged countryside; but it also produced environmental pressure groups and efforts to undo the damage, at first nationally and then by international agreement. Predictably, persuading Germans to accept reduced speed limits on their autobahns or Britons to enforce stricter controls on emissions being carried to Norway still causes disagreements. But in Northern and Western Europe the rivers and air are less polluted than a quarter century ago, and even in Mediterranean lands there is growing environmental consciousness. After all, northwestern Europe and Scandinavia are rich enough to pay for an environmentally friendly economy, possess an articulate middle class concerned about such issues, and have a tradition of state intervention for the common good; thus, enacting measures to protect the environment is like legislating worker safety or child welfare. Already the European Commission is pressing for much higher "clean energy" taxes, pointedly noting that Europe is more willing to pay the cost of reducing carbon dioxide emissions than America.[41]

The effects of global warming upon EC and EFTA countries are probably also containable, at least locally. Some studies suggest that Western Europe's climate might become drier, with decreased soil moisture affecting grain output[42]—although that might well be balanced by the enhanced yields from biotech farming discussed below. As in the United States, hotter temperatures could cause crops to migrate northward, hurting some European farmers while benefiting others. Rising sea levels could harm certain low-lying areas like the Netherlands and the Fenlands of Britain, but most of these societies have the engineering and financial resources to protect their coasts, if they choose to do so; competent hydraulic engineering could probably also prevent Venice from meeting its oft-forecast death by drowning. In fact, the biggest impact of global warming on Europe might be to reduce water supplies, as saltwater intrusion expands upriver and into lower-lying regions.

Europe's most serious environmental concerns, therefore, will once again arise from developments elsewhere, in Eastern Europe and the developing world. As noted earlier, heavy-handed industrialization by COMECON countries has left a legacy of poisoned lakes and streams, soil full of chemicals and metals, unsafe power plants, ravaged woodlands, and industrial pollution drifting across the Baltic to Scandinavia. With the collapse of Communism, this can now be arrested and recovery begun. However, given the scale of the damage and the task of upgrading the industrial structures of Eastern Europe, it is doubtful that even the wealthy EC and EFTA will be able to do all they want during the next decade, especially if there are shortages in global liquidity.

Equally worrying environmentally is the massive growth in the populations surrounding the Mediterranean (especially in Turkey, Syria, and North African states), and the even swifter migration from inland villages to water-short, polluted coastal settlements. In Algeria, for example, 53 percent of the fast-growing population squeezes into 3 percent of the land area, and the sewage is untreated—as it is, for that matter, in Athens, Sicily, and other parts of the Mediterranean's northern coastline. Add to this pollution a myriad of small oil spills and the draining of wetlands, the fact that Mediterranean waters (being virtually enclosed) do not renew themselves very swiftly, and the boom in tourism all along its crowded coasts, and the resultant environmental pressures are appalling. While a "Blue Plan" exists to arrest this damage, it is not clear from where the tens of billions of dollars required will come—and all reform measures run a desperate race against population growth. By contrast, being both far less populous and much richer, the Baltic and North Sea states clearly have an easier "clean-up" task ahead of them than Mediterranean countries.[43]

Most societies in northwest Europe and Scandinavia demonstrate a concern, *relatively speaking,* for the developing world as well as for global warming, presumably because they possess well-educated populations with a liberal, humanistic culture and an interest in world affairs. Some of this concern—as in France's case—may also reflect a desire to preserve influence over former colonial territories. Nevertheless, because some European states have recognized that the developing world requires attention, technical assistance, and financial aid, they contribute more than the targeted average (0.7 percent of GNP annually) that OECD nations agree to give (see Chart 11).

In absolute amounts, of course, 1 percent of Norway's or Sweden's GNP may not amount to much; but it offers an example which, if ever copied by larger economies like those of Britain, Germany, Japan, and

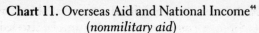

Chart 11. Overseas Aid and National Income[44]
(*nonmilitary aid*)

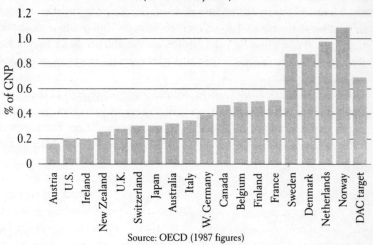

Source: OECD (1987 figures)

(especially) the United States, could massively boost the flow of resources from rich to poor nations. On the other hand, compared with the *needs* of developing countries—and the fact that someday their burgeoning populations and exhausted ecologies may drive families en masse toward the wealthier regions of the globe—even the allocation of 1 percent of GNP to overseas aid may in retrospect appear a totally inadequate premium for achieving global stability.

A much more mixed picture emerges regarding Europe's preparedness to deal with technologically driven global changes. For example, the biotech revolution in agriculture and food processing may at first seem to benefit Europe: the region contains the world's largest chemical companies, which produce one-third of the world's chemical output; it has hundreds of institutes, university departments, and private companies engaged in food research, agricultural studies, biotechnology, marine biology, and so on; and it possesses national governments, and the European Commission itself, working to improve the region's competitiveness. Yet biotech is turning into a political minefield, because of the social structure of European agriculture and the workings of the CAP described above.* Compared to the United States, the EC possesses many more farmers, especially peasant farmers with extremely small plots; in Greece and Portugal, for example, the average farm size is only 4.3 hectares, and the Community's average is just 13 hectares.† Then there is the special way in which the EC supports agriculture, described by *The Economist* as "the single most idiotic system of economic mismanagement that the rich western countries have ever devised."[45] Still, the fact is that the system will not readily disappear, because 10 million farmers possess enormous political weight and enhance Europe's tendency to try to insulate itself.

The biotech revolution in agriculture and food processing threatens these already strained arrangements in numerous ways. First, it promises large increases in output per unit, whether milk, beef, or grain crops; the average annual milk yield per cow in the Netherlands, for example, is forecast to rise from its mid to late 1980s figure of 5,000 kilograms to 8,000–8,500 kilograms by the year 2000.[46] This will place enormous, perhaps impossible strains upon the existing structure of price supports; since the European Commission is trying to *reduce* overall output, a surge in yields would lead to more items (milk powder, butter) put into storage, more cattle stock taken out of production, more farmers leaving agriculture. While one might imagine that countries with large dairy herds (the U.K. average is fifty-seven cows per farm, the Netherlands average forty) would benefit more than those with small herds (Greece's average is three cows per farm, Italy's seven), the 1984 quota system assigns a maximum output for each country, so that productivity rises "will force producers out of the market where the increases are *highest.*"[47] Given the nature of CAP financing and the social and political implications of declining agriculture in many parts of the EC, spending on this sector may have to rise, not fall, as biotech advances over the next decade.

Studies of the biotech revolution suggest that most farmers will become increasingly dependent upon giant agrochemical conglomerates. This may occur fairly swiftly in a laissez-faire economy like that of the United States, but the European record indicates that there will

---

*See above, pp. 264–65.
†1 hectare equals 2.47 acres.

be a much greater degree of official protection of traditional agriculture. The British government's 1988 decision not to approve the bovine growth hormone BST, ostensibly on public-health grounds, but also for economic reasons; the EC's opposition to isoglucose (seen as a rival to sugar beets), its banning of genetically altered tomatoes, and other regulatory controls upon biotech research are slowing the spread of new products in Europe relative to elsewhere in the developed world. This will not stop further intensive research by biotech companies, but most of that will be done in North American rather than European laboratories.[48]

Still, prohibitions are not going to stop the advance of biotechnology in agriculture and foodstuffs. Banning the bovine growth hormone is one thing; but a whole gamut of improvements such as new seed varieties, advances in animal stockbreeding, increased protein content in plants, and extracting more from by-products is already approved of, steadily pushing up average yields in every area. Moreover, as each sector grapples with its surplus, biotechnology offers ingenious ways (through fermentation, fragmentation, recomposition, protein enhancement) to turn that product into something else, and then to invade *another* sector's traditional market. Starch, for example, previously drawn from maize (imported, and French) and domestically grown potatoes, is increasingly derived from surplus wheat; dairy proteins are being replaced by vegetable proteins, so that condensed milk loses ground to coffee creamers. In consequence, Europe's agricultural "lobby" may dissolve into warring factions, each struggling for market share in an age of increasingly interchangeable materials.[49]

One escape from this crisis might be greater agricultural exports, as well as the near-complete substitution of imports. Some calculations show that it is technically feasible to replace all the EC's animal feed imports (over 20 million tons per year), as well as oil and vegetable fat (over 4 million tons per year), *and* cut imports of forestry products (over 120 million cubic meters per year).[50] Whether or not that would mop up all of Europe's future agricultural surpluses is unclear; but a policy of enhanced exports and diminished imports would certainly produce enormous rows with the United States and other major food-exporting nations and would hurt producers in the developing world.[51] Perhaps the only bright spot is the potential of Europe's farmland to produce energy biomass—to perhaps 100 million tons of coal equivalent a year, according to one estimate.[52] As at present, however, the surpluses remain and the demands for CAP funds grow.

Given the travails of the existing EC agricultural system, one can understand the European Commission's alarm at the idea of membership by the nations of Central and Eastern Europe. Already the absorption of the DDR has cost billions of dollars and increased overall agricultural output, as farmers in Germany's eastern provinces responded to the high CAP prices. The same may be expected elsewhere in Eastern Europe, where farming can be very productive when not hampered by collectivization and Eastern European farmers imitate the more efficient techniques of the West. Such surpluses would put further pressure on CAP's troubled finances and, as agriculture in Eastern and Central Europe modernized and shed workers, on the Community's regional and social funds.* Here, then, is yet another example of how Europe's existing problems are complicated by transnational developments and new technologies.[53]

While the robotics revolution also challenges European societies, it probably will not become as politically controversial and entangled in the debate on the EC's future as advances in biotech. Automating production is a long-standing and incremental process and tends to occur in decentralized fashion, from factory to factory. Also, it has affected only a few European industries (automobile assembly, painting, etc.); and the robots used have engaged chiefly in dirty and dangerous work, so that although Europe's trade unions remain suspicious of automation, they have offered less opposition than might have been expected. Finally, the robotics industry itself, along with the computerized machine-tool industry, has created employment for a considerable number of skilled and highly paid workers.

The likelihood is, therefore, that there will be a steady but undramatic increase in robots employed by European industry, particularly in Germany; but investment in them will follow the usual business criteria—labor-saving potential, expected improvement in quality production, increased output—and will be on a plant-by-plant basis. The

*In the late 1980s, agriculture's share of Eastern Europe's labor force averaged 13 percent—in Romania, 24 percent—which can be compared with 2.6 percent in the EC and 0.8 percent in the United States.

rate of installation might increase more swiftly if Japanese factories *inside* Europe automate at significantly higher rates (say, close to the levels of automation in Japanese home plants), because that would put pressure upon European firms in the same industry. In health care, the use of intelligent mobile robots might also expand steadily, because of shortages of skilled nursing staff for a rapidly aging population. Finally, it is conceivable that automation could become part of the debate over immigration from developing countries. Will some nationalist politicians, observing what is happening in Japan, press for similar levels of automation to obviate the need to import guest workers as the work force shrinks? And will those businesses and service industries which are labor-intensive, not capital-intensive, press instead for continued immigration? Will "white" trade unions prefer robots to working alongside Arabs?

On the whole, Europe is unlikely to follow Japan's systemic move into automation simply because it is not at present facing a general labor shortage. Admittedly, shortages of skilled workers exist in specific EC industries and regions; but officials, businessmen and unions generally believe that the correct response is to increase the skill levels of the work force and to encourage job mobility within the EC.[54] Given the structural unemployment in many EC nations—which would be augmented by the inclusion of the Eastern European states—there would be widespread concern if automation threw lots of industrial workers out of their jobs. Robots may increasingly be used in the wealthier EC countries, but operating alongside human beings rather than replacing them en masse. Whether this will permit European industry to remain competitive with hyperefficient, fully automated Japanese rivals, instead of relying on protection and experiencing relative decline, is much less clear.

More challenging to European societies are the financial and communications revolution and the emergence of the truly multinational corporation. Those transnational developments are, in many fields, partly Europe's own achievements. Its bankers have learned to globalize themselves and to engage in twenty-four-hour-a-day trading. Its giant companies, like their American and Japanese counterparts, have set up assembly plants, research laboratories, and distribution centers in the major world markets. Its consultants, engineers, and merchant bankers offer their services in every continent. Its deep-pocketed media conglomerates buy out foreign newspapers and book publishers. Its airlines (British Airways, Lufthansa, SAS) span the globe. While it receives significant amounts of foreign investment—American and Japanese companies getting into the EC before 1992—it also exports enormous sums of capital to purchase land, companies, equities, and bonds overseas, as well as to finance joint ventures. Theoretically, therefore, Europe is well positioned to become a major beneficiary of the globalization of finance, industry, and commerce, provided, of course, that worldwide financial instabilities do not occur.

However, two serious problems remain. First, the move toward unrestricted globalization might create the social gulf that Robert Reich notes in the United States; that is, the emergence of an upper stratum of lawyers, engineers, consultants, and other "symbolic analysts" catering to transnational demand for their services, while the lower four-fifths of society is increasingly at the mercy of multinational companies moving production *in and out* of regions for the sake of comparative advantage. Yet, while there has been a great expansion of symbolic analysts in Europe in recent years and European countries have shifted some production to countries like the United States to ensure continued access to those countries' markets, the social consequences Reich discusses may not perhaps be so severe in Europe.[55] A deeper sense of company roots and more interventionist state traditions could deter the full-scale transfer of production from one country to another. In any case, relocation of plants to other parts of the EC would make less economic sense if there is "harmonization" of social welfare, minimum wages, and general living standards; whereas if production is moved *outside* the EC the goods may be unable to enter Europe's protected markets. Finally, the EC's higher social security "net" for the unemployed would ease the impact of business closures upon workers.

Secondly, to what extent does the emergence of a "borderless world" contradict the EC's aim of deepening its economic and political unity? As noted already, there has always been tension between those favoring a strong Europe and those wanting a less centralized body. To the former, the EC should steadily eliminate discriminations among its member states (tariffs, capital controls, national subsidies, immigration barriers) and move toward integration *while maintaining and in some ways enhancing the barriers between Europeans and non-Europeans;* after all, there was no sense in creating a unified "Europe" if virtually everyone else could enjoy its privileges. The latter, by contrast, prefer a less exclusive Europe because they do not like walls between it and non-European bodies (the Commonwealth, the United States) and the latter's goods and services.

On the whole, and despite such setbacks as the Danish referendum against Maastricht, the integrationists have been gaining ground, with important consequences for Europe's future and the international economy. The theory of the borderless world implies that a "sovereign" European customer ought to be free to purchase U.S. beef rather than French beef, or a car made in Japan rather than a car made in Italy, if the price is right.[56] By contrast, the CAP's purpose is that the customer should consume European (if not solely French) beef, while many politicians and businessmen clearly intend Europe's industrial tariffs and quotas to deter the customer from buying a Japanese car rather than a native European (if not solely Italian) one. The larger implication here is that far from national borders being dismantled, they are simply being folded into a bigger entity—the EC, a North American free-trade zone, a yen-dominated area—with the world economy increasingly dominated by three enormous regional trading blocs. This would leave the countries outside desperately begging for market access, which they would be unlikely to get if European protectionist lobbies have their way. It would also presumably reduce employment prospects in those countries, and therefore *increase* the pressures to migrate to Europe in search of jobs.

Isn't there, then, an underlying contradiction between what the EC is striving to become and where the global economy is headed? As we have seen, this dialectic between national purposes and transnational changes exists in all countries; but perhaps the contradiction is greater in this case because European nations are moving toward integration into a new "superstate" just when trends in technology and communications loosen state controls, erode all borders, and question our traditional concern with national or regional identities as opposed to membership in the entire human race. In effect, trends in technology—like those in demography—threaten to make redundant the traditional agenda items which have been the focus of EC politics for the past four decades.

European integrationists often deny that they wish to distance their countries from the rest of the world; but they may have to consider more carefully than hitherto what the various policies for deepening Europe's unity mean *in practice* for others. Much of the world worries that access to markets in the advanced economies will be restricted. There is also considerable mistrust among political and business circles in Japan and (especially) the United States concerning European protectionism.[57] In sum, a broad international feeling exists that the EC, in pursuit of its own destiny, is less interested in boosting global commerce by opening markets and more willing to protect its own farmers and industrial workers, even at the cost of worsening trade relations with the developed world and hurting the prospects of the developing world. This concern may be unjustified, and the forecasts (especially prominent in the American press) that a "trade war" will replace the Cold War could also turn out to be exaggerated. Still, as the rest of the world watches Europe's integration, it clearly is concerned by its meaning for others.

It is not simply for economic reasons that great attention ought to be paid to Europe's future. It is engaged in a political experiment of the highest importance concerning how human societies think about themselves and relationships with others. As many experts on world affairs have pointed out, we seem to be witnessing a decline in the traditional loyalties, structures, and associations which have made *nations* the focal point of political and economic identity; instead, there is a growing "relocation of authority" discussed earlier, a relocation which concerns both larger (transnational) and smaller (regional, ethnic) units as politicians and peoples strive to discover what size state will work best in our present and future world. This sounds fine in theory, but one wonders what it means in practice. If a civilized and sophisticated people like the Danes vote against further measures of European integration, will there ever come a time when an organization like the EC will appear legitimate in the eyes of its peoples as national governments were? And how will such an organization relate in a meaningful way to the needs of regional units like Wallonia, Tuscany, the Upper Rhine, and South Wales? Are, in fact, the upward and downward relocations of authority contradictory—or complementary? As we know, the world of the late twentieth century is being moved by two currents. One, driven by technology and communications and trade, tends toward ever greater economic integration. The second is the revived tendency toward ethnic separatism, currently exacerbated by the collapse of a transcendent creed (Communism), the rise of religious fundamentalism, and increasing internal questioning (from Croatia to Somalia) of national borders that were superimposed, often from outside, upon very different ethnic groups; it is also exacerbated at times by economic fears.

In both respects, Europe's role has been critical historically. In the first half of this century, Europe offered dreadful examples of how excessive nationalism, ethnic prejudices, and desire for gain could plunge so-called civilized societies into war. After 1950, however, Europeans have been seeking to learn from past mistakes, creating a structure which would produce economic integration and sink national differences. Considering the fractured relationships elsewhere (East Asia, the Middle East, Central Africa, South Asia), Europe's march towards unity has been remarkable despite its flaws and offers an example to all strife-torn regions. If the leaders of states like Germany and France now wish to be at lasting peace with their neighbors after centuries of conflict and to embed themselves in larger, transnational units, might that not also happen at some time in the future to clusters of countries elsewhere, from South Asia to Latin America? And if it did, would that not be an advance upon today's regional fractures?

Of course, Europe still has a long way to travel and there are innumerable obstacles in the way, not least those thrown up by the new global forces that challenge all societies and—as argued above—pose perhaps special problems for the EC at this stage in its development. Yet it is precisely because of those global forces for change that the integrationists' argument *ought* to prevail over those who merely desire to erect a large trading consortium. In the light of all that is happening in world affairs—the disappearance of the USSR and the possibility of regional conflicts in the successor territories, the rise of East Asian economic power, the emergence of nuclear-armed local Great Powers (India, China), the protracted social and economic difficulties of the United States, the chances of demographically driven struggles, resource wars, and mass migration, the looming population imbalances between North and South, the long-term dangers of environmental damage—Europe surely has no real alternative to *moving forward*, seeking to create an influential and responsible entity capable of meeting these challenges collectively in a way that twelve or twenty separate nation-states simply cannot do. No one will deny that the task is enormous, especially given the tension between "deepening" the Community and "widening" its membership. Yet the profundity of international change, demanding new thinking and new structures, strengthens the position of those who argue that Europe simply cannot stay still.

While the larger logic of historical change favors the integrationists, they in turn need to respond imaginatively to the challenge and opportunity offered. At present, far too much of the rhetoric about Europe's destiny is accompanied by self-serving political maneuvers, bureaucratic infighting, blatant efforts to protect economic inefficiencies, national interests seeking to control and divert pan-European purposes, and protectionist, inward-looking tendencies—all confirming the worst suspicions of the anti-integrationists as well as those of other countries. Furthermore, the typical agenda of EC politics—how to reduce the "butter mountains," for example, or regulate accountancy standards—appears as excessively nitpicking and inward-focused in the light of the enormous demographic and technological forces that are changing the world. Whether any country or group of countries *can* respond effectively to the new transnational developments—some of which may manifest themselves swiftly and unpredictably—is unclear. But if European leaders spend so much time arguing over integration that little or none remains to consider coherent responses to demographic trends, migration, global warming, and the impact of new technologies, then their countries may be completely unprepared to handle the challenges ahead. Even in the early 1990s, it is clear that Europe cannot stand apart from the rest of the world's problems. How much clearer will that be in 2010 or 2030?

In sum, the burden is upon European federalists to outline how they can create a thriving unified body which will assume a responsible world role *without* hiding behind walls, adopting selfish policies, and running against the trends toward globalization; how they can further the EC's internal development at the same time as they seek to cope—and help poorer nations to cope—with global changes. Should it actually manage to reconcile those aims, Europe might find that the next century will be kinder to it than the present century has been. As things now stand, however, resolving such a cluster of major challenges seems unlikely— in which case, both Europe and the rest of the world will suffer the consequences.

13

THE AMERICAN DILEMMA

ALTHOUGH DEBATES ABOUT THE FUTURE of this and that country occur from France to Japan, perhaps nowhere are they more widespread than in the United States. In this large, decentralized, media-rich society, all sorts of controversies from abortion to "the end of History," from race to education, are vigorously debated, in books and newspapers and on radio and television, by pundits, pressure groups, op-ed writers, and lecture-circuit regulars. The controversy over America's future is also fueled by ideological differences: most (but certainly not all) conservatives emphasize American achievements—"winning" the Cold War, the success of capitalism—whereas liberal critics point to a growing legacy of problems—debt, social and educational decay, decline of middle-class standards of living, erosion of the country's economic leadership, and an overly large military presence abroad.[1] Because the debate over American "decline or renewal" has become politicized, the contenders proffer alternative measures of comparison and point to different aspects of the economy or society to support their positions,[2] which makes the matter more complicated.

This debate over the future of the United States is also intense because it occurs among a people who had believed—even before Henry Luce first used the term in 1941—that this is the "American century."[3] However accurate that expression will appear to future historians, it possessed an immense psychological and cultural power, providing emotional reinforcement to the American people. It gave them a sense of being "special," even superior; and once such feelings are acquired, it is difficult to let them go. It was predictable, therefore, that the appearance of books entitled *The End of the American Century, Beyond American Hegemony,* and *America as an Ordinary Power*[4] would provoke responses such as *The Myth of America's Decline, America's Economic Resurgence, Bound to Lead,* and *The Third Century: America's Resurgence in the Asian Era.*[5] Each new study is welcomed as reinforcement by a particular school—"a timely and forceful response to the doomsayers,"[6] etc., etc.—and the debate continues. Whether this outpouring will fade from natural exhaustion is impossible to forecast. What it suggests is a national mood very changed from that of Truman's time or even the experience of the Sputnik shock.[7] The United States is clearly more concerned about its future now than it was a generation or two ago.

What are America's strengths and weaknesses, and how well is it prepared to meet the global challenges outlined earlier in this study? In the traditional domain of "hard" or military-based power, the United States is unequaled by any other nation, including Russia and China. Both possess larger land forces, but there must be serious doubt about their overall quality. In any case, numbers are not as important as morale and training, sophistication of equipment, and capacity to project force to distant theaters; in all those aspects, the United States has devoted large resources during the 1980s to ensure the required standards. Strategically, it retains a panoply of air-, land-, and sea-based missile systems to intimidate another power from attacking it or its allies. Technologically, its armed services are equipped to fight "smart" wars, using everything from Stealth bombers and fighters to AEGIS cruisers and sophisticated night-fighting battlefield weapons. Through satellites, early-warning aircraft, and an extensive oceanic acoustical detection system, its forces usually have the means to spot what potential rivals are up to.[8]

Finally, it is the only country with a truly global "reach," with fleets and air bases and ground forces in every strategically important part of the world, plus the capacity to reinforce those positions in an emergency. Its response to the 1990 invasion of Kuwait by Iraq demonstrated the flexibility and extent of those abilities; in dispatching over 1,500 aircraft and 500,000 men (including heavy armored units) to Saudi Arabia in a matter of months, and in filling the Mediterranean, Persian Gulf, and Indian Ocean with carrier task forces, the United States displayed military power unequaled in recent times. Perhaps the only modern historical equivalent was Britain's "force projection" of over 300,000 soldiers, safely protected by the Royal Navy's command of the seas, to fight in the South African war at the beginning of this century.

As the Cold War fades away, the size and extent of U.S. deployments are being cut significantly; but it would be remarkable if the United States returned to its pre-1941 policy, under which no American military units were based outside the United States and its insular dependencies. As it is, the existence of regimes like those in Iraq and Libya aids the Pentagon in arguing the need to retain considerable and flexible armed forces.[9] Whatever reduction in American military power occurs, it is likely to possess far greater capacity than medium-sized countries like France and Britain and to retain a technological edge over Chinese and Russian forces.

Yet while this military power boosts the United States' place in world affairs, that may not necessarily be a blessing for the nation as a whole. Defense costs have caused some economic damage, and America's ability to handle nonmilitary threats is low. The Cold War provided the political "cement" to bind a majority of Americans, Republicans and Democrats alike, to large defense budgets and entangling alliances. With the Soviet threat removed, this consensus may disintegrate; at the least, it may be difficult for American leaders to justify a worldwide military presence to its own public. While some strategic thinkers debate whether forces should be withdrawn from Europe and concentrated against "out-of-area" threats in the developing world, others wonder about the *utility* of military force in general, since the threats to America may now come not from nuclear weapons but from environmental hazards, drugs, and the loss of economic competitiveness.[10]

As a consequence, the relief that the Soviet Union is no longer an "enemy" is overshadowed by uncertainties about the United States' proper world role.[11] To the traditionalists, it is important that America is present, in Europe, the Pacific, and elsewhere, in order to prevent any return to the anarchic conditions of the 1930s;[12] to the critics, the argument that the United States is "bound to lead" places burdens upon the American people, diverts resources from domestic needs, and takes American democracy further away from its original foreign-policy principles.[13] Such a debate is easily recognizable to historians. In general, the leading power favors international stability, to preserve the system in which it enjoys great influence and wealth; usually it has inherited a vast legacy of obligations and treaties, promissory notes to distant allies, and undertakings to keep open the world's seaways. But executing a special leadership role includes the danger of becoming the world's policeman, combating threats to "law and order" wherever they arise, and finding ever more "frontiers of insecurity" across the globe that require protection.[14] This suggests, therefore, that the debate over the future of American external policy will go on.

Such a debate cannot be separated from domestic concerns, simply because of the cost of maintaining such a global position; $300 billion a year bought military security for the United States, but it also diverted resources—capital, armed forces personnel, materials, skilled labor, engineers, and scientists—from nonmilitary production. In 1988, for example, over 65 percent of federal R&D monies were allocated to defense, compared with 0.5 percent to environmental protection and 0.2 percent to industrial development. Moreover, while engaging Moscow in an expensive arms race, America has had to compete for world market shares against allies like Japan and Germany which have allocated smaller percentages of their national resources to the military, thus freeing capital, personnel, and R&D for commercial manufacture that has undermined parts of the American industrial base. Not surprisingly, this has provoked American demands that allies contribute more to the common defense, or that major retrenchments occur in American defense spending in favor of domestic needs.[15]

Although this controversy usually focuses on the question of whether high defense spending causes economic slowdown, the issue is not as simple as that.* Much more important is the structure of an economy that bears large defense expenditures. If that economy is growing briskly, possesses a flourishing manufacturing base, is at the forefront of new technologies, enjoys a strong flow of skilled labor, scientists and technologists, invests heavily in R&D, is in balance (or surplus) on its current accounts, and is not an international debtor, then it is far better *structured* to allocate 3 or 6 or even 9 percent of its GNP to defense than if it lacks those advantages.[16]

In fact, given the size and complexity of the American economy, it is impossible to categorize it as either hopelessly weak or immensely strong; it is a mixture of strengths and weaknesses.

The single most important fact is that rates of growth have slowed considerably in the final third of this century compared with the middle third, as shown in Chart 12.

Whatever the explanation for this slowdown, the consequences are serious for the United States, with its internal and external obligations. With a high, fairly evenly distributed standard of living, a favorable current-accounts balance, and no foreign commitments, a country like Switzerland, perhaps, or Luxembourg, might suffer a long period of sluggish economic growth and the results, although depressing, might not be serious. But the United States is the world's foremost military power, with commitments all over the globe; its wealth, while considerable, is unevenly distributed, resulting in immense social problems at home; it has a large current-accounts deficit and needs to borrow from foreigners. Given those circumstances, a prolonged period of slow growth compounds its existing problems, making it unlikely that the United States can continue to fund the same level of military security *and* attend to its social needs *and* repay its debts. A country where *real* weekly incomes have fallen steadily since 1973—as in this case—is ever less inclined to fund even the worthiest needs.

Such a dilemma is intensified if other nations are growing faster, leading to changes in economic relationships. The leading Great Power

---

*In some cases, defense spending can boost economic growth, as the United States discovered in World War II. Again, a reduction in defense expenditures may do little or nothing to assist a country's economic growth if the amount "saved" is then returned into a society which spends it upon imported automobiles, wines, and VCRs; whereas if the same amount were channeled toward productive investment, the economic results could be very different.

Chart 12. Rates of Growth of U.S. Gross Domestic Product[17]
(annual average)

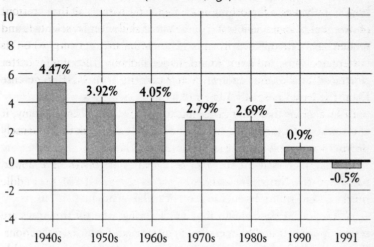

simply cannot maintain its status indefinitely if its economy is in relative decline.[18] Moreover, because this decline is relative and gradual, it is insidious, not dramatic; as one economic historian has noted, "a country whose productivity growth lags 1 percent behind other countries over one century can turn, as England did, from the world's undisputed industrial leader into the mediocre economy it is today."[19] It also turned from a first-class to a second-class power. Presumably, that reasoning was behind Mrs. Thatcher's recent declaration that it would be a "disaster" if the American economy were to grow—as some forecast—more slowly than Japan's in the 1990s.[20] From a realist viewpoint, that would erode America's world position, causing a further shift in the balance from Washington to Tokyo.*

This suggests that the fundamental strategic objective of the United

*Statistically, this is relatively easy to calculate. Suppose the American economy of $4.8 trillion (1988) grew at an average annual pace of 2 percent for the rest of the century: its size would reach $6.1 trillion by 2000, adjusted for inflation. If the Japanese economy of $2.8 trillion (1988) grew at an average annual pace of 4 percent, its size would then be $4.56 trillion. This simple projection makes no allowance for a possible strengthening of the yen—in consequence of greater growth—which would close the gap even more.

States as it moves toward the twenty-first century ought to be to enhance its per capita productivity for the sake of long-term growth. It is not that economic expansion is good in itself—it can damage environments and societies, if it is pursued wantonly—but without growth many desirable aims cannot be met.

In recent years, however, American productivity has become a cause of concern. Since the nineteenth century, the United States has enjoyed the world's highest labor productivity, which is why American national income and "war potential" were much larger than anybody else's when it fought the two world wars.[21] At present, its overall productivity is still larger than Japan's and Germany's, but other nations have increased productivity at a swifter pace since the 1960s, narrowing the American lead.

Moreover, improvements in American labor productivity in recent years have taken place chiefly in manufacturing, whereas the American economy is increasingly dependent upon services,* whose average value of output per employee is low compared with manufacturing or agriculture. Thus an annual increase in manufacturing productivity of 3 percent probably translates into a national rate of growth of 1 percent. Furthermore, much of the enhanced productivity of American industry in the 1980s came not—as in Japan—from higher output per *existing* worker, but from closing factories and cutting the work force, for productivity can increase faster during a recession when lots of jobs are lost than in a period of growth when cost-cutting is less urgent; and productivity increases often accompany actual reductions in overall output.[22]

America's growing indebtedness, the frailty of its financial system, and its persistent deficits in trade and current accounts would also be relieved by increased productivity. Indebtedness occurs at various levels. Nationally, it results from the U.S. government and Congress declining to pay the increasing cost of defense and social programs by additional taxes, a trend already evident in the 1960s, and perpetuated by both Democratic and Republican administrations; it was greatly accelerated by the Reagan government's decision to decrease taxation and increase defense spending during the 1980s. In 1960 the federal

---

*A few years ago, services accounted for roughly 68 percent of GNP and 71 percent of jobs.

deficit totaled $59.6 billion and the national debt $914.3 billion.[23] In 1991, despite pledges by White House and Congress to get spending "under control," additional expenditures—cleaning up nuclear facilities, bank bailouts—pushed the deficit well over $300 billion, while the national debt itself approached $4 *trillion,* which does *not* include the federal government's other obligations of around $6 trillion under various programs (crop guarantees, loans to farmers and students, insurance programs). Interest payments on the national debt are around $300 billion annually and represent 15 percent of government spending. As the economics editor of the *Wall Street Journal* has noted, interest payments now exceed "the combined amounts that government spends on health, science, space, agriculture, housing, the protection of the environment, and the administration of justice." Not only are these charges likely to increase,* at the expense of other government outlays, but a rising amount of those interest payments are to *foreign* owners of U.S. Treasury bonds, further reducing America's wealth. Finally, if slow economic growth persists throughout the 1990s, the deficit may rise further, since federal receipts will not grow as fast as expenditures.[24]

It was not only the national debt which soared during the 1980s, but every other form of debt. State and local governments began to experience deficits from 1986 onward—a trend exacerbated by cuts in federal grants. Consumer debt, fueled by "easy money" incentives, reached $4 trillion, while repayments diminished personal income. Corporate debt was even worse: "as the 1990s began, about 90 percent of the total after-tax income of U.S. corporations went to pay interest on their debt." Although beginning to slow due to rising economic worries, public and private debt equaled roughly 180 per cent of GNP, a level not seen since the 1930s.[25]

Deficits in the balance of payments and current accounts represented a further change from the 1950s and 1960s, when America had large surpluses in merchandise trade and current accounts.[26] Since 1971—when the United States recorded its first merchandise-trade deficit in over a century—it has consistently bought more than it has

---

*These totals will also be exacerbated by the coming of Social Security deficits, discussed on pp. 311–12 below.

sold. By 1987 the trade deficit reached a staggering $171 billion, and although the decline in the value of the dollar brought the total down by the later 1980s, deficits of over $100 billion were still being recorded. If the American economy was able to cover its "visible" trade deficit through earnings in "invisibles" such as services, investment income, and tourism, as Britain did before 1914, the position would be less serious; but American invisible earnings are insufficient to close the gap. As a result, the United States now pays its way by borrowing from foreigners roughly $100 billion each year. Once the world's largest creditor, the United States has by some measures become the world's largest debtor nation within less than a decade.[27] The longer this continues, the more American assets—equities, land, industrial companies, Treasury bonds, media conglomerates, laboratories—are acquired by foreign investors.

The heart of the trade deficit problem lies in the long-term erosion of America's relative manufacturing position, which may seem a curious fact when so much of the economy is in services. Yet, by their nature, many service activities (landscape gardening, catering, public transport) cannot be exported, and even where earnings from services are considerable (consultancy, legal work, patents, banking fees), the total doesn't pay for the goods and services imported each year.* Manufacturing is vital for other reasons: it accounts for virtually all of the research and development done by American industry, and a flourishing and competitive manufacturing base is still "fundamentally important to national security."[28]

Any attempt to summarize the present condition and future prospects of American manufacturing, however, is confronted by its extraordinary diversity. Some of its largest companies are world leaders, and many smaller firms (in computer software, for example) are unequaled in what they do. Others, however, are reeling from foreign competition, and their plight is the subject of innumerable commissions, studies, working parties, and congressional hearings. An entire industry (alas, not very distinguished either in manufacturing productivity or in its contribution to the balance of payments) has now

---

*For example, the total value of goods and services imported into the United States in 1987 was $550 billion, whereas the gross export of services was about $57 billion.

emerged devoted to studying American "competitiveness."[29] The overall picture that emerges is of an industrial structure which, though it has many strengths, no longer occupies the unchallenged position it did in the first two postwar decades.

While this is not a picture of unrelieved gloom, the rise of foreign competition in industry after industry has obviously increased the American merchandise-trade deficit. As Chart 13 reveals, out of eight key manufacturing sectors only chemicals and commercial aircraft were producing an export surplus by the late 1980s.

These deficits occur across a range of industries, from low-per-capita-value-added products like textiles to high-technology goods such as computer-controlled machine tools and luxury automobiles. This does not suggest an economy deliberately moving out of low-level production into more sophisticated sectors, as some have suggested, but one battling at all levels.

Unsurprisingly, the debate over "competitiveness" has not produced unanimity. Appeals for protection from hard-hit industries are opposed by those who fear retaliation in export markets, and by laissez-faire economists. Attacks upon foreigners' buying into America are countered by the argument that Japanese and European companies bring expertise, job opportunities, and much-needed capital. "Buy American" campaigns are resisted by those who feel that consumers should be free to purchase goods regardless of their nationality of origin. Calls for an industrial policy are denounced by groups who feel that government-led actions would be inefficient and contrary to American traditions. Some claim that the relative economic decline is due to a single cause, whereas others offer many reasons, from poor management to low levels of investment, from insufficient technical skills to excessive government regulations. The debate echoes one which took place a century ago in Britain, when a "national efficiency" movement emerged in response to the growing evidence that Britain's lead in manufacturing was being lost.[30]

The present concern about the condition of the U.S. economy is also fueled by a broader unease regarding the implications for national security, for American *power*, and for its position in world affairs. What if foreigners acquire a monopoly in industries that make strategic products for the Pentagon, or if an important military-related item is made

Chart 13. Trade Balances in Eight U.S. Industries[31]

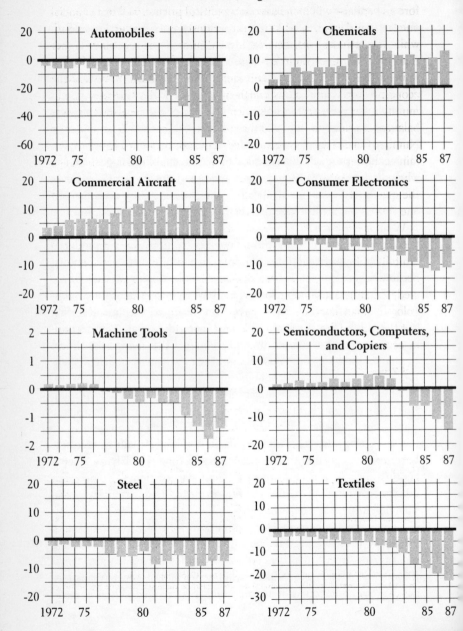

only abroad? What if the country becomes ever more reliant upon foreign capital—will it one day pay a political price as well as a financial one for that dependency? What if its industrial base is further eroded, while it continues with defense expenditures six or ten times higher than those of other countries—will it, instead of "running the risk" of imperial overstretch, finally have reached that condition?[32] What if the economy grows only half as swiftly as Japan's, or the European Community's, for the next decade or two—will not the productive power balances continue to shift,* so that the United States will no longer be Number One? These apprehensions may appear old-fashioned to certain economists—in their view, a sign of "residual thinking" in an age where the nation-state is no longer central and the key issues are about the quality of life rather than rank in the global pecking order[33]—but one suspects that they will remain deeply felt, for all that.

What is one to make of this controversy? To the optimists, what has been happening is perfectly understandable. In the postwar decades the United States occupied an artificially high position in world affairs, because other powers had been damaged by the conflict; as they recovered, the American share of world product, manufacturing, high technologies, financial assets, and even military capacity was bound to fall. Yet the United States remains the most important nation in the world, in economic and military power, diplomatic influence, and political

---

*J. Zysman, "U.S. Power, Trade and Technology," *International Affairs*, vol. 67, no. 1 (January 1991), p. 90, records the following shifts:

U.S. Output as Percentage of Output in:

	1970	1975	1980	1986	1987
Japan	495	317	254	214	188
Germany	547	371	330	469	401
France	706	462	409	576	507
U.K.	820	673	502	764	649
Japan and France	291	188	156	167	137
Japan and Germany	260	173	144	147	128
EEC	158	113	93	131	104
EEC and Japan	113	77	64	77	67

Although the short-lived rise in the value of the dollar (see 1986 column) caused a certain recovery for a while, the overall trend is unmistakable—and would be more marked were the statistics updated to 1991.

culture, though certain domestic reforms are needed.[34] American industry was unprepared for the intensity of foreign competition—and paid a price for that—but since the 1980s it has become leaner and fitter, its productivity has shot up, and it is moving into new technologies and products with unequaled strengths, especially research personnel. The advantages of such competitors as Japan will not last for long. With the dollar's reduced exchange rate and continuous upgrading of American manufacturing, the economy will rebound into prolonged growth, turn the deficits into surpluses, and respond vigorously to what were merely temporary difficulties.[35]

To the pessimists, such reasoning is a sign that many Americans have failed to understand the seriousness of the problem. It is not the country's relative economic decline in the two decades following 1945 that concerns them, since that clearly was the "natural" result of the rebuilding of other economies; it is the evidence that the American position relative to other nations has continued to erode *since* the 1960s in new technologies and patents, key manufacturing industries, financial assets and current-account balances, and international purchasing power. Most pessimists would, no doubt, be delighted to be proved wrong and dislike being called "defeatists" or "declinists." But they remain skeptical of the vague argument that America's "specialness" or "genius" or "capacity to respond to challenge" will somehow restore its position, seeing in such rhetoric the same ethnocentric pride which prevented earlier societies from admitting and responding to decline. While writing about the future, therefore, the pessimists are affected by a sense of the past, and worry that the leadership's indifference to the processes of global historical change may damage America's long-term prospects.[36]

While much of the controversy over American "decline and renewal" naturally focuses upon the economy, failures in the educational system, the social fabric, the people's well-being, even their political culture, are also much debated—presumably for fear that the causes of noncompetitiveness may be more profound than, for example, an inadequate savings rate. Characteristic of this thinking is the assumption that

somehow the American people have taken a wrong path. As the popular television commentator John Chancellor expresses it:

> The strength is there, but it is being sapped by a combination of weak-
> nesses—a thousand wounds we find difficult to heal. We have weakened
> ourselves in the way we practice our politics, manage our businesses, teach
> our children, succor our poor, care for our elders, save our money, protect
> our environment, and run our government.[37]

His conclusion is, therefore, that all sorts of changes are required before
the United States can return to its earlier state of well-being.[38] Yet how
likely such a recovery would be—even if there were a broad public
response to his call—is entirely unclear.

To the daily readers of American newspapers, the list of ailments will
be drearily familiar: for example, a health-care industry which doubled
the number of its employees in the 1980s—thus *worsening* overall labor
productivity—and which consumes around 12 percent of GNP, more
than twice the share for defense, yet does not provide decent health
care for many citizens. In fact, some 37 million Americans lack health
insurance, and suffer accordingly. By the end of the 1980s, the number
of poor people with health problems—such as babies born with syphilis
or AIDS—was steadily rising; in the black community, where half the
children under six live below the poverty line, health problems are
severe and compounded by poverty. Lacking a national health system,
"the U.S. occupies last place among the major industrialized countries
. . . in child mortality, life expectancy, and visits to the doctor,"
although it probably leads the world in politicians who talk about
"family values."[39] While life expectancy for older white men and
women has increased (much of the rise in health-care spending has
gone to those over seventy-five), that for black women and especially
black men has fallen.*[40] Because of this widespread poverty, Oxfam
America—famous for its aid to developing countries—announced in
1991 that it would also focus, for the first time ever, upon the United
States itself.

---

*The only other example of this decline in life expectancy in a developed society, as noted above
(p. 235), was among Russian males. Is it simply coincidence that this took place among the world's
two military superpowers?

This uneven health care reflects the structure of wealth and income in contemporary America, where on average managers earn over ninety times as much as industrial workers (up from forty times as much in 1980), but where 30 percent of African-Americans and 20 percent of Hispanics earn less than the official poverty line and live in slums. It is exacerbated by the amount of drugs Americans consume; according to one estimate, the United States—with 4 to 5 percent of the world's population—consumes 50 percent of the world's cocaine. Such addictions strain health-care services, and not simply in the treatment of adults; in 1989 alone, approximately 375,000 Americans were *born* addicted to drugs, mainly cocaine and heroin.[41]

Drugs in turn feed crime, which is significantly higher in the United States than anywhere else in the developed world. Thanks to the political power of the National Rifle Association, Americans have access to deadly weapons—and use them—to a degree that astounds observers abroad. Americans possess an estimated 60 million handguns and 120 million long guns, and kill one another at a rate of around 19,000 each year, chiefly with handguns. Homicide rates per capita are four to five times higher than in Western Europe (while rape rates are seven times higher, and forcible robbery rates some four to ten times higher).[42] Experts suggest that this violence has cultural roots, and cannot simply be linked to poverty; New York's homicide rate is far larger than that in the slums of Calcutta, for example, and in prosperous Seattle—recently rated number one city in the United States for "livability"—the murder rate is seven times that of Birmingham, England.[43] Nor is violence due to lack of police efforts and deterrents; at the last count, American prisons were holding over a million convicted prisoners, a proportion of the population larger even than in South Africa or the former USSR.* Three thousand out of every 100,000 black American males are in prison, whereas South Africa managed to preserve apartheid by imprisoning 729 black males per 100,000.[44]

Doubling the number of people behind bars during the 1980s has not been very effective, therefore, in dealing with the erosion of America's social fabric, partly because of the difficulty of attempting major

---

*The United States imprisons criminals at a rate of 426 per 100,000 of its population. The rate in Australia is 72, in the Netherlands only 40. The Soviet rate was 268 per 100,000. Blacks, who form 12 percent of America's population, supply nearly half of its prisoners.

social reforms in a politically decentralized, libertarian society.[45] Any attempt to alleviate homelessness and poverty in the inner cities—and the rural South—might cost a great deal of money, and a transfer of resources from the better off (who vote) to the poor (who don't). Since the Boston Tea Party, middle-class Americans have had a deep aversion to paying taxes—with some justification, since unlike Europeans they do not enjoy in return such middle-class benefits as free college tuition, health care, subsidized cultural events, efficient public-transport systems, and so on.[46] Because politicians who favor tax rises are punished at the polls, the temptation is ever present to meet unavoidable fresh demands such as the S&L bailout and rising interest charges on the national debt by borrowing rather than by increasing revenues; and it is almost as tempting to suggest that money is unavailable for social and health-care reforms, however desirable. Perhaps funds could be made available if productivity and real growth were bounding upward; when they are not, changes in spending priorities become part of a "zero-sum game," blocked by groups who would lose out.[47]

But Americans have been willing to invest heavily in education. In 1989 over $350 billion was spent on public and private education, to support 45 million pupils enrolled in primary and secondary schools, as well as nearly 13 million college and university students. In absolute terms, only Switzerland allocates more money per pupil; relatively, the United States devotes 6.8 percent of GNP to education, which is equal to that of Canada and the Netherlands and ahead of education's share in Japan, France, or Germany.[48]

In return the United States could claim, with some justification, to have one of the finest systems of higher education in the world. Apart from many superb liberal-arts colleges, it boasts state university systems that educate an impressive number of students. Above all, it possesses the world's greatest array of research universities and scientific institutes, with faculty recruited from around the globe, achieving disproportionately high international recognition (e.g., Nobel Prizes) and attracting students from many lands. The resources of intellectual powerhouses like Harvard, Yale, and Stanford—with endowments of billions of dollars—are equaled by their high performance and their global reputation. From them emerge annual cohorts of scientific and creative personnel upon which the American economy depends.

Apart from higher education, however, the picture is less favorable. Many Americans are worried by the growing evidence that *general* levels of pre-eighteen public education are relatively mediocre. Since the early 1960s, the scores achieved on Scholastic Aptitude Tests—for what they are worth—have fallen considerably. Despite the opportunities offered by the free mass public education system, pupils are abandoning it in record numbers; between 600,000 and 700,000 drop out of high school each year, which is one-fifth of all high school pupils (and closer to one-half of those at inner-city high schools).[49] Moreover, although the 1980 U.S. census ambitiously and perhaps misleadingly reported a literacy level of almost 100 percent, various studies claim that millions of Americans—the figures range from 23 to 84 (!) million—are functionally illiterate; according to one, 25 million adults cannot read well enough to understand a warning label on a medicine bottle, and 22 percent of adults are unable to address a letter correctly.[50]

How does this compare *internationally*? In a recent standardized science test administered to ninth-graders in seventeen countries, American students finished behind those of Japan, South Korea, and every Western European country, and ahead only of those in Hong Kong and the Philippines. In a test of mathematical proficiency (1988), American eighth-graders were close to the bottom. Other tests reveal that the American ranking *worsens* as children get older—although, ironically, over two-thirds of the high school pupils felt that they were "good" at mathematics whereas less than one-quarter of the South Koreans (who actually scored much higher) felt that way.[51] Only 15 percent of high school students study *any* foreign language, and a minuscule 2 percent pursue one for more than two years.[52] Surveys of the average high school pupil's knowledge of basic history have also revealed great ignorance (for example, of what the Reformation meant), eclipsed only by their geographical illiteracy; one in seven adult Americans tested recently could not locate his or her own country on a world map, and 75 percent could not place the Persian Gulf—even though in the late 1980s many of them favored dispatching U.S. forces to that region.[53] The National Commission on Excellence in Education noted in its landmark 1983 report *A Nation at Risk*, "If an unfriendly foreign power had attempted to impose on America the mediocre educational performance that exists today, we might well have viewed it as an act of war."[54]

Despite the many studies devoted to the problem, the root cause is still not clear. Certain experts caution against drawing too severe conclusions from the declining SAT scores and international tests, recalling that the United States is educating a far larger proportion of its population for much longer than it was forty years ago; by the same token, it may be erroneous to compare the knowledge of the average American high school pupil with that of children in more selective systems overseas.[55] It may also be misleading to compare educational standards of a melting-pot society with demographically stable and ethnically homogeneous countries like Sweden and Japan.

More prosaically, one might note that although America spends large amounts on education as a whole, a disproportionate 40 percent goes to higher education (which may explain why American universities rate high internationally), whereas the share going to other education is less than in other countries.*[56] Again, American pupils attend school for considerably *fewer* days each year (175 to 180 is normal) than their equivalents in Western Europe (200+) and Japan (220+). If by the age of eighteen the average Japanese or South Korean has had the equivalent of three or four years more school than the average American, is it surprising that they know much more algebra and physics?[57] Finally, while the United States is one of the few developed societies lacking nationally mandated education standards which are assessed by uniform national exams—the chief reason a National Research Council investigation on mathematics education felt that "the top-down systems have beaten us hands down"[58]—any suggestion of copying the other democracies is resisted by school boards, education authorities, teachers' unions, and all who celebrate the country's decentralized traditions.

To other experts, technical alterations are less significant than the social culture within which American education has to operate. Displaying nostalgia for what seemed better days—when high school pupils supposedly worked harder and achieved higher scores—some

---

*The United States spends 4.1 percent of GNP upon primary and secondary education, lagging behind Switzerland (5.8 percent), Japan (4.8 percent), Germany (4.6 percent), and most other industrial nations.

critics suggest, "The crisis is not in the schools but in us. The society we have constructed has given us the education we deserve."[59] The "trivialization" of American culture, meaning the emphasis upon consumer gratification, pop culture, cartoons, noise, color, and entertainment over serious reflection, is portrayed as a self-inflicted wound. Apparently, the average American child has watched five thousand hours of television even before entering school, and by graduation that total will be nearly twenty thousand hours. This anti-intellectual youth culture—continued later by the fascination with sports or "soap" shows—is not helped by the disintegration of the family, especially among African-Americans, which requires so many mothers to cope on their own; or by the great rise in female employment, so that (as is not the case in East Asian societies) the "first educator," the mother, is absent from the home for most of the day. Apart from certain groups who place strong emphasis on the value of education (Jews, Asian-Americans), the average American child is said to be picking up the value system of a shallow entertainment industry rather than the moral standards, discipline, and intellectual curiosity that equip a person to learn. To ask the schools, especially in the inner cities, to remedy this social-cum-cultural crisis is simply to demand too much.[60]

While a fair-minded reader of this gloomy literature may think it too cataclysmic—are the education systems in *other* countries free of problems?—the chief fact is that the literature exists, affecting the national debate about the future. If the average American is poorly educated, does that not also contribute to a trivialization of electoral campaigns, with slogans like "Read my lips," "Make my day," and "Morning in America"? Does an inadequate school system lead to an erosion of proper democratic debate to meet television's demands for quick answers? Is this why fewer and fewer citizens vote?[61] If the average American has little interest in foreign cultures and cannot locate the Persian Gulf on a map, how is he or she to comprehend issues of intervention abroad, or to understand the need for increases in development aid, or to learn about globally driven changes? Is that sort of knowledge to be left to a minority (say, 15 percent of the population, as at the time of the Founding Fathers) consisting of professional-class families whose members *did* go to the right schools and colleges, and whose standards of living, frequency of foreign travel, and access to the international economy have increased nicely throughout the 1980s?[62]

Despite these worrying tendencies, many commentators stress the positive features of their bustling, variegated society. The United States is still the largest economy in the world (unless one counts the European Community as a whole). It is attractive to millions of immigrants each year, and many more who can't get in. Its popular culture is visible around the world, and its language is dominant in business, science, and entertainment. Its commitment to liberty and democracy has inspired oppressed peoples everywhere from China to Czechoslovakia. It is the exemplar of the capitalist system, which its ideological foes challenged and lost. Because of its great military power and diplomatic influence, all eyes usually turn to Washington when an international crisis occurs. Americans, according to the unabashed optimists, should be celebrating their triumphs, their culture, their ideology, their way of life, their "noble national experience . . . the most universally attractive of our era."[63] Even the more cautious "revivalists" may admit that domestic reforms are needed, but argue that the chief danger is that the American people *think* the country is poor and impotent when it is in fact rich and powerful. If it can simply shake off its present mood and make certain adjustments, it will be the world's leading nation in the twenty-first century, just as it has been for the past fifty years.[64]

Despite such optimism, a widespread *Angst* remains. When a conservative columnist such as George Will objects to the levels of poverty and crime across the nation and notes "a gnawing, growing sense that savagery and second-ratedness are increasing in America,"[65] it is clear that the debate about the country's future is no longer one between right and left as in the Vietnam War years, but cuts across traditional party and ideological lines.[66] Discussions over an "industrial policy" or school reform or protectionism reveal new internal groupings and alliances, in its way a sort of domestic counterpart to the changing, uncertain shape of international politics. The very fact that by the late 1980s more Americans thought the Japanese economic challenge to be a greater danger than the Soviet military challenge inevitably provoked a debate over spending and policy priorities different from that of the Nixon years.

All this presents the United States with a dilemma. Apart from a few unreconstructed optimists like George Gilder or Ben Wattenberg who hold that the country is moving effortlessly upward, opinion polls show that most citizens feel things have worsened—in the social fabric, race relations, public education, economic performance, the conditions of the average American family—and will be worse for their children and grandchildren. This has led to a demand for changes: some want the tax system altered, others want the schools overhauled, or a transformation in health-care provision, or changes in industrial policy, or an all-out assault on poverty, or on crime; many Americans would like all of the above. But since most reforms would require a transfer of resources, and since some of them would imply a change in life-styles (a longer school year, for example, or much higher energy taxes), each individual reform provokes opposition.

Reforms that challenge existing arrangements are never easy in a democracy; but the American political structure in particular offers the most marvelous opportunities to *obstruct* changes. The constitutional division of powers means that the president lacks the authority of, say, the British prime minister and cabinet to get legislation swiftly enacted. The relative absence of party discipline makes each member of Congress more independent, but the unrestrained costs of electoral campaigning also make that member reliant upon funding from supporters and interest groups (Political Action Committees) and highly sensitive to the threat that a powerful lobby—the pro-Israel coalition, the National Rifle Association, pro- and anti-abortion movements, the groups representing retired Americans—will campaign against a congressman if it is offended by his or her policies. Consequently, efforts to slash the budget deficit, or trim Medicaid costs, or restrict gun sales usually founder in the "gridlock" of Washington politics.[67] A fragmented political system, coexisting in a social culture which asserts, "Let everyone do his or her own thing," is not the ideal location in which to push through reforms. The very notion of reforming or retooling American society to *make* it more competitive is itself a contradiction of the laissez-faire ethos.

Because of this gridlock, many frustrated citizens seem ready for drastic change, as could be seen in the surge of support for Ross Perot's populist policies in the summer of 1992. Other critics call for some form of national shock therapy. In John Chancellor's words, "What the country needs is a peacetime Pearl Harbor to shake it up, to make Americans aware of the trouble they're in, to tap their energy and their willingness to work."[68] Yet, although it is often claimed that the United States is in a commercial "war" with rival countries, the military analogy is unconvincing, for individual Americans benefit from selling things to Japan, buying that country's products, and receiving its capital. In any case, whatever one believes has "gone wrong" with America, the decline has been a steady and insidious process, quite different from the dramatic aerial assault on Pearl Harbor. One is also bound to wonder whether the circumstances surrounding a major national crisis—one of the favorite scenarios is a banking or stock market collapse—will really lead to bold structural reforms in public education, inner-city poverty, and the level of R&D investment.

How will American society in its present condition interact with the broad forces for global change described in Part One of this book? How well prepared is the United States for the twenty-first century?

Clearly, the United States is going to be affected in many ways by demographic trends. While its population is forecast to grow steadily over the next few decades,* significant changes will occur *within* that population. There will, for example, be many more elderly people by the early twenty-first century. Whereas there were only 16.6 million Americans aged sixty-five and over in 1960, the figure had virtually doubled to approximately 31 million by 1990; after slow rises over the next decade or two, it is then forecast to leap to 52 million in 2020 and 65.5 million in 2030—by which time there will be more elderly people than children.[69] The numbers of people over seventy-five and even over eighty-five—an age group for which the health-care costs per person are disproportionately high—will grow the fastest of all. This means not only that the political power of retirees' organizations will be greater, but also that there could be a further diversion of resources toward

---

*According to *World Resources 1990–91*, p. 254, America's population will rise from 249 million (1990) to 301 million by 2025. Much depends, of course, upon the annual inflow of legal and illegal immigrants over the next thirty years.

elderly care*—resources that, economically at least, would be better employed in preventing child poverty or improving infrastructure.[70] Over the longer term, however, the most serious consequence will be that the Social Security funds—at present still in surplus, and helping to disguise the true size of the federal deficit—will simply run out, causing a crisis not only in health provisions for the average elderly American, but also in the fiscal system. The politicians then in charge, facing a federal deficit worsened by Social Security losses, will have to make unpleasant choices: slash Social Security provisions *or* other forms of federal spending, or vastly increase taxes upon the relatively smaller proportion of "productive" Americans to pay for the swollen costs of caring for the fast-growing numbers of over-sixty-five-year-olds. The only other alternative would be to risk enormous federal deficits and consequent financial instability.

Meanwhile, the ethnic composition of the United States is also changing. Although the forecasts are subject to amendment—many earlier predictions of the future population of the United States have tended to be notoriously inaccurate—demographers are reasonably confident that the white, Caucasian segment will continue to shrink. This is partly due to the expectation of further large-scale immigration, both legal and illegal, chiefly from Latin America and Asia; as "have-not" families stream to "have" societies, America is seen as the most desirable *and* accessible destination to many migrants. The second reason is the differential birth rate between white and most non-white ethnic groups, which has socioeconomic causes but is also af-fected by different gender roles, women's expectations, and access to higher education. In consequence, some demographers refer to the "browning" of America by 2050, as Caucasians become a minority.[71]

Other experts forecast that this transformation will be less swift because over time immigrants and minorities will conform to white reproductive patterns.[72] Nevertheless, these trends toward the simulta-neous "graying" and "browning" of America are going to have lasting consequences. Some writers worry that an aging United States will stagnate economically and call for increased immigration, reminding

---

*Already (i.e., in 1987), Congress "spent $10,010 per capita on the elderly and only $854 per child." R. D. Lamm, "Again, Age Beats Youth," *New York Times*, 2 December 1990, p. E19.

readers that successive waves of migrants have fueled the country's rise in the past; this argument is often accompanied by gloomy prognoses about Europe's and Japan's long-term prospects as they grapple with demographic decline, yet seek to prevent an inflow of newcomers. Others point uneasily to the fact that most recent immigrants to America have relatively low educational and skill levels, congregate in the inner cities—few of them help to compensate for the declining populations of Great Plains townships—and impose additional demands upon the social and educational services of the poorest parts of the American administrative structure. Demographers predict that perhaps as many as 15 million immigrants will arrive each decade for the next thirty years, and calls are now being made to "bar the door."[73]

Demographic change can also exacerbate ethnic tensions, as between African-Americans and Hispanic-Americans (over jobs), or Asian-Americans and African-Americans (over educational access), as well as stimulate the racial worries of poor whites. Over the longer term, the graying/browning tendency may be setting up a massive contest over welfare and entitlement priorities between predominantly Caucasian retirees and predominantly nonwhite children, mothers, and unemployed, each with its vocal advocacy organizations.* Perhaps predictably, some authors now call for a debate about the implications of "bright, well-educated American women" giving birth to fewer and fewer children.[74]

These outcomes are, at the moment, hypothetical, whereas the political and economic consequences of America's demographic transformation are easier to estimate. Simply because the regional electoral balances (e.g., share of seats in the House of Representatives) do, over time, reflect population change, there is likely to be a further shift in voting power from the North and East to the South and West, from Caucasian to non-Caucasian districts, from Europe/Israel-centered issues to Hispanic/Pacific concerns. The executive, judiciary, and legislative branches, at present with a mere sprinkling of nonmale, nonwhite members, will find it difficult to halt their metamorphosis into bodies

---

*California, whose population rose by 30 percent in the 1980s alone, is still the favored destination of millions south of the border. In consequence of higher birth rates and continued immigration, half of all children in the state are forecast to be Hispanic by 2030, when whites will compose 60 percent of the elderly population—a troublesome mismatch.

containing many more women and minorities. Schools and colleges, already grappling with the demands to teach both "multiculturalism" and "Western civilization," may come under further social and cultural pressures as the demographic tide advances.[75]

Demographic change will also affect the American economy, both in the composition of its work force and in the larger issue of American competitiveness in a future which, forecasters assert, will be dominated by knowledge-based societies. According to a common economic theory, the United States rose to world preeminence because of its vast, easily accessible raw materials (oil, iron, coal) and foodstuffs, giving it an advantage over resource-poor Japan and Europe. Now that ample supplies of raw materials and food are produced all over the globe, that advantage is shrinking; and it will shrink further with the "dematerialization" of production and the many other changes in the way things are manufactured. Moreover, the continued explosion of scientific knowledge will be best exploited by societies that are steadily raising *overall* educational standards, technical training, and work-force skills, which America is not.[76]

Since the 1970s, the composition of the work force has changed significantly. While manufacturing cut many skilled and relatively high-paying blue-collar jobs, the boom in services created ever more low-paid, low-skill jobs (cleaners, restaurant personnel, drivers, health-care assistants, and the like), most of which paid less than $15,000 a year.[77] The other trend was the growth in white-collar, technical jobs, especially in information and research sectors of the economy, requiring advanced training and higher education. According to the Hudson Institute survey *Workforce 2000,* by the end of this century as many as 52 percent of *new* jobs may require at least some college education.[78]

Yet the supply of so many educated individuals is in doubt. For years the number of American Ph.D.s in mathematics and engineering (and faculty instructing them) has been inadequate, but while that may be another sign of a declining manufacturing culture, the shortfall can be made up by recruiting foreign doctoral students and professors. On the other hand, American industry has found it difficult to recruit workers to fill jobs not requiring a college education. The chairman of Xerox Corporation has declared that the skill levels of American society have "the makings of a natural disaster," while New York Telephone reports that it had to test a staggering 57,000 applicants to find 2,100 people qualified to fill entry-level jobs. As business spends ever more on training (the total may now be over $50 billion annually), there is increasing concern over the extent to which America's educational deficits will reduce economic competitiveness.[79]

Demographic trends suggest the worst is yet to come. Part of America's economic growth since World War II was simply the result of increases in both the overall population and the percentage entering the work force. However, during the 1990s the number of entrants into the work force will grow more slowly than in past decades,[80] unless boosted by a great influx of immigrants. The point here is not race per se, but educational access. Of the new entrants into the work force, white males—currently the best-educated sector of the population, especially in science, technology, and engineering—will constitute only 15 percent, and the rest will be women, minorities, and immigrants.[81] Since the latter two categories have generally gone into low-paid, unskilled jobs, there exists a potentially enormous mismatch between educational levels and the forecast demand for jobs requiring advanced technical or higher education. Unlike Germany, Sweden, or Japan, however, the United States does not possess a systematic approach to remedial training or, the experts say, to vocational education as a whole, preferring instead to retain haphazard, laissez-faire methods.[82]

It appears unlikely that in the near future deliberate federal policies will address this problem by giving additional funds to cities and states in the Southwest to help absorb the tide of immigrants, subsidizing Midwestern and Appalachian states to prevent further rural drift, or above all by a national scheme to finance training, remedial education, apprenticeships and the rest for the millions of poorly educated immigrants and minority schoolchildren who will become a steadily larger share of the work force. The states themselves, and local businesses, will bear the chief responsibility, and most of the costs—if anything is done at all.

Demographic trends also influence the long-term American response to robotics and automated manufacture. While intelligent robots are being designed for specialized circumstances (space exploration, undersea mining, hazardous-waste disposal) and the spiraling costs of U.S. health care may also compel the increasing use of field robots,* manufacturing as a whole has less incentive to automate production than in Japan. Although one might imagine that the "graying" of the Caucasian males among the American population would stimulate automation, the simultaneous "browning" trend provides a cheap labor pool in many repetitive jobs. Just as the relative cost of manual versus automated production hurt America's early lead in robotics, so is it likely that demography and work-force composition will slow any overall move to automated manufacturing.

This generality may not apply to certain sectors of industry—for example, to American factories owned by a Japanese multinational, or companies under pressure from East Asian competition *and* able to raise the capital to make large-scale investments in automation, or firms preferring robots to poorly trained workers. However, with the collapse of America's indigenous robotics industry, around 75 to 80 percent of robots sold to U.S. firms each year are imported, worsening the trade gap. Moreover, if the investment in robots is not accompanied by retraining the redundant workers by either the company itself (as in Japan) or the state (as in Sweden), then the decline in well-paid blue-collar employment would intensify, just as if the surviving workers are not trained to work with robots, the increases in output will be much less than expected.

American agriculture will also be challenged by the newer global forces for change, certainly by biotechnology and possibly by global warming. As argued earlier, the biotech revolution in farming and food processing appears to offer enticing prospects to the large pharmaceutical and agrochemical firms that have invested heavily in both research and production in this field and are constructing large factory complexes or "refineries" which, in essence, replace the traditional farm. As they also increasingly link up with giant food distribution and chain stores, conglomerates are emerging that will control every part of the process of providing food, from the seeds and fertilizer (or the *in vitro* hormones and genes) to the tinned and packaged goods in the supermarket.

*See pp. 84–85 above.

For American farmers themselves—and their communities—these trends are disturbing. Abundant agricultural output made the United States the reserve breadbasket of the world for the past century, earning large amounts of foreign currency. Because of improved technology, American farming is becoming *more* efficient each year; in fact, according to the U.S. Office of Technology Assessment, the United States has the capacity "not only to meet domestic demand, but also to contribute significantly to meeting world demand in the next twenty years," enough indeed to meet the expected 1.8 percent annual growth in world population.[83] While that forecast would be contested by environmental groups that believe that U.S. agriculture's long-term prospects are being damaged by overgrazing, loss of topsoil, decline in water supplies, excessive use of fertilizers, and other unwise methods which aided the original expansion of output,[84] there is no disputing that present productivity per hectare is impressive. But that itself is now a problem.

The challenges facing American farming are large-scale and structural. Even if only 3 percent of the total population is nowadays involved in farming, far more is produced than can be consumed at home. To avoid a crisis of agricultural overproduction—there have been several such crises since the late nineteenth century—farmers have pressed U.S. administrations to discover and open markets overseas. At present, however, such a solution is clouded by chronic imbalances in global supply and demand for farm products. Dozens of poor countries would welcome the continued flow of American food supplies, but have no funds to pay for them. Similarly, the erstwhile USSR and certain of its former Eastern European satellites require food to make up for their own farming deficiencies, but there is no way that those societies can themselves provide the hard currency required; they will need international aid. (In any case, if they do eventually manage to restructure agriculture, all or most of them could well become surplus food producers.) Efforts to lower or remove tariff barriers to American food imports into, say, Japan or Korea provoke violent reactions from local farmers.

Meanwhile the EC's common agricultural policy, which subsidizes and protects millions of farmers, has eroded American farm export shares in both European and third markets—compelling the U.S. gov-

ernment to subsidize its own farmers in expensive ways. Even if agreement were reached to phase out all such subsidies and price supports—
which is highly unlikely—the greatest beneficiaries would probably be
countries like Australia, New Zealand, and Argentina, whose farmers
are efficient enough to oppose agricultural tariffs. While consumers
might rejoice at the drop in food prices, many American farming
communities would wither away.

With access to foreign markets limited and agricultural prices generally low—though boosted occasionally by drought or reports of fresh
credits for Soviet purchases—American farmers struggle against the
rising costs of energy and equipment, interest payments and depressed
land prices, and the ultimate threat of foreclosure—all this in addition
to the scourges of nature and the fact that much farmland is marginal
and depends on tapping desert aquifers, the massive use of fertilizers,
and so on. Meanwhile farmers are continually being offered improved
seeds, newer strains of fruit and vegetables, more efficient fertilizers,
all intended to increase local output—but with the macroeconomic
effect of exacerbating the national food surplus.

It is upon this already troubled agricultural sector that biotechnology's innovations will make their impact. With artificial sweeteners
having cut heavily into the American sugar market over the past decade, and with forecasts that the use of the bovine growth hormone to
increase milk production could lead to a 50 percent reduction in the
number of dairy farms by 2000, it is not surprising that some groups
of farmers are campaigning against the new technologies. However,
unless these innovations can be proved positively harmful to health or
the environment—and are therefore banned by federal agencies—the
response is likely to be mixed. Many better-capitalized farms could be
attracted by the promise of greatly enhanced yields from "designer"
herbicide-resistant seeds and the accompanying herbicides, or the
greater productivity that will flow from new information-technology
equipment, reckoning that they will survive the "shakeout" that this
increased competition—and decreased prices—will bring.

What might this mean in overall numbers? One study by the U.S.
Office of Technology Assessment calculated that the new biotechnology and information technologies would be adopted by more than 70
percent of the largest farms in the United States, but by only 40

percent of the moderate-sized farms and about 10 percent of small farms. Many of the nation's 2 million small farms are run by people with other income, so the impact there might be less. For the moderate-size full-time farms, traditionally the backbone of American agriculture, the results would be very serious as they struggled to compete. By 2000, the number of such farms might have shrunk to 75,000, compared with 180,000 in 1982. By contrast, the largest farms are expected to grow in size and efficiency, and by the end of the century a mere 50,000 of them could be producing around three-quarters of all agricultural output.[85] Whether they will still be regarded as farms or simply as the upstream production facilities of food-processing companies, with wage laborers supervised by corporate-style managers, is an open question.[86] In any case, the traditional style of farming, in middle America no less than rural France, is little prepared for the next century.

Given these prospects, it is to be hoped that the "greenhouse effect" does not result in the temperature rises forecast in the gloomier studies on global warming, for that would increase the pressures upon farmers whose livelihoods are already endangered by the biotech revolution. Consider, for example, the challenges which farms growing feed grains in the southern Great Plains will face over the next few decades. Not only do they have to confront the emergence of agribusinesses, they also face the depletion of water supplies from the Ogallala Aquifer and the possible effects of global warming—a swifter snowmelt in the mountains and less available river-fed water, higher evaporation rates and drier soils, and a northward movement of the growing regions. Although different in form, both the depletion of the aquifers and the rise in CO_2 result from the excessive use of a "shared resource" and contribute to a drying-out of the Great Plains.[87]

It is not simply the water resources and growing areas of the Plains states that would be affected by a significant rise in temperatures. Marine geologists, engineers, and hydrologists estimate that coastal shoreline retreat, which for various reasons is already taking place, will be accelerated by rising sea levels. According to one local study, Massachusetts may lose between three thousand and ten thousand acres of coastal upland by 2025. Since the higher figure assumes a sea-level rise of 1.57 feet over the next few decades, and the same study estimates that by 2100 Massachusetts will have experienced a sea-level rise between 5.5 and 8 feet (!), a considerable further retreat of the shoreline is implied.[88] In other, lower-lying coastal regions, from South Carolina to New Jersey, the retreat would be proportionately greater. Moreover, as coastal bluffs are eroded by higher waves and storm surges, salt water will move farther upstream and into coastal aquifers, contaminating water supplies at the same time that higher average temperatures create greater demand.[89] Some environmentalists suggest that it is a waste of time and resources to seek to check coastal erosion (by building seawalls, reinforcing the foundations of coastal properties, etc.), but local communities and property owners will obviously press for costly protection and restoration measures.

It is not just food crops that might migrate northward in response to global warming. Were carbon dioxide levels to double over the next century, some scientists predict that certain trees (beech, birch, hemlock, and sugar maple) would move five hundred kilometers north to find a more suitable habitat, so that beech forests would disappear from the southeastern United States. There is even more concern among biologists for the impact of such changes upon wildlife, particularly rare birds and animals attached to specialized and limited habitats. While human beings can at least plan to shift locations, plants and wildlife cannot; and although it is known that migration of trees has taken place (e.g., during post-ice-age warming), it occurred over thousands of years, not in the century or half century assumed in the global warming models.*[90]

Clearly, while some rural areas would lose from these migrations, others—in the northern states—would benefit from the rise in temperatures and longer growing seasons. Increased levels of CO_2 can stimulate plant yields. It is also likely that farmers would adjust by changing crop types and using plants with greater drought resistance. Since the global warming process is gradual—though it may be attended, some researchers claim, by increasing volatility and ferocity in the weather— American agriculture _as a whole_ can adjust almost as well as American industry;[91] but for some regions and many traditional farmers adjust-

---

*At the end of the Pleistocene era ten to twelve thousand years ago, as the glaciers retreated and temperatures rose 3°–5°C, beech forests moved about twenty kilometers per century, far less than the five hundred kilometers forecast in the models for the next century.

ment may simply not be possible—for financial as much as ecological reasons.

Environmental changes *outside* the national boundaries are also affecting American society. For example, the recent flood of Haitian refugees to the United States was prompted by political turbulence, but a more important cause is that peasant landowners have eliminated the forests (only 2 percent of the land is still forested) and the subsequent exploitation and loss of topsoil have worn some areas down to the bedrock. With farmable land (only 11 percent of the whole) continuing to shrink, total fertility rates still very high, and population control negligible, more and more people—among a population already the poorest in the western hemisphere—are left with fewer and fewer resources. Given the mass unemployment rates of 30 percent, is it any surprise that many of them struggle to get to the United States and regard repatriation as close to a death sentence? And once they arrive in Florida or New York, is it a further surprise that—through no fault of their own—these immigrants are additional burdens upon the sorely pressed educational and social systems of the inner cities? Here, in microcosm, is an example of how entwined demographic growth, environmental damage, social and economic catastrophe, and mass migration have become.

It is while they confront these challenges that citizens of the United States are being urged to adjust to the borderless world of twenty-four-hour-a-day financial flows, electronic trading, and the globalization of business and communications. Since American society is regarded as the trailblazer in all these developments and their socioeconomic implications have been widely discussed,* there is no need to repeat the conclusions in detail here. The general sense is that America enjoys massive advantages in the form of giant multinationals and banks, traders, consultants and service industries, the dominance of the English language and (though declining) the U.S. dollar, an entrepreneurial culture, and numerous highly educated scientists, engineers, designers, lawyers, and other "symbolic analysts" whose skills are in global demand. On the other hand, the relocation of industries abroad, the increasing redundancy of various occupations, and the inadequate

*See above, pp. 58–60.

educational levels of many workers for high-tech employment suggest
that the lower four-fifths (or more) of Americans may not enjoy the
oft-proclaimed benefits of globalization. If demographic trends lead to
a relative decline in the number of Americans with high scientific skills,
if U.S. multinationals find themselves increasingly pitted against foreign rivals with larger capital resources and better-trained labor and
conclude that they can only compete by moving production to (say)
Mexico, and if American banks, media conglomerates, software companies, and R&D establishments continue to sell out to overseas firms,
those benefits may appear ever less obvious.

If the above analysis is generally accurate, the United States may not
be a "loser" in the face of global changes, as many desperate societies
in the developing world will be; but because of its social and economic
structure—its altering demographic pattern, its environmental problems, its educational and social deficits, its political-constitutional gridlock, its fiscal problems—it could be less than a clear "winner." What
emerges instead is a mixed picture: some industries rising as others fall,
traditional farms losing as agribusinesses gain, consultants flourishing
as blue-collar workers face fewer opportunities, the slow growth in
overall per capita GNP barely concealing the widening gap between
those whose skills are in demand and those whose are not.

Despite expressions of concern by various reform movements at the
implications of global and internal trends for the United States, and
despite the possibility of some corrective measures implemented here
and there as the 1990s advance, the nature of American society and
politics makes it unlikely that a national "plan" for the twenty-first
century will emerge such as may be formulated in France or Japan.
Instead, there will be differentiated responses and local initiatives, in
the traditional American way: states and school districts will push
ahead with their individual schemes; communities will grapple with
local environmental problems; towns and cities will attack urban poverty in various ways; some regions will benefit from fresh foreign investment, others will suffer as American companies transfer production
overseas; in the business world especially, "preparing for the twenty-

first century" will be seen as a matter of individual company strategy, not the result of a plan conceived by Washington.

There is a lot to be said for this sort of differentiated, decentralized, individualistic response to change: it is in the tradition of American free enterprise and its libertarian culture; and it is what the nation is used to. The United States is, after all, a demi-continent, not a small country like Japan, which finds it necessary to stress social harmony and organization in order for everyone to exist on its mountainous, crowded island chain. America, by contrast, is the home of those fleeing from constraints elsewhere; it offered an open frontier to dissatisfied people; and its sheer size, "escapist" culture, and lack of serious external threat combined to foster dislike of organized, central government. This cultural heritage means that as the United States turns to meet the broad forces for global change, its response is also likely to be differentiated, decentralized, and individualistic, a "muddling through" rather than a coordinated, centralized attack upon the problems. After all, a country like Great Britain "muddled through" for a very long time.

But that returns us to historical analogy as well as to the core of the American dilemma. One hundred years ago, Britain, which was widely regarded then as Number One, was engaged in a similar debate about its future prospects. It was, of course, a very different society from America today, and occupied a different geographical position as the island center of a worldwide empire rather than a resource-rich continental landmass. Nevertheless, the dilemma Britain faced was like the one facing the United States now. Both were preeminent world powers whose economic competitiveness and general international position seemed less assured at the century's end than five decades earlier. In both, alarmed citizens called for changes to improve national competitiveness and "prepare" for the next century. The difficulty was, however, that the proposed reforms would threaten many vested interests. Britain's spending priorities, its public educational system, the efficiency of its industry, its treatment of poverty, its levels of investment, and even its pattern of career choice (not enough engineers, too many lawyers and bankers) might all have to be altered to match the new global competition.

While reformers in turn-of-the-century Britain urged the need for tough solutions and cultural pessimists bemoaned the evidence of "de-

cline" and "decay," many disliked the idea of change. It would mean
the loss of institutions and work habits that were familiar, cozy, and
reassuring. It implied that national traditions had to be amended in
imitation of foreign ones. It upset powerful vested interests and made
for uncertainty. It involved costs, or a redistribution of national resources, when economic growth was moderate. Besides, there were
many other academic "experts," journalists, and economists who said
that things were still fine, that the declinists were too alarmist, and that
Britain still had the energies and resourcefulness to remain ahead. All
this made sense to a people taught that it occupied a unique historical
place, and was an example to others. In sum, there was an understandable and deep-rooted antipathy, both psychological and cultural, to the
idea that great changes were needed, especially if they involved pain
or money. Rejecting the calls for change, the British people thought
it was better to "muddle through."[92] Why, then, cannot America
today do the same?

In fact, the evidence above suggests that the United States *will*
continue to muddle through, as the debate about "decline or renewal"
continues. But the long-term implication of muddling through is slow,
steady, relative *decline*—in comparative living standards, educational
levels, technical skills, social provisions, industrial leadership, and, ultimately, *national power,* just as in Britain. The British may have avoided
hard choices by "muddling through" policies, but that evasion ultimately caused the loss of their place in the world.

While an impressive array of American individuals, companies,
banks, investors, and think tanks are scrambling to prepare for the
twenty-first century, the United States as a whole is not and indeed
cannot, without becoming a different kind of country. Perhaps a serious
program of reforms might be undertaken following a sufficient shock
to complacency, like a financial crash or a broadly perceived external
threat; but just how likely that is to happen is impossible to say. Even
if there should be such a catalyst, there surely could be no coherent
response by the United States unless the political leadership—especially the president—recognized the larger challenges facing the country and had the courage and the ability to mobilize opinion to accept
changes which many would find uncomfortable. That, in turn, would
require leadership very different from the sort demonstrated by recent

incumbents of the White House, whether it concerned domestic deficits or global population and environmental issues. It remains to be seen, therefore, whether traditional approaches will carry the American people successfully into the twenty-first century—or whether they will pay a high price in assuming that things can stay the same at home while the world outside changes more swiftly than ever before.

PART 3

CONCLUSION

14

PREPARING FOR THE
TWENTY-FIRST CENTURY

THE PROBLEM RESTATED

THIS BOOK BEGAN WITH A HISTORICAL example from two hundred years ago—Malthus's concern with England's eighteenth-century population explosion—to introduce the reader to themes that would run throughout the rest of the study. This final chapter begins with a more recent example that may illuminate both the continuities and the changes in our modern world condition. In October 1930, a year after the Wall Street Crash but before the Manchurian crisis and the Nazi seizure of power, the London *Economist* somberly surveyed contemporary global problems, and concluded:

> The supreme difficulty of our generation . . . is that our achievements on the economic plane of life have outstripped our progress on the political plane to such an extent that our economics and our politics are perpetually falling out of gear with one another. On the economic plane, the world has been organized into a single, all-embracing unit of activity. On the political plane, it has not only remained partitioned into sixty or seventy sovereign national States, but the national units have been growing smaller and more numerous and the national consciousnesses more acute. The tension between these two antithetical tendencies has been producing a series of jolts and jars and smashes in the social life of humanity. . . .[1]

As it turned out, World War II, with its heightened nationalism and demands upon citizenry everywhere, was soon to resolve that tension between the "two antithetical tendencies" in favor of the nation-state, at least temporarily. The following half century of Cold War, plus numerous regional conflicts, also emphasized political nationalism at the cost of economic cosmopolitanism. At the same time, the collapse of Western colonial empires, and more recently the disintegration of the USSR, meant that national units did indeed become "smaller and more numerous," so that almost three times as many states existed by the early 1990s as there had been sixty years earlier. Without exception, whether a former Soviet republic or French West African colony, the new state established all the usual attributes of sovereignty—national government, armed forces, border/customs posts, budgets, currency, and so on.

Yet this revival of nationalism as old empires dissolved could not alter the fact that the lengthy Great Power peace after 1945, with an American-led coalition protecting a relatively open trading order across much of the globe, was once again pushing trade, finance, and technology toward "a single all-embracing unit of activity," as the pace of economic integration increased from year to year. As a result, today's global society, even more than its predecessor sixty years ago, confronts the task of reconciling technological change and economic integration with traditional political structures, national consciousness, social needs, institutional arrangements, and habitual ways of doing things.

Moreover, efforts to harmonize economic and political structures will be complicated by trends which were scarcely evident three generations ago but now threaten to exacerbate social relations in all manner of ways, and may even threaten the long-term existence of humankind itself.[2]

The first and most important of these is the surge in the earth's population and the rising demographic imbalances between rich and poor countries. When *The Economist* was making its 1930 survey of the world scene, overall population was around 2 billion people. Europe, North America, and such Caucasian offshoots as Australia contained a considerable share of world population (perhaps about one-third), and their fertility rates were well above replacement level.* The populations of Asia, Africa, and Latin America were also growing, but their higher fertility rates were held in check by extremely high mortality rates. All that has now changed: world population has surged to well past 5 billion and may be heading toward 10 billion or more by the middle of next century, and most of that growth occurs in the poorest regions of the world, whereas developed societies have slow-growing or declining populations containing a rising share of older people. The result is a growing mismatch between where the world's riches, technology, good health, and other benefits are to be found and where the world's fast-growing new generations, possessing few if any of those benefits, live. A population explosion on one part of the globe and a technology explosion on the other is not a good recipe for a stable international order.

Meanwhile, the population explosion also produces environmental challenges qualitatively different from those of sixty years ago. Of course, there was dreadful pollution then in the industrial cities of Europe and North America, carbon dioxide levels were rising, and prolonged droughts occasionally turned farmland into dust bowls. But over the past half century there has been exponential growth in industrial emissions, especially in newly developed countries intent upon flat-out growth; the draining of wetlands and aquifers, the onslaught on tropical forests, and the overgrazing of plains and savannahs are nowadays far more extensive; and evidence is at hand of a "greenhouse effect" that could change ecologies in all sorts of ways. As climate changes and sea levels rise, even the most environmentally responsible societies will be affected. It is inconceivable that the earth can sustain a population of 10 billion people devouring resources at the rate enjoyed by richer societies today—or at even half that rate. Well before total world population reaches that level, irreparable damage to forests, water supplies, and animal and plant species will have occurred, and many environmental thresholds may have been breached.

Another trend more in evidence today than in our grandparents' time is technology's way of making redundant traditional jobs, replac-

---

*France, with its notoriously slow population increase in the nineteenth and early twentieth centuries, might be the exception here.

ing them with entirely new systems of production. This is not unwelcome, of itself; the economic history of the world, and of humankind's growing overall prosperity, flows from the invention of newer, improved ways of making things, from steam-driven textile production to computerized automobile design. But some changes are more sweeping than others; and over the coming decades it is possible that the biotech revolution will make traditional agriculture redundant while the robotics revolution changes a way of manufacturing and a structure of industrial employment that have existed for the past two centuries.

The transformation of agriculture and manufacturing as we know them, should that occur, will not take place in a vacuum, for this process will coincide with a demographic explosion, in which hundreds of millions of people will be seeking jobs that biotech farming and automated manufacturing may make redundant. It will also occur just as multinational corporations, freeing themselves from their local roots, increasingly compete for global market shares and employ every device—relocating production, installing automation, adopting new laboratory-created technologies—to achieve that aim. Such companies are simply acting according to the "rules" of laissez-faire capitalism; the point is that local communities in the developed world, and entire societies in the developing world, will have difficulty in accepting the logic of the global marketplace if it works to their disadvantage. Rather than economic and technological trends leading to that all-embracing unit of activity, the borderless world, they could provoke the commercial clashes and social instability which *The Economist* was noting in 1930. They could also provoke immense bouts of violence, as tens of millions crowd into cities in the developing world and find no work available.

Today's global financial and communications revolution is also more intense than in that earlier era, although even then there were severe currency crises and mass withdrawals of capital (as when U.S. dollars were recalled from Europe in the late 1920s), which made for instability and exacerbated interstate relations. It is unclear nowadays whether our more sophisticated official controls have kept pace with the risk of financial turbulence built into twenty-four-hour-a-day electronic/computerized trading in sums far in excess of most countries' GNP. The greater change, however, is in the realm of global communications.

Fifty or sixty years ago, radio and television were beginning to make their impact, but only among a relatively few rich societies; as our century closes, they are affecting peoples—especially younger generations—across the globe. Moreover, while it once appeared that the new media would enhance the power of governments (as, for example, Orwell argued in *1984*), their effect recently has been the opposite: breaking state monopolies of information, permeating national boundaries, allowing peoples to hear and see how others do things differently. It has also made richer and poorer countries more aware of the gap between them than was possible a half century ago, and stimulated legal and illegal migration.

As a result of these changes, communities and even entire countries appear to have less and less control of their own destinies. Traditional power structures are baffled by below-replacement fertility rates, illegal immigration, and massive currency flows; they have unsatisfactory answers—or no answers at all—to the threat of large-scale redundancy in farming and manufacturing; they find it hard to prevent companies from relocating to other regions, or to muffle information from transnational television and radio; they pause, and worry, at the implications of global warming. And because the established structures are fumbling with these challenges, people are responding with resignation (witnessed in the decreased percentages of voters in many elections), searching for new structures (from the EC experiment to the dismantling of the USSR and Yugoslavia), demanding protection from the global forces for change (as seen in the pressures from French farmers and American textile workers), and turning angrily against recent immigrants. In sum, we are facing again that "series of jolts and jars and smashes in the social life of humanity" noted by *The Economist*; and there seems every likelihood that such shocks will continue in the future.

In view of the speed and complexity of these changes, is *any* social group really "prepared" for the twenty-first century? Clearly, there exist companies (engaged in everything from pharmaceuticals to aerospace) and individuals (chiefly professionals providing high-added-value services) who benefit from current socioeconomic developments and are keenly positioning themselves to gain further advantages. Their prospects are the basis for the many optimistic works by Kenichi

Ohmae, George Gilder, Ben Wattenberg, and others that forecast humankind's ever-increasing prosperity. On the other hand, there are billions of impoverished, uneducated individuals in the developing world, and tens of millions of unskilled, nonprofessional workers in the developed world, whose prospects are poor, and in many cases getting worse. Their plight is the concern of the pessimistic writings about the demographic explosion and environmental catastrophes by the Ehrlichs, the Worldwatch Institute, and others, and it also inspires studies on future career trends and their social implications, like the work of Robert Reich. Initially, it might seem that only one school of thought must be right, but it could be that each has examined different aspects of a single phenomenon, so that the optimists are excited about the world's "winners" whereas the pessimists worry at the fate of the "losers." But if both *are* correct, the gap between rich and poor will steadily widen as we enter the twenty-first century, leading not only to social unrest within developed countries but also to growing North-South tensions, mass migration, and environmental damage from which even the "winners" might not emerge unscathed.

Whereas many individuals and firms seem well positioned for the twenty-first century, relatively few nations appear to be. Of those covered in this survey, the most likely at the moment appear to be Japan, Korea, and certain other East Asian trading states, Germany, Switzerland, some of the Scandinavian states, and *perhaps* the EC as a whole. What they have in common, more or less, are high savings rates, impressive levels of investment in new plant and equipment, excellent educational systems (especially for those *not* going to college), a skilled work force and good retraining systems, a manufacturing culture with many more engineers than lawyers, a commitment to producing well-designed, high-added-value manufactures for the global market, and fairly consistent trade surpluses in "visible" goods. They also enjoy cultural homogeneity and ethnic coherence; but that may not be as important a factor, since cultural and linguistic homogeneity also exist in societies which are much less successful economically.*

However, even technologically better-prepared countries face diffi-

---

*And Switzerland, arguably one of the "best-prepared" countries, contains three linguistic divisions.

culties in dealing with certain forces for global change: the decline in fertility rates; population imbalances; global warming; financial volatility; the need to cushion farming communities from increasing obsolescence. The fact that they have ample funds to pay for retraining workers or environmental protection is a great benefit, but it is unlikely that money will solve every difficulty. Nevertheless, it is obvious that societies which possess technical and educational resources, ample funds, and cultural solidarity are better positioned for the next century than those lacking all those strengths.

THE DIFFICULTIES OF REFORM

What can be done? How could nations better prepare themselves for the century ahead? Before attempting to answer, we should note the two greatest difficulties facing any program of systematic reforms. The first is the apparent inevitability of overall demographic and environmental trends. With around a billion new mouths being born each decade, does it matter much if there are 100 million more or less; or whether there will be 9 billion human beings on this planet in 2050 instead of 10 billion? In either case the consequences will be enormous, yet, simply because of the number of females who will reach child-bearing age over the next twenty years, large increases are probably unavoidable. Similarly, because atmospheric emissions are rising from year to year, and will expand further because of growing industrialization and global population, CO_2 levels seem bound to increase over time; for this reason, most reforms can merely hope to slow down the rise in greenhouse emissions, not halt them, which is widely regarded as impossible. Again, if India's population growth has already led to the loss of over two-thirds of its forests during this century, shouldn't we expect the current demographic surge to wipe out the remainder, as has happened in Ethiopia and Haiti?* In other words, far from a stimulus to preventive actions, global trends are so large as to induce despair. Since it is unlikely that these trends can be altered much, should we

---

*Only 14 percent of India is covered by forest today, compared with over 50 percent last century. Forty years ago, Ethiopia had a 30 percent forest cover, which has now shriveled to a mere 1 percent.

not try policies of reaction and adaptation—including, in the case of richer, developed societies, the cruel if necessary policy of blocking the rising migratory floods from overpopulated, impoverished lands?

The second difficulty lies both in the timing and the instrumentality of proposed reforms, from the viewpoint of practical politics. Even if it is worth trying to curb global warming—by banning gas-guzzling cars, curbing factory emissions, halting forest clearing, etc.—the problem is that these actions have to be implemented now for the sake of consequences twenty-five or forty years ahead. Apart from saving for old age (which directly benefits the savers), human beings are usually unwilling to make short-term sacrifices to achieve a distant (and uncertain) improvement in the general good—and most politicians' perspectives are shorter still. Unlike traditional threats to national security, these dangers are less obvious and therefore less likely to induce a unified, determined response. In addition, the usual mechanisms by which nation-states respond to threats seem inappropriate to some of the challenges posed here. To halt global warming requires international cooperation, while the introduction of robots is properly the task of individual manufacturers; in each case, the nation-state is either too small or too large.

Yet even if these newer forces for global change make many national instruments irrelevant, we know that states still remain the chief locus of authority and loyalty. They raise, and dispense, a large share of a society's product. They possess a deliberative system to discuss policies, and a command system to implement them. They establish policy priorities. Only states have the authority to enter international agreements to reduce CO_2 emissions and regulate biotech farming. Furthermore, if a society desires to improve its general preparedness for the next century—by encouraging a skilled work force, or the lowering (or raising) of fertility rates—no other structures possess the *potential* effectiveness of the state itself.* Actively preparing a people for the future as Korea and Singapore have done, or preferring laissez-faire methods to do that job as in the United States, is the decision of national governments and their publics—which is why we should not

---

Potential effectiveness, of course, because of the actual differences between strong states (Korea) and weaker ones (Ethiopia). The discussion above assumes reasonably strong and capable societies which can decide for or against changes.

expect to see uniform responses to these transnational challenges, but a mixture of responses instead; as some states feverishly seek to improve themselves, others will be either unwilling or unable to do much.

Given the difficulties of reform, humankind's instinctive avoidance of uncomfortable changes and its preference to make only minor ones is likely to prevail. Still, for societies willing to prepare for the twenty-first century, a range of measures can be considered. Most of them are specific to the type of country—Botswana obviously has different needs from Britain—but others require international cooperation to be effective. Such reforms will cost money, and thus involve a debate upon spending priorities, but the sums involved are unlikely to equal those devoted to the Cold War arms race.

Since this book is intended as a guide to understanding global changes, *not* as a technical primer for responses to them, it will not recount the many studies which outline in detail actual programs of change. For example, organizations like the Worldwatch Institute have recommended an array of reforms to halt the growing damage to the environment: cutting factory emissions by more efficient use of energy, filter systems, and extraction devices; investing in public transport, developing alternative fuels for automobiles, and taking other measures to reduce dependence upon petroleum; husbanding water resources and cutting reliance upon aquifers; boosting international technology transfers and training to countries in the developing world; and negotiating a pact between rich and poor countries, whereby the latter would protect their forests in return for increased aid, assistance in creating alternative employment, and guaranteed access to markets.[3] Some of the proposals from the environmentalist lobby may be impractical,[4] but others appear perfectly feasible, and cheap; with the "appropriate technology" of a simple solar oven, for example, families in the developing world can cook most meals without the daily scavenging of fuel wood which causes so much deforestation.[5]

There is also no need to repeat here the findings of innumerable works upon how to make one's society more competitive technologically and industrially in an age of globalized production. Every study of "competitiveness" in the United States, where the issue is keenly studied, concludes with virtually the same agenda: increase national savings rates and slash budgetary deficits which drain funds from productive investment; enhance the levels of *commercial* R&D; avoid the diversion of too many resources to the military; escape (but how?) from a business culture that has become too dependent upon Wall Street's expectation of short-term profits; focus upon making well-designed, reliable products for the world's most demanding markets; vastly improve the levels of skill and training among the work force at large and provide opportunities for thorough retraining; and raise educational standards, especially for those not going to college.[6] Either implicitly or explicitly, unfavorable comparisons are made in these studies to Japan and Germany, which are regarded as leading examples of highly skilled, technology-based societies possessing good prospects as the decade unfolds.

Finally, a detailed proposal for dealing with the demographic explosion in developing countries would simply repeat what numerous studies by international agencies have pointed out: that the only practical* way to ensure a decrease in fertility rates, and thus in population growth, is to introduce cheap and reliable forms of birth control—as has happened, for example, in Brazil, where the fertility rate fell from 4.7 children per woman in the 1970–75 period to 3.5 children per woman by the 1983–86 period.[7] This is also true of other developing countries where active family-planning programs have been established. Such a solution obviously faces difficulties—local cultural mores, the disapproval of the Vatican, the opposition of conservative U.S. governments which have not distinguished contraception from abortion—but that does not change the fact that population growth is dangerously high in societies where little family planning is practiced, yet is ebbing in countries where birth control occurs. To be sure, elements like urbanization and the changing role of women also contribute to a demographic transition, but the swiftest way to stabilize family size—and head off the threat posed by a doubling of the world's population in the next few decades—is measures to reduce conception in the first place.

In short, it is not that solutions to such transnational challenges are lacking, but that publics and politicians are equally reluctant to imple-

---

*In theory, of course, there are other ways, such as abstinence from intercourse and marrying later (which was what Malthus meant when urging "moral restraint"). How that is possible for fifteen-year-old brides in male-dominated societies in Africa or India is difficult to see.

ment changes which cause short-term personal costs to secure long-term general benefits. In many cases such reluctance is perfectly understandable. It is all very well for, say, ecologically conscious and well-educated Swedes to press for drastically reduced CO_2 emissions, higher fuel taxes, abolition of nuclear power stations, and large-scale increases in development aid; given their country's relative advantages, the costs would probably not be crushing. But it would be quite different politically to require farmers in the southern Great Plains, already threatened by biotech and global warming, to cease drawing water from aquifers, switch from automobiles to cycles, invest in energy-saving devices, and so on; it would also be politically unwise to expect support from such farmers for increased foreign aid to enable poorer countries to boost agricultural output. Similarly, while Western liberals agree that improving the role of women in Muslim and sub-Saharan African countries is long overdue, such a transformation poses a great challenge to traditional male-dominated cultures and is likely to be strongly resisted. Since it would be counterproductive for richer nations to try to impose such social changes, the issue will have to be decided within developing societies themselves—and the signs point to a looming clash between secularists and fundamentalists in these sensitive areas.[8] Whether reforms are accepted or rejected will depend upon context, not upon abstract logic.

Yet while this book is not a primer of technical solutions to global developments, it is important to emphasize three key elements in any *general* effort to prepare global society for the twenty-first century: the role of education, the place of women, and the need for political leadership.

THE ROLE OF EDUCATION AND THE POSITION OF WOMEN

If my analysis is roughly correct, the forces for change facing the world could be so far-reaching, complex, and interactive that they call for nothing less than the reeducation of humankind. This is not a new conclusion. Social thinkers from Wells to Toynbee have repeatedly argued that global society is in a race between education and catastrophe; and those stakes are higher at the century's end, simply because population pressures, environmental damage, and humankind's capacity to inflict mass destruction are all far greater.

An enhanced role for education implies many things, both philosophical and practical. For example, since technological innovation creates new jobs as it destroys old ones, developed countries which do not possess a national system for training *and* retraining—on the lines of Germany's apprenticeship scheme or of Sweden's methods of preparing discharged workers to learn a new skill—will probably find themselves more disadvantaged than they are now. Moreover, not only economic productivity but also the social fabric suffers from, say, Britain's inadequate job-training program, or the even less organized American efforts. But the systems that work rely upon planning and cooperation among schools, business, and government, which laissez-faire political cultures dislike and poorer countries lack the resources to sustain.

Still, the challenges facing nations like Britain or Italy in restructuring their educational systems are nothing like those facing the developing countries. In Somalia, where the adult male literacy rate is only 18 percent and the female literacy rate a mere 6 percent, only 37,000 pupils are in secondary education (1986 figures); of the very few professionally trained personnel, several hundred were doctors and, presumably, hardly any were engineers, computer-software designers, and others needed to bring Somalia into the modern world.[9] In South Korea, by contrast, where the male and female literacy rates are 96 and 88 percent respectively, and where 5 million are in secondary and 1.3 million in higher education, large numbers of professionals enter productive employment each year.[*][10] Clearly, those developing countries which manage to follow Korea's path can look forward to a bright economic future; but, as we have seen earlier, very few poorer societies are in such a favorable position. Backwardness has many causes, but a leading one is that education is regarded as less important in many cultures than it is in East Asia.

Yet education in the larger sense means more than technically "re-

---

*Korea's population is about five times larger than Somalia's, but even proportionately, the differences are immense.

tooling" the work force, or the emergence of professional classes, or even the encouragement of a manufacturing culture in the schools and colleges in order to preserve a productive base. It also implies a deep understanding of why our world is changing, of how other people and cultures feel about those changes, of what we all have in common—as well as of what divides cultures, classes, and nations. Moreover, while this process of inquiry ought if possible to be tolerant and empathetic, it cannot be value-free. In the end, it is not enough merely to understand what we are doing to our planet, as if we were observing the changes through a giant telescope on Mars. Because we are all members of a world citizenry, we also need to equip ourselves with a system of ethics, a sense of fairness, *and* a sense of proportion as we consider the various ways in which, collectively or individually, we can better prepare for the twenty-first century.[11] In societies where fundamentalist forces block open inquiry and debate, where politicians, to attract the support of special interests, inveigh against foreign peoples or ethnic minorities, and where a commercialized mass media and popular culture drive serious issues to the margins, the possibility that education will introduce deeper understanding of global trends is severely limited.

Enhancing the role of education is inextricably linked to an even greater issue, namely, the position of women in both developing and developed countries. In the former case, the evidence linking the depressed status of women to population explosion, acute poverty, and economic retardation seems clear.* As the United Nations Population Division's statistics show, in country after country there is a strong inverse correlation between the adult female literacy rate and the total fertility rate (see Table 13).

There are a few interesting exceptions to this rule—Mongolia claims both an adult female literacy rate of 88 percent and a total fertility rate of 5.4—but the evidence overwhelmingly suggests that when education is widely available to women, average family size drops sharply and the demographic transition sets in. The obvious explanation for this—marrying older, postponing the birth of children, choosing a career—is confirmed by an even more thought-provoking set of statistics, shown

---

*The only exceptions, one suspects, are certain oil-rich Arab states where the woman's status is low, but per capita GNP is high—the latter because of geological accident rather than indigenous creative energies.

Table 13. Adult Female Literacy Rate and Total Fertility Rate,
Selected Countries[12]

Country	Adult Female Literacy Rate	Total Fertility Rate
Afghanistan	8%	6.9
Oman	12%	7.2
Yemen Arab Republic	3%	7.0
Honduras	58%	5.6
Burkina Faso	6%	6.5
Sudan	14%	6.4
Singapore	79%	1.7
Canada	93%	1.7
Chile	96%	2.7
Hungary	98%	1.8
Thailand	88%	2.6

in Table 14, on the relationship between a mother's education and the
number of children born in developing countries.

In general, women in developing countries with seven or more years
of education (and presumably from the better-off classes?) marry approximately four years later than those without education, have higher
rates of contraceptive use, *and* enjoy lower maternal and child mortality rates[13]—so both they and their offspring have better chances in life.
This clearly implies that a change in the status of women would significantly reduce population growth in the developing world. But how
likely is that in those parts of South Asia, Africa, and the Muslim world
where gender restrictions are so pronounced?

In the developed world, where elderly males bemoan the below-
replacement fertility rates and ask why "bright, well-educated women"

Table 14. Average Number of Children by Mother's
Years of Education, Selected Countries[14]

Country	No Education	Seven+ Years of Education
Benin	7.4	4.3
Sudan	6.5	3.4
Haiti	6.0	2.8
Ecuador	7.8	2.7
Jordan	9.3	4.9
Pakistan	6.5	3.1
Portugal	3.5	1.8

are having fewer children (or none at all),* the challenge is different—but still involves the position of women in society. Assuming that it is *not* good for a society to fail to renew its numbers—if only because of the strains of the burgeoning "elderly dependency" ratio—then politicians who worry about such trends may need to reassess their own cultural and social norms. In Japan, for example, the evidence suggests that a rising generation of educated women resent the traditional expectation that they become full-time housewives after college, bringing up children in cramped accommodations while their husbands are absent from early morning to late evening.[15] A similar resentment probably exists in Italy and Spain, where total fertility rates have plunged in recent years. No doubt the consequent labor shortages can be partially handled, in Japan's case at least, by the growing use of robots; but if Japan wants to return to replacement fertility rates, more than technical fixes will be needed. In this connection, Japanese and Italian politicians may care to study the case of Sweden, where, after decades of demographic slowdown, the fertility rate has steadily risen from 1.6 (1983) to 2.1 (1990).[16] Initial researches of this development—which also appears in several other Northern European countries—suggest that the reason could be a mixture of excellent social provisions (paid maternity *and* paternity leave, child care, kindergarten, comfortable housing) together with a significant degree of overall gender equality, measured, for example, in the numbers of female politicians and cabinet ministers.

Ironically, then, if the world is to move toward a better demographic balance—lowering fertility rates in poorer societies and raising them in richer ones—the lesson seems to be that while African and Middle Eastern nations need to educate women to Korean levels, countries like Japan, Portugal, Spain, and Italy need to imitate Scandinavian practices. Each involves a change in gender roles and a different set of challenges.

*See above, pp. 154–55, 313–14.

THE ISSUE OF POLITICAL LEADERSHIP

It may seem curious to conclude this work with a discussion of political leadership, since demographic trends and new technologies often appear so irresistible that nothing can be done to affect them. In fact, the thrust of this chapter is not about their inevitability, but about the difficulty of changing entrenched structures and ideas and the danger of remaining culturally blind, given the transformation of global society. After all, there clearly is a broad and lively concern in many countries about where the world in general and one's own nation in particular are headed. Technological challenges, gender issues, migration, the future of agriculture, environmental damage, the implication of globalization, and the impact of all this upon policies, spending priorities, even values and culture, are the subject of intense interest, from France to Japan, from Kansas to Cairo. They explain, at least in part, the search for newer transnational and subnational political structures, the innumerable committees investigating national educational systems, the calls for joint action over global warming or development aid, the anxious debates about commercial open-ness or protection. The man and woman in the street *know* that their world is changing and worry about it. Above all, unease about present or impending changes is behind the widespread disenchantment with political leaderships, whether in advanced industrial nations like America, France, and Japan, in existing or recently dissolved Marxist regimes, in large parts of Latin America and Africa, in the Asian giants of India and China, or, for that matter, in the Muslim world, where discontented youths turn to fundamentalist prescriptions. Much of this is suppressed in authoritarian states, but in both the older and the newer democracies the demand for political *responses* to the new challenges is immense.

Such responses can often be reactionary. Protectionism, anti-immigrant policies, blocking new technologies, and finding new enemies to replace Cold War foes are common reactions at a time of "jolts and jars and smashes in the social life of humanity." Clearly, a society which desires to be better prepared for the twenty-first century will pay a price to achieve that transition; it will need to retool its national skills and infrastructure, challenge vested interests, alter many old habits, and perhaps amend its governmental structures. But this assumes long-term

vision at a time when most politicians—in both rich and poor countries—can hardly deal with even short-term problems; and it means
political risk, since many of the reforms proposed would be unpopular
among vested interests. Alongside voices calling for change there exist
large constituencies wanting things to stay as they are, to freeze things
rather than respond. Moreover, there is much scholarly disagreement
over critical issues. Can we sustain a world of 8 to 10 billion people?
Can food supplies keep pace? How fast, if at all, is global warming
occurring? Is "managed trade" better than laissez-faire? Should globalization have no checks? And given the differences of view on these
questions, why rush ahead with controversial changes?

Since most politicians, especially in such countries as Japan, the
United States, France, Italy, and Germany, have risen to the top
through a process of compromise, making deals and alliances, and
taking care not to annoy powerful interests, they are hardly prepared
to endorse controversial policies now for purported benefits twenty
years away—especially when experts argue that there is little or no
cause for alarm (e.g., over world food supplies), or that further study
is needed. As "cornucopians" since Godwin and Condorcet two centuries ago have pointed out, Malthus's forecasts about Britain's future
were wrong, because of humankind's capacity to develop new resources
through technology. If his predictions for the nineteenth century were
false, why should any more notice be taken of the alarmist cries of
today's "neo-Malthusians" concerning the twenty-first century?[17] It is,
moreover, only a couple of decades since the last wave of gloomy
predictions (*The Silent Earth,* the "Club of Rome" report, etc.), which
provoked widespread concern before it faded away.

Perhaps we should distinguish here between reformers who advocate
prudent measures in the near future to control population and limit
vehicle emissions, for example, and apocalyptic writers who argue that
all will be lost unless a drastic change in human behavior occurs now.[18]
In denouncing the latter as both alarmist and erroneous, some conservatives tend to lump all reformers into the same camp. Yet it is proper
to note a distinction between the moderate and more radical reform
proposals, especially since it is the former that have better prospects of
swaying politicians.

Despite divided opinions over where our world is heading, societies ought to take seriously the challenge of preparing for the twenty-first century for three main reasons. The first concerns relative competitiveness. Though economic growth is hardly all that matters, it surely is true that a decent standard of living provides a foundation for much else that groups and individuals deem important—good health, education, leisure, etc. Yet those benefits, deriving from technological innovation and increased growth, do not flow equally to all; they come instead as rewards to successful societies. An economy increasingly unable to keep up with new technologies, experiencing slow (or negative) rates of growth, with per capita income levels static or falling just as demographic changes impose fresh social demands, is less happily placed than one which remains competitive and adaptable. A failure to rethink, retrain, and retool for the future will thus produce yet another crop of History's economic losers.

The second is the need to respond to demographic and environmental challenges, instead of simply hoping that a solution will turn up on its own.[19] Today's consumption of the earth's resources is far greater than in Malthus's day—or even in the 1960s—because of the size of the population, the sheer amounts of material it consumes, and the complexity of economic activities. Consequently, the *speed* of the human assault upon nature has greatly increased: "Whole countries may be deforested in a few decades; most of a region's topsoil can disappear in a generation; and critical ozone depletion may occur in as little as twenty years."[20] In other words, it might be that while the pessimists of several decades ago were wrong in their timing, their overall arguments about the damage increasingly inflicted upon the planet are becoming more valid—and ought not to be ignored. Finally, there is the point that societies best able to adapt are those (like Malthus's England or Japan today) with capital, scientific knowledge, technical expertise, and skilled and inventive personnel, whereas the countries facing the most serious problems in today's world are much less well equipped to respond.

This concern about environmental damage does not, of course, imply that *all* economic growth should be halted, for this would hurt poorer societies most and, in any case, contradicts the argument for enhanced competitiveness. Instead, politicians and publics ought to take far more seriously the proposals for "sustainable growth" which development experts have formulated.[21]

The third and final reason for reforming our existing global condition is a very traditional one: to reduce the chances of political instability, with concomitant threats of violence and war. Admittedly, many such convulsions are impossible to anticipate beforehand; if five years ago we would not have expected the degree of bloodshed and violence that has torn Yugoslavia to pieces, how can we hope to know what wars and tumults will be taking place in a decade's time? Still, many social explosions, such as the outbreak of the French or Russian revolutions, are preceded by a steady buildup of pressures, akin to the increased tensions along the edges of tectonic plates before an earthquake occurs, or, for that matter, the outbreak of an environmental disaster once incremental damage passes a certain threshold. While it is usually impossible to know exactly where or when the irruption will take place, scientists can make a plausible forecast that an explosion *will* someday occur, given the general buildup of pressures. By analogy, it is not unreasonable to suggest that as pressures increase within human societies—rapid population growth, diminishing resources, unemployment, migration to shanty cities, lack of education—social and political explosions are likely to occur, especially if the environmental causes of acute conflicts interact with traditional quarrels over boundaries, water and grazing rights, and so on.[22]

Civil or external wars—with their heavy casualties—were, like famine and disease, among the Malthusian antidotes to a population explosion, and perhaps the most effective of all because they killed people in the prime of life. Such turbulence is not only of local importance. Instabilities could nowadays take place in regions where the possession of advanced weaponry such as medium-range missiles with chemical, biological, or even nuclear warheads by ambitious and threatened regimes makes a potentially lethal combination, with implications that would be far from local.

In sum, we need to be concerned about the condition of our planet as a whole not simply because we face a new agenda of security risks such as global warming and mass migration, but also because these phenomena could interact with and exacerbate older threats to international stability such as regional wars, hostage-taking, and closure of sealanes. While the newer transnational forces for global change appear to be on a different plane from the traditional concerns of the nation-states—as analyzed, for example, in my work *The Rise and Fall of the Great Powers*—they constitute additional causes for social conflict.

Given this array of problems, it may seem that our merely human political leadership has no chance of doing much; that instead we ought to brace ourselves for a continuation of jolts and jars and smashes in the social life of humanity—and on an increasingly global and intense scale. If so, it would be foolish for any country—or social class—to assume that it can isolate itself from future changes, some of which may be unexpected and perhaps dramatic, in the worlds of politics, economics, and the environment. Moreover, in the unlikely event that governments and societies do decide to transform themselves, we ought to recognize that our endeavors might have only a marginal effect on the profound driving forces of today's world. We also ought to be aware that interventions (like enhancing female education in developing countries) could produce their own unforeseen and unintended changes. Nothing is certain except that we face innumerable uncertainties; but simply recognizing that fact provides a vital starting point, and is, of course, far better than being blindly unaware of how our world is changing.

Thus, despite the size and complexity of the global challenges facing us, it is too simple and too soon to conclude gloomily that nothing can be done. Even Malthus was careful enough to end his *Essay on Population* by suggesting that despite the ominous demographic trends, the astounding technical advances of his day could have a positive influence upon the moral and political dimensions of society. Far from over-whelming human beings with a sense of despair, he pointed out that science might actually stimulate constructive responses and alter social habits.[23] While he may have regarded that possibility as unlikely, he was at least willing to admit that *theoretically* humankind could change its ways and avoid the fate predicted for it. The same is as true today.

Many earlier attempts to peer into the future concluded either in a tone of unrestrained optimism, or in gloomy forebodings, or (as in Toynbee's case) in appeals for spiritual renewal. Perhaps this work should also finish on such a note. Yet the fact remains that simply because we do not know the future, it is impossible to say with certainty whether global trends will lead to terrible disasters or be diverted by astonishing advances in human adaption. What is clear is that as the Cold War fades away, we face not a "new world order" but a troubled and fractured planet, whose problems deserve the serious attention of politicians and publics alike. As the above chapters suggest, the pace and complexity of the forces for change are enormous and daunting; yet it may still be possible for intelligent men and women to lead their societies through the complex task of preparing for the century ahead. If these challenges are not met, however, humankind will have only itself to blame for the troubles, and the disasters, that could be lying ahead.

APPENDIX
HUMAN DEVELOPMENT INDEX

THE FOLLOWING TABLE, ASSEMBLED BY the United Nations Development Program, measures three elements— life expectancy at birth, adult literacy rate, and GNP per capita—to produce a composite "human development" ranking of 130 countries. The ranking is in ascending order, so that Niger actually rates lowest and Japan highest. These are based on mid-to-late-1980s statistics, and the position of individual peoples—in South Korea on the one hand, or in the erstwhile Soviet Union on the other—will have changed significantly since then.

	Life expectancy at birth (years) '87	Adult literacy rate (%) '85	Real GDP per head (PPP-adj'd) '87, $	HDI	Rank by GNP per head	Rank by HDI		Life expectancy at birth (years) '87	Adult literacy rate (%) '85	Real GDP per head (PPP-adj'd) '87, $	HDI	Rank by GNP per head	Rank by HDI
Niger	45	14	452	0.116	20	1	China	70	69	2,124	0.716	22	66
Mali	45	17	543	0.143	15	2	Libya	62	66	7,250	0.719	103	67
Burkina Faso	48	14	500	0.150	13	3	South Africa	61	70	4,981	0.731	82	68
Sierra Leone	42	30	480	0.150	27	4	Lebanon	68	78	2,250	0.735	78	69
Chad	48	26	400	0.157	4	5	Mongolia	64	90	2,000	0.737	57	70
Guinea	43	29	500	0.162	31	6	Nicaragua	64	88	2,209	0.743	54	71
Somalia	46	12	1,000	0.200	23	7	Turkey	65	74	3,781	0.751	71	72
Mauritania	47	17	840	0.208	40	8	Jordan	67	75	3,161	0.752	76	73
Afghanistan	42	24	1,000	0.212	17	9	Peru	63	85	3,129	0.753	74	74
Benin	47	27	665	0.224	28	10	Ecuador	66	83	2,687	0.758	68	75
Burundi	50	35	450	0.235	18	11	Iraq	65	89	2,400	0.759	96	76
Bhutan	49	25	700	0.236	3	12	United Arab Emirates	71	60	12,191	0.782	127	77

	Life expectancy at birth (years) '87	Adult literacy rate (%) '85	Real GDP per head (PPP-adj'd) '87, $	HDI	Rank by GNP per head	Rank by HDI		Life expectancy at birth (years) '87	Adult literacy rate (%) '85	Real GDP per head (PPP-adj'd) '87, $	HDI	Rank by GNP per head	Rank by HDI
Mozambique	47	39	500	0.239	10	13	Thailand	66	91	2,576	0.783	55	78
Malawi	48	42	476	0.250	7	14	Paraguay	67	88	2,603	0.784	65	79
Sudan	51	23	750	0.255	32	15	Brazil	65	78	4,307	0.784	85	80
Central African Republic	46	41	591	0.258	29	16	Mauritius	69	83	2,617	0.788	75	81
Nepal	52	26	722	0.273	8	17	North Korea	70	90	2,000	0.789	67	82
Senegal	47	28	1,068	0.274	43	18	Sri Lanka	71	87	2,053	0.789	38	83
Ethiopia	42	66	454	0.282	1	19	Albania	72	85	2,000	0.790	61	84
Zaire	53	62	220	0.294	5	20	Malaysia	70	74	3,849	0.800	80	85
Rwanda	49	47	571	0.304	26	21	Colombia	65	88	3,524	0.801	72	86
Angola	45	41	1,000	0.304	58	22	Jamaica	74	82	2,506	0.824	62	87
Bangladesh	52	33	883	0.318	6	23	Kuwait	73	70	13,843	0.839	122	88
Nigeria	51	43	668	0.322	36	24	Venezuela	70	87	4,306	0.861	95	89
Yemen Arab Rep.	52	25	1,250	0.328	47	25	Romania	71	96	3,000	0.863	84	90
Liberia	55	35	696	0.333	42	26	Mexico	69	90	4,624	0.876	81	91
Togo	64	41	670	0.337	24	27	Cuba	74	96	2,500	0.877	66	92
Uganda	52	58	511	0.354	21	28	Panama	72	89	4,009	0.883	88	93
Haiti	55	38	775	0.356	34	29	Trinidad and Tobago	71	96	3,664	0.885	100	94
Ghana	55	54	481	0.360	37	30	Portugal	74	85	5,597	0.899	94	95
Yemen, PDR	52	42	1,000	0.369	39	31	Singapore	73	86	12,790	0.899	110	96
Côte d'Ivoire	53	42	1,123	0.393	52	32	South Korea	70	95	4,832	0.903	92	97
Congo	49	63	756	0.395	59	33	Poland	72	98	4,000	0.910	83	98
Namibia	56	30	1,500	0.404	60	34	Argentina	71	96	4,647	0.910	89	99
Tanzania	54	75	405	0.413	12	35	Yugoslavia	72	92	5,000	0.913	90	100
Pakistan	58	30	1,585	0.423	33	36	Hungary	71	98	4,500	0.915	87	101
India	59	43	1,053	0.439	25	37	Uruguay	71	95	5,063	0.916	86	102
Madagascar	54	68	634	0.440	14	38	Costa Rica	75	93	3,760	0.916	77	103
Papua New Guinea	55	45	1,843	0.471	50	39	Bulgaria	72	93	4,750	0.918	99	104
Kampuchea, Dem.	49	75	1,000	0.471	2	40	USSR	70	99	6,000	0.920	101	105
Cameroon	52	61	1,381	0.474	64	41	Czechoslovakia	72	98	7,750	0.931	102	106
Kenya	59	60	794	0.481	30	42	Chile	72	98	4,862	0.931	73	107
Zambia	54	76	717	0.481	19	43	Hong Kong	76	88	13,906	0.936	111	108
Morocco	62	34	1,761	0.489	48	44	Greece	76	93	5,500	0.949	98	109
Egypt	62	45	1,357	0.501	49	45	East Germany	74	99	8,000	0.953	115	110
Laos	49	84	1,000	0.506	9	46	Israel	76	95	9,182	0.957	108	111
Gabon	52	62	2,068	0.525	93	47	USA	76	99	17,615	0.961	129	112
Oman	57	30	7,750	0.535	104	48	Austria	74	99	12,386	0.961	118	113
Bolivia	54	75	1,380	0.548	44	49	Ireland	74	99	8,566	0.961	106	114
Burma	61	79	752	0.561	11	50	Spain	77	95	8,989	0.965	105	115
Honduras	65	59	1,119	0.563	53	51	Belgium	75	99	13,140	0.966	116	116
Zimbabwe	59	74	1,184	0.576	45	52	Italy	76	97	10,682	0.966	112	117
Lesotho	57	73	1,585	0.580	35	53	New Zealand	75	99	10,541	0.966	109	118
Indonesia	57	74	1,660	0.591	41	54	West Germany	75	99	14,730	0.967	120	119
Guatemala	63	55	1,957	0.592	63	55	Finland	75	99	12,795	0.967	121	120
Vietnam	62	80	1,000	0.608	16	56	Britain	76	99	12,270	0.970	113	121
Algeria	63	50	2,633	0.609	91	57	Denmark	76	99	15,119	0.971	123	122
Botswana	59	71	2,496	0.646	69	58	France	76	99	13,961	0.974	119	123
El Salvador	64	72	1,733	0.651	56	59	Australia	76	99	11,782	0.978	114	124
Tunisia	66	55	2,741	0.657	70	60	Norway	77	99	15,940	0.983	128	125
Iran	66	51	3,300	0.660	97	61	Canada	77	99	16,375	0.983	124	126
Syria	66	60	3,250	0.691	79	62	Holland	77	99	12,661	0.984	117	127
Dominican Rep.	67	78	1,750	0.699	51	63	Switzerland	77	99	15,403	0.986	130	128
Saudi Arabia	64	55	8,320	0.702	107	64	Sweden	77	99	13,780	0.987	125	129
Philippines	64	86	1,878	0.714	46	65	Japan	78	99	13,135	0.996	126	130

NOTES

CHAPTER 1
PROLOGUE: OLD CHALLENGES AND NEW CHALLENGES

1. See the broad estimates in G. T. Trewartha, *A Geography of Population: World Patterns* (New York, 1969), p. 30.
2. N. Tranter, *Population Since the Industrial Revolution: The Case of England and Wales* (New York, 1973), pp. 41–42.
3. See the discussion in W. H. McNeill, *Plagues and Peoples* (New York, 1976), ch. 6; and in P. E. Razzell, "Population Growth and Economic Change in Eighteenth- and Early Nineteenth-Century England and Ireland," in E. L. Jones and G. E. Mingay (eds.), *Land, Labour and Population in the Industrial Revolution* (London, 1967), pp. 260–81.
4. T. R. Malthus, *An Essay on the Principle of Population as It Affects the Future Improvement of Society* (London, 1798); reprinted with notes by J. Bonar, New York, 1965, p. 13.
5. Ibid., p. 22.
6. R. L. Heilbroner, *The Worldly Philosophers* (New York, 1986 edn.), pp. 77–78.
7. P. Mathias, *The First Industrial Nation* (London, 1969), p. 452; W. D. McIntyre, *Colonies into Commonwealth* (London, 1966), p. 345.
8. There is a good brief description in Mathias, *First Industrial Nation*, pp. 64–80; see also J. D. Chambers and G. E. Mingay, *The Agricultural Revolution 1750–1880* (New York, 1966).
9. D. S. Landes, *The Unbound Prometheus: Technological Change and Industrial Development in Western Europe from 1750 to the Present* (Cambridge, 1969), p. 1.
10. P. Kennedy, *The Rise and Fall of the Great Powers* (New York, 1987), pp. 146–47; and see the more general discourse in C. M. Cipolla, *The Economic History of*

World Population, 7th edn. (Harmondsworth, Mddsx., 1978), pp. 70ff., 115; W. H. McNeill, *Population and Politics Since 1750* (Charlottesville, Va., 1990).

11. Mathias, *First Industrial Nation*, Table 15, p. 466.

12. Quoted in R. Hyam, *Britain's Imperial Century 1815–1914* (London, 1975), p. 47.

13. This is the theme of Landes, *Unbound Prometheus*.

14. T. S. Ashton, *The Industrial Revolution, 1760–1830* (Oxford, 1968 edn.), p. 129.

15. This figure comes from P. Bairoch, "International Industrialization Levels from 1750 to 1980," *Journal of European Economic History* 11 (1982), p. 294.

16. Ashton, *Industrial Revolution*, p. 129.

17. For this argument, see W. H. McNeill, *The Pursuit of Power* (Chicago, 1983), ch. 6.

18. See in particular E. L. Jones, *The European Miracle: Environments, Economies and Geopolitics in the History of Europe and Asia* (Cambridge, 1981); and C. M. Cipolla (ed.), *The Economic Decline of Empires* (London, 1970).

19. As argued in K. Mendelssohn, *Science and Western Domination* (London, 1976).

20. For a flavor of that concern, see J. Fallows, *More Like Us* (New York, 1989); D. Burstein, *Yen!* (New York, 1988); R. Rosecrance, *America's Economic Resurgence* (New York, 1990); S. Schlossstein, *The End of the American Century* (New York, 1989).

CHAPTER 2
THE DEMOGRAPHIC EXPLOSION

1. Cipolla, *Economic History of World Population*, quoting H. Brown, *The Challenge of Man's Future* (New York, 1954), p. 3.

2. These commonly accepted figures are reproduced in H. Thomas, *A History of the World* (New York, 1979), pp. 49–50. See also W. W. Rostow, *The World Economy—History and Prospects* (Austin, Texas, 1978), pp. 3–7. The 1990 figure comes from *World Population Prospects 1988* (United Nations Population Division, New York, 1989), p. 28.

3. *World Population Prospects 1988*, p. 28; and see also N. Sadik, *The State of the World Population* (U.N. Population Fund, New York, 1990).

4. *Population Today*, vol. 16, no. 1 (January 1988), p. 3; "World Population Pace Quickens," *Wall Street Journal*, 14 May 1991, p. A18.

5. *World Population Prospects 1988*, pp. 27–32. The population totals of the countries referred to were taken from *World Resources 1990–91* (New York/Oxford, 1990), pp. 254–55.

6. *World Population Prospects 1988*, p. 37, Table 2.5.

7. Ibid.; M. Southeimer, "Die Erde ist voll," *Die Zeit*, 28 December 1990, *Dossier*, p. 13.

8. Cipolla, *Economic History of World Population*, pp. 89–90; and see also the discussion in McNeill, *Plagues and Peoples*, passim.

9. *World Resources 1990–91*, pp. 254, 258.

10. Ibid., p. 254.

11. Ibid., pp. 254–55.

12. J. Axelbank, "The Crisis of the Cities," *Populi*, vol. 15, no. 4 (1988), pp. 28–35; Sadik, *State of the World Population*, p. 9. For the "centers of wealth . . . centers of poverty" argument, see R. Wright and D. MacManus, *Flashpoints* (New York, 1991), p. 168.

13. Sadik, *State of the World Population*, p. 8.

14. T. J. Goliber, "Africa's Expanding Population: Old Problems, New Policies," *Population Bulletin*, vol. 44, no. 3 (November 1989), p. 18.

15. T. C. Quinn et al., "AIDS in Africa: An Epidemiological Paradigm," *Science* 234 (November 1986), pp. 955–58; K. Hunt, "Scenes from a Nightmare," *New York Times Magazine*, 12 August 1990, pp. 24–26, 50–51.

16. L. K. Altman, "W. H. O. Says 40 Million Will Be Infected with AIDS Virus by 2000," *New York Times*, 18 June 1991, p. C3.

17. "AIDS in Africa," *Economist*, 25 November 1989, p. 16.

18. Goliber, "Africa's Expanding Population," p. 22, referring to a 1988 unpublished AAAS conference paper by J. Bougaarts, "Modeling the Demographic Impact of AIDS in Africa."

19. See the comparative statistics in *World Resources 1990–91*, pp. 244–65. For analyses of the East Asian "boom," see S. B. Linder, *The Pacific Century* (Stanford, Cal., 1986); J. W. Morley (ed.), *The Pacific Basin* (New York, 1986); M. Smith et al., *Asia's New Industrial World* (London, 1985).

20. R. Rosecrance, *The Rise of the Trading States* (New York, 1985), covers this aspect of history *and* current trends.

21. See A. J. Coale and E. M. Hoover, *Population Growth and Economic Development in Low Income Countries* (Princeton, N.J., 1958), as well as the arguments in D. H. Meadows et al., *The Limits to Growth* (New York, 1972); P. R. Ehrlich, *The Population Bomb* (New York, 1968); and H. E. Daly, *Steady State Economics* (San Francisco, 1977).

22. J. Simon, *The Ultimate Resource* (Princeton, N.J., 1981), p. 6, and passim. See also the more technical comments by D. A. Ahlburg, "The Impact of Population Growth on Economic Growth in Developing Nations: The Evidence From Macroeconomic-Demographic Models," in D. G. Johnson and R. D. Lee, *Population Growth and Economic Development: Issues and Evidence* (Madison, Wis., 1987), pp. 479–522.

23. P. R. Ehrlich and A. E. Ehrlich, *The Population Explosion* (New York, 1990), p. 134. The oil consumption figures come from M. L. Wald, "America Is Still Demanding a Full Tank," *New York Times*, 12 August 1990, p. E3.

24. Apart from the Ehrlichs' *Population Explosion* and P. R. Ehrlich, *The Population Bomb* (New York, 1968), see also L. R. Brown et al., *State of the World 1990*, passim; *World Resources 1990–91;* and *Our Common Future* (World Commission on Environment and Development, Oxford, 1987).

25. Simon, *Ultimate Resource*, passim.

26. See M. S. Teitelbaum and J. M. Winter, *The Fear of Population Decline* (Orlando, Fla./London, 1976), ch. 2.

27. G. D. Foster, "Global Demographic Trends to the Year 2010: Implications for U.S. Security," *Washington Quarterly* 12 (Spring 1989), p. 10.

28. See, for example, K. R. Andrews, *Elizabethan Privateering* (Cambridge, 1974), passim; W. H. McNeill, *The Pursuit of Power* (Chicago, 1983), pp. 185ff.

29. B. J. Wattenberg, *The Birth Dearth* (New York, 1987), passim.

30. *Wall Street Journal*, 5 June 1991, p. A10.

31. *World Resources 1990–91*, p. 257.

32. Ibid., pp. 256–57.

33. "Ten Billion Mouths," *Economist*, 20 January 1990.

34. Teitelbaum and Winter, *Fear of Population Decline*, passim.

35. For one good example, see G. R. Searle, *Eugenics and Politics in Britain, 1900–1914* (Leyden, 1976), passim, but many more are offered in Teitelbaum and Winter, *Fear of Population Decline*.

36. Teitelbaum and Winter, *Fear of Population Decline*, esp. chs. 5–7. See also K. Davis et al. (eds.), *Below-Replacement Fertility in Industrial Societies*, Supplement to *Population and Development Review* 12 (1986).

37. Foster, "Global Demographic Trends to the Year 2010," passim, and N. Eberstadt, "Population Change and National Security," *Foreign Affairs*, vol. 70, no. 3 (Summer 1991), pp. 115–31, are best here.

38. G. V. Scammell, *The World Encompassed: The First European Maritime Empires, c. 800–1650* (Berkeley, Cal., 1981); J. H. Parry, *The Age of Reconnaissance*, 2nd edn. (London, 1966).

39. Cipolla, *Economic History of World Population*, p. 120.

40. T. H. Von Laue, *The World Revolution of Westernization* (New York/Oxford, 1987), passim.

41. "The Would-Be European," *Economist*, 4 August 1990, pp. 14–15.

42. These comments are based on McNeill, *Population and Politics Since 1750*, pp. 60–71; Teitelbaum and Winter, *Fear of Population Decline*, passim; many of the essays in W. Alonso (ed.), *Population in an Interacting World* (Cambridge, Mass., 1987); and S. Castles et al., *Here for Good: Western Europe's New Ethnic Minorities* (London, 1984). See also T. Horwitz and C. Forman, "Immigrants to Europe from the Third World Face Racial Animosity," *Wall Street Journal*, 14 August 1990, pp. A1, A8.

43. *World Resources 1990–91*, pp. 254–55. The Australian projection here already looks conservative, given that country's high rate of population growth: see C. Young, "Australia's Population: A Long-Term View," *Current Affairs Bulletin* (Sydney) 65 (May 1989), pp. 4–11.

44. Eberstadt, "Population Change and National Security," p. 125.

45. D. Johnston, "Rise in Crossings Spurs New Actions to Seal U.S. Border," *New York Times*, 9 February 1992, pp. 1, 30; A. Riding, "France Unveils Strict New Rules on Immigration," *New York Times*, 11 July 1991, p. A5.

46. "One Sign of Our Times: World's Refugee Flood," *New York Times*, 12 August 1990, p. 16 (main section).

47. McNeill, *Population and Politics*, p. 69.

48. Eberstadt, "Population Change and National Security," p. 128.

49. Ibid., p. 129.

CHAPTER 3
THE COMMUNICATIONS AND FINANCIAL REVOLUTION AND THE RISE OF THE MULTINATIONAL CORPORATION

1. Both the statistics in the text and this table come from Bairoch, "International Industrialization Levels from 1750 to 1980," p. 273.

2. M. Moynihan, *Global Consumer Demographics* (New York, 1991), p. 28.

3. *World Resources 1990–91*, pp. 244–45.

4. *World Development Report 1990* (Washington, D.C., 1990), p. iii.

5. R. Aggarwal, "The Strategic Challenge of the Evolving Global Economy," *Business Horizons*, July–August 1987, pp. 38–44; W. B. Wriston, "Technology and Sovereignty," *Foreign Affairs*, vol. 67, no. 2 (Winter 1988–89), p. 71. For other comments about these transformations, see B. C. Resnick, "The Globalization of World Financial Markets," *Business Horizons* 32 (November–December 1989), pp. 34–41; "The Stateless Corporation," *Business Week*, 14 May 1990, pp. 98–105; H. B. Malmgren, "Technology and the Economy," in W. E. Brock and

R. D. Hormats (eds.), *The Global Economy: America's Role in the Decade Ahead* (New York/London, 1990), pp. 92–119. More generally, see the important article by P. Drucker, "The Changed World Economy," *Foreign Affairs* 64 (Spring 1984), pp. 768–91.

6. See again Resnick, "Globalization of World Currency Markets," passim; "International Banking," *Economist* (Survey), 25 March 1989; K. Pierog, "How Technology Is Tackling 24-Hour Global Markets," *Futures*, vol. 17, no. 6 (June 1989), pp. 68–74; G. A. Keyworth II, "Goodbye, Central: Telecommunications and Computing in the 1990s," Vital Speeches of the Day, vol. 56, no. 12 (1 April 1990), pp. 358–61.

7. C. F. Bergsten, *America in the World Economy: A Strategy for the 1990s* (Washington, D.C., 1988), pp. 59–60.

8. K. Ohmae, *The Borderless World: Management Lessons in the New Logic of the Global Marketplace* (New York/London, 1990), passim. See also Wriston, "Technology and Sovereignty"; Keyworth, "Goodbye Central," passim.

9. James N. Rosenau, "The Relocation of Authority in a Shrinking World," unpublished paper, 1990.

10. A. W. Pessin, "Communications and Revolution: 1989, the Year Communications Got a Good Name," *Vital Speeches of the Day*, vol. 56, no. 14 (1 May 1990), p. 425.

11. Ohmae, *Borderless World*, p. 3.

12. Ibid.

13. R. B. Reich, *The Work of Nations* (New York, 1990), pp. 3–4, 8–9.

14. Ibid., pp. 115–16, 126.

15. Ohmae, *Borderless World*, p. 170.

16. S. Strange, "Finance, Information, and Power," *Review of International Studies*, vol. 16, no. 3 (July 1990), p. 274. For a more cautionary viewpoint, see E. Helleiner, "States and the Future of Global Finance," *Review of International Studies*, vol. 18, no. 1 (January 1992), pp. 31–49.

17. For the increasing precariousness of the pre-1914 system, for example, see M. de Cecco, *Money and Empire: The International Gold Standard, 1890–1914* (Oxford, 1974). See also the interesting comments of R. P. Gilpin, *The Political Economy of International Relations* (Princeton, 1987), chs. 4 and 9.

18. I have borrowed this sentence from a commentary by my editor Jason Epstein on the first draft of the manuscript of this book.

19. The executive was from Colgate-Palmolive: see Reich, *Work of Nations*, p. 141, quoting from Louis Uchitelle's important article "U.S. Businesses Loosen Link to Mother Country," *New York Times*, 28 May 1984.

20. The Danville/Portland example is provided by Reich, *Work of Nations*, pp. 295–96. The Arlington/Ypsilanti example comes from C. Harlan and J. Mitchell, "Rage, Relief and Warning to UAW Mark GM Decision on Closing Plant," *Wall Street Journal*, 25 February 1992, p. A8; and G. A. Patterson, "How GM's Car Plant in Arlington, Texas, Hustled to Avoid Ax," *Wall Street Journal*, 6 March 1992, pp. A1, A4.

21. Reich, *Work of Nations*, pp. 295–98, gives many examples of this competitive bidding.

22. Ibid., p. 213. Reich's book offers a very clear analysis of these social and occupational trends.

23. Ohmae, *Borderless World*.

24. Ibid., p. xii.

25. Rosenau, "Relocation of Authority," passim.

CHAPTER 4
WORLD AGRICULTURE AND THE BIOTECHNOLOGY REVOLUTION

1. L. R. Brown et al., *State of the World 1990*, p. 5.
2. B. Johnstone, "Fading of the Miracle," and "Sowing for the Future," *Far East Economic Review*, 1 December 1988, pp. 72–75.
3. These causes are discussed in L. R. Brown and J. E. Young, "Feeding the World in the Nineties," ch. 4 of *State of the World 1990;* and in Ehrlich and Ehrlich, *Population Explosion*, chs. 4–5. For a critique of this "alarmism," see D. T. Avery, "Mother Earth Can Feed Billions More," *Wall Street Journal*, 19 September 1991 (op-ed), and J. L. Simon, *Population Matters* (New Brunswick, N.J., 1990), pt. 2.
4. Johnstone, "Fading of the Miracle," passim.
5. Figures from *World Resources 1990–91*, p. 86.
6. These figures can be found in L. R. Brown et al., *State of the World 1990*, p. 65, and *World Resources 1990–91*, p. 87, respectively.
7. *World Resources 1990–91*, p. 87; and N. Calder, *The Green Machines* (New York, 1986), pp. 109–18.
8. Johnstone, "Sowing for the Future," p. 72.
9. *Technology, Public Policy, and the Changing Structure of American Agriculture* (U.S. Congress, Office of Technology Assessment, Washington, D.C., 1986), p. 4.
10. For descriptions of these techniques, see "Biotechnology Survey," *Economist*, 30 April 1988. See also J. L. Marx (ed.), *A Revolution in Biotechnology* (Cambridge, 1989); S. Prentis, *Biotechnology: A New Industrial Revolution* (New York, 1984); R. Teitelman, *Gene Dreams* (New York, 1989); B. D. Davis (ed.), *The Genetic Revolution: Scientific Prospects and Public Perceptions* (Baltimore/London, 1991).
11. "Biotechnology Survey," *Economist*, 30 April 1988, p. 6; *Agricultural Biotechnology: The Next Green Revolution?*, World Bank Technical Paper no. 133 (Washington, D.C., 1991).
12. For the above, see S. Browlee, "The Best Banana Bred," *Atlantic* 264 (September 1989), pp. 22, 24, 28; K. Schneider, "Betting the Farm on Biotech," *New York Times Magazine*, 10 June 1990, "Business World," pp. 26–28, 36, 38–39; J. M. Nash, "A Bumper Crop of Biotech," *Time*, 1 October 1990, pp. 92–94; "The Tomatoes of the Tree of Knowledge," *Economist*, 14 July 1990, p. 83; D. E. Hanke, "Seeding the Bamboo Revolution," *Nature*, 22 (1990).
13. *Science*, 16 June 1989, p. 1281.
14. J. Doyle, "Sustainable Agriculture and the Other Kind of Biotechnology," p. 173; testimony to *Reform and Innovation of Science and Education: Planning for the 1990 Farm Bill* (U.S. Senate, Committee on Agriculture, Nutrition, and Forestry, Washington, D.C., 1989); M. Mellon, "An Environmentalist Perspective," in Davis (ed.), *Genetic Revolution*, pp. 60–76. For the issue of biodiversity vs. genetic uniformity, see R. E. Rhoades, "The World's Food Supply at Risk," *National Geographic* (April 1991), pp. 74–105.
15. L. Busch et al., *Plants, Power, and Profit: Social, Economic and Ethical Consequences of the New Biotechnologies* (Cambridge, Mass./Oxford, 1991), p. 186 (quoting Balandrin et al).
16. See again Schneider, "Betting the Farm on Biotech," passim.
17. Busch et al., *Plants, Power, and Profit*, p. 184.
18. This is a paraphrase of J. Doyle, "DNA—It's Changing the Whole Economy," *Christian Science Monitor*, 30 September 1987, and "Who Will Gain from

Biotechnology?" in S. M. Gendel et al., *Agricultural Bioethics* (Ames, Iowa, 1990), p. 185—a remarkable article. See also M. Kenney, *Biotechnology: The University-Industrial Complex* (New Haven/London, 1986), ch. 10.

19. D. Goodman et al., *From Farming to Biotechnology: A Theory of Agro-Industrial Development* (Oxford, 1987), p. 138 and passim; E. Yoxen, *The Gene Business* (New York, 1983), esp. pp. 140–48.

20. The calculation is by G. Junne and J. Birman, "The Impact of Biotechnology on European Agriculture," in E. Yoxen and V. Di Martino, *Biotechnology in Future Society* (Aldershot, 1989), p. 79.

21. "Biotechnology Survey," *Economist*, 30 April 1988, p. 17.

22. See K. Schneider, "Biotechnology Enters Political Race," *New York Times*, 21 April 1990; G. Gugliotta, "Bovine Growth Hormone Stirs a Debate in Wisconsin," *Washington Post*, National Weekly Edition, July 2–8, 1990, p. 39; and the letters in the *New York Times* of 19 May and 12 June 1990.

23. D. Dickson, "German Biotech Firms Flee Regulatory Controls," *Science*, 16 June 1990, pp. 1251–52.

24. As suggested in Busch et al., *Plants, Power, and Profit*, pp. 175, 178.

25. "Yesterday's Farming," *Economist*, 20 August 1988, passim; M. L. LaGanga, "U.S. Agriculture, Biotech Firms Cut Good Deals with Japanese," *Los Angeles Times*, 9 April 1990, p. D3; H. Yamaguchi, "Biotechnology: New Hope for Japan's Farmers," *Business Japan*, April 1987, pp. 36–40.

26. See again Dickson, "German Biotech Firms Flee Regulatory Controls," passim.

27. A. Gibbons, "Biotechnology Takes Root in the Third World," *Science*, 25 May 1990, p. 962.

28. C. Juma, *The Gene Hunters: Biotechnology and the Scramble for Seeds* (London/Princeton, N.J., 1989), pp. 117–24—an excellent account.

29. L. R. Brown et al., *State of the World 1990*, p. 71.

30. Ibid.

31. J. R. Kloppenburg, "The Social Impacts of Biogenetic Technology in Agriculture: Past and Future," in G. M. Berardi and C. C. Geisler (eds.), *The Social Consequences and Challenges of New Agricultural Technologies* (Boulder, Colo., 1984), p. 318.

32. Busch et al., *Plants, Power, and Profit*, pp. 172, 175, 181–82, provides these examples and statistics in its fine analysis of the problem.

33. Ibid., pp. 183–85. See also the running commentary in J. R. Kloppenburg, *First the Seed: The Political Economy of Plant Biotechnology 1492–2000* (Cambridge, 1988).

34. Contrast, for example, L. R. Brown's "Reexamining the World Food Prospect," *State of the World 1989*, pp. 41–58, with D. T. Avery, "The Green Revolution Is Our Real Food Security," Hudson Institute, Briefing Paper 112, 18 October 1989. See also the various articles in Davis (ed.), *Genetic Revolution*.

CHAPTER 5
ROBOTICS, AUTOMATION, AND A NEW INDUSTRIAL REVOLUTION

1. Landes, *Unbound Prometheus*, p. 41.

2. Kennedy, *Rise and Fall of the Great Powers*, pp. 126–39.

3. This is nicely discussed in T. S. Harmerow, *Restoration, Revolution, Reaction: Economics and Politics in Germany, 1815–1871* (Princeton, N.J., 1958), chs. 2, 5, and 8.

4. According to P. B. Scott, *The Robotics Revolution* (Oxford/New York, 1982), p. 10.
5. Ibid.; and especially W. B. Gevarter, *Intelligent Machines* (Englewood Cliffs, N.J., 1985), p. 161.
6. See the breakdown of the industries using robots in *Annual Review of Engineering Industries and Automation, 1988*, vol. 1 (UN Economic Commission for Europe, N.Y., 1989), p. 53.
7. *Robotics Technology and Its Varied Uses*, Hearing Before the Subcommittee on Science, Research and Technology, U.S. Congress, 25 September 1989 (Washington, D.C., 1989), testimony of Mr. K. G. Engelhardt; see also K. G. Engelhardt, "Innovations in Health Care: Roles for Advanced Intelligent Technologies," *Pittsburgh High Technology Journal*, vol. 2, no. 5, pp. 69–72.
8. *Robotics Technology and Its Varied Uses*, pp. 15, 19, 24.
9. J. Baranson, *Robots in Manufacturing* (Mt. Airy, Md., 1983), p. 67.
10. Ibid., pp. 39–41, 111–27; *Robotics Technology and Its Varied Uses*, p. 76; P. T. Kilborn, "Brave New World Seen for Robots Appears Stalled by Quirks and Costs," *New York Times*, 1 July 1990, p. 16.
11. Kilborn, "Brave New World Seen."
12. Baranson, *Robots in Manufacturing*, p. 86.
13. *Robotics Technology and Its Varied Uses*, p. 172.
14. *Annual Review of Engineering Industries and Automation*, p. 53.
15. "Japan's New Idea: Technology for the 21st Century," *Industry Week* Special Report, 5 September 1990, p. 42.
16. "Bodybuilding Without Tears," *Economist*, 21 April 1990, p. 138.
17. FANUC's operations have been described in innumerable articles, for example, F. L. Schodt, "In the Land of Robots," *Business Month* 132 (November 1988), pp. 67–75; F. Hiatt, "Japanese Robots Reproducing Like Rabbits: High-Tech Capital Investment Helps Fuel Economic Miracle," *Washington Post*, 2 January 1990, pp. A1, A13.; and more technically, D. F. Urbanials, "The Unattended Factory," *13th International Symposium on Industrial Robots, and Robots 7: Conference Proceedings*, vol. 1 (Dearborn, Mich., 1983), pp. I-18 to I-24.
18. See the extremely stimulating article by M. J. E. Cooley, "Robotics—Some Wider Implications," *The World Yearbook of Robotics Research and Development* (1985), pp. 95–104.
19. See again the articles by Schodt and Hiatt (note 17 above).
20. See Table 11 below.
21. M. Carnoy, "High Technology and International Labour Markets," *International Labour Review*, vol. 124, no. 6 (1985), p. 649.
22. Ibid., p. 650.
23. Ibid., p. 653.
24. "Japan's New Idea," *Industry Week*, p. 69.
25. See the argument in Chapter 3.

CHAPTER 6
THE DANGERS TO OUR NATURAL ENVIRONMENT

1. This early narrative is based upon the following key works: B. L. Turner et al., *The Earth As Transformed by Human Action: Global and Regional Changes in the Biosphere over the Past 300 Years* (Cambridge, Mass., 1990); *World Resources 1990–91*, pp. 1–10; L. R. Brown et al., *State of the World 1990*, esp. ch. 1, "The

Illusion of Progress," pp. 3–16; M. Oppenheimer and R. H. Boyle, *Dead Heat: The Race Against the Greenhouse Effect* (New York, 1990), ch. 2; and Rostow, *World Economy: History and Prospects*, esp. pts. 1 and 6.

2. L. R. Brown et al., *State of the World 1990*, p. 6.

3. S. Hecht and A. Cockburn, *The Fate of the Forest: Developers, Destroyers and Defenders of the Amazon* (London/New York, 1989), passim; K. Maxwell, "The Tragedy of the Amazon," *New York Review of Books* 38 (7 March 1991), pp. 24–29.

4. *World Resources 1990–91*, p. 106.

5. See the discussion in J. D. Ives and B. Messerli, *The Himalayan Dilemma: Reconciling Development and Conservation* (London/New York, 1989), ch. 1. (It ought to be noted that while admitting the impact of deforestation, Ives and Messerli argue that there are also profound geophysical reasons for the siltation and floodings.)

6. L. R. Brown et al., *State of the World 1990*, p. 5.

7. *World Resources 1990–91*, pp. 101–2. The 20.4 million hectares figure is based upon a very uncertain extrapolation to *all* tropical forests from the deforestation rate in the Amazon.

8. Well explained in W. V. Reid and K. R. Miller, *Keeping Options Open: The Scientific Basis for Conserving Biodiversity* (Washington, D.C., 1989), passim.

9. "A Latin American Ecological Alliance" (paid advertisement), *New York Times*, 22 July 1991, p. A11.

10. F. Painton, "Where the Sky Stays Dark," *Time*, 28 May 1990, pp. 40–41.

11. L. R. Brown et al., *State of the World 1990*, p. 100.

12. Ibid., p. 109.

13. For a summary of the various studies of this topic, see *World Resources 1990–91*, ch. 10, "Freshwater."

14. L. R. Brown et al., *State of the World 1990*, p. 43, from the chapter "Saving Water for Agriculture," an excellent introduction to this problem.

15. Ibid., pp. 44–45.

16. *World Resources 1990–91*, p. 171, "The Dying Aral Sea."

17. Ibid., pp. 176–77.

18. S. Postel, *Water: Rethinking Management in an Age of Scarcity*, Worldwatch Paper 62 (December 1984), esp. pp. 20–22; and the witty analysis in M. Reisner, *Cadillac Desert* (New York, 1986), passim.

19. The reason global warming has to be seen as *the* environmental problem of our time is articulated in *World Resources 1990–91*, ch. 2, "Climate Change: A Global Concern," pp. 11–31; P. H. Gleick, "Climate Change and International Politics: Problems Facing Developing Countries," *Ambio* 18 (1989), pp. 333–39; P. H. Gleick, "The Implications of Global Changes for International Security," *Climatic Change* 15 (1989), pp. 309–25.

20. This paragraph and the following rely heavily upon a letter to the author by Kenneth Keller, Senior Fellow for Science and Technology, Council on Foreign Relations, 30 January 1992.

21. S. H. Schneider, *Global Warming* (San Francisco, 1989), esp. pp. 18–19. See also "Under the Sun—Is Our World Warming?" *National Geographic*, vol. 178, no. 4 (October 1990), p. 73—an excellent introductory article.

22. *World Resources 1990–91*, p. 14.

23. S. Shulman, "Hot Air—or What?," *Nature* 345 (14 June 1990), p. 4562; D. L. Wheeler, "Scientists Studying 'The Greenhouse Effect' Challenge Fears of Global Warming," *Journal of Forestry*, vol. 88, no. 7 (1989), pp. 34–36; W. K. Stevens,

"Carbon Dioxide Rise May Alter Plant Life, Researchers Say," *New York Times,* 18 September 1990, pp. C1, C9. For critical comments upon this viewpoint, see the entire issue of the journal *Climatic Change* 6 (1985). Note also Avery, "The Green Revolution Is Our Real Food Security," a sustained attack on Lester Brown's Worldwatch Institute; Simon, *Population Matters,* passim; and W. Tucker, *Progress and Privilege* (New York, 1982).

24. For this "consensus," see the U. S. National Research Council's report *Changing Climate* (Washington, D.C., 1983); J. Hansen et al., "Global Climate Changes as Forecast by the Goddard Institute for Space Studies Three-Dimensional Model," *Journal of Geophysical Research* 93 (1988), pp. 9341–64, a very technical piece; and R. A. Kerr, "New Greenhouse Report Puts Down Dissenters," *Science* 249 (3 August 1990), pp. 481–82, an advance summary of the October 1990 report of the International Panel on Climate Change.

25. D. Goleman, "Antarctica Sheds Ice and Scientists Wonder Why," *New York Times,* 14 August 1990, pp. C1, C8.

26. The Intergovernmental Panel on Climate Change apparently believes that "barring strict controls on greenhouse gas emissions, sea level will rise between 8 and 29 centimeters by 2030," which is a rather modest increase (Kerr, "New Greenhouse Report," p. 481). By contrast, a National Academy of Sciences study, which takes "into account the possibility of further polar ice melting, forecast the rise of roughly 1.5 to 3.5 feet in the next century," which is a very different matter (Goleman, "Antarctica Sheds Ice," p. C8). See also the table in S. Hoffman, "Estimates of Future Sea Level Rise," in M. C. Barth and J. G. Titus (eds.), *Greenhouse Effect and Sea Level Rise* (New York, 1984).

27. See E. D. Fajer et al., "The Effects of Enriched Carbon Dioxide Atmospheres on Plant–Insect Herbivores Interactions," *Science* 243 (1989), pp. 1198–1200. This concerns, however, a single plant-insect interaction.

28. J. Broadus et al., "Rising Sea Level and Damming of Rivers: Possible Effects in Egypt and Bangladesh," in J. G. Titus (ed.), *Effects of Changes in Stratospheric Ozone and Global Climate,* vol. 4, *Sea Level Rise* (Washington, D.C., 1986).

29. Figures from *World Resources 1990–91,* pp. 244–45.

30. J. Hoffman et al., *Projecting Future Sea Level Rise: Methodology, Estimate to the Year 2000, and Research Needs* (Washington, D.C., 1983), passim.

31. *World Resources 1990–91,* pp. 254–55.

32. T. F. Homer-Dixon, "On the Threshold: Environmental Changes as Causes of Acute Conflict," *International Security,* vol. 16, no. 2 (Fall 1991), pp. 76–116; Gleick, "Implications of Global Change for International Security," passim.

33. Hoffman et al., *Projecting Future Sea Level Rise.*

34. See, for example, S. Manabe and R. T. Wetherald, "Large-Scale Changes of Soil Wetness Induced by an Increase in Atmospheric Carbon Dioxide," *Journal of Atmospheric Sciences* 44 (1987), pp. 1211–35.

35. Gleick, "Implications of Global Climate Changes for International Security," passim.

36. D. V. Williams, "Estimated Bioresource Sensitivity to Climate Change in Alberta, Canada," *Climatic Change* 7 (1985), pp. 55–69; B. Smit et al., "Sensitivity of Crop Yields and Land Resource Potential to Climate Change in Ontario, Canada," *Climatic Change* 14 (1989), pp. 153–74.

37. See the illustrations and text on pp. 86–87 of "Under the Sun—Is Our World Warming?"

38. "Energy and the Environment," *Economist* Survey, August 1991; M. W. Browne,

"93 Nations Agree to Ban Chemicals That Harm Ozone," *New York Times*, 30 June 1990, p. A1.

39. C. Flavin, "Slowing Global Warming," in L. R. Brown et al., *State of the World 1990*, p. 21.

40. What follows is based upon J. MacNeill et al., *Beyond Interdependence* (New York/Oxford, 1991), chs. 4–5; Flavin, "Slowing Global Warming," pp. 17–38: *World Resources 1990–91*, pp. 24–30; Oppenheimer and Boyle, *Dead Heat*, passim; Schneider, *Global Warming*, pp. 260ff. For the potentialities of photovoltaic energy, see Y. Hamakawa, "Photovoltaic Power," *Scientific American* 256 (April 1987), pp. 87–92.

41. *World Resources 1990–91*, p. 105.

42. L. R. Brown et al., *State of the World 1990*, p. 20.

43. An important exception here: Senator Albert Gore, *Earth in the Balance: Ecology and the Human Spirit* (New York, 1992)—an excellent overview of the environmental crisis. Will he now, as vice president, be able to translate his ideas into policies?

44. See the articles referred to in note 23 above; and "How to Find an Ozone Hole," *Wall Street Journal*, 28 February 1992, p. A14.

45. W. D. Nordhaus, "Global Warming: Slowing the Greenhouse Express," Cowes Foundation Paper no. 758 (Yale University, New Haven, 1990), passim.

46. M. D. Lowe, "Cycling into the Future," in L. R. Brown et al., *State of the World 1990*, ch. 7.

47. P. Lewis, "Balancing Industry with the Ecology," *New York Times*, 2 March 1992, p. A3.

CHAPTER 7
THE FUTURE OF THE NATION-STATE

1. C. Tilly (ed.), *The Formation of National States in Western Europe* (Princeton, N.J., 1975); J. H. Shennan, *The Origins of the Modern European State 1450–1725* (London, 1974); H. Lubasz (ed.), *The Development of the Modern State* (New York, 1964).

2. For details, see P. Dollinger, *La Hanse* (Paris, 1964), and the shorter analysis in Scammell, *World Encompassed*, ch. 2.

3. See V. G. Kiernan, "State and Nation in Western Europe," *Past and Present* 31 (1965), pp. 20–38; and esp. D. Kaiser, *Politics and War: European Conflict from Philip II to Hitler* (Cambridge, Mass., 1990), ch. 2.

4. For a good example, see C. Wilson, *Profit and Power: A Study of England and the Dutch Wars* (London, 1957); and, more generally, Kennedy, *Rise and Fall of the Great Powers*, chs. 2 and 3.

5. O. Ranum (ed.), *National Consciousness, History and Political Culture in Early-Modern Europe* (Baltimore/London, 1975); C. Jones (ed.), *Britain and Revolutionary France: Conflict, Subversion and Propaganda*, Exeter Studies in History, no. 5 (Exeter, 1983); L. Colley, "The Apotheosis of George III: Loyalty, Royalty and the British Nation 1760–1820," *Past and Present* 102 (February 1984), pp. 94–129; idem., *Britons* (New Haven/London, 1992).

6. M. Howard, *The Lessons of History* (New Haven, Conn., 1991), chs. 4–7; J. Joll, *The Origins of the First World War* (London/New York, 1984), chs. 4–5 and 7–8.

7. Well covered in A. Marwick, *War and Social Change in the Twentieth Century* (London, 1974); and A. Calder, *The People's War* (London, 1969).
8. G. Adama, *The Iron Triangle* (New York, 1981); R. W. DeGrasse, *Military Expansion, Economic Decline* (Armonk, N.Y., 1985 edn.); L. Thurow, "How to Wreck the Economy," *New York Review of Books*, 14 May 1981, pp. 3–8; M. Kaldor, *The Baroque Arsenal* (London, 1982); R. Cohen and P. A. Wilson, *Superpowers in Economic Decline* (New York, 1990).
9. J. Joffe, "Germany After NATO," *Harper's Magazine*, September 1990, p. 31; E. N. Luttwak, "From Geopolitics to Geo-Economics," *National Interest* 20 (Summer 1990), p. 19; N. Munro, "Atwood: New Power Found in Economies," *Defense News*, 4 December 1989, p. 18 (reporting on a speech by U.S. Deputy Secretary of Defense Donald Atwood); C. V. Prestowitz et al., (eds.), *Powernomics: Economics and Strategy After the Cold War* (Lanham, Md., 1991).
10. See the articles in A. H. Westing, *Global Resources and International Conflict* (Oxford/New York, 1986), as well as the specific case study by J. R. Starr and D. C. Stoll, *The Politics of Scarcity: Water in the Middle East* (Boulder, Colo., 1988).
11. T. H. Moran, "International Economics and National Security," *Foreign Affairs*, vol. 69, no. 5 (Winter 1990–91), pp. 80–82; T. H. Moran, "The Globalization of America's Defense Industries: Managing the Threat of Foreign Dependence," *International Security* 15 (Summer 1990), pp. 57–100.
12. See the references in note 9 above, as well as T. C. Sorensen, "Rethinking National Security," *Foreign Affairs*, vol. 69, no. 3 (Summer 1990), pp. 1–18; W. Greene, "An Idea Whose Time Is Fading," *Time*, 28 May 1990, p. 90 (on the changing concept of national security).
13. See S. Hassan, "Environmental Issues and Security in South Asia," *Adelphi Papers* 262 (Autumn 1991), passim; and, more generally, the essays in Westing (ed.), *Global Resources and International Conflict.*
14. See the more extensive discussion in J. T. Mathews, "Redefining Security," *Foreign Affairs*, vol. 68, no. 2 (Spring 1989), pp. 174–77; and the articles in L. Brown et al., *State of the World 1990*, passim.
15. Moran, "International Economics and National Security," p. 90.
16. These paragraphs borrow from Rosenau's discussion of "the relocation of authority" (referred to in Chapter 3, note 9, above).
17. Immanuel Kant, *Zum Ewigen Frieden* (1795); (Stuttgart, 1954 edn.), p. 49. This quotation was brought to my attention by H. W. Smith, "Nationalism and Religious Conflict in Imperial Germany 1887–1914," Ph.D. dissertation, Yale University, 1991), pp. 1–2.

CHAPTER 8
THE JAPANESE "PLAN" FOR A POST–2000 WORLD

1. See H. Kahn, *The Emerging Japanese Superstate* (London, 1971); E. F. Vogel, *Japan as Number One; Lessons for America* (New York, 1980 edn.); E. F. Vogel, "Pax Nipponica," *Foreign Affairs*, vol. 64, no. 4 (Spring 1986), pp. 752–67; Burstein, *Yen!* T. R. Zengage and C. T. Ratcliffe, *The Japanese Century* (Hong Kong, 1988). There is also a good analysis in R. M. Morse, "Japan's Drive to Pre-eminence," *Foreign Policy* 69 (Winter 1987–88), pp. 3–21.
2. J. S. Nye, Jr., *Bound to Lead* (New York, 1990), pp. 154–70; K. E. House, "Though Rich, Japan Is Poor in Many Elements of Global Leadership," *Wall Street Journal*, 30 January 1989, pp. 1, 9; R. Taggert Murphy, "Power Without

Purpose," *Harvard Business Review* 66 (March–April 1988), pp. 71–83; Fallows, *More Like Us;* K. van Wolferen, *The Enigma of Japanese Power* (London/New York, 1989); B. Emmott, *The Sun Also Sets: The Limits to Japan's Economic Power* (New York, 1989).

3. See Vogel, *Japan as Number One,* chs. 3–9.

4. For what follows, see Ibid., ch. 7; T. P. Rohlen, *Japan's High Schools* (Berkeley, Cal., 1983), passim; R. P. Dore and M. Sako, *How the Japanese Learn to Work* (London, 1989); M. White, *The Japanese Educational Challenge* (New York, 1989). See also the interesting article by M. and J. Sayle, "Why We Send Our Children to a Japanese School," *Tokyo Journal,* August 1990, pp. 78–83, for an empathetic description of the system; and "Why Can't Little Taro Think?" *Economist,* 21 April 1990, pp. 21–24, which is much more critical.

5. 1987 statistics: see *Education in Japan,* Foreign Press Center (Tokyo, 1988), p. 17.

6. For these figures, see Dore and Sako, *How the Japanese Learn to Work,* p. 1 (percentage in school); *Education in Japan,* pp. 18–19 (number of school days); *Fortune,* 6 November 1989, p. 88 (science scores); "Why Can't Little Taro Think?" p. 23 (intelligence scores).

7. For these figures, see *UNESCO Statistical Yearbook 1989,* tables 5.15 and 5.17; and Kennedy, *Rise and Fall of the Great Powers,* p. 464. For signs of the Japanese turn toward scientific innovation, see G. Bylinsky, "Trying to Transcend Copycat Science," *Fortune,* 30 March 1987, pp. 42–46; and "Who Are the Copycats Now?" *Economist,* 20 May 1989, pp. 91–94. Also very important is "Japanese Technology," *Economist* Survey, 2 December 1989, with many additional statistics.

8. There is good coverage of this in Burstein, *Yen!;* Emmott, *Sun Also Sets;* and van Wolferen, *Enigma.* See also "The New Global Top Banker: Tokyo and Its Mighty Money," *New York Times,* 27 April 1986, pp. 1, 16.

9. See, for example, J. Womack et al., *The Machine That Changed the World* (London, 1990), passim; "Japan's New Idea," Special Report to *Industry Week,* 3 September 1990, pp. 34–69; B. Bowonder and T. Miyake, "Technology Development and Japanese Industrial Competitiveness," *Futures,* vol. 22, no. 1 (January–February 1990, pp. 21–45.

10. This "ideal" is well argued in M. Porter, *The Competitive Advantage of Nations* (New York, 1990), esp. ch. 5.

11. According to the U.S. Council on Competitiveness, in 1989 Japanese investment in plant and equipment totaled $549 billion, compared with the American total of $513 billion: *New Haven Register,* Associated Press report, 24 June 1990, p. A9. For the yen-to-dollar exchange rate, see "The Joy of High Costs," *Economist,* 4 March 1989, p. 66.

12. See in particular the coverage in Zengage and Ratcliffe, *Japanese Century,* ch. 2; and "Japanese Technology," *Economist* Survey, 2 December 1989.

13. P. Revzin, "Japanese Systematically Invest in Europe Prior to 1992 Changes," *Wall Street Journal,* 10 December 1990, p. A7A.

14. See the table in Linder, *Pacific Century,* p. 12, quoting from a *Japan in the Year 2000* study; C. F. Bergsten, "The World Economy After the Cold War," *Foreign Affairs,* vol. 69, no. 3 (Summer 1990), p. 96.

15. The classic study remains Chalmers Johnson, *MITI and the Japanese Miracle* (Stanford, Cal., 1982); but see also van Wolferen's negative comments upon MITI in *Enigma,* ch. 5, "The Administrators."

16. This is covered in E. A. Olsen, *U.S.–Japanese Strategic Reciprocity: A Neo-*

Nationalist View (Stanford, Cal., 1985), passim; G. Segal, *Rethinking the Pacific* (Oxford, 1990), pp. 242–45.

17. This is also the argument in H. W. Maull, "Germany and Japan: The New Civilian Powers," *Foreign Affairs*, vol. 69, no. 5 (Winter 1990–91), p. 92.

18. See R. Robinson and J. Gallagher, *Africa and the Victorians* (London, 1961), ch. 1, "The Spirit of Victorian Expansion."

19. J. Steingold, "Japan Builds East Asia Links, Gaining Labor and Markets," *New York Times*, 8 May 1990, pp. A1, D18; Segal, *Rethinking the Pacific*, p. 365; the articles in *Far East Economic Review*, 3 May 1990, pp. 46–55; "The Yen Block," *Economist* Survey, 15 July 1989; "Japan Builds a New Power Base," *Business Week*, 20 March 1989, pp. 18–23. I also benefited from Richard P. Cronin, "Japan's Expanding Role and Influence in the Asia-Pacific Region: Implications for U.S. Interests and Policy," Congressional Research Service paper, Washington, D.C., September 1990.

20. See again van Wolferen, *Enigma*, passim; Fallows, *More Like Us*, passim; J. Taylor, *Shadows of the Rising Sun: A Critical View of the "Japanese Miracle"* (New York, 1984); S. Kamata, *Japan in the Passing Lane* (New York, 1984).

21. D. Moisi, "If Japan Is So Successful, Where Are Its Imitators?" *International Herald Tribune*, 24 October 1990, p. 7; Nye, *Bound to Lead*, pp. 166–69. For comments upon racism, see van Wolferen, *Enigma*, passim; and I. Buruma, *Behind the Mask* (New York, 1984).

22. This is most systematically covered in C. Prestowitz, *Trading Places: How We Allowed Japan to Take the Lead* (New York, 1988); but see also the coverage in van Wolferen, *Enigma*, pp. 393ff.

23. "Pity Those Poor Japanese," *Economist*, 24 December 1988; "Japan's Silent Majority Starts to Mumble," *Business Week*, 23 April 1990, pp. 52–54.

24. This is particularly well developed in Emmott, *Sun Also Sets;* but see also "Tokyo Sings the Blues," *Economist*, 24 November 1990, p. 31; and "Can Japan Cope?" *Business Week*, 23 April 1990, pp. 46–51. The demographic changes are covered in L. G. Martin, "The Graying of Japan," *Population Bulletin*, vol. 44, no. 2 (July 1989). The most pessimistic of all accounts is B. Reading, *Japan: The Coming Collapse* (London, 1992).

25. Which is the thrust of van Wolferen's argument in *Enigma*, and in "The Japan Problem," *Foreign Affairs*, vol. 62, no. 2 (Winter 1986–87), pp. 288–303.

26. See D. Halberstam, "Can We Rise to the Japanese Challenge?" *Parade*, 9 October 1983; and Fallows, *More Like Us*.

27. Morse, "Japan's Drive to Pre-eminence," has some interesting comments upon the misunderstandings of non-Japanese-speaking experts. See also van Wolferen, "The Japan Problem Revisited," *Foreign Affairs*, vol. 69, no. 4 (Fall 1990), pp. 42–55.

28. For a discussion of this problem, see M. L. Balfour, *Britain and Joseph Chamberlain* (London/Boston, 1985), pp. 17–19, 207–210, 298–300; and P. Kennedy, *The Realities Behind Diplomacy* (London, 1980), pp. 22–24.

29. See again Emmott, *Sun Also Sets*. For Japan's financial troubles, see "Japanese Finance: Falling Apples," *Economist* Special Survey, 8 December 1990.

30. "Japan's New Idea," *Business Week*, 3 September 1990; Vogel, "Pax Nipponica," passim; Zengage and Ratcliffe, *Japanese Century;* Morse, "Japan's Drive to Pre-eminence," passim; "Japanese Technology," *Economist* Survey, 2 December 1989; "Japan, At Your Service," *Economist*, 20 October 1990, pp. 83–84.

31. See again Fallows, *More Like Us* (although note that his argument is chiefly about *America's* need to change).

32. For examples of this in the United States, see P. Choate, *Agents of Influence* (New York, 1990).

33. Van Wolferen, *Enigma*, pp. 403–5, offers the interesting observation "Although there is no convincing reason to suspect that the [Japanese] administrators have worked out a grand master-plan for industrial domination of the world, what they are doing has the same effect as if there were such a plan." Zengage and Ratcliffe, *Japanese Century*, refers frequently to the Japanese "game plan"; see pp. 192–93. See also T. H. White's alarmist piece "The Danger from Japan," *New York Times Magazine*, 28 July 1985.

34. "Reconsider Japan," *Economist*, 26 April 1986, pp. 19–22.

35. See again Porter, *Competitive Advantage of Nations*.

36. This is suggested in Morse, "Japan's Drive to Pre-eminence." I also benefited from Okazaki Hisahiko's paper "The Restructuring of the U.S.-Japan Alliance," 29 July 1989, an English-language translation of his July 1988 *Bungei Shinju* article on the same topic.

37. See Burstein, *Yen!* ch. 11; D. S. Zakheim, "Japan's Emerging Military-Industrial Machine," *New York Times*, 27 June 1990, p. A23; and G. R. Packard, "The Coming U.S.-Japan Crisis," *Foreign Affairs* 66 (Winter 1987–88), pp. 356–57. Also useful is F. C. Iklé and T. Nakanishi, "Japan's Grand Strategy," *Foreign Affairs*, vol. 69, no. 3 (Summer 1990), pp. 81–95.

38. See again Morse, "Japan's Drive to Pre-eminence," passim; and "From Superrich to Superpower," *Time*, 4 July 1988, pp. 28–31. There is also a very useful analysis of Japan's future options in K. B. Pyle, "Japan, the World, and the Twenty-first Century," in *The Political Economy of Japan*, vol. 2, *The Changing International Context*, eds. T. Inoguchi and D. I. Okimoto (Stanford, Cal., 1988), pp. 446–86.

39. "Rankings," *Wall Street Journal*, World Business Report, 20 September 1991, pp. R8–R9.

40. Ibid.

41. W. J. Broad, "In the Realm of Technology, Japan Looms Ever Larger," *New York Times*, 28 May 1991, pp. C1, C8. (*Influential* patents refers to those cited frequently in subsequent papers and patents, as opposed to eccentric and unimportant patents.)

42. *CIA Handbook of Economic Statistics, 1990* (Washington, D.C., 1990), p. 162.

43. Martin, "Graying of Japan," p. 7.

44. D. E. Sanger, "Tokyo Official Ties Birth Decline to Education," *New York Times*, 14 June 1990; D. E. Sanger, "Minister Denies He Opposed College for Japanese Women," *New York Times*, 19 June 1990.

45. "The Silvering of Japan," *Economist*, 7 October 1989, p. 81.

46. Ibid.; "The Dwindling Japanese," *Economist*, 26 January 1991, p. 36; Martin, "Graying of Japan"; and R. S. Jones, "The Economic Implications of Japan's Aging Population," *Asian Survey*, vol. 28, no. 9 (September 1988), pp. 958–69—an excellent summary.

47. "No Way to Treat a Guest," *Economist*, 2 June 1990, p. 36; "Revised Immigration Law Is Criticized as Foreign Workers Wait to Be Deported," *Japan Times*, Weekly International Edition, 11–17 June 1990, p. 3.

48. Sanger, "Minister Denies . . . ," passim (quoting Professor Kuniko Inoguchi); Jones, "Economic Implications," p. 969; "The Dwindling Japanese."

49. "The Dwindling Japanese."

50. For the following, see M. Maruyama, "Japan's Agricultural Policy Failure," *Food Policy* (May 1987), pp. 123–26; "Yesterday's Farming," *Economist*, 20 August

1988, pp. 58–59; "Here Comes Farmer Giles-san," *Economist,* 8 June 1991, pp. 35–36.

51. M. L. LaGanga, "U.S. Agriculture, Biotech Firms Cut Good Deals with Japanese," *Los Angeles Times,* 9 April 1990, p. D3; Yamaguchi, "Biotechnology: New Hope for Japan's Farmers," pp. 36–40.

52. F. J. Galde and D. G. Aubrey, "Changing Climate and the Pacific," *Oceanus,* vol. 32, no. 4 (Winter 1989–90), pp. 72–73.

53. M. Prowse, "Japan Deserves a Little Respect," *Financial Times,* 7 May 1991, p. 38.

54. Van Wolferen, *Enigma,* passim; House, "Though Rich, Japan Is Poor in Many Elements of Global Leadership," passim.

55. C. Johnson, "Japan in Search of a 'Normal' Role," Institute on Global Conflict and Cooperation (U.C., San Diego), Policy Paper no. 3, July 1992, provides a very useful summary of Japan's dilemmas.

CHAPTER 9
INDIA AND CHINA

1. *World Resources 1990–91,* p. 345.

2. Ibid., pp. 244–45. Since these are national averages, the implication is that many millions survive on less than $100 a year.

3. *Trends in Developing Economies 1990,* p. 244, gives Korea's 1989 per capita GNP as $4,400, which presumably means that the past two years of growth will have brought it close to $5,000 at current prices. Using the *World Resources 1990–91* table of China and India's population (see note 1 above), a per capita GNP of $5,000 for each would produce totals of $5.6 trillion for China and $4.2 trillion for India.

4. *Trends in Developing Countries 1990,* pp. 113–269.

5. Ibid., p. 108.

6. A. Coale, "Fertility and Mortality in Different Populations with Special Attention to China," *Proceedings of the American Philosophical Society,* vol. 132, no. 2 (1988), p. 186. H. Angang and Z. Ping, *China's Population Development* (Beijing, 1991), gives the total as "more than 15 million," p. 13.

7. "China: The Mewling That They'll Miss," *Economist,* 13 August 1988, p. 31; Z. Yi, "Population Policies in China: New Challenge and Strategies," in J. M. Eekelaar and D. Pearl (eds.), *An Aging World: Dilemmas and Challenges for Law and Social Policy* (Oxford, 1989), pp. 61–62.

8. "Peasants' Revolt," *Economist,* 30 January 1988, p. 27.

9. "China: The Mewling That Tyey'll Miss," p. 63.

10. "China: The Mewling That They'll Miss."

11. S. WuDunn, "China, with Even More to Feed, Pushes Anew for Small Families," *New York Times,* 16 June 1991, p. 12.

12. Yi, "Population Policies in China," p. 65.

13. Coale, "Fertility and Mortality in . . . China," p. 189.

14. Ibid., p. 188; and see esp. N. Ogawa, "Aging in China: Demographic Alternatives," *Asia-Pacific Population Journal,* vol. 3, no. 3 (September 1988), pp. 21–64. The above section also benefited from Angang and Ping, *China's Population Development.*

15. M. Tain and R. Menon, "The Greying of India," *India Today,* 30 September 1991, pp. 24–33.

16. The figures for life expectancy at independence come from B. L. C. Johnson, *Development in South Asia* (Harmondsworth, Mddsx., 1983), p. 169; for the late 1980s, from *World Resources 1990–91*, p. 257.

17. B. Crossette, "Why India Is Still Failing to Stop Its Population Surge," *New York Times*, 9 July 1989, Week in Review, p. 3.

18. Statistics from *World Resources 1990–91*, pp. 255, 257.

19. B. J. McCormick, *The World Economy: Patterns of Growth and Change* (Oxford, 1988), p. 251.

20. These are the categories examined in B. L. C. Johnson, *Development in South Asia*, ch. 12, "Levels of Living and the Plight of the Poor."

21. *World Resources 1990–91*, p. 245 (1987 figures).

22. For what follows, see Johnson, *Development in South Asia*, chs. 5–8; McCormick, *World Economy*, pp. 246–48; B. H. Farmer, "Perspectives on the Green Revolution in South Asia," *Modern Asian Studies* 20 (1986), pp. 175–99.

23. See in particular the detailed analysis by P. S. Mann, "Green Revolution Revisited: The Adoption of High Yielding Variety Wheat Seeds in India," *Journal of Development Studies*, vol. 26, no. 1 (October 1989), pp. 131–44.

24. Johnson, *Development in South Asia*, chs. 6–7.

25. L. Kaye, "The White Revolution," *Far Eastern Economic Review*, 24 March 1988, p. 112.

26. J. McMillan et al., "The Impact of China's Economic Reforms on Agricultural Productivity Growth," *Journal of Political Economy*, vol. 97, no. 4 (1989), pp. 781–85; N. R. Lardy, "Agricultural Reforms in China," *Journal of International Affairs* 39 (Winter 1986), pp. 91–104.

27. *The Economist World Atlas and Almanac 1989*, p. 222.

28. This figure, originally taken from U.S. Department of Agriculture, was also reproduced in Kennedy, *Rise and Fall of the Great Powers*, p. 442.

29. Y. Yang and R. Tyers, "The Economic Costs of Self-Sufficiency in China," *World Development*, vol. 17, no. 2 (1989), p. 234.

30. This is the argument in ibid.

31. For this list, see Johnson, *Development in South Asia*, p. 141; and K. Marton, *Multinationals, Technology, and Industrialization* (Lexington, Mass., 1982), ch. 10, "India."

32. "Asia," *Economist*, 23 June 1990, p. 27.

33. A. Vaidyanathan, "Indian Economic Performance and Prospects," in P. K. Ghosh (ed.), *Developing South Asia* (Westport, Conn., 1984), pp. 10–11.

34. The 1950 and 1978–79 figures are from Johnson, *Development in South Asia*, p. 136; the 1989 figure from *Trends in Developing Economies 1990*, p. 264.

35. *Trends in Developing Economies 1990*, p. 269, gives industry's share of the labor force as 13.2 percent in 1980, which suggests that manufacturing's share might be less than 10 percent. See also *The Statesman's Yearbook 1990–91* J. Paxton (ed.), (New York/London, 1990), p. 644, which states that in 1984 only 7.4 million were employed in manufacturing out of a labor force of 222.5 million workers.

36. "Asia," *Economist*, 23 June 1990, p. 27.

37. I. J. Ahluwalia, "Industrial Growth in India: Performance and Prospects," *Journal of Development Economics* 28 (1986), p. 8; "Asia," *Economist*, 23 June 1990, p. 27.

38. For a lively account of this transformation, see O. Schell, *To Get Rich Is Glorious: China in the '80s* (New York, 1985).

39. J. P. Sterba, "Long March," *Wall Street Journal*, 16 June 1989, p. A4.

40. "China," *Economist,* 20 October 1990, p. 40; *Trends in Developing Economies 1990,* pp. 114, 270.

41. For some of those rosy projections, see Kennedy, *Rise and Fall of the Great Powers,* pp. 454–58.

42. "Rich China, Poor China: The Gap Keeps Growing," *Business Week,* 5 June 1989, pp. 40–41; "Amid the Sourness, a Portion of China That Is Still Sweet," *Economist,* 19 August 1989, pp. 21–22. For more details, see also E. F. Vogel, *One Step Ahead in China: Guangdong Under Reform* (Cambridge, Mass., 1990); and D. Goodman, *China's Regional Development* (London, 1989).

43. "When the Reforming Spirit Flags," *Economist,* 1 April 1989, pp. 29–30; J. P. Sterba, "How the Twisting Path of China's Reform Led to Guns of Tiananmen," *Wall Street Journal,* 16 June 1989, pp. A1, A4.

44. "China Begins a New Long March," *Business Week,* 5 June 1989, pp. 38–46.

45. "China's Economy: Joyless Christmas Tidings," *Economist,* 24 November 1990, pp. 32–33; and N. D. Kristof, "At the Businesses Owned by Beijing: The Ink Is Red," *New York Times,* 18 November 1990, Week in Review, p. 2.

46. P. H. B. Goodwin, "Soldiers and Statesmen: Chinese Defense and Foreign Policies in the 1990s," in S. S. Kim (ed.), *China and the World* (Boulder, Colo., 1989), p. 192.

47. For more details, see G. Segal, *Defending China* (Oxford, 1985); Segal, *Rethinking the Pacific,* chs. 12–13; J. Keegan and A. Wheatcroft, *Zones of Conflict* (New York, 1978), ch. 15, "China: The Zones of Vulnerability"; G. Chaliand and J. P. Rageau, *A Strategic Atlas* (New York, 1985), pp. 67, 143–50; R. Delfs, "A Two-Front Threat: China Sees Danger from Japan, Soviet Union," *Far Eastern Economic Review,* 13 December 1990, pp. 28–30.

48. For these criticisms, see the series of related articles by J. Clad, "Power Amid Poverty: India Puts National Pride Before Defence Efficiency," *Far Eastern Economic Review,* 7 June 1990, pp. 47–51; and A. Gupta, "The Indian Arms Industry: A Lumbering Giant," *Asian Survey,* vol. 30, no. 9 (September 1990), pp. 847–61.

49. See the argument in Kennedy, *Rise and Fall of the Great Powers,* esp. pp. 536ff. A good example of this traditional thinking can be seen in A. Prakosh, "A Carrier Force for the Indian Navy," *Naval War College Review,* vol. 43, no. 4 (Autumn 1990), pp. 58–71.

50. Statistics from "Development Brief," *Economist,* 26 May 1990, p. 81; Paxton (ed.), *Statesman's Yearbook 1990–91,* p. 364.

51. "Development Brief"; Paxton (ed.), *Statesman's Yearbook 1990–91,* p. 650, gives the literacy rate (1981 census) as being 47 percent male and 25 percent female, both of which probably increased somewhat during the 1980s.

52. See the details in N. Kristof, "In Rural China, Road to School Is All Uphill," *New York Times,* 3 December 1990, pp. A1, A15.

53. *UNESCO Statistical Yearbook 1989* (Paris, 1989), Table 1, "Educational Attainment."

54. Ibid.; see also Paxton (ed.), *Statesman's Yearbook 1990–91,* p. 364.

55. *UNESCO Statistical Yearbook 1989,* Table 3.11, "Third level: teachers and institutions by type of institution."

56. Johnson, *Development in South Asia,* pp. 213–15.

57. *UNESCO Statistical Yearbook 1989,* Table 5.3, "Scientific and technical personnel in R&D."

58. *UNESCO Statistical Digest 1987* (Paris, 1987), p. 188 (China) and p. 196 (India).

59. Johnson, *Development in South Asia,* p. 214.

60. D. Ernst and D. O'Conner, *Technology and Global Competition* (OECD; Paris, 1989), p. 53.

61. Marton, *Multinationals, Technology, and Industrialization*, p. 236. See also S. Lall, *Developing Countries as Exporters of Technology: A First Look at the Indian Experience* (London, 1982), p. 19 (Table 3.1), which gives details of the geographical destination of engineering goods exports; and *World Link*, vol. 3, nos. 9/10 (September–October 1990), which includes a special "Area Profile" on India, full of declarations about liberalization and competitiveness.

62. See again Johnson, *Development in South Asia*, for consideration of what technologies might be appropriate for India's stage of development.

63. See the comments by Sam Pitroda (Rajiv Gandhi's science adviser) on investing in the "software" of female education rather than the hardware of steel mills, as reported in Crossette, "Why India Is Still Failing to Stop Its Population Surge."

64. See esp. J. Polumbaum, "Dateline China: The People's Malaise," *Foreign Policy* 20 (Winter 1990–91), pp. 163–81; L. W. Pye, "China: Erratic State, Frustrated Society," *Foreign Affairs*, vol. 69, no. 4 (Fall 1990), pp. 56–74.

65. M. P. Singh, "The Crisis of the Indian State," *Asian Survey*, vol. 30, no. 8 (August 1990), p. 815; B. Weinraub, "India Peers at Its Future with a Sense of Gloom," *New York Times*, 14 July 1991, p. E2.

66. B. Crossette, "As Violent Year Ends, India Pleads for Peace," *New York Times*, 1 January 1991, p. A5; A. S. Abraham, "The Failure of India's Fling with V. P. Singh," *Wall Street Journal*, 14 November 1990, p. A16 (op-ed).

67. "India's Upheavals," *Wall Street Journal*, 14 November 1990, p. A16 (lead article).

68. "The South China Miracle," *Economist*, 5 October 1991, pp. 19–44.

69. Ibid.

70. 1987 figures: from *World Resources 1990–91*, pp. 244–45.

71. C. Nickerson, "China Copies Worst Polluters," *Boston Globe*, 20 December 1989, pp. 1, 16. See also "Pollution in Asia," *Economist*, 6 October 1990, pp. 21–26.

72. These measures are described in W. Yuging, "Natural Conservation Regions in China," *Ambio*, vol. 16, no. 6 (1987), pp. 326–31; H. Yuanjun and Z. Zhongzing, "Environmental Pollution and Control Measures in China," *Ambio*, vol. 16, no. 5 (1987), pp. 257–61. Nickerson, "China Copies Worst Polluters," gives details of the tree-planting schemes and the disappointing results.

73. H. Govind, "Recent Developments in Environmental Protection in India: Pollution Control," *Ambio*, vol. 18, no. 8 (1989), p. 429. The exclamation mark is mine; presumably a very broad definition of "victims of environmental pollution" is being used here, and not merely people with respiratory problems. The loss of forest cover in the New Delhi area is reported in T. Wicker, "Battered and Abused," *New York Times*, 25 November 1988, p. A31.

74. Govind, "Recent Developments in Environmental Protection in India," p. 430.

75. "Pollution in Asia," p. 22.

76. Nickerson, "China Copies Worst Polluters," p. 16.

77. Ibid.

CHAPTER 10
WINNERS AND LOSERS IN THE DEVELOPING WORLD

1. *World Tables 1991* (World Bank, Washington, D.C., 1991), pp. 268–69, 352–53.

2. Ibid.

3. See the World Bank publication *Trends in Developing Economies 1990*, pp. 299–303, for Korea.

4. For descriptions, see F. Braudel, *Civilization and Capitalism*, vol. 3, *The Perspective of the World* (New York, 1986), pp. 506–11.

5. See P. Lyon, "Emergence of the Third World," in H. Bull and A. Watson (eds.), *The Expansion of International Society* (Oxford, 1983), pp. 229ff.; G. Barraclough, *An Introduction to Contemporary History* (Harmondsworth, Mddsx., 1967 edn.), ch. 6, "The Revolt Against the West."

6. J. Ravenhill, "The North-South Balance of Power," *International Affairs*, vol. 66, no. 4 (1990), pp. 745–46. See also J. Cruickshank," The Rise and Fall of the Third World: A Concept Whose Time Has Passed," *World Press Review* 38 (February 1991), pp. 28–29.

7. Ravenhill, "North-South Balance of Power," p. 732.

8. W. L. M. Adriaansen and J. G. Waardensburg (eds.), *A Dual World Economy* (Rotterdam, 1989).

9. S. Fardoust and A. Dhareshwan, *Long-Term Outlook for the World Economy: Issues and Projections for the 1990s* (World Bank, Washington, D.C., February 1990), p. 9, Table 3.

10. P. Drysdale, "The Pacific Basin and Its Economic Vitality," in Morley (ed.), *Pacific Basin*, p. 11.

11. See esp., "Taiwan and Korea: Two Paths to Prosperity," *Economist*, 14 July 1990, pp. 19–21; also "South Korea," *Economist* Survey, 18 August 1990. There is a useful comparative survey in L. A. Veit, "Time of the New Asian Tigers," *Challenge* 30 (July–August 1987), pp. 49–55.

12. N. D. Kristof, "In Taiwan, Only the Strong Get U. S. Degrees," *New York Times*, 26 March 1989, p. 11.

13. Figures taken, respectively, from J. Paxton (ed.), *Statesman's Yearbook 1990–91;* and from R. N. Gwynne, *New Horizons? Third World Industrialization in an International Framework* (New York/London, 1990), p. 199.

14. Lest this 1987 figure appear too distant, note that Korea's sixth Five-Year Plan calls for a national savings rate of 33.5 percent in the early 1990s: see *Trends in Developing Economies*, p. 300. Table 7 is taken from T. Fukuchi and M. Kagami (eds.), *Perspectives on the Pacific Basin Economy: A Comparison of Asia and Latin America* (Tokyo, 1990), p. 31 (Table 10).

15. Fukuchi and Kagami (eds.), *Perspectives on the Pacific Basin Economies*, p. 4 (Table 1), shows the different rates of growth, and of export's share of total GDP, of the Asian Pacific nations compared with those of Latin America. See also H. Hughes, "Catching Up: The Asian Newly Industrializing Economies in the 1990s," *Asian Development Review*, vol. 7, no. 2 (1989), p. 132 (and Table 3).

16. "The Yen Block," *Economist* Survey, 15 July 1989; "Japan Builds a New Power Base," *Business Week*, 20 March 1989, pp. 18–25.

17. "Taiwan and Korea: Two Paths to Prosperity," p. 19; "South Korea: A New Society," *Economist*, 15 April 1989, pp. 23–25.

18. "Development Brief," *Economist*, 26 May 1990, p. 81, for the first two columns; the GNP per capita comes from *World Development Report 1990*, pp. 178–79.

19. "When a Miracle Stalls," *Economist*, 6 October 1990, pp. 33–34 (on Taiwan); *Trends in Developing Economies 1990*, pp. 299–300 (Korea); R. A. Scalapino, "Asia and the United States: The Challenges Ahead," *Foreign Affairs*, vol. 69, no. 1 (1989–1990), esp. pp. 107–12; "Hong Kong, in China's Sweaty Palm," *Economist*, 5 November 1988, pp. 19–22.

20. See the detailed forecasts in "Asia 2010: The Power of People," *Far Eastern*

Economist Review, 17 May 1990, pp. 27–58. On industrial retooling, see "South Korea," *Economist* Survey, 18 August 1990, pp. 8–9.

21. *Population: The UNFPA Experience*, (New York, 1984), ch. 4, "Latin America and the Caribbean," pp. 51–52.

22. A. F. Lowenthal, "Rediscovering Latin America," *Foreign Affairs*, vol. 69, no. 4 (Fall 1990), p. 34.

23. Figure from "Latin America's Hope," *Economist*, 9 December 1989, p. 14.

24. Taken from G. W. Landau et al., *Latin America at a Crossroads* (Trilateral Commission, New York/Paris/Tokyo, 1990), p. 5, which reports the source as *Economic and Social Progress in Latin America: 1989 Report* (Inter-America Development Bank, Washington, D.C., 1989), Table B-1, p. 463.

25. For details, see the various national entries in Paxton (ed.), *Statesman's Yearbook 1990–91;* and *Economist World Atlas and Almanac*, pp. 131–157. Gwynne, *New Horizons*, has useful comments on Latin America's "inward-oriented industrialization" (ch. 11), which it then contrasts with East Asia's "outward orientation" (ch. 12).

26. *World Resources 1990–91*, p. 39.

27. Ibid., p. 246.

28. For the above, see *World Resources 1990–91*, pp. 33–48, "Latin America at a Crossroads," passim; McCormick, *World Economy*, ch. 13; "Latin American Debt: The Banks' Great Escape," *Economist*, 11 February 1989, pp. 73–74.

29. For educational details, see Paxton (ed.), *Statesman's Yearbook 1990–91*, pp. 95, 236; for literacy rates, see especially those of Uruguay, Costa Rica, Argentina, and Venezuela in the table "Development Brief," *Economist*, 26 May 1990, p. 81.

30. T. E. Martinez, "Argentina: Living with Hyperinflation," *Atlantic Monthly* 266 (December 1990), p. 36.

31. Paxton (ed.), *Statesman's Yearbook 1990–91*, pp. 584, 605.

32. T. Kamm, "Latin America Edges Toward Free Trade," *Wall Street Journal*, 30 November 1990, p. A10.

33. C. Farnsworth, "Latin American Economies Given Brighter Assessments," *New York Times*, 30 October 1990; "Latin America's New Start," *Economist*, 9 June 1990, p. 11; N. C. Nash, "A Breath of Fresh Economic Air Brings Change to Latin America," *New York Times*, 13 November 1991, pp. A1, D5.

34. "Latin America's Hope," *Economist*, 9 December 1989, p. 15; Nash, "Breath of Fresh Economic Air Brings Change to Latin America," passim.

35. J. Brooke, "Debt and Democracy," *New York Times*, 5 December 1990, p. A16; P. Truell, "As the U.S. Slumps, Latin America Suffers," *Wall Street Journal*, 19 November 1990, p. 1.

36. For these arguments, see especially Lowenthal's fine summary, "Rediscovering Latin America," passim; also G. A. Fauriol, "The Shadow of Latin American Affairs," *Foreign Affairs*, vol. 69, no. 1 (1989–90), pp. 116–34; and M. D. Hayes, "The U.S. and Latin America: A Lost Decade?" *Foreign Affairs*, vol. 68, no. 1 (1988–89), pp. 180–98.

37. This is the subdivision preferred by *Economist World Atlas and Almanac*, pp. 256–71, which discusses the North African states (except Egypt) in a later section, under "Africa."

38. "The Arab World," *Economist* Survey, 12 May 1990.

39. See "Major Religions of the World," Hammond *Comparative World Atlas* (Maplewood, N.J., 1986 edn.), p. 41.

40. G. Brooks and T. Horwitz, "Shaken Sheiks," *Wall Street Journal*, 28 December 1990, pp. A1, A4.

41. "Arab World," p. 12.

42. M. A. Heller, "The Middle East: Out of Step with History," *Foreign Affairs*, vol. 69, no. 1 (1989–90), pp. 153–71.

43. See also the remarks by S. F. Wells and M. A. Bruzonsky (eds.), *Security in the Middle East* (Boulder, Colo./London, 1987), pp. 1–3.

44. D. E. Duncan, "Africa: The Long Goodbye," *Atlantic Monthly*, July 1990, p. 20.

45. J. A. Marcum, "Africa: A Continent Adrift," *Foreign Affairs*, vol. 68, no. 1 (1988–89), p. 177. See also the penetrating article by K. R. Richburg, "Why Is Black Africa Overwhelmed While East Asia Overcomes?" *International Herald Tribune*, 14 July 1992, pp. 1, 6.

46. C. H. Farnsworth, "Report by World Bank Sees Poverty Lessening by 2000 Except in Africa," *New York Times*, 16 July 1990, p. A3; Marcum, "Africa: A Continent Adrift," passim; Duncan, "Africa: The Long Goodbye," passim; "The Bleak Continent," *Economist*, 9 December 1989, pp. 80–81.

47. B. Fischer, "Developing Countries in the Process of Economic Globalization," *Intereconomics* (March–April 1990), p. 55.

48. J. S. Whitaker, *How Can Africa Survive?* (New York, 1988).

49. Goliber, "Africa's Expanding Population: Old Problems, New Policies," pp. 4–49. This is an outstandingly good article.

50. *World Resources 1990–91*, p. 254.

51. Ibid., p. 254 (overall population growth to 2025) and p. 258 (infant mortality). L. K. Altman, "WHO Says 40 Million Will Be Infected with Aids by 2000," *New York Times*, 18 June 1991, p. C3 (for percentage of GNP devoted to health care).

52. See Whitaker, *How Can Africa Survive?* esp. ch. 4, "The Blessings of Children," for a fuller analysis; and J. C. Caldwell and P. Caldwell, "High Fertility in Sub-Saharan Africa," *Scientific American* (May 1990), pp. 118–25.

53. "The Bleak Continent," passim; Whitaker, *How Can Africa Survive?* chs. 1 and 2; Goliber, "Africa's Expanding Population," pp. 12–13.

54. Whitaker, *How Can Africa Survive?*; Duncan, "Africa: The Long Goodbye," passim.

55. "Fruits of Containment," *Wall Street Journal*, 18 December 1990 (op-ed), p. A14, for the Africa-Belgium comparison; H. McRae, "Visions of Tomorrow's World," *Independent* (London), 26 November 1991, for Africa's share of world GDP.

56. "Aid to Africa," *Economist*, 8 December 1990, p. 48.

57. *Economist World Atlas and Almanac* (1989), p. 293.

58. Apart from the country-by-country comments in *Economist World Atlas and Almanac*, see also K. Ingham, *Politics in Modern Africa: The Uneven Tribal Dimension* (London/New York, 1990), passim; K. Ingham, "Africa's Internal Wars of the 1980s—Contours and Prospects," United States Institute of Peace, *In Brief* 18 (May 1990).

59. Paxton (ed.), *Statesman's Yearbook 1989*, p. 84; Goliber, "Africa's Expanding Population," p. 15.

60. Paxton (ed.), *Statesman's Yearbook 1989*, pp. 1159–60 (certain smaller groups of students are excluded from these totals).

61. T. R. Odhiambo, "Human Resources Development: Problems and Prospects in Developing Countries," *Impact of Science on Society* 155 (1989), p. 214.

62. Odhiambo, "Human Resources Development," p. 215.

63. P. Lewis, "Nyere and Tanzania: No Regrets at Socialism," *New York Times*, 24 October 1990.

64. "Wind of Change, but a Different One," *Economist*, 14 July 1990, p. 44. See also the encouraging noises made—on a country-by-country basis—in the World

Bank's own *Trends in Developing Economies 1990*, as well as in its 1989 publication *Sub-Saharan Africa: From Crisis to Sustainable Growth*, summarized in "The Bleak Continent," *Economist*, 9 December 1989, pp. 80–81.

65. See esp. P. Pradervand, *Listening to Africa: Developing Africa from the Grassroots* (New York, 1989); B. Schneider, *The Barefoot Revolution* (London, 1988); K. McAfee, "Why the Third World Goes Hungry," *Commonweal* 117 (15 June 1990), pp. 384–85.

66. Duncan, "Africa: The Long Goodbye," p. 24; G. Hancock, *Lords of Poverty: The Power, Prestige, and Corruption of the International Aid* (Boston, 1990); G. B. N. Ayittey, "No More Aid for Africa," *Wall Street Journal*, 18 October 1991 (op-ed), p. A14.

67. Whitaker, *How Can Africa Survive?* p. 231.

68. See, for example, the conclusions in Fischer, "Developing Countries in the Process of Economic Globalization," pp. 55–63.

69. Caldwell and Caldwell, "High Fertility in Sub-Saharan Africa," p. 88.

70. "AIDs in Africa," *Economist*, 24 November 1989, p. 1b; E. Eckholm and J. Tierney, "AIDs in Africa: A Killer Rages On," *New York Times*, 16 September 1990, pp. 1, 4; C. M. Becker, "The Demo-Economic Impact of the AIDs Pandemic in Sub-Saharan Africa," *World Development* 18 (1990), pp. 1599–1619.

71. *World Resources 1990–91*, p. 254.

72. Ibid.

73. Apart from Chapters 2 and 4 above, see again *World Resources 1990–91*, pp. 33–48; T. Wicker, "Bush Ventures South," *New York Times*, 9 December 1990, p. E17; T. Golden, "Mexico Fights Cholera but Hates to Say Its Name," *New York Times*, 14 September 1991, p. 2.

74. "Arab World," p. 4.

75. Ibid., p. 6; Y. F. Ibrahim, "In Algeria, Hope for Democracy but Not Economy," *New York Times*, 26 July 1991, pp. A1, A6.

76. *World Resources 1990–91*, pp. 258–59.

77. As quoted in "Arab World," p. 5.

78. See again Pradervand, *Listening to Africa*, passim. Also important is D. Pearce et al., *Sustainable Development: Economics and Environment in the Third World* (Aldershot, Hants, 1990).

79. F. Gable, "Changing Climate and Caribbean Coastlines," *Oceanus*, vol. 30, no. 4 (Winter 1987–88), pp. 53–56; G. Gable and D. G. Aubrey, "Changing Climate and the Pacific," *Oceanus*, vol. 32, no. 4 (Winter 1989–90), pp. 71–73.

80. "Arab World," p. 12.

81. *World Resources 1990–91*, pp. 176–77; L. R. Brown et al., *State of the World 1990*, pp. 48–49.

82. Juma, *Gene Hunters*, pp. 226–28.

83. D. Pirages, *Global Technopolitics* (Belmont, Cal., 1989), p. 152.

84. McAfee, "Why the Third World Goes Hungry," p. 380.

85. See P. K. Ghosh (ed.), *Technology Policy and Development* (Westport, Conn., 1984), p. 109.

86. A. Smith, *The Geopolitics of Information: How Western Culture Dominates the World* (Oxford/New York, 1980), p. 13.

87. Ibid.

88. C. J. Dixon et al. (eds.), *Multinational Corporations and the Third World* (London/Sydney, 1986), passim.

89. For a good example, B. Onimode, *A Political Economy of the African Crisis* (London/New Jersey, 1988), esp. pp. 310ff.

90. M. Clash, "Development Policy, Technology Assessment, and the New Technologies," *Futures* 22 (November 1990), p. 916.

91. L. Cuyvers and D. Van den Bulcke, "Some Reflections on the 'Outward-oriented'
Development Strategy of the Far Eastern Newly Industrialising Countries," esp.
pp. 196–97, in Adriaansen and Waardenburg (eds.), *Dual World Economy*.

92. *World Development Report 1991: The Challenge of Development* (World Bank/
Oxford University Press, Washington, D.C., 1991). See also the World Bank's
Global Economic Prospects and the Developing Countries (Washington, D.C.,
1991).

CHAPTER 11
THE ERSTWHILE USSR AND ITS CRUMBLED EMPIRE

1. J. Paxton (ed.), *The Statesman's Yearbook, 1982–83*, p. 1228. For current shares
of energy and mineral production see *Economist World Atlas and Almanac 1989*,
pp. 96–97.

2. Quoted in P. Dibb, *The Soviet Union: The Incomplete Superpower* (London,
1986), p. 67.

3. Basic statistics from *Statesman's Yearbook 1982–83*, p. 1240. For a different
breakdown of rather similar overall figures, see *UNESCO Statistical Digest 1987*,
pp. 330–31.

4. Calculated from *UNESCO Statistical Digest 1987*, p. 331, where the figures are
presented as "scientists and engineers per million inhabitants." One suspects that
the definition of the word "scientist" employed here is a wide one, and not
restricted to people possessing Ph.D.s and engaged in laboratory work.

5. J. Paxton (ed.), *Statesman's Yearbook 1982–83*, p. 1240, which can be compared
with the U.S. totals on p. 1424. The number of physicians attending the needs
of China's 1.1 billion people may be larger again, if one includes those who did
not receive a "Western-style" medical education (ibid., p. 355).

6. There are some useful remarks on the achievements—as well as the problems—of
Soviet science in V. Z. Kresin, "Soviet Science in Practice: An Inside View," in
J. Cracraft (ed.), *The Soviet Union Today: An Interpretive Guide*, 2nd edn. (Chi-
cago/London, 1988), ch. 24.

7. These long-term aims are nicely traced in C. Rice, "The Evolution of Soviet Grand
Strategy," in P. Kennedy (ed.), *Grand Strategies in War and Peace* (New Haven/
London, 1991), ch. 9.

8. See *Soviet Military Power* (U.S. Department of Defense, Washington, D.C.,
annual) or *The Military Balance* (International Institute of Strategic Studies,
London, annual), as well as the reports by the Stockholm International Peace
Research Institute. For analyses pointing to Soviet military strength, see the
various essays in H. S. Rowen and C. Wolf, Jr. (eds.), *The Future of the Soviet
Empire* (New York, 1987); for an analysis of its weaknesses, see Dibb, *Soviet
Union*.

9. See H. S. Rowen and C. Wolf, Jr. (eds.), *The Impoverished Superpower* (San
Francisco, 1990); A. Aganbegyan, *The Economic Challenge of Perestroika*, ed. M.
Barratt Brown (Bloomington, Ind., 1988), p. 2; the discussion in Cohen and
Wilson, *Superpowers in Economic Decline*, pp. 10ff.; and Meyerson, "Soviet
Economic Morass," p. 5.

10. This is a composite table, based upon the following sources: Cracraft (ed.), *Soviet
Union Today*, p. 179 (for 1956–84); P. Passell, "Where Communist Economics

Fell Short," *New York Times*, 17 December 1989, p. E3 (for 1985–88); A. R. Myerson, "The Soviet Economic Morass," *New York Times*, 16 September 1990, p. F5 (for 1989); C. H. Farnsworth, "Soviet Economic Output Off Sharply," *New York Times*, 22 December 1990, p. 8 (for 1990, and the forecast for 1991). Because of the intensifying economic crisis, later estimates of 1991 GNP are suggesting declines of 13 percent, 18 percent, or even 25 percent: see "The Soviet Economy: Still Bust," *Economist*, 24 August 1991, p. 21; J. Sterngold, "Coup Is Linked to Debt Crisis by Soviet Aide" (reporting on Grigory Yalinsky's economic statement), *New York Times*, 16 October 1991, pp. A1, A10.

11. See the very good discussion in R. W. Judy and V. L. Clough, *The Information Age and Soviet Society* (Indianapolis, 1989), esp. ch. 1.

12. This is discussed in Cohen and Wilson, *Superpowers in Decline*, pp. 9ff. See also the acute remarks by "Z," "To the Stalin Mausoleum," *Daedalus*, vol. 119, no. 1 (Winter 1990), pp. 311–12, 317–18.

13. "Russia Drills Less Oil, OPEC Keeps It Cheap," *Economist*, 8 June 1985, p. 65.

14. P. R. Gregory and R. C. Stuart, *Soviet Economic Structure and Performance*, 3rd edn. (New York, 1986), p. 325.

15. For the above, see R. W. Campbell, "Energy," in A. Bergson and H. S. Levine (eds.), *The Soviet Economy: Towards the Year 2000* (London, 1983); L. Dienes, "An Energy Crunch Ahead in the Soviet Union?" in M. Bornstein (ed.), *The Soviet Union: Continuity and Change* (Boulder, Colo., 1981); M. I. Goldman, *The Enigma of Soviet Petroleum* (London, 1980).

16. P. Truell, "Western Study Says Soviet Aid May Be Futile," *Wall Street Journal*, 24 December 1990, p. 2.

17. See especially Bergson and Levine (eds.), *Soviet Economy*, chs. 4 and 5; M. I. Goldman, *Gorbachev's Challenge: Economic Reform in the Age of High Technology* (New York, 1987), pp. 32ff.; D. G. Johnson, "Agriculture," in Cracraft (ed.), *Soviet Union Today*, pp. 198–209; B. Keller, "Soviet System Dooms a Bumper Crop," *New York Times*, 20 August 1990.

18. P. Torday, "Chaos Looms for Soviet Economy," *Independent* (London), 29 August 1991, p. 6.

19. See Eberstadt, "Health of an Empire," in Rowen and Wolf (eds.), *The Future of the Soviet Empire*, pp. 221–45; "Sick Men of Europe," *Economist*, 22 March 1986, p. 53; J. Lloyd, "Soviet Citizens' Plight Exposed," *Financial Times*, 18 August 1988.

20. V. Bukovsky, "The Political Condition of the Soviet Empire," in Rowen and Wolf (eds.) *The Future of the Soviet Empire*, pp. 11–39; D. E. Powell, "A Troubled Society," in Cracraft (ed.), *Soviet Union Today*, ch. 30; "Z," "To the Stalin Mausoleum," passim.

21. For impressions of this growing public disarray, see P. Gumbel, "Gorbachev Urges Soviet Congress to Expand Powers," *Wall Street Journal*, 17 December 1990; N. Gardels: "Helping to Diminish the Perils of Perestroika," *Wall Street Journal*, 30 January 1989 (op-ed.); B. Keller, "Soviet Economy: A Shattered Dream," *New York Times*, 13 May 1990, pp. A1, A12.

22. R. S. Clem, "Ethnicity," in Cracraft (ed.), *Soviet Union Today*, p. 306.

23. Ibid., pp. 304–5, provides a full list.

24. E. Keenan, "Rethinking the USSR, Now That It's Over," *New York Times*, 8 September 1991, p. E3.

25. "Gorbachev's Turbulent South," *Economist*, 13 January 1990, p. 45; F. X. Clines, "In Soviet Union, Dizzying Disunion," *New York Times*, 26 October 1990, p. A6.

26. P. Gumbel, "Soviets Are at a Loss About Ethnic Unrest," *Wall Street Journal*,

21 July 1989, p. A12; "The Battle Lines of the Republics," *Economist,* 23 September 1989, p. 58.

27. Clem, "Ethnicity," p. 306. See also M. Hauner, *What Is Asia to Us?* (Boston/London, 1990), esp. pp. 9, 233–34, 247–52; and D. Lieven, "Gorbachev and the Nationalities," *Conflict Studies* 216 (November 1988).

28. See the important discussion of these issues in D. Lieven, "The Soviet Crisis," *Conflict Studies* 241 (May 1991), esp. pp. 20ff.

29. V. Kvint, "Russia as Cinderella," *Forbes,* 19 February 1990, pp. 103–8; B. Keller, "Selling Soviet Unity," *New York Times,* 19 December 1990, pp. A1, A11; B. Keller, "Russia Cuts Share of Soviet Budget," *New York Times,* 28 December 1990, pp. A1, A10.

30. Torday, "Chaos Looms for Soviet Economy."

31. For details, see N. Mansergh, *The Commonwealth Experience* (London, 1969); and B. Porter, *The Lion's Share: A Short History of British Imperialism 1850–1970* (London, 1976). For the Ukraine, see S. Greenhouse, "To Ukrainians, Separation Follows Laws of Nature," *New York Times,* 20 December 1990, p. A10; and Lieven, "Soviet Crisis," passim.

32. See B. D. Porter and J. G. Roche, "The Expanding Military Power of the Soviet Union," in Rowen and Wolf (eds.), *The Future of the Soviet Empire,* pp. 143–61; F. J. Gaffney, "Is Moscow Cutting Its Military? No, It's Building Up," *New York Times,* 17 November 1989 (op-ed.); J. Churba, *Soviet Breakout* (Washington/London, 1988)—a particularly egregious example.

33. A. Karatnycky, "The Many Armies of the Soviet Union," *Wall Street Journal,* 28 August 1990 (op-ed.); J. Fialka, "Soviets Begin Moving Nuclear Warheads out of Volatile Republics," *Wall Street Journal,* 22 June 1990, pp. A1, A4.

34. See D. Ross, "Where Is the Soviet Union Heading?" and H. S. Rowen and C. Wolf, "The Future of the Soviet Empire," in Rowen and Wolf (eds.), *Future of the Soviet Empire,* pp. 259–79, 279–324; T. J. Colton, *The Dilemma of Reform in the Soviet Union,* 2nd edn. (New York, 1986), ch. 4, "Reform and the Soviet Future." See also Cohen and Wilson, *Superpowers in Economic Decline,* pp. 90ff.

35. C. H. Fairbanks, "Russian Roulette: The Danger of a Collapsing Empire," *Policy Review* 57 (Summer 1991), pp. 7–8.

36. M. Feshbach, "Population and Labor Force," in Bergson and Levine (eds.), *Soviet Economy: Towards the Year 2000,* p. 79. See also M. S. Bernstam, "Trends in the Soviet Population," in Rowen and Wolf (eds.), *Future of the Soviet Empire,* pp. 185–214.

37. Colton, *Dilemma of Reform in the Soviet Union,* p. 42.

38. Clem, "Ethnicity," pp. 304–5.

39. M. S. Bernstam, "Trends in the Soviet Population," p. 209.

40. Ibid., p. 208.

41. See M. Feshbach and A. Friendly, *Ecocide in the USSR* (New York, 1992), for harrowing details.

42. "A Way of Life Evaporates," *Economist,* 21 September 1991, p. 59.

43. Judy and Clough, *Information Age and Soviet Society,* p. 29.

44. Quoted in ibid., p. 15.

45. Ibid.

46. "If Gorbachev Dares," *Economist,* 6 July 1985.

47. *Economist World Atlas and Almanac 1989,* p. 209.

48. For details, see Kennedy, *Rise and Fall of the Great Powers,* pp. 320–23.

49. For background analysis, see W. E. Griffith (ed.), *Central and Eastern Europe: The Opening Curtain* (Boulder, Colo., 1984); C. Gati, *The BLOC That Failed*

(Bloomington, IN, 1990); and the essay collections by T. Garton Ash, *The Uses of Adversity* (New York, 1989) and *The Magic Lantern* (New York, 1990).

50. As of December 1990: see "Trade, Exchange Rates and Reserves," *Economist*, 15 December 1990, p. 100.

51. "Democracy in Eastern Europe," *Economist*, 15 December 1990, p. 5 (referring in particular to the National Salvation Front in Romania). For the political debates, see "Eastern Europe Moves Right," *Economist*, 24 March 1990, pp. 21–23.

52. C. Bohlen, "Ethnic Rivalries Revive in Eastern Europe," *New York Times*, 12 November 1990, pp. A1, A12; C. Bohlen, "3 East Europe States Grope for Union," *New York Times*, 16 December 1990, p. 16.

53. V. Meier, "Yugoslavia: Worsening Economic and Nationalist Crisis," in Griffith (ed.), *Central and Eastern Europe*, p. 276. See also I. Banac, "Political Change and National Diversity," *Daedalus*, vol. 119, no. 1 (Winter 1990), pp. 141–59.

54. C. R. Whitney, "Burst of Freedom in Czechoslovakia May Split Czechs from Slovaks," *New York Times*, 3 June 1990, p. 14. See also "Slovakia Pressing Czechs for an Equal Partnership," *New York Times*, 18 May 1990.

55. See again Bohlen, "Ethnic Rivalries Revive in Eastern Europe," passim; and the useful survey "Perestroika: And Now for the Hard Part," *Economist*, 28 April 1990.

56. S. Greenhouse, "Long, Painful Road Ahead to Free Markets for East," *New York Times*, 10 November 1990, pp. 1, 4.

57. J. Dempsey, "Lights Going Dim in Eastern Europe," *Financial Times*, 13 September 1990, p. 27.

58. *Financial Times*, 17 July 1990, p. 2.

59. R. D. Hormats, "Don't Let the West Erect a New Iron Curtain," *Wall Street Journal*, 27 December 1990, p. A8.

60. This is well discussed in the various articles in *Daedalus*, vol. 121, no. 2 (Spring 1992), entitled "The Exit from Communism."

61. F. Barringer, "Birth Rates Plummeting in Some Ex-Communist Regions of Eastern Europe," *New York Times*, 31 December 1990, p. A3.

62. "Europe in Turmoil," *Agricultural Outlook* (July 1990), pp. 28–32.

CHAPTER 12
EUROPE AND THE FUTURE

1. T. L. Friedman, "Old Feuds and the New Order," *International Herald Tribune*, 13 July 1992, p. 1.

2. See, for example, the quote in D. Burstein, *Euroquake: Europe's Explosive Challenge Will Change the World* (New York, 1991), p. 11.

3. S. P. Huntington, "The U.S.—Decline or Renewal?" *Foreign Affairs*, vol. 67, no. 2 (Winter 1988–89), pp. 93–94.

4. S. Hoffmann, "The European Community and 1992," *Foreign Affairs*, vol. 68, no. 4 (Fall 1989), p. 27.

5. There is a useful summary of these mixed positions in "Who Wants What in the Brave New Europe," *Economist*, 1 December 1990, pp. 46–47.

6. G. Agnelli, "The Europe of 1992," *Foreign Affairs*, vol. 68, no. 4 (Fall 1989), pp. 61–70; J. Joffe, "Reunification II: This Time, No Hobnail Boots," *New York Times*, 30 September 1990, p. E3.

7. C. R. Whitney, "Gulf Fighting Shatters Europeans' Fragile Unity," *New York Times*, 25 January 1991, p. A11.

8. The tenth is, admittedly, Switzerland and not a member of the EC: see *Economist World Atlas and Almanac 1989*, p. 87. The greater part of this trade is, of course, with other EC members. For the banking statistics, see ibid., p. 90, "Top International Banks."

9. See the various tables in *Annual Review of Engineering Industries and Automation 1988*, vol. 1.

10. Hoffmann, "European Community and 1992," p. 28.

11. See again Agnelli's arguments in "Europe of 1992," passim.

12. Burstein, *Euroquake*, pp. 129–30.

13. Hoffmann, "European Community and 1992," pp. 27–28.

14. Burstein, *Euroquake*, pp. 25–28.

15. *World Resources 1990–91*, p. 245.

16. *Economist World Atlas and Almanac 1989*, p. 159.

17. G. Bolte, "How Stubborn Can You Get?" *Time*, 8 October 1990, p. 65. The statistics come from T. Roth, "Europe's Small Farmers See Bleak Future," *Wall Street Journal*, 24 April 1992, p. A11A.

18. See, for example, the population figures for virtually every one of the villages included in D. Reperant, *The Most Beautiful Villages of France* (New York, 1990), passim.

19. Quoted in Burstein, *Euroquake*, p. 150, which has a fine analysis of both personalities and issues involved.

20. Ibid., pp. 40ff, 155ff.

21. See "European Community," *Economist* Survey, 7 July 1990, especially pp. 29–30, for a discussion of those constitutional difficulties.

22. Ibid., p. 24.

23. Ibid., p. 5.

24. For coverage of these debates, see G. F. Treverton, *Making the Alliance Work: The United States and Western Europe* (Ithaca, N.Y., 1985); J. Joffe, *The Limited Partnership: Europe, the United States, and the Burdens of Alliance* (Cambridge, 1987); C. McInnes, *NATO's Changing Strategic Agenda* (London/Boston, 1990); J. J. Mearsheimer, *Conventional Deterrence* (Ithaca, N.Y., 1983); R. W. Tucker and L. Wrigley (eds.), *The Atlantic Alliance and Its Critics* (New York, 1983).

25. K. Gottfried and P. Bracken (eds.), *Reforging European Security* (Boulder, Colo., 1990), pp. 3–4—part of the editors' excellent analysis.

26. Ibid., pp. 23ff, as well as the section by J. Dean and S. R. Resor, "Constructing European Security System," in the same volume.

27. For the Concert of Europe idea, see C. A. Kupchan and C. A. Kupchan, "After NATO: Concert of Europe," *New York Times*, 6 July 1990, p. A25 (op-ed). For the above remarks generally, see the analyses in C. R. Whitney, "NATO, Victim of Success, Searches for New Strategy," *New York Times*, 26 October 1991, pp. 1, 5; S. Hoffmann, "Today's NATO—and Tomorrow's," *New York Times*, 27 May 1990, p. E13 (op-ed); A. Riding, "The New Europe," *New York Times*, 20 November 1990, p. A14.

28. See D. Calleo, *The German Question Reconsidered* (New York, 1978); W. Gruner, *Die deutsche Frage* (Munich, 1985).

29. "Saying the Unsayable About the Germans" (interview with British minister Nicholas Ridley), *Spectator*, 14 July 1990, pp. 8–10; W. Safire, "Defending Germany," *New York Times*, 22 June 1990, p. A27.

30. B. Geremek, "The Realities of Eastern and Central Europe," in *Change in Europe* (Washington, D.C.: Plenary of the Trilateral Commission, April 1990), p. 10.

31. Quoted in F. Lewis, "The Bane of Nations," *New York Times*, 28 November 1990 (op-ed); and see Burstein, *Euroquake*, ch. 5.

32. "The Unpopularity of Two-Speed Europe," *Economist*, 14 September 1991, pp. 89–90.

33. "The Graying of Europe," *Business Week*, 6 February 1989, pp. 12–16; A. Riding, "Western Europe, Its Births Falling, Wonders Who'll Do All the Work," *New York Times*, 22 July 1990, pp. 1, 12; H. de Jouvenel, "Europe at the Dawn of the Third Millennium: A Synthesis of the Main Trends," *Futures*, vol. 20, no. 5 (October 1988), p. 515.

34. Quotations from "Graying of Europe"; and Riding, "Western Europe, Its Births Falling. . . ."

35. "The Missing Children," *Economist*, 3 August 1991, pp. 43–44; D. J. van de Kaa, "Europe's Second Demographic Transition," *Population Bulletin*, vol. 42, no. 1 (March 1987), pp. 3–57; J. Gapper, "Skills Shortage Stalls the Workers' March," *Financial Times*, 5 September 1990; Riding, "Western Europe, Its Births Falling . . . ," passim.

36. "West Germany's Unexpected Boost from the East," *Commerzbank* Viewpoint, reproduced in *Economist*, 13 January 1990, p. 62.

37. T. Carrington, "Central Europe Borders Tighten as Emigrés Flood In from East," *Wall Street Journal*, 8 February 1991, p. A8.

38. "Italy: The Numbers Game," *Economist*, 26 May 1990, p. 25.

39. "Graying of Europe," p. 15.

40. Burstein, *Euroquake*, p. 137. See also F. Heisbourg, "Population Movements in Post–Cold War Europe," *Survival*, vol. 33, no. 1 (January–February 1991), pp. 31–43.

41. P. L. Montgomery, "European Community Asks Heavy Energy Tax to Curb Emissions," *New York Times*, 26 September 1991, p. D3.

42. See two technical pieces, C. A. Wilson and J. F. B. Mitchell, "Simulated Climate and CO_2-Induced Climate Change over Western Europe," *Climatic Change* 8 (1986), pp. 11–42; F. Bultot et al., "Estimated Annual Regime of Energy-Balance Components, Evapotranspiration and Soil Moisture for a Drainage Basin in the Case of a CO_2 Doubling," *Climatic Change* 12 (1988), pp. 39–56 (a Belgian study).

43. "Cleaning Up the Mediterranean," *Economist*, 21 December 1991, pp. 19–24.

44. *Economist World Atlas and Almanac 1989*, p. 105.

45. "Europe's Farm Farce," *Economist*, 29 September 1990, p. 17.

46. P. Bye, "Biotechnology and Food/Agricultural Complexes," in Yoxen and Di Martino (eds.), *Biotechnology in Future Society*, p. 77. This volume contains many fine essays.

47. Ibid.

48. Ibid.; *Economist*, 20 October 1990, p. 15; "German Regulatory Firms Flee Regulatory Climate," *Science*, 16 June 1989, pp. 1251–52; K. Green and E. Yoxen, "The Greening of European Industry: What role for biotechnology?" *Futures* (June 1990), pp. 475–95.

49. See G. Junne and J. Bijman, "The Impact of Biotechnology on European Agriculture," in Yoxen and Di Martino (eds.), *Biotechnology in Future Society*, esp. p. 83.

50. Bye, "Biotechnology and Food/Agricultural Complexes," p. 69.

51. "Europe's Farm Farce," passim; Bolte, "How Stubborn Can You Get?" p. 65.

52. Junne and Bijman, "Impact of Biotechnology on European Agriculture," p. 84.

53. See the excellent article "Europe in Turmoil" in *Agricultural Outlook*, July 1990, pp. 28ff, for an analysis of the recovery of Eastern Europe's agriculture.
54. Gapper, "Skills Shortage Stalls the Workers' March," passim.
55. This Reich himself suggests in *Work of Nations*, passim.
56. See again the argument throughout Ohmae, *Borderless World*.
57. For a good example, see P. Brimelow, "The Darker Side of 1992," *Forbes*, 22 January 1990, pp. 85–89.

CHAPTER 13
THE AMERICAN DILEMMA

1. This debate can be followed, virtually on a weekly basis, by comparing the criticisms of liberal *New York Times* op-ed writers such as Anthony Lewis and Tom Wicker with the assertions of *Wall Street Journal* lead articles.
2. See the thoughtful comments by S. Huntington, "The U.S.—Decline or Renewal?" pp. 76–96.
3. See the discussion on this theme by H. Grunwald, "The Second American Century," *Time*, 8 October 1990, pp. 70–75.
4. Schlosstein, *End of the American Century;* D. Calleo, *Beyond American Hegemony* (New York, 1987); R. Rosecrance (ed.), *America as an Ordinary Power* (Ithaca, N.Y., 1976).
5. H. R. Nau, *The Myth of America's Decline* (New York, 1990); Rosecrance, *America's Economic Resurgence;* Nye, *Bound to Lead;* and J. Kotkin and Y. Kishimoto, *The Third Century: America's Resurgence in the Asian Era* (New York, 1988). It will be noted that one of these "responses" is by the editor of *America as an Ordinary Power*, Professor Richard Rosecrance. For his further commentary upon the American position in world affairs, see Rosecrance, *Rise of the Trading States*.
6. Z. Brzezinski's quoted extract on the dust jacket of Nye, *Bound to Lead*.
7. For lengthier analyses of the United States' prospects, see Nye, *Bound to Lead;* Rosecrance, *America's Economic Resurgence;* A. Anderson and D. L. Bork (eds.), *Thinking Abc .c America: The United States in the 1990s* (Stanford, Cal., 1988); E. K. Hamilton (ed.), *America's Global Interests: A New Agenda* (New York, 1989); M. Green and M. Pinsky (ed.), *America's Transition: Blueprints for the 1990s* (Lanham, Md., 1990). These are, of course, only a sampling of a now enormous body of literature.
8. Details and analyses of U.S. armed forces can be found in the standard sources: *Report of the Secretary of Defense . . . to the Congress* (annual, Washington, D.C.); *The Military Balance* (International Institute of Strategic Studies, London, annual); *RUSI and Brassey's Defence Yearbook* (annual); *American Defense Annual*, and so on.
9. P. E. Tyler, "Pentagon Imagines New Enemies to Fight in Post-Cold-War Era," *New York Times*, 17 February 1992, pp. A1, A8. See also F. C. Iklé and A. Wohlstetler (eds.), *Discriminate Deterrence: Report of the Commission on Integrated Long-Term Strategy*, (Washington, D.C., 1988), pp. 13–22, for an earlier recommendation along those lines; and M. T. Klare, "The U.S. Military Faces South," *Nation*, 18 June 1990, pp. 841, 858–62.
10. See the references to this literature in Chapter 7 above, especially the articles by Mathews, "Redefining Security," and Sorensen, "Rethinking National Security," as well as R. J. Barnett's thoughtful piece "After the Cold War," *New Yorker*, 1

January 1990, pp. 65–76. For the strategic debate, see the excellent analysis and bibliography in S. Van Evera, "Why Europe Matters, Why the Third World Doesn't; American Grand Strategy After the Cold War," *Journal of Strategic Studies,* vol. 13, no. 2 (June 1990), pp. 1–51.

11. As one of Gorbachev's early foreign-policy advisers, Giorgi Arbatov, put it in 1988, the USSR was going to deprive the United States of its "enemy," thereby confusing American conservative circles in particular.

12. Nye, *Bound to Lead,* p. 239 and passim; P. A. Gigot, "After Communism, World Still Needs U.S. Troops," *Wall Street Journal,* 11 February 1990 (op-ed).

13. For samples of these criticisms, see A. Lewis, "When Decline Hurts," *New York Times,* 26 September 1990 (op-ed); D. Boren, "New Decade, New World, New Strategy," *New York Times,* 2 January 1990; T. Wicker, "The 'Super' Concept," *New York Times,* 25 November 1990, p. E11.

14. For the classic analysis of this tendency, see Robinson and Gallagher, *Africa and the Victorian,* esp. the concluding chapter, with its remarks about the "frontiers of insecurity." For a critique of the current U.S. tendency in that direction, see again Van Evera, "Why Europe Matters, Why the Third World Doesn't," pp. 15ff.

15. See, for example, E. Mortimer, "Sharing the Bill for Peace," *Financial Times,* 14 September 1990, p. 17; A. Ireland, "A Hawk Says: Pull Our Troops Out," *New York Times,* 7 March 1989 (op-ed); W. L. Schlosser, "Let's Cut the Subsidies for Allies Defense," *New York Times,* 27 November 1988 (letters); "Time to Share the Burden," *Economist,* 7 May 1988, pp. 23–24. The 1988 R&D figures come from M. Prowse, "Scales Out of Balance," *Financial Times,* 13 August 1991, p. 10.

16. There is a wealth of literature upon this theme. For samples, see Cohen and Wilson, *Superpowers in Economic Decline,* passim; L. J. Dumas, *The Overburdened Economy* (Berkeley/Los Angeles, 1986), esp. pp. 57–63, 297ff.; B. Russett, "Defense Expenditures and National Well-Being," *American Political Science Review,* vol. 76, no. 4 (December 1982), pp. 767–77; DeGrasse, *Military Expansion, Economic Decline* (Armonk, N.Y., 1985), passim.

17. The decade-by-decade averages can be calculated from *Economic Report of the President* (Washington, D.C., 1990) and, for 1989, *Survey of Current Business* (Bureau of Economic Analysis, July 1990), Table 1.2. I am grateful to Professor Charles L. Ballard for advice here; see also his letter in *Wall Street Journal,* 12 December 1990, p. A17. The 1991 figure is a provisional OECD one, as reported in *Wall Street Journal,* 13 December 1991, p. A10, although a slightly later *Journal* report (10 March 1992, p. A2) gives a 1990–91 figure of 0.4 percent growth in GDP.

18. See Kennedy, *Rise and Fall of the Great Powers,* esp. Introduction and Epilogue, for the full argument.

19. "The Elusive Boom in Productivity," *New York Times,* 8 April 1984, business section, pp. 1, 26. See also "Richer Than You," *Economist,* 25 October 1986, pp. 13–14.

20. D. Gergen, "Can America Stay on Top?" *U. S. News & World Report,* 16 July 1990, p. 68. See also L. Silk, "Who Is No. 1? It's Hard to Say," *New York Times,* 27 July 1990, p. D2; A. Murray, "U.S. Economy Leads Japan's—But For How Long?" *Wall Street Journal,* 13 June 1990.

21. For the comparative statistics, see Kennedy, *Rise and Fall of the Great Powers,* Tables 21, 31, 32.

22. L. H. Clark and A. L. Malabré, "Productivity Indicates Sluggish Economy," *Wall*

Street Journal, 6 July 1989, p. A2; and the table "Output per Employee" (covering 1960 to 1986) in the excellent MIT analysis M. L. Dertouzos et al., *Made in America: Regaining the Productive Edge* (Cambridge, Mass., 1989), p. 29. Note that the latter, p. 31, estimates that 36 percent of the recorded improvement in labor productivity between 1979 and 1986 came from loss of jobs.

23. Kennedy, *Rise and Fall of the Great Powers*, p. 527.

24. For these figures, see A. L. Malabré, *Within Our Means* (New York, 1991), pp. xix–xx; and D. P. Calleo, *The Bankrupting of America* (New York, 1992).

25. The quotations and statistics are from Malabré, *Within Our Means*, pp. 3–5, 11–12. See also B. Friedman, *Day of Reckoning* (New York, 1988); but note "Defining the Debt Bomb," *Economist*, 3 November 1990, p. 75, for a more reassuring picture of corporate indebtedness.

26. See the breakdown in M. S. Feldstein (ed.), *The United States in the World Economy* (Cambridge, Mass., 1987), pp. 562–63, together with the analysis by J. A. Frankel, pp. 560ff.

27. H. Stout, "U.S. Foreign Debt Widened Last Year," *Wall Street Journal*, 2 July 1990, p. 42. The status of being the "world's largest debtor" may be a nominal one at the moment, since American purchases of overseas assets several decades ago ought to yield a far higher value than the actual purchasing price—although it is the latter which is recorded in the totals.

28. Dertouzos et al. (eds.), *Made in America*, pp. 40–41. For the longer argument, see also S. S. Cohen and J. Zysman, *Manufacturing Matters* (New York, 1987); and R. Dornbusch et al., *The Case for Manufacturing in America's Future* (Rochester, N.Y., 1987).

29. For samples, see the many releases and publications of the Office of Technology Assessment (U.S. Congress) and the Council on Competitiveness; Dertouzos et al. (eds.), *Made in America;* M. G. Barons, *Competing for Control* (Cambridge, Mass., 1988); J. S. Yudken and M. Black, "Targeting National Needs: A New Direction for Science and Technology Policy," *World Policy Journal* 7 (Spring 1990), pp. 251–88; G. N. Hatsopoulos et al., "U.S. Competitiveness: Beyond the Trade Deficit," *Science* 241 (15 July 1988), pp. 299–307; and P. Krugman, *The Age of Diminished Expectations* (Cambridge, Mass., 1990), passim.

30. See G. R. Searle, *The Quest for National Efficiency, 1899–1914*, 2nd edn. (Atlantic Highlands, N.J., 1990), passim; F. Crouzet, *The Victorian Economy* (London, 1982), pp. 371ff; E. J. Hobsbawm, *Industry and Empire* (Harmondsworth, Mddsx., 1969), pp. 136–53, 172–85.

31. Taken from Dertouzos et al., *Made in America*, p. 7.

32. Kennedy, *Rise and Fall of the Great Powers*, p. 515.

33. See H. Stein, "Who's Number One? Who Cares?" *Wall Street Journal*, 1 March 1990 (op-ed); Ohmae, *Borderless World*, passim; and Reich, *Work of Nations*, ch. 13 and passim.

34. See esp. Nye, *Bound to Lead*, passim.

35. For examples, W. Hummer, "A Contrarian View: A Short, Mild Recession," *Wall Street Journal*, 7 January 1990; the important series of articles by K. House in *Wall Street Journal* in early 1989, esp. 27 January 1989; C. R. Morris, "The Coming Global Boom," *Atlantic*, October 1989, pp. 51–64.

36. P. Kennedy, "Fin-de-Siecle America," *New York Review of Books*, 28 June 1990, pp. 31–40; Lewis, "When Decline Hurts," passim; H. Allen, "Red, White, and Truly Blue," *Washington Post*, 26 November 1990, pp. B1, B4; R. Bernstein, "Euphoria Gives Way to Fractured Feelings of Gloom," *New York Times*, 23

December 1990, p. E3; H. Carter, "U.S. Could Well Snatch Defeat from the Jaws of Victory," *Wall Street Journal*, 29 March 1990, p. A13.

37. J. Chancellor, *Peril and Promise: A Commentary upon America* (New York, 1990), p. 23.

38. Ibid.

39. W. Meyer-Larsen, "America's Century Will End with a Whimper," *World Press Review*, January 1991, p. 27. (I've amended the sentence order here.) See also R. Pear, "Study Says U.S. Needs to Battle Infant Mortality," *New York Times*, 6 August 1990, pp. A1, B9; W. B. Maher, "Reform Medicine: The Rest Will Follow," *New York Times*, 9 July 1989, business section, p. 3.

40. C. C. Douglas, "In Black America, Life Grows Shorter," *New York Times*, 2 December 1989, p. 84.

41. D. R. Gergen, "Remember the Drug War?" *U.S. News & World Report*, 18 December 1989, p. 84.

42. "Crime in America," *Economist*, 22 December 1990, pp. 29–32.

43. Ibid.; and K. E. Meyer, "A Good Word for Calcutta," *New York Times*, 6 January 1991, p. 18.

44. T. Wicker, "The Iron Medal," *New York Times*, 9 January 1991, p. A21; "U.S. Incarceration Rate Highest in World," *Wall Street Journal*, 7 January 1991, p. B5.

45. L. Uchitelle, "Not Getting Ahead? Better Get Used to It," *New York Times*, 16 December 1990, Week in Review, pp. 1, 6; A. Murray, "Losing Faith: Many Americans Fear U.S. Living Standards Have Stopped Rising," *Wall Street Journal*, 1 May 1989, pp. 1, 10.

46. See the important arguments in Calleo, *Beyond American Hegemony*, pp. 109–113.

47. See L. Thurow's classic, *The Zero-Sum Society* (New York, 1980), passim.

48. "U.S. Is Said to Lag in School Spending," *New York Times*, 16 January 1990, p. A23; J. Hood, "Education: Money Isn't Everything," *Wall Street Journal*, 2 February 1990.

49. "The Stupidification of America," *New Perspectives Quarterly*, vol. 7, no. 4 (Fall 1990), p. 47.

50. J. Kozol, *Illiterate America* (New York, 1985), pp. 4, 8–9.

51. B. O'Reilly, "America's Place in World Competition," *Fortune*, 6 November 1989, p. 88; C. O. Baker (ed.), *The Condition of Education 1989*, vol. 1, *Elementary and Secondary Education* (Washington, D.C., 1989), p. 78; A. Shanker, "U.S. Rock Bottom," *New York Times*, 5 February 1989, p. E7 (advertisement).

52. Kozol, *Illiterate America*, p. 212.

53. C. D. Baker (ed.), *The Condition of Education 1989*, vol. 1, p. 84; G. M. Grosvenor, "Those Panamanian Pandas," *New York Times*, 31 July 1988, p. 25.

54. *A Nation at Risk* (National Commission on Excellence in Education, Washington, D.C., 1983), p. 5.

55. R. Hoffmann, "Ignorance, Ignorantly Judged," *New York Times*, 14 September 1989 (op-ed); *A Nation at Risk*, p. 11. On the other hand, the U.S. twelfth-graders who scored low in mathematics in international tests were themselves a select group.

56. See again "U.S. Is Said to Lag in School Spending," *New York Times*, 16 January 1990.

57. See M. J. Barnett, "The Case for More School Days," *Atlantic*, November 1990, pp. 78–106—an excellent general survey; "Japan–243, United States–180," *Washington Post*, 15 October 1990, p. A14 (editorial).

58. *Everybody Counts: A Report to the Nation of the Future of Mathematics Education* (National Research Council, Washington, D.C., 1989), p. 90. See also D. P. Doyle, "Time for America to Set National Education Norms," *Hudson Opinion*, October 1989, p. 1.

59. N. Gardels, "The Education We Deserve," *New Perspectives Quarterly*, vol. 7, no. 4 (Fall 1990), pp. 2–3.

60. The quotations and statistics are from ibid., pp. 52–55, 18–19. That same issue of *New Perspectives Quarterly* offers an excellent sampling of seventeen articles about the education/social/cultural crisis. See also Senator Daniel Moynihan's op-ed piece "Half the Nation's Children Born Without a Fair Chance," *New York Times*, 25 September 1988, p. E25; and the remarks in E. D. Hirsch, *Cultural Literacy: What Every American Needs to Know* (Boston, 1987).

61. In that latter connection, see the interesting discussion by S. Knack, "Why We Don't Vote—Or Say Thank You," *Wall Street Journal*, 31 December 1990, p. 6; and H. Carter, "We Have Seen the Enemy, and It Is Ignorance," *Wall Street Journal*, 17 November 1988, p. A23.

62. This is well traced in K. Phillips, *The Politics of Rich and Poor* (New York, 1990), passim; and Reich, *Work of Nations*, chs. 14, 17–18, 23–24.

63. M. Novak, "What Became of the Ugly American?" *Forbes*, 30 April 1990, p. 120. See also B. Wattenberg, *The First Universal Nation* (New York, 1990); G. Gilder, "You Ain't Seen Nothing Yet," *Forbes*, 4 April 1988, pp. 89–93; A. Balk, "America Is No. 1. It'll Stay No. 1," *New York Times*, 31 July 1990 (op-ed); and many of the triumphalist pieces (Gilder's especially) in *Commentary*, September 1990, entitled "The American 80s: Disaster or Triumph?"

64. Nye, *Bound to Lead*, passim; Grunwald, "Second American Century," passim; "Yes, You Are the Superpower," *Economist*, 24 February 1990, p. 11.

65. G. F. Will, "Who Will Stoke the Fires?" *Newsweek*, 9 April 1990, p. 78.

66. See M. Lind, "America as an Ordinary Country," *American Enterprise* (September–October 1990), pp. 19–23; and J. B. Judis, "The Conservative Crackup," *American Prospect*, Fall 1990, pp. 30–42.

67. See Chancellor's readable (and angry) description in *Peril and Promise*, passim.

68. Ibid., p. 23.

69. These are the "middle series" estimates: see the table on p. 7 of "Projection of the Population of the United States, by Age, Sex, and Race: 1988 to 2080," *Current Population Reports*, Series P-25, no. 1018 (U.S. Bureau of the Census, Washington, D.C., 1989).

70. J. M. Guralnik et al., "Projecting the Older Population of the United States," *Milbank Quarterly*, vol. 66, no. 2 (1988), pp. 283–308; "On the Economic Implications of Demographic Change in the United States," *Population and Development Review*, vol. 15, no. 2 (June 1989), pp. 379–89.

71. W. A. Henry, "Beyond the Melting Pot," *Time*, 9 April 1990, pp. 28–35.

72. S. Thornstrom, "The Minority Majority Will Never Come," *Wall Street Journal*, 26 July 1990 (op-ed).

73. D. James, "Bar the Door," *New York Times*, 25 July 1992, p. 21.

74. P. Francese, "Aging America Needs Foreign Blood," *Wall Street Journal*, 27 March 1990 (op-ed); F. Barringer, "A Land of Immigrants Gets Uneasy About Immigration," *New York Times*, 14 October 1990, p. E4; R. J. Herrnstein, "IQ And Falling Birth Rates," *Atlantic*, May 1989, pp. 73 et see.; D. E. Bloom and N. G. Bennett, "Future Shock," *New Republic*, 19 June 1989, pp. 18–22.

75. Henry, "Beyond the Melting Pot," passim.

76. G. Wright, "Where America's Industrial Monopoly Went," *Wall Street Journal*, 20 December 1990, p. A16.

77. See again Reich, *Work of Nations.*

78. *Workforce 2000: Work and Workers for the 21st Century*, Hudson Institute (Indianapolis, 1987), p. 98; see also *New Perspectives Quarterly*, Fall 1990, p. 37.

79. The quotation and statistic are from the Report of the Comparison of the Skills of the Average Work Force, *America's Choice: High Skills or Low Wages!* (Rochester, N.Y., 1990), p. 23. See also N. J. Perry, "How to Help America's Schools," *Fortune*, 4 December 1989, pp. 137–42. For the shortages at the higher levels, see R. Atkinson, "Supply and Demand for Scientists and Engineers: A National Crisis in the Making," *Science*, 27 April 1990, pp. 425–32; and "Needed: Home-Grown Talent," *New York Times*, 26 December 1990, p. A30 (editorial).

80. *America's Choice: High Skills or Low Wages!* pp. 19–21.

81. Ibid., p. 21; *Workforce 2000*, p. 25; "On the Economic Implication of Demographic Change in the United States," passim.

82. *America's Choice: High Skills or Low Wages!* has frequent comparisons with what occurs in the European and Japanese educational and worker-training programs. See also J. Jacobs, "Training the Workforce of the Future," *Technology Review* 93 (August–September 1990), pp. 66–72, pointing to the potential in community colleges.

83. *Technology, Public Policy, and the Changing Structure of American Agriculture*, pp. 3, 11. (The 1.8 percent annual increase referred to in this report concerns "world agricultural demand by the year 2000," but that figure is clearly related to expected population growth.)

84. See L. R. Brown et al., *State of the World 1990*, chs. 1 and 4.

85. *Technology, Public Policy, and the Changing Structure of American Agriculture*, p. 20.

86. See the description of agricultural "refineries" in F. Rexen and L. Munck, *Cereal Crops for Industrial Use in Europe* (Copenhagen, 1984).

87. M. H. Glantz and J. E. Ausubel, "The Ogallala Aquifer and Carbon Dioxide: Comparison and Convergence," *Environmental Conservation*, vol. 11, no. 2 (Summer 1984), pp. 123–130.

88. G. S. Giese and D. G. Aubrey, "Losing Coastal Upland to Relative Sea-Level Rise: 3 Scenarios for Massachusetts," *Oceanus*, vol. 30, no. 3 (Fall 1987), pp. 16–22.

89. H. E. Schwarz and L. A. Dillard, "The Impact on Water Supplies," *Oceanus*, vol. 32, no. 2 (Summer 1989), pp. 44–45.

90. J. P. Cohn, "Gauging the Biological Impacts of the Greenhouse Effect," *Bio-Science*, vol. 39, no. 3 (March 1989), pp. 142–46.

91. W. D. Nordhaus, "Greenhouse Economics: Count Before You Leap," *Economist*, 7 July 1990, pp. 21–24, esp. p. 22.

92. See the account in C. Barnett, *The Collapse of British Power* (New York/London, 1972).

CHAPTER 14
PREPARING FOR THE TWENTY-FIRST CENTURY

1. *Economist*, 11 October 1930, p. 652. (I am obliged to Dr. Maarten Pereboom for this reference.)

2. For a further discussion of these trends, see J. L. Gaddis, "Toward the Post–Cold War World," *Foreign Affairs*, vol. 70, no. 2 (Spring 1991), pp. 102–22; Wright and McManus, *Flashpoints.*

3. L. R. Brown et al., *State of the World 1989*, ch. 10, "Outlining a Global Action Plan."

4. Ibid., *1990*, ch. 7, "Cycling into the Future."

5. D. M. Kamimen, "Technology for Development: Sustaining, not Obliterating, the Environment," *Research & Exploration*, Winter 1991, pp. 3–5.

6. For recent examples, see W. S. Dietrich, *In the Shadow of the Rising Sun* (University Park, Pa., 1991), passim; *Competing Economies: America, Europe, and the Pacific Rim* (Office of Technology Assessment, Congress of the United States, Washington, D.C., October 1991), esp. pp. 13–14; Malabré, *Within Our Means*, ch. 6.

7. *World Resources 1990–91*, pp. 61–62, 256. For a more critical view of Brazilian conditions, see L. R. Brown et al., *State of the World 1992*, p. 96.

8. P. Waldman, "Conflict in Algeria over Islamic Military Pits Father Against Son," *Wall Street Journal*, 23 January 1992, pp. A1, A8.

9. *World Resources 1990–91*, p. 262; Paxton (ed.), *Statesman's Yearbook 1990–91*, p. 1087.

10. Paxton (ed.), *Statesman's Yearbook 1990–91*, p. 785; *World Resources 1990–91*, p. 263.

11. Nicely argued in H. Küng, *Global Responsibility: In Search of a New World Ethic* (New York, 1991).

12. *World Resources 1990–91*, pp. 256–57, 262–63.

13. Ibid., p. 266 (notes to Table 16.5).

14. Ibid.

15. D. E. Sanger, "Minister Denies He Opposed College for Japanese Women," *New York Times*, 19 June 1990; "The Dwindling Japanese," *Economist*, 26 January 1991, p. 36.

16. "The Missing Children," *Economist*, 3 August 1991, pp. 43–44.

17. For use of the terms "cornucopians" and "neo-Malthusians," see the excellent survey by T. F. Homer-Dixon, "On the Threshold," pp. 76–116.

18. See, for example, J. Bellini, *High Tech Holocaust* (San Francisco, Cal., 1986), p. 251; Ehrlich and Ehrlich, *Population Explosion*, chs. 1 and 12. In many ways, the tone of this literature replicates that of the antinuclear lobby: see, for example, J. Cox, *Overkill* (Harmondsworth, Mddsx., 1981 edn.).

19. This closely follows Homer-Dixon, "On the Threshold," pp. 100–101.

20. Ibid.

21. As is repeatedly argued in the annual issues of L. R. Brown et al., *State of the World:* see the 1992 edition, chs. 3, 9, 11.

22. Homer-Dixon, "On the Threshold," passim; Eberstadt, "Population Change and National Security," passim; Foster, "Global Demographic Trends to the Year 2010," passim.

23. T. R. Malthus, *An Essay on Population*, 2 vols. (London, 1914 edn.), pp. 261–62. Malthus continued to produce newer versions of his first *Essay* for another few decades, and was therefore able to amend certain of his arguments.

BIBLIOGRAPHY

Note: Articles in daily newspapers and weekly magazines like *The Economist*—much used for this study—and unsigned articles in other periodicals are not included here but are fully cited in the endnotes.

INSTITUTIONAL WORKS, GOVERNMENT PUBLICATIONS, ETC.

Agricultural Biotechnology: The Next Green Revolution? World Bank, Technical Paper no. 133. Washington, D.C., 1991.

American Defense Annual. Lexington, Mass.

America's Choice: High Skills or Low Wages! The Report of the Comparison of the Skills of the Average Work Force. Rochester, N.Y., 1990.

Annual Review of Engineering Industries and Automation 1988, vol. 1. U.N. Economic Commission for Europe. New York, 1989.

Changing Climate. U.S. National Research Council. Washington, D.C., 1983.

CIA Handbook of Economic Statistics, 1990. Central Intelligence Agency. Washington, D.C., 1990.

Competing Economies: America, Europe, and the Pacific Rim. U.S. Congress, Office of Technology Assessment. Washington, D.C., 1991.

Current Population Reports, Series P-25, no. 1018. U.S. Bureau of the Census. Washington, D.C., 1989.

The Diffusion of Power: An Era of Realignment. Report of the National Security Group. Chicago, Ill., 1988.

Draft Report on Military Dependency on Foreign Technologies. National Security Council. Washington, D.C., April 1987.

Economic and Social Progress in Latin America: 1989 Report. Inter-America Development Bank. Washington, D.C., 1989.

Economic Report of the President. Washington, D.C., 1990.

The Economist World Atlas and Almanac 1989. London, 1989.

Education in Japan. Foreign Press Center. Tokyo, 1988.

Everybody Counts: A Report to the Nation of the Future of Mathematics Education. National Research Council. Washington, D.C., 1989.

Global Economic Prospects and the Developing Countries. World Bank. Washington, D.C., 1991.

The Military Balance 1990–91. International Institute of Strategic Studies. London, 1990.

A Nation at Risk. The National Commission of Excellence in Education. Washington, D.C., 1983.

Our Common Future. World Commission on Environment and Development. Oxford, 1987.

Population: The UNFPA Experience. United Nations Fund for Population Activities. New York, 1984.

Reform and Innovation of Science and Education: Planning for the 1990 Farm Bill. U.S. Senate, Committee on Agriculture, Nutrition, and Forestry. Washington, D.C., 1989.

Report of the Secretary of Defense. U.S. Congress. Washington, D.C., Annual.

Robotics Technology and Its Varied Uses. U.S. Congress, Hearing Before the Subcommittee on Science, Research, and Technology, 25 September 1989. Washington, D.C., 1989.

RUSI and Brassey's Defence Yearbook. Royal United Services Institute for Defence Studies. New York. Annual.

Soviet Military Power. U.S. Department of Defense. Washington, D.C. Annual.

State of the Environment: A View Towards the Nineties. Conservation Foundation. Washington, D.C., 1987.

The Statesman's Yearbook, 1990–91. J. Paxton, ed. New York and London, 1990.

Statistical Abstract of the United States 1990. U.S. Bureau of the Census. Washington, D.C., 1990.

Survey of Current Business. Bureau of Economic Analysis. Washington, D.C., July 1990.

Technology, Public Policy, and the Changing Structure of American Agriculture. U.S. Congress, Office of Technology Assessment. Washington, D.C., 1986.

Trends in Developing Economies 1990. World Bank. Washington, D.C., 1990.

UNESCO Statistical Digest 1987. Paris, 1987.

UNESCO Statistical Yearbook 1989. Paris, 1989.

Workforce 2000: Work and Workers for the 21st Century. Hudson Institute. Indianapolis, Ind., 1987.

World Development Report 1990. World Bank. Washington, D.C., 1990.

World Development Report 1991. World Bank. Washington, D.C., 1991.

World Population Prospects 1988. United Nations Population Division. New York, 1989.

World Resources 1990–91. World Resources Institute and International Institute for Environment and Development. New York/Oxford, 1990.

World Tables 1991. World Bank. Washington, D.C., 1991.

Year Book of Labor Statistics 1988. International Labor Office. Geneva, 1988.

AUTHORED WORKS

Adama, G. *The Iron Triangle*. New York, 1981.

Adriaansen, W. L. M., and J. G. Waardensburg, eds. *A Dual World Economy: Forty Years of Development Experience*. Rotterdam, 1989.

Aganbegyan, A. *The Economic Challenge of Perestroika*. M. Barratt Brown, ed. Bloomington, Ind., 1988.

Aggarwal, R. "The Strategic Challenge of the Evolving Global Economy." *Business Horizons*, July–August 1987.

Agnelli, G. "The Europe of 1992." *Foreign Affairs* 68 (Fall 1989).

Ahluwalia, I. J. "Industrial Growth in India: Performance and Prospects." *Journal of Development Economics* 28 (1986).

Alexander, I., and P. Burnett. *Reinventing Man: The Robot Becomes Reality*. New York, 1983.

Alonso, W., ed. *Population in an Interacting World*. Cambridge, Mass., 1987.

Anderson, A., and D. L. Bork, eds. *Thinking About America: The United States in the 1990s*. Stanford, Cal., 1988.

Andrews, K. R. *Elizabethan Privateering: English Privateering During the Spanish War, 1585–1603*. Cambridge, 1964.

Angang, H., and Z. Ping, *China's Population Development*. Beijing, 1991.

Ashton, T. S. *The Industrial Revolution, 1760–1830*. Oxford, 1968.

Atkinson, R. "Supply and Demand for Scientists and Engineers: A National Crisis in the Making." *Science* 248 (27 April 1990).

Attali, J., "Lines on the Horizon: A New Order in the Making." *New Perspectives Quarterly*, Spring 1990.

Avery, D. "The Green Revolution Is Our Real Food Security." Hudson Institute Briefing Paper no. 112. Indianapolis, 1989.

Axelbank, J. "The Crisis of the Cities." *Populi*, 15 (1988).

Baark, E., and A. Jamison. *Technical Development in China, India and Japan*. London, 1986.

Bairoch, P. "International Industrialization Levels from 1750 to 1980." *Journal of European Economic History* 11 (1982).

Baker, C. O., ed. *The Condition of Education 1989. vol. 1, Elementary and Secondary Education*. Washington, D.C., 1989.

Balfour, M. L. G. *Britain and Joseph Chamberlain*. London/Boston, 1985.

Banac, I. "Political Change and National Diversity." *Daedalus* 119 (1990).

Baranson, J. *Robots in Manufacturing: Key to International Competitiveness*. Mt. Airy, Md., 1983.

Barnett, C. *The Collapse of British Power*. New York/London, 1972.

Barnett, M. J. "The Case for More School Days." *Atlantic* 266 (November 1990).

Barraclough, G. *An Introduction to Contemporary History*. Harmondsworth, Mddsx., 1967 edn.

Barth, M. C., and J. G. Titus, eds. *Greenhouse Effect and Sea Level Rise: A Challenge for This Generation*. New York, 1984.

Becker, C. M. "The Demo-Economic Impact of the AIDs Pandemic in Sub-Saharan Africa." *World Development* 18 (1990).

Bellini, J. *High Tech Holocaust*. San Francisco, Cal., 1986.

Berardi, G. M., and C. C. Geisler, eds. *The Social Consequences and Challenges of New Agricultural Technologies*. Boulder, Colo., 1984.

Bergson, A., and H. S. Levine, eds. *The Soviet Economy: Towards the Year 2000.* London, 1983.

Bergsten, C. F. *America in the World Economy: A Strategy for the 1990s.* Washington, D.C., 1988.

———. "The World Economy After the Cold War." *Foreign Affairs* 69 (Summer 1990).

Bloom, D. E., and N. G. Bennett. "Future Shock." *New Republic*, 19 June 1989.

Bornstein, M., ed. *The Soviet Economy: Continuity and Change.* Boulder, Colo., 1981.

Borrus, M. G. *Competing for Control: America's Stake in Microelectronics.* Cambridge, Mass., 1988.

Bowonder, B., and T. Miyake. "Technology Development and Japanese Industrial Competitiveness." *Futures* 22 (January–February 1990).

Braisted, W. R. *The United States Navy in the Pacific, 1909–1922.* Austin, Tex., 1971.

Braudel, F. *Civilization and Capitalism.* vol. 3, *The Perspective of the World.* New York, 1986.

Briggs, A. *Victorian Cities.* London, 1963.

Brock, W. E., and R. D. Homats, eds. *The Global Economy: America's Role in the Decade Ahead.* New York/London, 1990.

Browlee, S. "The Best Banana Bred." *Atlantic* 264 (September 1989).

Brown, H. *The Challenge of Man's Future: An Inquiry Concerning the Condition of Man During the Years That Lie Ahead.* New York, 1954.

Brown, L. R., et al. *State of the World.* New York. Annual.

Bull, H., and A. Watson, eds. *The Expansion of International Society.* Oxford, 1983.

Bultot, F., et al. "Estimated Annual Regime of Energy-Balance Components, Evapotranspiration and Soil Moisture for a Drainage Basin in the Case of a CO_2 Doubling." *Climatic Change* 12 (1988).

Burstein, D. *Euroquake: Europe's Explosive Economic Challenge Will Change the World.* New York, 1991.

———. *Yen! Japan's New Financial Empire and Its Threat to America.* New York, 1988.

Buruma, I. *Behind the Mask: On Sexual Demons, Sacred Mothers, Transvestites, Gangsters, Drifters, and Other Japanese Cultural Heroes.* New York, 1984.

Busch, L., et al. *Plants, Power, and Profit: Social, Economic, and Ethical Consequences of the New Biotechnologies.* Oxford, 1991.

Bylinsky, G. "Trying to Transcend Copycat Science." *Fortune* 115 (30 March 1987).

Calder, A. *The People's War: Britain, 1939–1945.* London, 1969.

Calder, N. *The Green Machines.* New York, 1986.

Caldwell, J. C., and P. Caldwell. "High Fertility in Sub-Saharan Africa." *Scientific American* 262 (May 1990).

Calleo, D. P. *The Bankrupting of America: How the Federal Budget is Impoverishing the Nation.* New York, 1992.

———. *Beyond American Hegemony: The Future of the Western Alliance.* New York, 1987.

———. *The German Question Reconsidered: Germany and the World Order, 1870 to the Present.* New York, 1978.

Carnoy, M. "High Technology and International Labour Markets." *International Labour Review* 124 (1985).

Castles, S., et al. *Here for Good: Western Europe's New Ethnic Minorities.* London, 1984.

Chaliand, G., and J. P. Rageau. *A Strategic Atlas: Comparative Geopolitics of the World's Powers.* New York, 1985.

Chambers, J. D., and G. E. Mingay. *The Agricultural Revolution 1750–1880.* New York, 1966.

Chancellor, J. *Peril or Promise: A Commentary upon America.* New York, 1990.

Choate, P. *Agents of Influence.* New York, 1990.

Chu, L., "The Chimera of the China Market." *Atlantic* 266 (October 1990).

Churba, J. *Soviet Breakout: Strategies to Meet It.* Washington, D.C./London, 1988.

Cipolla, C. M. *Before the Industrial Revolution.* 2nd edn. London, 1981.

———, ed. *The Economic Decline of Empires.* London, 1970.

———. *The Economic History of World Population.* 7th edn. Harmondsworth, Mddsx., 1978.

Clash, M. "Development Policy, Technology Assessment, and the New Technologies." *Futures* 22 (November 1990).

Coale, A. J. "Fertility and Mortality in Different Populations with Special Attention to China." *Proceedings of the American Philosophical Society* 132 (1988).

———, and E. M. Hoover. *Population Growth and Economic Development in Low-Income Countries.* Princeton, N.J., 1958.

Cohen, E. A. "When Policy Outstrips Power—American Strategy and Statecraft," *Public Interest* 75 (1984).

Cohen, R., and P. A. Wilson. *Superpowers in Economic Decline: U.S. Strategy for the Transcentury Era.* New York/London 1990.

Cohen, S. S., and J. Zysman. *Manufacturing Matters: The Myth of the Post-Industrial Economy.* New York, 1987.

Cohn, J. P., "Gauging the Biological Impacts of the Greenhouse Effect," *BioScience* 39 (March 1989).

Colley, L. "The Apotheosis of George III: Loyalty, Royalty, and the British Nation, 1760–1820." *Past and Present* 102 (February 1984).

———. *Britons.* (New Haven/London, 1992).

Colton, T. J. *The Dilemma of Reform in the Soviet Union.* 2nd edn. New York, 1986.

Cooley, M. J. E. "Robotics—Some Wider Implications." *The World Yearbook of Research and Development.* 1985.

Cox, J. *Overkill.* Harmondsworth, Mddsx., 1981 edn.

Cracraft, J., ed. *The Soviet Union Today: An Interpretive Guide.* 2nd edn. Chicago/London, 1988.

Crouzet, F. *The Victorian Economy.* London, 1982.

Cruickshank, J. "The Rise and Fall of the Third World: A Concept Whose Time Has Passed." *World Press Review* 38 (February 1991).

Daly, H. E. *Steady State Economics: The Economics of Biophysical Equilibrium and Moral Growth.* San Francisco, 1977.

———, and J. B. Cobb. *For the Common Good: Redirecting the Economy Toward Community, the Environment and a Sustainable Future.* Boston, Mass., 1989.

Davis, B. D., ed. *The Genetic Revolution: Scientific Prospects and Public Perceptions.* Baltimore/London, 1991.

Davis, K., et al., eds. *Below-Replacement Fertility in Industrial Societies.* New York, 1987.

de Cecco, M. *Money and Empire: The International Gold Standard 1890–1914.* Oxford, 1974.

Decker, W. L., et al. *The Impact of Climate Change from Increased Atmospheric Carbon Dioxide on American Agriculture.* Washington, D.C., 1986.

DeGrasse, R. W. *Military Expansion, Economic Decline: The Impact of Military Spending on U.S. Economic Performance.* Armonk, N.Y., 1985 edn.

Dehio, L. *The Precarious Balance: Four Centuries of the European Power Struggle.* London, 1963.

de Jouvenel, H. "Europe at the Dawn of the Third Millennium: A Synthesis of the Main Trends." *Futures* 20 (October 1988).

Dertouzos, M. L., et al., eds. *Made in America: Regaining the Productive Edge.* Cambridge, Mass., 1989.

Dibb, P. *The Soviet Union: The Incomplete Superpower.* London, 1986.

Dickson, D. "German Biotech Firms Flee Regulatory Controls." *Science* 248 (16 June 1990).

Dietrich, W. S. *In the Shadow of the Rising Sun: The Political Roots of American Economic Decline.* University Park, Pa., 1991.

Dixon, C. J., et al., eds. *Multinational Corporations and the Third World.* London/Sydney, 1986.

Dollinger, P. *La Hanse.* Paris, 1964.

Dore, R. P., and M. Sako. *How the Japanese Learn to Work.* London, 1989.

Dornbusch, R., et al. *The Case for Manufacturing in America's Future.* Rochester, N.Y., 1987.

Doyle, D. P. "Time for America to Set National Education Norms." *Hudson Opinion,* October 1989.

Drucker, P. "The Changed World Economy." *Foreign Affairs* 64 (Spring 1986).

Dumas, L. J. *The Overburdened Economy: Uncovering the Cause of Chronic Unemployment, Inflation, and National Decline.* Berkeley/Los Angeles, 1986.

Duncan, D. E. "Africa: The Long Goodbye," *New Republic* 203 (July 1990).

Eberstadt, N. "Population Change and National Security." *Foreign Affairs* 70 (Summer 1991).

Eekelaar, J. M., and D. Pearl, eds. *An Aging World: Dilemmas and Challenges for Law and Social Policy.* Oxford, 1989.

Ehrlich, P. R. *The Population Bomb.* New York, 1968.

——, and A. E. Ehrlich. *The Population Explosion.* New York, 1990.

Emmott, B. *The Sun Also Sets: The Limits to Japan's Economic Power.* New York, 1989.

Engelhardt, K. G., "Innovations in Health Care: Roles for Advanced Intelligent Technologies." *Pittsburgh High Technology Journal* 2 (1987).

Ernst, D., and D. O'Conner. *Technology and Global Competition: The Challenge for Newly Industrializing Economies.* OECD. Paris, 1989.

Fairbanks, C. H. "Russian Roulette: The Danger of a Collapsing Empire." *Policy Review* 57 (Summer 1991).

Fajer, E. D., et al., "The Effects of Enriched Carbon Dioxide Atmospheres on Plant-Insect Herbivores Interactions." *Science* 243 (1989).

Fallows, J. *More Like Us: Making America Great Again.* New York, 1989.

Fardoust, S., and A. Dhareshwan. *Long-Term Outlook for the World Economy: Issues and Projections for the 1990s.* World Bank. Washington, D.C., 1990.

Farmer, B. H. "Perspectives on the Green Revolution in South Asia." *Modern Asian Studies* 20 (1986).

Fauriol, G. A. "The Shadow of Latin American Affairs." *Foreign Affairs* 69 (1989–90).

Feldstein, M. S., ed. *The United States in the World Economy.* Cambridge, Mass., 1987.

Feshbach, M., and A. Friendly. *Ecocide in the U.S.S.R.* New York, 1992.

Fieldhouse, D. K. *Unilever Overseas: The Anatomy of a Multinational.* Stanford, Cal., 1978.

Fischer, B. "Developing Countries in the Process of Economic Globalization." *Intereconomics* 25 (March–April 1990).

Fjermedal, G. *The Tomorrow Makers: A Brave New World of Living-Brain Machines.* New York, 1986.

Foster, G. D. "Global Demographic Trends to the Year 2010: Implications for U.S. Security." *Washington Quarterly* 12 (Spring 1989).

Friedman, B. M. *Day of Reckoning: The Consequences of American Economic Policy Under Reagan and After.* New York, 1988.

Friedman, G., and M. Lebard. *The Coming War with Japan.* New York, 1991.

Fukuchi, T., and M. Kamagi, eds. *Perspectives on the Pacific Basin Economy: A Comparison of Asia and Latin America.* Tokyo, 1990.

Gable, F. "Changing Climate and Caribbean Coastlines." *Oceanus* 30 (Winter 1987–88).

———, and D. G. Aubrey. "Changing Climate and the Pacific." *Oceanus* 32 (Winter 1989–90).

Gaddis, J. L. "Toward the Post–Cold War World." *Foreign Affairs* 70 (Spring 1991).

Gardels, N. "The Education We Deserve." *New Perspectives Quarterly* 7 (1990).

Garton Ash, T. *The Magic Lantern: The Revolution of '89 Witnessed in Warsaw, Budapest, Berlin and Prague.* New York, 1990.

———. *The Uses of Adversity: Essays on the Fate of Central Europe.* New York, 1989.

Gati, C. *The BLOC That Failed: Soviet-East European Relations in Transition.* Boulder, Colo., 1984.

Gellner, E. *Nations and Nationalism.* Oxford, 1983.

Gendel, S. M., et al. *Agricultural Bioethics: Implications of Agricultural Biotechnology.* Ames, Iowa, 1990.

Geremek, B. "The Realities of Eastern and Central Europe," in *Change in Europe.* Washington, D.C.: Plenary of the Trilateral Commission, April 1990.

Gevarter, W. B. *Intelligent Machines: An Introductory Perspective of Artificial Intelligence and Robotics.* Englewood Cliffs, N.J., 1985.

Ghosh, P. K., ed. *Developing South Asia: A Modernization Perspective.* Westport, Conn., 1984.

———, ed. *Technology Policy and Development: A Third-World Perspective.* Westport, Conn., 1984.

Gibbons, A. "Biotechnology Takes Root in the Third World." *Science* 248 (25 May 1990).

Giese, G. S., and D. G. Aubrey. "Losing Coastal Upland to Relative Sea-Level Rise: 3 Scenarios for Massachusetts." *Oceanus* 30 (Fall 1987).

Gilder, G. "You Ain't Seen Nothing Yet." *Forbes* 141 (4 April 1988).

Gill, S., and D. Law. *The Global Political Economy: Perspectives, Problems and Policies.* Baltimore, Md., 1988.

Gilpin, R. *The Political Economy of International Relations.* Princeton, N.J., 1987.

———. *War and Change in World Politics.* Cambridge, Mass., 1981.

Glantz, M. H., and J. E. Ausubel. "The Ogallala Aquifer and Carbon Dioxide: Comparison and Convergence." *Environmental Conservation* 11 (Summer 1984).

Gleick, P. H. "Climate Change and International Politics: Problems Facing Developing Countries." *Ambio* 18 (1989).

———. "The Implications of Global Changes for International Security." *Climatic Change* 15 (1989).

Goldman, C. S., ed. *The Empire and the Century: A Series of Essays on Imperial Problems and Possibilities, by Various Writers.* London, 1905.

Goldman, M. I. *Gorbachev's Challenge: Economic Reform in the Age of High Technology.* New York, 1987.

———. *The Enigma of Soviet Petroleum: Half-Full or Half-Empty?* London, 1980.

———. *U.S.S.R. In Crisis: The Failure of an Economic System.* New York, 1983.

Goliber, T. J. "Africa's Expanding Population: Old Problems, New Policies." *Population Bulletin* 44 (1989).

Goodman, D. S. G. *China's Regional Development.* London, 1989.

———, et al. *From Farming to Biotechnology: A Theory of Agro-Industrial Development.* Oxford, 1987.

Gore, Albert. *Earth in the Balance: Ecology and the Human Spirit.* New York, 1992.

Gottfried, K., and P. Bracken, eds. *Reforging European Security: From Confrontation to Cooperation.* Boulder, Colo., 1990.

Govind, H. "Recent Developments in Environmental Protection in India: Pollution Control." *Ambio* 18 (1989).

Green, K., and E. Yoxen. "The Greening of European Industry: What Role for Biotechnology?" *Futures* 22 (June 1990).

Green, M., and M. Pinsky, eds. *America's Transition: Blueprints for the 1990s.* Lanham, Md., 1990.

Gregory, P. R., and R. C. Stuart. *Soviet Economic Structure and Performance.* 3rd edn. New York, 1986.

Griffith, W. E., ed. *Central and Eastern Europe: The Opening Curtain.* Boulder, Colo., 1989.

Gruner, W. *Die deutsche Frage: Ein Problem der Europaischen Geschichte seit 1800.* Munich, 1985.

Gupta, A. "The Indian Arms Industry: A Lumbering Giant." *Asian Survey* 30 (1990).

Guralnik, J. M., et al. "Projecting the Older Population of the United States." *Milbank Quarterly* 66 (1988).

Gwynne, R. N. *New Horizons? Third World Industrialization in an International Framework.* New York/London, 1990.

Hamakawa, Y. "Photovoltaic Power." *Scientific American* 256 (April 1987).

Hamerow, T. S. *Restoration, Revolution, Reaction: Economics and Politics in Germany, 1815–1871.* Princeton, N.J., 1958.

Hamilton, E. K., ed. *America's Global Interests: A New Agenda.* New York, 1989.

Hancock, G. *Lords of Poverty: The Power, Prestige, and Corruption of the International Aid Business.* Boston, Mass., 1990.

Hanke, D. E. "Seeding the Bamboo Revolution." *Nature* 22 (1990).

Hansen, J., et al. "Global Climate Changes as Forecast by the Goddard Institute for Space Studies Three-Dimensional Model." *Journal of Geophysical Research* 93 (1988).

Hartley, J. "Are There Really So Many Robots in Japan?" *Decade of Robotics.* Special 10th Anniversary Issue of *Industrial Robot Machine.* Berlin, 1983.

Hassan, S. "Environmental Issues and Security in South Asia." *Adelphi Papers* 262 (Autumn 1991).

Hatsopoulos, N., et al. "U.S. Competitiveness: Beyond the Trade Deficit." *Science* 241 (1988).

Hauner, M. *What Is Asia to Us? Russia's Asian Heartland Yesterday and Today.* Boston/London, 1990.

Hayes, M. D. "The U.S. and Latin America: The Lost Decade?" *Foreign Affairs* 68 (1988–89).

Hecht, S., and A. Cockburn. *The Fate of the Forest: Developers, Destroyers, and Defenders of the Amazon.* London/New York, 1989.

Heilbroner, R. L. *The Worldly Philosophers: The Lives, Times, and Ideas of the Great Economic Thinkers.* New York, 1986 edn.

Heisbourg, F. "Population Movements in Post–Cold War Europe." *Survival* 33 (January–February 1991).

Helleiner, E. "States and the Future of Global Finance." *Review of International Studies* 18 (January 1992).

Heller, M. A. "The Middle East: Out of Step with History." *Foreign Affairs* 69 (1989–90).

Herrnstein, R. J. "IQ and Falling Birthrates." *Atlantic* 263 (May 1989).

Hirsch, E. D. *Cultural Literacy: What Every American Needs to Know.* Boston, 1987.

Hoagland, J. "Europe's Destiny." *Foreign Affairs* 69 (1989–90).

Hobsbawm, E. J. *Industry and Empire: The Making of Modern English Society.* Harmondsworth, Mddsx., 1969.

Hobson, J. A. *Imperialism: A Study.* London, 1902.

Hoffman, J., et al. *Projecting Future Sea Level Rise: Methodology, Estimate to the Year 2000, and Research Needs.* Washington, D.C., 1983.

Hoffmann, S. "The European Community and 1992." *Foreign Affairs* 68 (Fall 1989).

Holzman, F. D. "Soviet Military Spending: Assessing the Numbers Game." *International Security* 6 (1982).

———. *Financial Checks on Soviet Defense Expenditures.* Lexington, Mass., 1975.

Homer-Dixon, T. F. "On the Threshold: Environmental Changes as Causes of Acute Conflict." *International Security* 16 (Fall 1991).

Houghton, R. A., and Woodwell, G. M. "Global Climatic Change." *Scientific American* 260 (1989).

Howard, M. *The Lessons of History.* New Haven, Conn., 1991.

Hughes, H. "Catching Up: The Asian Newly Industrializing Economies in the 1990s." *Asian Development Review* 7 (1989).

Hunt, H. A., and T. L. Hunt. *Human Resource Implications of Robotics.* Kalamazoo, Mich., 1983.

Huntington, S. P. "The U.S.—Decline or Renewal?" *Foreign Affairs* 67 (Winter 1988–89).

Iklé, F. C., and T. Nakanishi. "Japan's Grand Strategy." *Foreign Affairs* 69 (Summer 1990).

———, and A. Wohlstetter, eds. *Discriminate Deterrence: Report of the Commission on Integrated Long-Term Strategy.* Washington, D.C., 1988.

Ingham, K. "Africa's Internal Wars of the 1980s: Contours and Prospects." United States Institute of Peace. *In Brief* 18 (1990).

———. *Politics in Modern Africa: The Uneven Tribal Dimensions.* London/New York, 1990.

Inoguchi, T., and D. I. Okimoto, eds. *The Political Economy of Japan.* Vol. 2, *The Changing International Context.* Stanford, Cal., 1988.

Ishihara, Shintaro. *The Japan That Can Say No.* New York, 1991.

Ives, J. D., and B. Messerli. *The Himalayan Dilemma: Reconciling Development and Conservation.* London/New York, 1989.

Jacobs, J. "Training the Workforce of the Future." *Technology Review* 93 (August–September 1990).

Joffe, J. *The Limited Partnership: Europe, the United States, and the Burdens of Alliance.* Cambridge, 1987.

———. "Germany After NATO." *Harper's* 281 (September 1990).

Johnson, B. L. C. *Development in South Asia.* Harmondsworth, Mddsx., 1983.

Johnson, C. "Japan in Search of a 'Normal' Role." *Institute on Global Conflict and Cooperation* 3 (July 1992), U.C. San Diego.

———. *MITI and the Japanese Miracle: The Growth of Industrial Policy, 1925–1975.* Stanford, Cal., 1982.

Johnson, D. G., and R. D. Lee. *Population Growth and Economic Development: Issues and Evidence.* Madison, Wis., 1987.

Joll, J. *The Origins of the First World War.* London/New York, 1984.

Jones, C., ed. *Britain and Revolutionary France: Conflict, Subversion, and Propaganda.* Exeter Studies in History, no. 5. Exeter, 1983.

Jones, E. L. *The European Miracle: Environments, Economies and Geopolitics in the History of Europe and Asia.* Cambridge, Mass., 1981.

———, and G. E. Mingay, eds. *Land, Labour and Population in the Industrial Revolution.* London, 1967.

Jones, R. S. "The Economic Implications of Japan's Aging Population." *Asian Survey* 28 (September 1988).

Judy, R. W., and V. L. Clough. *The Information Age and Soviet Society.* Indianapolis, 1989.

Juma, C. *The Gene Hunters: Biotechnology and the Scramble for Seeds.* London/ Princeton, N.J., 1989.

Kahn, H. *The Emerging Japanese Superstate: Challenge and Response.* London, 1971.

Kaiser, D. *Politics and War: European Conflict from Philip II to Hitler.* Cambridge, Mass., 1990.

Kaldor, M. *The Baroque Arsenal.* London, 1982.

Kamata, S. *Japan in the Passing Lane: An Insider's Account of Life in a Japanese Auto Factory.* New York, 1984.

Kamimen, D. M. "Technology for Development: Sustaining, Not Obliterating, the Environment." *Research & Exploration,* Winter 1991.

Kant, Immanuel. *Zum Ewigen Frieden.* Stuttgart, 1954 edn.

Keegan, J., and A. Wheatcroft. *Zones of Conflict: An Atlas of Future Wars.* New York, 1978.

Kenney, M. *Biotechnology: The University-Industrial Complex.* New Haven, Conn., 1986.

Kennedy, P. M. "Fin-de-Siecle America." *New York Review of Books* 37 (28 June 1990).

———, ed. *Grand Strategies in War and Peace.* New Haven/London, 1991.

———. *The Realities Behind Diplomacy: Background Influences on British External Policies.* London, 1980.

———. *The Rise and Fall of the Great Powers: Economic Change and Military Conflict from 1500 to 2000.* New York, 1987.

———. *The Rise of the Anglo-German Antagonism 1860–1914.* London/Boston, 1980.

Kerr, R. A. "New Greenhouse Report Puts Down Dissenters." *Science* 249 (1990).

Kiernan, V. G. "State and Nation in Western Europe." *Past and Present* 31 (1965).

Kim, S. S., ed. *China and the World: Chinese Foreign Policy in the Post-Mao Era.* Boulder, Colo., 1989.

Kindleberger, C. *The World in Depression, 1929–1939.* Berkeley, Cal., 1973.

Kloppenburg, J. R. *First the Seed: The Political Economy of Plant Biotechnology, 1492–2000.* Cambridge, 1988.

Kotkin, J., and Y. Kishimoto. *The Third Century: America's Resurgence in the Asian Era.* New York, 1988.

Kozol, J. *Illiterate America.* New York, 1985.

Krauthammer, C. "The Unipolar Moment." *Foreign Affairs* 70 (1990–91).

Krugman, P. *The Age of Diminished Expectations: U.S. Economic Policy in the 1990s.* Cambridge, Mass., 1990.

Küng, H. *Global Responsibility: In Search of a New World Ethic.* New York, 1991.

Kvint, V. "Russia as Cinderella." *Forbes* 145 (19 February 1990).

Lall, S. *Developing Countries as Exporters of Technology: A First Look at the Indian Experience.* London, 1982.

Landau, G. W., et al. *Latin America at a Crossroads: The Challenge to the Trilateral Countries.* Trilateral Commission, New York/Paris/Tokyo, 1990.

Landes, D. S. *The Unbound Prometheus: Technological Change and Industrial Development in Western Europe from 1750 to the Present.* Cambridge, 1969.

Lardy, N. R. "Agricultural Reforms in China." *Journal of International Affairs* 39 (1986).

Larson, T. B. *Soviet-American Rivalry.* New York, 1978.

Lieven, D. "Gorbachev and the Nationalities." *Conflict Studies* 216 (1988).

———. "The Soviet Crisis." *Conflict Studies* 241 (1991).

Lind, M. "America as an Ordinary Country." *American Enterprise* 1 (September–October 1990).

Linder, S. B. *The Pacific Century: Economic and Political Consequences of Asian-Pacific Dynamism.* Stanford, Cal., 1986.

Liverman, D. M., et al. "Climatic Change and Grain Corn Yields in the North American Great Plains." *Climatic Change* 9 (1986).

Lowenthal, A. F. "Rediscovering Latin America." *Foreign Affairs* 69 (Fall 1990).

Lubasz, H., ed. *The Development of the Modern State.* New York, 1964.

Luttwak, E. N. "From Geopolitics to Geo-Economics." *National Interest* 20 (Summer 1990).

MacNeill, J., et al. *Beyond Interdependence: The Meshing of the World's Economy and the Earth's Ecology.* New York/Oxford, 1991.

Malabré, A. L. *Within Our Means: The Struggle for Economic Recovery After a Reckless Decade.* New York, 1991.

Malthus, T. R. *An Essay on the Principle of Population As It Affects the Future Improvement of Society.* London, 1798; reprinted, with notes by J. Bonar, New York, 1965.

———. *An Essay on Population,* 2 vols. London, 1914.

Manabe, S., and R. T. Wetherald. "Large-Scale Changes of Soil Wetness Induced by an Increase in Atmospheric Carbon Dioxide." *Journal of Atmospheric Sciences* 44 (1987).

Mann, P.S. "Green Revolution Revisited: The Adoption of High Yielding Variety Wheat Seeds in India." *Journal of Development Studies* 26 (1989).

Mansergh, N. *The Commonwealth Experience.* London, 1969.

Marcum, J. A. "Africa: A Continent Adrift." *Foreign Affairs* 68 (1988–89).

Marien, M. "Driving Forces and Barriers to a Sustainable Global Economy." *Futures* 22 (December 1989).

Markin, J. H. "Japan's Investment in America: Is It a Threat?" *Challenge* (November–December 1988).

Martin, L. G. "The Graying of Japan." *Population Bulletin* 44 (1989).

Martinez, T. E. "Argentina: Living with Hyperinflation." *Atlantic* 266 (December 1990).

Marton, K. *Multinationals, Technology, and Industrialization: Implications and Impact in Third World Countries.* Lexington, Mass., 1986.

Maruyama, M. "Japan's Agricultural Policy Failure." *Food Policy* 12 (May 1987).

Marwick, A. *War and Social Change in the Twentieth Century.* London, 1974.

Marx, J. L., ed. *A Revolution in Biotechnology.* Cambridge, 1989.

Mathews, J. T. "Redefining Security." *Foreign Affairs* 68 (Spring 1989).

Mathias, P. *The First Industrial Nation: An Economic History of Britain, 1700–1914.* London, 1969.

Maull, H. W. "Germany and Japan: The New Civilian Powers." *Foreign Affairs* 69 (Winter 1991–92).

Maxwell, K. "The Tragedy of the Amazon." *New York Review of Books* 38 (7 March 1991).

McAfee, K. "Why the Third World Goes Hungry." *Commonweal* 117 (15 June 1990).

McCormick, B. J. *The World Economy: Patterns of Growth and Change.* Oxford, 1988.

McCormick, G. H., and R. E. Bissell, eds. *Strategic Dimensions of Economic Behavior.* New York, 1984.

McInnes, C. *NATO's Changing Strategic Agenda: The Conventional Defense of Central Europe.* London/Boston, 1990.

McIntyre, W. D. *Colonies into Commonwealth.* London, 1966.

McMillan, J., et al. "The Impact of China's Economic Reforms on Agricultural Productivity Growth," *Journal of Political Economy* 97 (1989).

McNeill, W. H. *Plagues and Peoples.* New York, 1976.

———. *Population and Politics Since 1750.* Charlottesville, Va., 1990.

———. *The Pursuit of Power: Technology, Armed Forces and Society Since 1000 A.D.* Chicago, 1983.

———. *The Rise of the West: A History of the Human Community.* Chicago, Ill., 1967.

Meadows, D. H., et al. *The Limits to Growth: A Report for the Club of Rome's Project on the Predicament of Mankind.* New York, 1972.

Mearsheimer, J. J. *Conventional Deterrence.* Ithaca, N.Y., 1983.

Mendelssohn, K. *Science and Western Domination.* London, 1976.

Meyer-Larsen, W. "America's Century Will End with a Whimper." *World Press Review* 38 (January 1991).

Moran, T. H., "International Economics and National Security," *Foreign Affairs* 69 (Winter 1990–91).

———. "The Globalization of America's Defense Industries: Managing the Threat of Foreign Dependence." *International Security* 15 (Summer 1990).

Morley, J. W., ed. *The Pacific Basin: New Challenges for the United States.* New York, 1986.

Morris, C. R. "The Coming Global Boom." *Atlantic* 264 (October 1989).

Morse, E. L. "The Coming Oil Revolution." *Foreign Affairs* 69 (Winter 1990–91).

Morse, R. M. "Japan's Drive to Pre-eminence." *Foreign Policy* 69 (1987–88).

Moynihan, M. *Global Consumer Demographics.* New York, 1991.

Mukerjie, D. "Economic Realities Forbid Sweeping Changes in Policy." *Asian Finance* 16 (15 April 1990).

Murphy, R. T. "Power Without Purpose." *Harvard Business Review* 66 (March–April 1988).

Nau, H. R. *The Myth of America's Decline: Leading the World Economy into the 1990s.* New York, 1990.

Nordhaus, W. D. "Global Warming: Slowing the Greenhouse Express." Cowes Foundation Paper no. 758. Yale University, New Haven, 1990.

Novak, M. "What Became of the Ugly American?" *Forbes* 145 (30 April 1990).

Nye, J. S. *Bound to Lead: The Changing Nature of American Power*. New York, 1990.

Odhiambo, T. R. "Human Resources Development: Problems and Prospects in Developing Countries." *Impact of Science on Society* 155 (1989).

Ogawa, N. "Aging in China: Demographic Alternatives." *Asia-Pacific Population Journal* 3 (1988).

Ohmae, K. *The Borderless World: Management Lessons in the New Logic of the Global Marketplace*. New York/London, 1990.

Olsen, E. A. *U.S.-Japan Strategic Reciprocity: A Neo-Nationalist View*. Stanford, Cal., 1985.

Onimode, B. *A Political Economy of the African Crisis*. London/New Jersey, 1988.

Oppenheimer, M., and R. H. Boyle. *Dead Heat: The Race Against the Greenhouse Effect*. New York, 1990.

O'Reilly, B. "America's Place in the World Competition." *Fortune* 120 (6 November 1989).

Packard, G. R. "The Coming U.S.–Japan Crisis." *Foreign Affairs* 66 (Winter 1987–88).

Parry, J. H. *The Age of Reconnaissance*. 2nd edn. London, 1966.

Pearce, D. W., et al. *Sustainable Development: Economics and Environment in the Third World*. Aldershot, Hants, 1990.

Perry, N. J. "How to Help America's Schools." *Fortune* 120 (4 December 1989).

Peterson, P. G., and N. Howe. *On Borrowed Time*. San Francisco, 1989.

Phillips, K. *The Politics of Rich and Poor: Wealth and the American Electorate in the Reagan Aftermath*. New York, 1990.

Pierog, K., "How Technology Is Tackling 24-Hour Global Markets." *Futures* 17 (1989).

Pirages, D. *Global Technopolitics: The International Politics of Technology and Resources*. Belmont, Cal., 1989.

Pollard, S. *Peaceful Conquest: The Industrialization of Europe, 1760–1970*. Oxford, 1971.

Polumbaum, J. "Dateline China: The People's Malaise." *Foreign Policy* 20 (1990–91).

Porter, B. *The Lion's Share: A Short History of British Imperialism 1850–1970*. London, 1976.

Porter, M. *The Competitive Advantage of Nations*. New York, 1990.

Postel, S. "Water: Rethinking Management in an Age of Scarcity." *Worldwatch Paper* 62 (December 1984).

Pradervand, P. *Listening to Africa: Developing Africa from the Grassroots*. New York, 1989.

Prakosh, A. "A Carrier Force for the Indian Navy." *Naval War College Review* 43 (Autumn 1990).

Prentis, S. *Biotechnology: A New Industrial Revolution*. New York, 1984.

Prestowitz, C. V. *Trading Places: How We Allowed Japan to Take the Lead*. New York, 1988.

Prestowitz, C. V., et al., eds. *Powernomics: Economics and Strategy After the Cold War*. Lanham, Md., 1991.

Pye, L. W. "China: Erratic State, Frustrated Society." *Foreign Affairs* 69 (Fall 1990).

Quester, G., ed. *Nuclear Proliferation*. Madison, Wis., 1981.

Quinn, T. C., et al. "AIDS in Africa: An Epidemiological Paradigm." *Science* 234 (November 1986).

Radharaman, R., ed. *Robotics and Factories of the Future '87*. Berlin/Heidelberg/New York, 1988.

Ranum, O., ed. *National Consciousness, History, and Political Culture in Early-Modern Europe.* Baltimore/London, 1975.

Ravenhill, J. "The North-South Balance of Power." *International Affairs* 66 (1990).

Reading, B. *Japan: The Coming Collapse.* London, 1992.

Reich, R. B. *The Work of Nations: Preparing Ourselves for the 21st-century Capitalism.* New York, 1990.

Reid, W. V., and K. R. Miller. *Keeping Options Open: The Scientific Basis for Conserving Biodiversity.* Washington, D.C., 1989.

Reisner, M. *Cadillac Desert: The American West and Its Disappearing Water.* New York, 1986.

Reperant, D. *The Most Beautiful Villages in France.* New York, 1990.

Resnick, B. C. "The Globalization of World Financial Markets." *Business Horizons* 32 (November–December 1989).

Rexen, F., and L. Munck. *Cereal Crops for Industrial Use in Europe.* Copenhagen, 1984.

Rhoades, R. E. "The World's Food Supply at Risk." *National Geographic* 179 (April 1991).

Roberts, J. *The Pelican History of the World.* Harmondsworth, Mddsx., 1980.

Robinson, R., and J. Gallagher. *Africa and the Victorians: The Official Mind of Imperialism.* London, 1961.

Rohlen, T. P. *Japan's High Schools.* Berkeley, Cal., 1983.

Rosecrance, R., ed. *America as an Ordinary Power.* Ithaca, N.Y., 1976.

———. *America's Economic Resurgence: A Bold New Strategy.* New York, 1990.

———. *The Rise of the Trading States: Commerce and Conquest in the Modern World.* New York, 1985.

Rosenau, J. N. "The Relocation of Authority in a Shrinking World." Unpublished paper. 1980.

Roskill, S. W. *Naval Policy Between the Wars.* Vol. 1. London, 1968.

Rostow, W. W. *The World Economy: History and Prospects.* Austin, Tex., 1978.

Rowen, H. S., and C. Wolf, Jr., eds. *The Future of the Soviet Empire.* New York, 1987.

———, eds. *The Impoverished Superpower: Perestroika and the Soviet Military Burden.* San Francisco, 1990.

Rudney, R. S. "Mitterand's New Atlanticism: Evolving French Attitudes Toward NATO." *Orbis* 28 (1984).

Russett, B. "Defense Expenditures and National Well-Being." *American Political Science Review* 76 (1982).

Sadik, N. *The State of the World Population.* U.N. Population Fund. New York, 1990.

Sayle, M., and J. Sayle. "Why We Send Our Children to a Japanese School." *Tokyo Journal,* August 1990.

Scalapino, R. A. "Asia and the United States: The Challenges Ahead." *Foreign Affairs* 69 (1989–90).

Scammell, G. V. *The World Encompassed: The First European Maritime Empires, c. 800–1650.* Berkeley, Cal., 1981.

Schell, O. *To Get Rich Is Glorious: China in the '80s.* New York, 1985.

Schlosstein, S. *The End of the American Century.* New York, 1989.

Schneider, B. *The Barefoot Revolution.* London, 1988.

Schneider, S. H. *Global Warming.* San Francisco, Cal., 1989.

Schodt, F. L. "In the Land of Robots." *Business Month* 132 (November 1988).

Schoenfeld, G. "The Soviet Union: Rad Storm Rising." *Atlantic* 266 (December 1990).

Schwarz, H. E., and L. A. Dillard. "The Impact on Water Supplies." *Oceanus* 32 (Summer 1989).

Scott, P. B. *The Robotics Revolution: The Complete Guide for Managers and Engineers.* Oxford/New York, 1984.

Searle, G. R. *Eugenics and Politics in Britain, 1900–1914.* Leyden, 1976.

———. *The Quest for National Efficiency, 1899–1914.* 2nd edn. Atlantic Highlands, N.J., 1990.

Segal, G. "As China Grows Strong." *International Affairs* 64 (1988).

———. *Defending China.* Oxford, 1985.

———. *Rethinking the Pacific.* Oxford, 1990.

Shennan, J. H. *The Origins of the Modern European State, 1450–1725.* London, 1974.

Sheridan, T. "Merging Mind and Machine." *Technology Review* 87 (October 1984).

Shulman, S. "Hot Air—or What?" *Nature* 345 (14 June 1990).

Simon, J. L. *Population Matters: People, Resources, Environment and Immigration.* New Brunswick, N.J., 1990.

———. *The Ultimate Resource.* Princeton, N.J., 1981.

Singer, H. W. "The African Food Crisis and the Role of Food Aid." *Food Policy* 14 (1989).

Singh, M. P. "The Crisis of the Indian State." *Asian Survey* 30 (1990).

Smit, B., et al. "Sensitivity of Crop Yields and Land Resource Potential to Climate Change in Ontario, Canada." *Climatic Change* 14 (1989).

Smith, A. *The Geopolitics of Information: How Western Culture Dominates the World.* Oxford/New York, 1980.

Smith, H. W. "Nationalism and Religious Conflict in Imperial Germany, 1887–1914." Ph.D. dissertation, Yale University, 1991.

Smith, M., et al. *Asia's New Industrial World.* London, 1985.

Snyder, J. C., and S. F. Wells, eds. *Limiting Nuclear Proliferation.* Cambridge, Mass., 1985.

Sorensen, T. C. "Rethinking National Security." *Foreign Affairs* 69 (Summer 1990).

Spence, J. *To Change China: Western Advisors in China, 1620–1969.* New York, 1969 edn.

Starr, J. R., and D. C. Stoll. *The Politics of Scarcity: Water in the Middle East.* Boulder, Colo., 1988.

Steinberg, J. *Why Switzerland?* Cambridge, 1976.

Strange, S. "Finance, Information, and Power." *Review of International Studies* 16 (1990).

Taylor, A. J. P. *The Struggle for Mastery in Europe 1848–1918.* Oxford, 1954.

———. *The Trouble Makers: Dissent Over Foreign Policy, 1789–1939.* London, 1969 edn.

Taylor, J. *Shadows of the Rising Sun: A Critical View of the "Japanese Miracle."* New York, 1984.

Taylor, P. A. M., ed. *The Industrial Revolution in Britain: Triumph or Disaster?* Lexington, Mass., 1970.

Teitelbaum, M. S., and J. M. Winter. *The Fear of Population Decline.* Orlando, Fla./London, 1976.

Teitelman, R. *Gene Dreams: Wall Street, Academia, and the Rise of Biotechnology.* New York, 1989.

Thomas, H. *A History of the World.* New York, 1979.

Thomas, R. G. C. *Indian Security Policy.* Princeton, N.J., 1986.

Thucydides. *The Peloponnesian War.* Harmondsworth, Mddsx., 1954 edn.

Thurow L. "How to Wreck the Economy." *New York Review of Books* 28 (14 May 1981).

————. *The Zero-Sum Society: Distribution and the Possibilities for Economic Change.* New York, 1980.

Tilly, C., ed. *The Formation of National States in Western Europe.* Princeton, N.J., 1975.

Titus, J. G., ed. *Effects of Changes in Stratospheric Ozone and Global Climate.* Vol. 4, *Sea Level Rise.* Washington, D.C., 1986.

Tolchin, M., and S. Tolchin. *Buying into America: How Foreign Money is Changing the Face of Our Nation.* New York, 1988.

Tranter, N. *Population Since the Industrial Revolution: The Case of England and Wales.* New York, 1973.

Treverton, G. F. *Making the Alliance Work: The United States and Western Europe.* Ithaca, N.Y., 1985.

Trewartha, G. T. *A Geography of Population: World Patterns.* New York, 1969.

Tucker, R. W., and L. Wrigley, eds. *The Atlantic Alliance and Its Critics.* New York, 1983.

Tucker, W. *Progress and Privilege: America in the Age of Environmentalism.* New York, 1982.

B. L. Turner et al. *The Earth As Transformed by Human Action: Global and Regional Changes in the Biosphere over the Past 300 Years* (Cambridge, 1990).

Urbanials, D. F. "The Unattended Factory: FANUC's New Flexibility Automated Manufacturing Plant Using Industrial Robots," *13th International Symposium on Industrial Robots and Robots 7: Conference Proceedings.* Vol. 1. Dearborn, Mich., 1983.

van de Kaa, D. J. "Europe's Second Demographic Transition." *Population Bulletin* 42 (1987).

Van Evera, S. "Why Europe Matters, Why the Third World Doesn't: American Grand Strategy After the Cold War." *Journal of Strategic Studies* 13 (1990).

Veit, L. A. "Time of the New Asian Tigers." *Challenge* 30 (July–August 1987).

Vogel, E. F. "Pax Nipponica." *Foreign Affairs* 64 (Spring 1986).

————. *Japan as Number One: Lessons for America.* New York, 1980 edn.

————. *One Step Ahead in China: Guangdong Under Reform.* Cambridge, Mass., 1990.

Von Laue, T. H. *The World Revolution of Westernization.* New York/Oxford, 1987.

Wattenberg, B. *The First Universal Nation: Leading Indicators and Ideas about the Surge of America in the 1990s.* New York, 1990.

————. *The Birth Dearth.* New York, 1987.

Wells, S. F., and M. A. Bruzonsky, eds. *Security in the Middle East: Regional Change and Great Power Strategies.* Boulder, Colo./London, 1987.

Westing, A. H. *Global Resources and International Conflict: Environmental Factors in Strategic Policy and Action.* Oxford/New York, 1986.

Wheeler, D. L. "Scientists Studying 'The Greenhouse Effect' Challenge Fears of Global Warming." *Journal of Forestry* 88 (1989).

Whitaker, J. S. *How Can Africa Survive?* New York, 1988.

White, M. *The Japanese Educational Challenge: A Commitment to Children.* New York, 1989.

Williams, D. V. "Estimated Bioresource Sensitivity to Climate Change in Alberta, Canada." *Climatic Change* 7 (1985).

Wilson, C. *Profit and Power: A Study of England and the Dutch Wars.* London, 1957.

Wilson, C. A., and J. F. B. Mitchell. "Simulated Climate and CO_2-Induced Climate Change Over Western Europe." *Climatic Change* 8 (1986).

Wolferen, K. van. "The Japan Problem." *Foreign Affairs* 65 (Winter 1986–87).

———. "The Japan Problem Revisited." *Foreign Affairs* 69 (Fall 1990).

———. *The Enigma of Japanese Power: People and Politics in a Stateless Nation.* New York, 1989.

Womack, J., et al. *The Machine That Changed the World: Based on the Massachusetts Institute of Technology 5-Million-Dollar 5-Year Study on the Future of the Automobile.* London, 1990.

Woodruff, W. *The Impact of Western Man: A Study of Europe's Role in the World Economy.* New York, 1967.

Wright, R., and D. MacManus. *Flashpoints: Promise and Peril in a New World.* New York, 1991.

Wriston, W. B. "Technology and Sovereignty." *Foreign Affairs* 67 (Winter 1988–89).

Yamaguchi, H. "Biotechnology: New Hope for Japan's Farmers." *Business Japan* (April 1987).

Yang, Y., and R. Tyers. "The Economic Costs of Self-Sufficiency in China." *World Development* 17 (1989).

Young, C. "Australia's Population: A Long-Term view." *Current Affairs Bulletin* (Sydney) 65 (May 1989).

Yoxen, E. *The Gene Business: Who Should Control Biotechnology?* New York, 1983.

———, and V. Di Martino. *Biotechnology in Future Society: Scenarios and Options for Europe.* Luxembourg, 1989.

Yuanjun, H., and Z. Zhongzing. "Environmental Pollution and Control Measures in China." *Ambio* 16 (1987).

Yudken, J. S., and M. Black. "Targeting National Needs: A New Direction for Science and Technology Policy." *World Policy Journal* 7 (Spring 1990).

Yuging, W. "Natural Conservation Regions in China." *Ambio* 16 (1987).

"Z." "To the Stalin Mausoleum." *Daedalus* 119 (Winter 1990).

Zengage, T. R., and C. T. Ratcliffe. *The Japanese Century: Challenge and Response.* Hong Kong, 1988.

Zysman, J. "U.S. Power, Trade, and Technology." *International Affairs* 67 (1991).

INDEX

The Identity of France

Volume Two
People and Production

Fernand Braudel
Translated by Siân Reynolds

The great unchanging geology of history, *la longue dureé*, is the context in which Braudel sees the changes and transformations not only of his own time but those of the centuries. The whole book is a dialogue, wonderfully enriched by images drawn from an exceptional consciousness and a depth of historical research that has never lost its sense of enjoyment. A flash of recollection sharpens his point and suddenly there is a vivid, sometimes elegaic, sketch of French life or landscape in all its particularity drawn from his own direct experience.

'The most revered of modern French historians, Braudel parades a stupendous breadth of knowledge and a passion for local detail. The book glows with a keen curiosity about the living past . . . much of it is as absorbing as a novel. Braudel's love of France shines through its pages.'   John Ardagh, *Daily Telegraph*

'Do feast your mind on this learned, provocative, and endlessly readable historical anatomy of France, delightfully translated by Siân Reynolds.'   Roy Porter, *New Statesman*

'This volume is wonderfully rich, informative, and intelligent. It is as nourishing as a *cassoulet*. There is indeed scarcely a page which does not stimulate thought or provoke speculation.'   Alan Massie, *Sunday Telegraph*

ISBN 0 00 686231 4

Fontana Press

Protestants

The Birth of a Revolution

Steven Ozment

'Magisterial . . . a successful and rather timely piece of polemic that has plenty of documentary stuffing.'

John Bossy, author of *Giordano Bruno and the Embassy Affair*

Protestants tells the story of the birth of Protestantism in sixteenth-
century Germany – the revolutionary event to which all modern Protestant communities ultimately trace their origins. But Steven Ozment takes that oft-told history and strips it of the crust of myth and ideology which has been grafted onto it to lay bare the
tale of a people both bewildered and inspired by the inflammatory ideas loosed upon the world by Martin Luther.

'Steven Ozment is the leader of those Reformation historians who have lifted the religious history of the sixteenth century out of the closed and sealed realm of disputation among competing, hairsplitting theologians and set it down in the hurly-burly of city streets, brought it to the fireside of family life, and followed its influences into the hearts of lay people young and old, princes, nobles, and common folk. Here is the Reformation as it depended on Everyman – and Everywoman – defining popular opinion and in turn defined by it. Ozment has given us a scholarly book, gracefully written, raising from the dead the audience of ordinary and extraordinary people to whom Luther's reform was addressed and by whom it was shaped and made to endure. To read Steven Ozment is to believe that history is a living art.'

Richard Marius, Harvard University, author of *Thomas More*

ISBN 0 00 686258 6

Hitler: The Führer and the People

J. P. Stern

His life, his times, his policies, his strategies, his influence have often been analysed. But rarely is the most elementary question of all raised – how could it happen?

How could a predominantly sober, hard-working and well-educated population have been persuaded to follow Hitler to the awful abyss of destruction? What was the image projected in his speeches, his writings, and his conversation? What were those elements from which the Hitler myth was constructed?

With terrifying logic the sequence of his career emerges as the creation of a man who translated the private sphere of sentiment into the public sphere of political action. *Hitler: The Führer and the People* is a compelling attempt to reconstruct the nature of Hitler's political ideology, its roots, its logic and its function.

'Who really wants or needs another book on Hitler? The short answer is, when the book is as good and original and brief as Professor Stern's, we all do.'   Donald Rae, *New Society*

'This is a book that tells us more about National Socialist Germany than many works three times as long.'
James Joll, *Times Literary Supplement*

'It is an excellent book, all the more so because it concerns itself, via Hitler, with the more general problem of the relationship between the ideas and action, between myth and reality.'
Douglas Johnson, *New Society*

'One of the most remarkable studies of Hitler and Nazism to have appeared.'   Christopher Sykes, *Observer*

ISBN 0 00 686195 4

Fontana Press

Fontana Press